TWELVE DAYS

TWELVE DAYS

REVOLUTION 1956

**How the Hungarians Tried to Topple
their Soviet Masters**

VICTOR SEBESTYEN

Weidenfeld & Nicolson
LONDON

First published in Great Britain in 2006
by Weidenfeld & Nicolson

1 3 5 7 9 10 8 6 4 2

A CIP catalogue record for this book
is available from the British Library.

ISBN-13: 978 0 297 847311
ISBN-10: 0 297 847317

Typeset by Input Data Services Ltd, Frome

Printed and bound by Butler & Tanner Ltd,
Frome and London

The Orion Publishing Group's policy is to use papers that
are natural, renewable and recyclable products and made
from wood grown in sustainable forests. The logging and
manufacturing processes are expected to conform to the
environmental regulations of the country of origin.

Weidenfeld & Nicolson

The Orion Publishing Group Ltd
Orion House
5 Upper Saint Martin's Lane
London, WC2H 9EA

www.orionbooks.co.uk

To Jess

CONTENTS

ILLUSTRATIONS

Sections of photographs appear between pages 100 & 101 and 228 & 229

Between pages 100 and 101:

Mikhail Suslov, Mátyás Rákosi and Kliment Voroshilov, 4 April 1954[1]

Achbishop of Esztergom, József Mindszenty is inaugurated, 16 August 1945[1]

Cardinal Mindszenty during his trial, 3 February 1949[1]

László Rajk[2]

László Rajk's widow, Julia, and son at his reburial, 6 October 1956[3]

Yuri Andropov and Ernõ Gerõ, 1 December 1955[1]

Imre Nagy dances with a peasant girl at a wine festival, 1955[2]

Nikita Khrushchev at the United Nations General Assembly, New York, 11 October 1960[4]

President Eisenhower and Secretary of State John Foster Dulles, 25 July 1955[2]

Crowds in Parliament Square, 23 October 1956[5]

The severed head from the statue of Josef Stalin, 24 October 1956[6]

The fallen statue of Josef Stalin in front of the National Theatre in Budapest, 24 October 1956[4]

Between pages 228 and 229:

Soviet tanks advance through the streets of Budapest, October 1956[7]

A Hungarian flag with a hole in Corvin Street, October 1956[1]

Shop window in Majakovszkij Street, October 1956[2]

Corvin Street, 26 October 1956[1]

Mikhail Suslov [1]

Anastas Mikoyan[8]

Freedom fighters wave the Hungarian national flag on a captured
    Soviet tank, 2 November 1956[8]
Pal Maleter at the rebel command headquarters, 31 October 1956[9]
János Szabó[3]
A crowd gathers around the body of an AVO member, 23 October
    1956[10]
The body of a lynched member of the AVO hangs from a tree in
    Budapest, 1November 1956[11]
János Kádár[7]
Defendants at the Imre Nagy trial at the pronouncing of the sentence,
    15 June 1958[1]
A lye-covered corpse of a member of the AVO, 31 October 1956.[9]

[1] Hungarian National Museum
[2] CORBIS
[3] The Institute for the History of the 1956 Revolution
[4] Empics
[5] Hungarium News Agency/Magyar Tavirati Iroda
[6] Keystone/France/Gamma, Camera Press London
[7] Topham Picturepoint
[8] akg-images
[9] Time & Life Pictures
[10] Gamma, Camera Press London
[11] Keystone/Getty Images

ACKNOWLEDGEMENTS

I have been returning to Hungary since the late 1970s, when the big taboo subject in Budapest was the 1956 Revolution. By Communist bloc standards of the time, the regime was relatively relaxed – 'the merriest barracks in the camp' it was called. Nevertheless, even within families and amongst dissidents producing samizdat publications, 1956 was a risky topic, seldom talked about and then in hushed tones. In the mid 1980s, the two or three years before Communism collapsed, people allowed themselves to speak more openly about the Revolution – and they did. I went to Hungary often as a reporter during those times and then began to hear the personal stories of many people who took part in the Revolution and stayed in the country afterwards. Some have since died, but I have liberally used their reminiscences here.

In Budapest now, people rarely talk about the four and a half Communist decades, which ended just half a generation ago. A collective amnesia has descended on the country – especially among the young. Hungarians like to think of themselves as a modern, go-ahead part of the EU. They do not wish to be associated with grimy Communism and something unfashionable, such as an heroic failure – even one on such a grand scale as the 1956 Revolution.

Many do wish to remember, however. The number of people in Hungary who went out of their way to help me is enormous. I have space to mention just a few of them here. Miklós Haraszti is one of the shrewdest men I know, and the possessor of one of the best contacts books in Mitteleuropa, which I raided with ruthlessness. Mária Vásárhelyi, Károly Makk, Nora Walko, Klara Kelémeri, Sándor Zsindely, László Eörsi, Csaba Békés, Agnes Gergely, Sándor Vas, Julia Gabor, Gergely Pongrácz, Sándor Revesz, Csilla Strbik, Mihály Szilágy, László Rajk, Janos Rainer and Géza Doromby, were immensely generous with their time, as were all the staff at the Institute for the History of the 1956 Revolution. Katalin Janosi gave me much useful additional

information about her grandfather Imre Nagy's domestic life as well as
a fascinating tour around his Budapest home. General Béla Király was
an invaluable source. The curatorial staff at the Hungarian National
Archive and National Library pointed me in the direction of large areas
of research I might otherwise have missed

I would like to thank the Columbia University Library in New York
for granting me access to the extraordinary Bakhmeteff archive, which
holds hundreds of interviews with refugees, most of them conducted
just days after they left their homes in 1956. Also in New York, I am
grateful for original ideas and advice from Joan Stein and Rebecca
Mead. From Russia, the Archive of the Russian President and the
Foreign Ministry Archive were vital for access to material about 1956
made available only after the collapse of the Soviet Union.

In London, I owe an enormous debt of thanks to Simon Sebag Monte-
fiore for encouraging me to start the book, and for his constant help
and advice, which enable to me to finish. He has been a loyal supporter.
Many Hungarian refugees in Britain, exiled in 1956, have been amazingly generous of their time, in particular Stephen Vizinczey and
Mátyás and Ilona Sárkozi. No detail of their memories of 1956 seemed
too trivial for them to consider. I also wish to thank Katalin Bogyay,
Peter Unwin, István Dénes, Andrew Roberts, George Schöpflin,
Amanda Sebestyen and Gizela Doromby for helping me with ideas and
tracking down vital leads. Piers Dixon very generously gave me access
to the personal diaries of his father, Sir Pierson Dixon. The staff at the
British Library, the London Library and the Bodleian Library in Oxford
were ever helpful.

I am particularly indebted, for insight and inspiration of various
kinds, to Janos Rainer's biography of Imre Nagy, György Litván's *The
Hungarian Revolution, Reform, Revolt and Repression*, and the Russian
General Yevgeny Malaschenko's Memoirs.

My agent, Georgina Capel, always lifted my spirits when they needed
raising. At Weidenfeld & Nicolson my wise editor, Ion Trewin, was a
constant source of reassurance and his Assistant Editor, Anna Hervé,
was also enormously helpful. Linden Lawson, my copy editor, showed
enormous enthusiasm and professionalism.

I thank my sister, Judith Maynard, for help with translations - and
am indebted to her and to my brother, John Walko, for their reflections
on the Revolution, still so vivid after nearly 50 years. Peter, Paul, Jayne
and Wendy Diggory have been a constant and vital support.

It is impossible to acknowledge all that I owe Jessica Pulay. Quite simply, without her this book could never have been written. With her passionate interest in Central Europe, her strategic judgment and her organised mind, she meticulously pored over the manuscript and suggested countless numbers of improvements. She could spot my logical inconsistencies, sometimes even before I had committed them to paper. Her loving encouragement was a constant spur for me to try harder. I found it extremely difficult living with myself while writing this book, thinking of almost nothing but the year 1956. I have no idea how Jess managed it. I'll be forever grateful that she did.

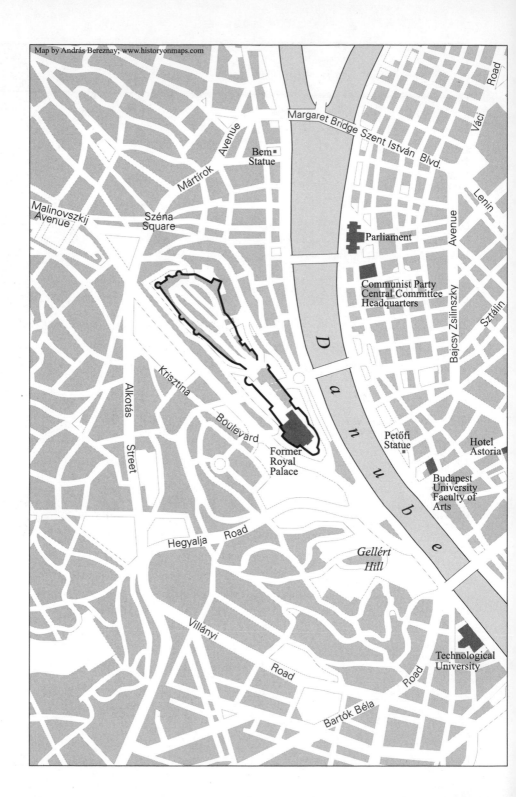

Map by András Bereznay; www.historyonmaps.com

Margaret Bridge Szent István Blvd.

Bem
Statue

Mártírok Avenue

Malinovszkij
Avenue

Széna
Square

Parliament

Communist Party
Central Committee
Headquarters

Váci Road

Lenin Avenue

Bajcsy Zsilinszky Avenue

Sztálin

D
a
n
u
b
e

Krisztina

Alkotás
Street

Boulevard

Former
Royal
Palace

Petőfi
Statue

Hotel
Astoria

Budapest
University
Faculty of
Arts

Hegyalja Road

Gellért
Hill

Villányi

Road

Technological
University

Bartók Béla

Road

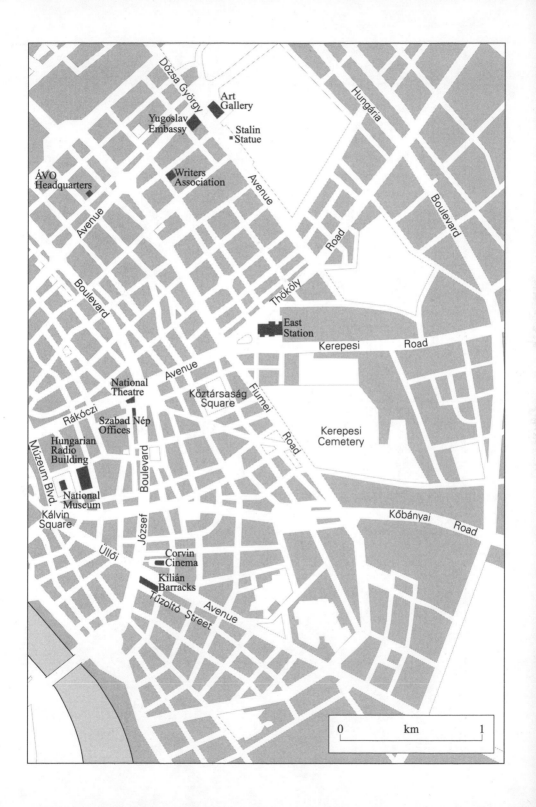

Dózsa György

Hungária

Art
Gallery

Yugoslav
Embassy

Stalin
Statue

ÁVO
Headquarters

Writers
Association

Avenue

Boulevard

Avenue

Road

Boulevard

Thököly

East
Station

Kerepesi   Road

Avenue

National
Theatre

Köztársaság
Square

Fiumei

Rákóczi

Kerepesi
Cemetery

Szabad Nép
Offices

Hungarian
Radio
Building

Boulevard

Road

Múzeum Blvd.

National
Museum

Kálvin
Square

József

Kőbányai   Road

Üllői

Corvin
Cinema

Kílián
Barracks

Tűzoltó   Street

Avenue

0   km   1

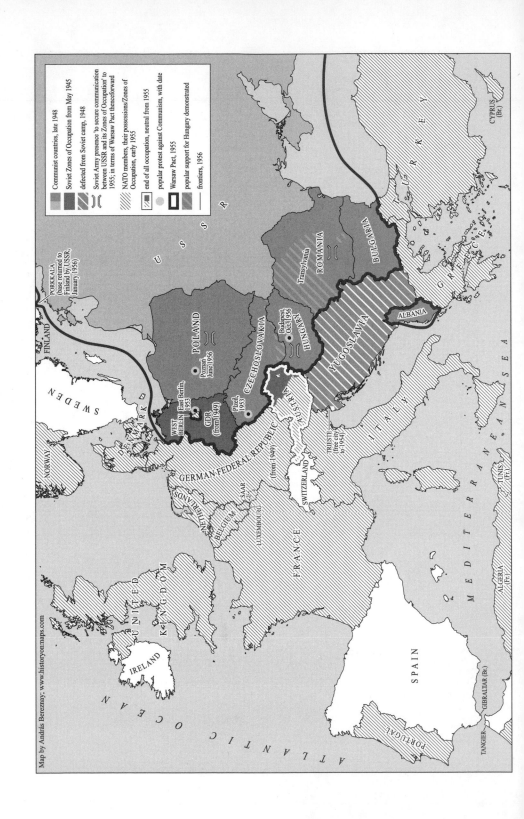

Map by András Bereznay; www.historyonmaps.com

Communist countries, late 1948

Soviet Zones of Occupation from May 1945

defected from Soviet camp, 1948

Soviet Army presence 'to secure communication between USSR and its Zones of Occupation to 1955; in terms of Warsaw Pact thenceforward

NATO members, their possessions/Zones of Occupation, early 1955

end of all occupation, neutral from 1955

popular protest against Communism, with date

Warsaw Pact, 1955

popular support for Hungary demonstrated

frontiers, 1956

PORKKALA
(base returned to Finland by USSR, January 1956)

FINLAND

SWEDEN

NORWAY

DENMARK

WEST BERLIN
East Berlin, 1953
GDR (from 1949)
Plzeň 1953

U S S R

POLAND
Poznań June 1956

CZECHOSLOVAKIA

Budapest, Oct 1956
HUNGARY

Transylvania
ROMANIA

BULGARIA

GREECE

ALBANIA

YUGOSLAVIA

AUSTRIA (from 1949)

TRIESTE (free city to 1954)

ITALY

T U R K E Y

CYPRUS (Br.)

GERMAN FEDERAL REPUBLIC

SAAR

NETHERLANDS
BELGIUM
LUXEMBOURG

SWITZERLAND

FRANCE

U N I T E D   K I N G D O M

IRELAND

SPAIN

PORTUGAL

TANGIER

GIBRALTAR (Br.)

ALGERIA (Fr.)

TUNIS (Fr.)

M E D I T E R R A N E A N   S E A

A T L A N T I C   O C E A N

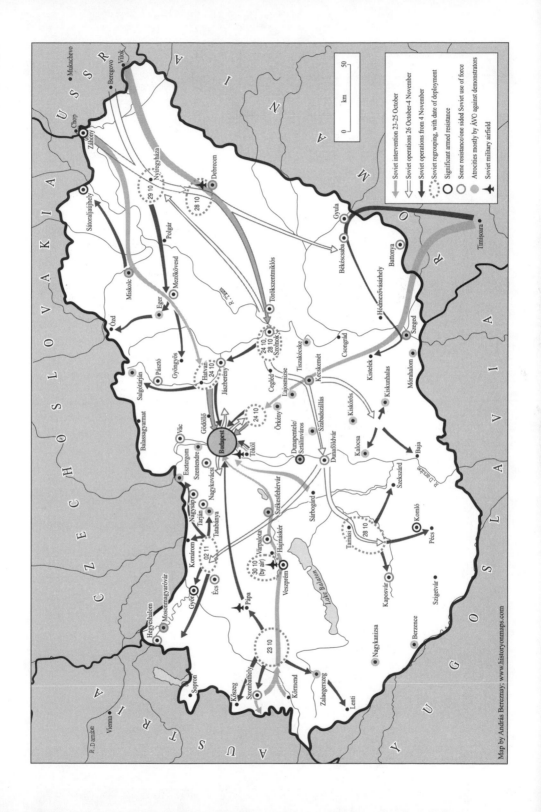

| Soviet intervention 23-25 October |
| Soviet operations 26 October-4 November |
| Soviet operations from 4 November |
| Soviet regrouping, with date of deployment |
| Significant armed resistance |
| Some resistance/one sided Soviet use of force |
| Atrocities mostly by ÁVO against demonstrators |
| Soviet military airfield |

50
km
0

U S S R

Mukacevo
Beregovo
Vilok
Záhony
Chop
Sátoraljaújhely

U K R A I N E

R O M A N I A

Nyíregyháza
29 10
Debrecen
28 10
Polgár
Mezőkövesd
Miskolc
Ozd
Eger
Mezőkövesd
Torökszentmiklós
R. Tisza

Timisoara

Gyula
Békéscsaba
Hódmezővásárhely
Battonya
Szeged
Csongrád
Szolnok
24 10,
28 10
Tiszakécske
Kecskemét
Kiskőrös
Kistelek
Mórahalom
Kiskunhalas

Pászló
Gyöngyös
Hatvan
24 10
Jászberény
Salgótarján
Balassagyarmat
Vác
Esztergom
Szentendre
Nagykovácsi
Gödöllő
Budapest
Cegléd
Orkény
Lajosmizse
Szabadszállás
24 10
Dunapentele/
Sztálinváros
Dunaföldvár
Kalocsa
Baja

Tököl
Székesfehérvár
Nagysáp
Tarján
Tatabánya
Komárom
02 11
Várpalota
30 10
(by air)
Hajmáskér
Veszprém
Ecs
Győr
Pápa
Mosonmagyaróvár
Hegyeshalom
Sopron

Sárbogárd
Szekszárd
Komló
Pécs
28 10
Tamási
Kaposvár
Szigetvár
Berzence
Nagykanizsa

Lake Balaton

23 10
Kőszeg
Szombathely
Körmend
Zalaegerszeg
Lenti

C Z E C H O S L O V A K I A

A U S T R I A

Vienna
R. Danube
R. Danube

Y U G O S L A V I A

Map by András Bereznay; www.historyonmaps.com

THE MAIN ACTORS

István Bibó (Isht-van Bee-bo) 1911–79. Minister of State for a day in Nagy's last Cabinet. The only Minister who refused to flee when Parliament was attacked by the Soviets on 4 November 1956. One of Hungary's most influential political thinkers. Sentenced to a life term in 1956. Released in the general amnesty of 1963.

József Dudás (Yo-zeff Do-dash) 1912–57. Revolutionary leader whose group of fighters occupied several strategic buildings in Budapest during the uprising. Was one of the first insurgent leaders to be executed, in January 1957.

Ernő Gerő (Jerr-owe) 1889–1980. In exile for two decades in USSR from mid 1920's. Senior KGB agent. After Hungary 'liberated' he was the second-ranking Communist 1945–56. Took over as Party leader in July 1956, but was ousted by the Russians on the second day of the revolution. Went into exile in Russia until 1961. Returned to Budapest where he worked as an occasional translator.

András Hegedüs (On-drash Heg-eh-dush) 1922–99. Hungarian Prime Minister 1955–6. Fled to the USSR on 28 October 1956 in the middle of the revolution. Returned to Hungary 1958 and taught sociology.

János Kádár (Yan-osh Kar-dar) 1912–89. Communist Interior Minister 1948–51 under Rákosi. Jailed 1951–4. Joined Imre Nagy's revolutionary government on 25 October 1956 but turned against it on 1 November. Installed by Soviets as Hungarian leader after the revolution was suppressed. Remained Party boss in Hungary until 1988.

Béla Király (Kir-rah-ee) 1912–. Army general sentenced to life imprisonment in a 1952 show trial. Released in September 1956. Appointed head of the Hungarian Revolutionary Armed Forces during October 1956. In charge of the defence of Budapest. Escaped to the West after the Soviet invasion in November 1956. Sentenced to death *in absentia*. Taught history at Brooklyn College, New York. Returned

to Hungary in 1989. Was an Independent Member of Parliament
1990–94.

Sándor Kopácsi (Shan-door Kop-ah-chi) 1922–2001. Chief of Budapest
police 1952–6. Tried with Imre Nagy as one of the ringleaders of the
revolution. Sentenced to life imprisonment. Amnestied in 1963 and
emigrated to Canada. Worked for twenty years as a mechanic at the
Toronto electricity works. Returned to Hungary 1989.

Géza Losonczy (Gay-za Losh-on-chi) 1917–57. Journalist. Imre Nagy's
closest political adviser and friend. Jailed and tortured in Rákosi
purges. Sought refuge with Nagy on 4 November at Yugoslav
Embassy. Interned and arrested with him. Died from forced feeding
while on hunger strike in detention in Budapest Central Prison on
21 December 1957.

Pál Maléter (Mal-eh-ter) 1917–58. Commander in Hungarian army.
Led the defence of the main revolutionary strongholds. Promoted to
Major-General and appointed Minister of Defence by Imre Nagy.
Sent to negotiate with the Soviets, he was kidnapped by the KGB
on 3 November 1956. Tried with Imre Nagy and executed on 16
June 1958.

Cardinal József Mindszenty (Mind-senty) 1892–1975. Catholic
Primate of Hungary. Jailed for life after show trial in 1949. Freed
on 31 October 1956 during the revolution. On 4 November, when
Russians invaded, given refuge at US Legation where he remained
until 1971.

Imre Nagy (Im-reh Nodge) 1896–1958. Hungarian Prime Minister
1953–5 and again from 24 October to 4 November 1956. Political
leader of the Hungarian revolution. Kidnapped by the Soviets after
they crushed the uprising. Deported to Romania. Arrested and
returned to Budapest 1957. Tried in secret the following year and
hanged on 16 June 1958.

Mátyás Rákosi (Mart-yarsh Rak-oh-she) 1892–1971. Leader of the
Hungarian émigrés in the Soviet Union 1940–44, First Secretary of
the Hungarian Communist Party 1945 to July 1956. Removed from
office by the Russians. Lived the rest of his days in the USSR in
Kirghizia. In 1970 was granted permission to return to Hungary if
he gave an undertaking not to engage in politics. He refused. His
body was returned from the Soviet Union and he was buried in
Budapest.

János 'Uncle' Szabó (Yan-osh Sa-bow) 1897–1957. Truck driver and best-known rebel commander. Led one of the main groups of armed freedom fighters. Arrested trying to escape to the West. Hanged January 1957.

Attila Szigetthy (Sig-et-ee) 1912–57. One of the main leaders of the revolution outside Budapest. Head of the Revolutionary Council in Győr, the principal city in western Hungary. After the failure of the revolution he committed suicide, in August 1957, a few days before his trial was due to be heard.

József Szilágyi (See-largey) 1917–57. Police colonel in Budapest, then leading opposition figure to Rákosi. Was Imre Nagy's secretary during the revolution. Tried and hanged in 1957.

Zoltán Tildy 1889–1961. President of Hungary 1946–8. Under house arrest 1948–56. Became Imre Nagy's deputy Prime Minister and close confidant. Arrested November 1956 and sentenced to six years' imprisonment. Released in 1959 on an individual amnesty.

INTRODUCTION

Even now, with Budapest a bustling, modern European Union capital, some of the city's public buildings and big apartment blocks are pock-marked by bullet holes. They are a deliberate reminder, to Hungarians and visitors alike, of a fifty-year-old tragedy that will always be an inspiration to those who have fought against tyranny: the 1956 Hungarian Revolution.

It is a story of heroic failure, of awe-inspiring courage in a doomed cause, and of ruthless cruelty. A small nation, its people armed with little more than rifles and petrol bombs, had the will to rise up against one of the world's superpowers. The passionate determination of the Hungarians to resist the Russians astonished outsiders. People of all kinds, throughout the Western world, became deeply involved in the fate of Hungary. For a few euphoric days it looked, miraculously, as though the revolutionaries might even win. Then reality bit back. The Soviets invaded with overwhelming force. The Hungarians were brutally crushed; their capital was devastated, thousands of their people died; their country was occupied for a further three decades.

The revolution was the defining moment of the Cold War, when the Soviet Union showed, beyond doubt, that it was prepared to use barbaric measures to keep its empire, and the West was content to let it do so. The free world looked on in horror and sympathy as Russian tanks turned once-beautiful parts of Budapest into rubble. But Western leaders did nothing.

Much new material has emerged about the uprising* since the collapse of communism. The more we know, the more clearly Hungary

---

*Entire books have been written on whether Hungary 1956 was a revolution or an uprising. Hungarians insist on revolution, even though it was so short-lived. I tend to agree; for a while it seemed everything had changed. But the two terms are not mutually exclusive and I have used them both throughout the text.

emerges as just one battleground in the great East-West struggle in the second half of the twentieth century. Hungary was a pawn, trapped between bigger powers. In 1956 its fate was not decided on the streets of Budapest by the Hungarian heroes, villains or charlatans who will appear in these pages. All the major decisions were made by the power-brokers in Moscow and in Washington. Therefore, scenes in this book shift regularly from Hungary to the Soviet Union and the United States.

The documents recently available from Russia refine views long held about the Soviet leaders' handling of Hungary '56. The heirs to Stalin, bitter rivals, vacillated for a few days and were surprisingly unsure of themselves, but finally displayed the ruthless savagery expected of tyrants. The methods they adopted in Budapest were ferocious. Yet the Red tsars in the Kremlin behaved as typical imperialists invariably have done, from the Romans onwards. They tried to keep what they held while they could. They were not fools and suffered from few delusions. They understood with great clarity how loathed communism was and they as Russians were in Eastern Europe. The edifice they had built since the war, that vast monolithic power bloc, looked terrifyingly strong. But the ageing men in the Kremlin were prescient enough to know that the whole empire could collapse within a matter of days, which is precisely what happened thirty-three years after the Hun-garian Revolution. By 1989 the Soviet Union had lost interest in keeping its vassal states in Europe. In 1956, maintaining its imperial possessions was a national and ideological priority. The Russians had no intention of letting any of their satellites leave the 'socialist camp'. From the perspective of Nikita Khrushchev and the other Communist magnates in Moscow, they did the 'right', or at least the predictable, thing in Budapest. They bought time, at a high cost in blood.

As for the role of the US in 1956, documents are more revealing. The Americans 'won' the Cold War and have dictated the way its history is written. The soldier-statesman President Dwight Eisenhower and his Secretary of State, the dour John Foster Dulles, are respected in the US today. The Hungarian Revolution was not their finest hour. It coincided with the last week of the President's re-election campaign and the Suez crisis. Eisenhower regarded Egypt as more important than Hungary, which was a reasonable judgment call. The perplexing thing, however, was his Janus-faced policy before the uprising. Throughout Eisen-hower's administration, his aides and spin doctors spoke with bellicose rhetoric about 'liberating' the 'captive peoples' behind the Iron Curtain and 'rolling back' communism. The CIA spent millions of dollars on propaganda to spread the gospel of democracy. Without a doubt the Hungarians were encouraged to rebel. But when the revolutionaries needed help, official Washington washed its hands of them; the Hungarians were left on their own. It is a gross exaggeration to say, as a freedom fighter did in Budapest, that American Cold Warriors were prepared to fight communism down to the last Hungarian. But in 1956 many Hungarians felt betrayed by the US.

It is easy to see why. The reputation of Richard Nixon, who makes a walk-on appearance in this drama, has undergone a major re-evaluation upwards, post-Watergate. He was Vice President in 1956 and was the author of an utterly chilling example of realpolitik. He said at a meeting in the White House, three months before the Hungarian Revolution began, that it would be no bad thing, from America's point of view, in public relations terms, if the 'Soviet iron fist were to come down hard again on the Soviet bloc'.

Russian troops slaughtered Hungarian civilians and it was the killers in the Kremlin who sent them; the US must not shoulder the blame for that. Yet, at the time, some leading figures in Washington felt uneasy about the way the Hungarian crisis was being handled and thought the administration bore greater responsibility for the tragedy than it accepted. The questions asked then, which were left unanswered, are still worth asking. The US was on the 'right side' in the great struggle of the 1950s. Far higher standards of honesty, integrity and decency were expected of the leader of the free world than from one of history's worst tyrannies.

One enduringly fascinating Cold War theme, espionage, plays an important part in this story. Vast sums were spent on the intelligence networks of the East and West and the spies seemed to be working hard. Yet it is astonishing how ignorant all these agencies were about what was really happening in the satellite states. The Russians, despite some shocks to their system elsewhere, were remarkably complacent about Hungary. Neither the CIA, MI6 nor the other Western spying organisations predicted any serious Hungarian disturbances in 1956, let alone that the most violent rebellion there would ever be against Soviet rule in Europe was about to erupt.

Why Hungary and why 1956? The most obvious reason is that in the early 1950s Hungary lived under the most oppressive dictatorship in the Eastern bloc. Its despot for eight years, Mátyás Rákosi, stood comparison with his great mentor Stalin, or Mao Zedong, as a monster. On the de Tocqueville principle, dictatorships are at their most vulnerable when they start to reform. By 1956 the regime had relaxed significantly, enough to make rage and loathing replace fear as the biggest motivating factor in political life. More important, though, Hungary felt different, culturally, historically and linguistically, from the other nations in the Eastern bloc. There was resentment against the Soviet Union in all the satellite countries after the war; Russia regarded them all as colonies and behaved towards them as such. But nowhere was the hatred as strong and deep as in Hungary. It was a defeated nation, treated like an enemy – a vital psychological factor. Hungary, under a fascist dictator of its own for two decades, had, unlike the Poles or the Czechs, invaded the Soviet Union in the Second World War. The background to the revolution explains much of the extreme brutality and nastiness displayed by both sides during those twelve autumn days.

Hungarian names can be terribly confusing and difficult to grasp for those unfamiliar with the language. Among them is Imre Nagy,* one of the principal characters in the 1956 story. He became the acknowledged leader of the revolution, died a supremely brave and honourable death on the scaffold, and is revered as a martyr to the cause of freedom. A strange role reversal has occurred in Hungary over the last few years. Nagy has been weighed in the balance again and the scales have slightly tilted. Nagy died better than he had lived. Some evidence suggests that he had been an agent of the KGB at the height of the Moscow purges in the 1930s. Contemporary Hungarians have come to regard him as a man worthy of great respect, but rather hopeless as a political leader. It seemed inevitable that his end would be tragic the moment he took a leading part in the revolution.

By contrast János Kádár betrayed the revolution, was installed by the Russians as their puppet in Hungary, and ensured that Nagy was hanged. He survived in power for thirty-two years, for most of them as a genuinely popular and admired figure. An opinion poll carried out

---

*Nagy means 'big'. It is one of the most common names in Hungary. In Hungarian, still, the surname is always placed before the forename. So, for example, he would have been addressed 'Nagy Imre'. Keeping to Hungarian tradition would probably confuse readers everywhere else, so here I will use the internationally recognised system of first names placed first.

in Budapest in 2003 placed him as the second most popular Hungarian in history (well ahead of Imre Nagy).

The Hungarian word for revolution is 'forradalom'. Literally it means a 'boiling over of the masses' and that is what happened in Budapest in October 1956. This revolution was marked by idealism and breathless excitement, as well as by violence and utter confusion. Sometimes it is not always entirely clear who was fighting whom, or for what. Some of the images, typically remembered in grainy black and white, have the capacity, even now, to shock: Russian guns firing shells across the Danube at anything that moved; lynch mobs of armed civilians meting out instant justice to police spies; children as young as twelve fighting against tanks. It has always disturbed me that these youngsters – and the adults who sent them out with arms – should be hailed as revolutionary heroes.

My mother used to attend a discussion group regularly with her friends from Budapest. Could the revolution have succeeded? Need 2,500 Hungarians have died in a struggle against hopeless odds? Was this in any sense, as Hungarians like to say, a 'victory in defeat'? I was brought up on the story of '56. It has been part of me since my family left Hungary as refugees, when I was a tiny child. From my earliest memories I have been asking the same kind of questions as my mother asked about the revolution that changed our lives.

PROLOGUE

Sunday, 4 November 1956

At 6.30 a.m. in the Associated Press newsroom in Vienna a series of telex messages began to arrive from Budapest. They were urgently sent from the office of the Hungarian newspaper *A Free People* (*Szabad Nép*). But they were not the words of an ordinary reporter. With one hand operating the teletype keyboard and another holding a gun, they were written by a young man who was seeing his desperate hopes for freedom crushed.

> Since the early morning hours Russian troops are attacking Budapest and our population . . .
> Please tell the world of the treacherous attack against our struggle for liberty . . .
> Our troops are already engaged in fighting.
> Help! – Help! – Help!
> SOS! SOS! SOS!
> The people have just overturned a tram to use as a barricade near this building. In the building young people are making Molotov cocktails and hand grenades to fight tanks. We are quiet, not afraid. Send the news to the public of the world and say it should condemn the aggression.
> The fighting is very close now and we haven't enough tommy-guns in the building. I don't know how long we can resist. They are fixing the hand grenades now. Heavy shells are exploding nearby. Above, jet planes are roaring . . .

There was a break in the line for half an hour. Then the anguished messages started again.

> At the moment there is silence. It may be the silence before the storm. We have almost no weapons, only light machine-guns, Russian-made long rifles and some carbines. We haven't any kind of heavy guns.

People are jumping up at the tanks, throwing hand grenades inside
and then slamming the drivers' windows. The Hungarian people
are not afraid of death. It is only a pity that we can't stand this for
long.
A man just came in from the street. He said that we should not think
that because the street is empty, people have taken shelter. They
are standing in the doorways, waiting for the right moment.

There was another break in the transmission for a few minutes. The
line reopened. It was now about two hours since Soviet tanks had
begun an assault on Budapest in massive force.

Now the firing is starting again. We are getting hits.
The tanks are getting nearer and there is heavy artillery. We have just
had a report that our unit is receiving reinforcements and ammunition.
But it is still too little. It can't be allowed that people attack tanks with
their bare hands. What is the United Nations doing?
There are between 200 and 250 people here in the newspaper building.
About 50 are women.
The tanks are coming nearer. Both radio stations are in rebel hands.
They have been playing the national anthem.
We will hold out to the last drop of blood. Downstairs there are men
who have only one hand grenade.
I am running over to the window in the next room to shoot. But I will
be back if there is anything new . . . or you ring me.
Don't be mad at the way I am writing. I am excited. I want to know
how this is going to end. I want to shoot but there is no target so far.
I will file to you as long as possible.
Where is the UN?
A Russian plane has just fired a machine-gun burst. We don't know
where. We just heard and saw it.
The building of barricades is going on. The Parliament and its vicinity
is crowded with tanks . . . Planes are flying overhead but can't be
counted there are so many. The tanks are coming in long lines.
Our building has already been fired on, but so far there are no
casualties. The roar of the tanks is so loud we can't hear each other's
voices.
Now I have to run over again to the next room to fire some shots from
the window. But I'll try to be back if there's anything new.

The young man took a 'rifle break', then returned.

> They just brought us a rumour that the American troops will be
> here within one or two hours.
> Bullets are hitting this building again. The tanks are now firing
> towards the Danube. Our boys are on the barricades and calling for
> more arms and ammunition. There is most bitter fighting in the inner
> city ... The tanks rolled away from our building and have gone
> somewhere else ...
> A shell just exploded nearby. Now there is heavy fighting in the
> direction of the National Theatre, near us in the centre of the city.
> In our building we have youngsters of fifteen and men of forty.
> Don't worry about us. We are strong even if we are a small nation.
> When the fighting is over we will rebuild our unhappy country.
> Send us any news you can about world action on Hungary's behalf.
> Don't worry ... we burn your despatches as soon as we have read
> them ...

Just before 11 a.m. the lines went dead. The reporter did not come
back.

PART ONE
PRELUDE

ONE

9 October 1944, Moscow

In his apartment in the Kremlin, Joseph Stalin hosted a war summit with Winston Churchill. Both men knew it was only a matter of months before Germany would be defeated. They wanted an understanding about the future of Europe after the conflict ceased.

Much to the annoyance of the British Prime Minster, who kept slightly more conventional hours, Stalin slept during the day and worked at night. The leaders met at 10 p.m., with only their Foreign Ministers, Vyacheslav Molotov and Anthony Eden, and two interpreters present. Churchill later described the scene: 'The moment was apt for business so I said "Let us settle our affairs in the Balkans. Your armies are in Romania and Bulgaria. We have interests, missions, agents there. Don't let us get at cross purposes in small ways. So far as Britain and Russia are concerned how would it do for you to have 90 per cent predominance in Romania, for us to have 90 per cent of the say in Greece and go 50/50 about Yugoslavia?"'

Churchill picked up some paper and wrote down on a half-sheet the deal he proposed. 'Hungary was another country to be split 50/50. Casting an eye over the paper, Stalin took his blue pencil and made a large tick upon it and passed it back to us. It was all settled in no more time than it takes to set down. After this there was a long silence. The pencilled paper lay in the centre of the table. At length I said "Might it not be thought rather cynical if it seemed we had disposed of these issues, so fateful to millions of people, in such an offhand manner? Let us burn the paper?" "No, you keep it," said Stalin.'[1] The next day Soviet troops crossed the border from Ukraine into eastern Hungary and they did not leave for a further forty-five years.

Diplomats and historians still argue about the significance of the 'percentage deal', or as Churchill called it, 'the naughty document'. Many say it was unimportant and simply recognised the reality of Russian troops on the ground. But taken together with US agreement at the Yalta Conference the following year, the post-war division of Europe had a massive psychological effect in Hungary. 'After the war we felt abandoned by the West,' Eva Walko, a well-informed and astute young woman who had travelled widely in the west between the wars noted. 'And our feeling proved to be right.' Eden minuted his Permanent Secretary, Alexander Cadogan, after the 'percentage deal' was struck: 'I expect the Russians will want to be very hard on the Hungarians.' He was a master of understatement.[2]

First, though, the Russians had to win their victory. The next six months in Hungary saw some of the most bitter fighting of the entire war. Two Soviet armies commanded by Marshal Rodion Malinowsky slowly encircled Budapest, while in the capital itself there was chaos and civil war.

Hungary, under its 'Regent' for the last quarter of a century, Admiral Miklós Horthy, had been a key ally of the Germans.* Horthy's manners were impeccable, but he was ruthless and violent. Thousands of his opponents were murdered or disappeared. His primary aim was simple: to win the return of historic Hungarian lands lost after the First World War. Hitler had promised to restore to Hungary most of Transylvania, Slovakia and Croatia, which had been ceded under the Treaty of Trianon. From the mid 1930s, with Horthy's blessing, Hungary became increasingly Nazified, and when the time came the Regent's army enthusiastically marched against Soviet Russia.

Hungarians escaped the worst of the war until March 1944, when the Germans occupied the country. They were desperate to bolster the steadily weakening Eastern Front and they wanted to make up for lost time in implementing the Final Solution in Central Europe. In barely six months 450,000 Hungarian Jews, those living outside Budapest, were sent to the gas chambers in Auschwitz-Birkenau. Even if Horthy had wanted to save them[3] – and the evidence is mixed, his private papers reveal him as a keen anti-Semite[4] – he could do nothing.

In September 1944 the Regent at last tried to do the decent thing. Knowing the Germans would lose the war, he made secret overtures to

---

* Horthy was in many ways the prototype *entre-deux-guerres* dictator. He took power in 1919 in a violent coup against a short-lived Soviet Republic after which thousands of leftists were killed and jailed. He ruled for nearly twenty-five years, narrowly avoiding prosecution after World War Two as a war criminal. He was the only Axis leader to die quietly in bed, enjoying peaceful retirement in Portugal.

Stalin about a separate Hungarian-Soviet peace. His attempt never came to anything. The Germans got wind of the plans. Commandos kidnapped his surviving son, Miklós junior, and on 15 October forced the Regent to abdicate. He was deported to Germany. Hitler replaced him as head of state with Ferenc Szálasi, the leader of the Arrow Cross, Hungary's home-grown fascist group, who unleashed an unprecedented reign of terror and destruction on the country that shocked even the German High Command by its barbarity.[5] The transports to the death camps had stopped in the summer. But the Arrow Cross continued the slaughter. Its gangs roamed Budapest rounding up Jews and anyone suspected of socialist sympathies. Scores of thousands were shot on the Danube quayside and thrown into the river.

As Malinowsky's troops tightened the circle around Budapest, the defeat of Hungary was an imminent prospect celebrated in anticipation by the Western allies. Unlike Poland or Czechoslovakia, Hungary was not then seen as a plucky little victim nation. Propaganda from London, Washington and Moscow remembered that the Hungarians had been on the 'wrong' side in two world wars and judged them to be among the chief troublemakers in Central Europe. The view of the Tory MP and diarist Harold Nicolson, a man of liberal opinions, was common at the time:

> When I learned that the Russian armies were within cannon-range of Budapest, I was conscious of delight, which I felt to be neither virtuous nor sane. My reason tells me that the Hungarians found themselves in a difficult position, and that it would have been hard indeed for them to maintain a stubborn neutrality. They were forced into the war by geographical necessity and by a burning resentment against the Treaty of Trianon. The fact is that since the day more than a thousand years ago, when Árpád first entered Hungary, the Magyars have done much harm and little good to Europe ... My satisfaction may be due to the quite rational feeling that this time the Hungarians will not again be able to disturb the peace.

The bloody siege of Budapest began on Christmas Eve and lasted fifty-one days. The Germans had transferred ten divisions to Hungary from the Western Front and Hitler's orders were to defend the city at all costs. More than 40,000 German troops and 70,000 Russians died in the battle, large numbers in hand-to-hand combat.[6] Uncounted thousands of civilians, hiding in basements, were killed in the crossfire. At the end Budapest lay in ruins. All the bridges spanning the two sides of the Danube had been blown up by the retreating Germans. After Berlin and Warsaw, Budapest was the most war-ravaged capital in Europe.[7] Ferenc Nagy,* shortly to become Prime Minister, described the sight as he came out of his hiding place on 14 February 1945: 'Man-high rubble covered the streets. High blockades of concrete, steel girders, lumber, brick and glass from the collapsed buildings jammed the thoroughfares. The wrecks of thousands of planes, tanks, armoured cars were everywhere . . . Merciful snow covered the uncounted dead. Animal carcasses littered the streets. Shop windows were full of the dead, while the wraith-like living ransacked the abandoned stores. Twisted tram rails jutted skyward like thin fingers of an imploring hand.'[8]

For a few days of joy the Russians were greeted rapturously as saviours. But the frontline army moved on for the final assault on Germany, leaving behind soldiers who made Hungarians understand very quickly what it meant to be a conquered enemy. The Red Army's occupation caused despair even among those who welcomed it as the defeat of fascism. Soon, hatred of the Soviet Union became stronger than before the defeat. The first Russian words most Hungarians learned was the phrase 'Davai tchassey' ('Give me your watch'). Looting was widespread, from officially sanctioned 'trophy brigades' which sought valuables that were sent back to Moscow, to soldiers emptying food stores.†

The great novelist Sándor Márai had his belongings stripped, as did many of his friends:

The Russian who dropped by in the morning, conversed amicably with the family, showed pictures of his wife and children back home, sentimentally patted the heads of the children and gave them candy, departed and then returned in the afternoon or late at night and robbed

---

* Not to be confused with Imre Nagy.
† The Hatvany family had the finest art collection in Hungary, with scores of works by Tintoretto, El Greco, both Cranachs, Delacroix, Manet, Corot, Rodin, Degas, Constable, Pissarro and Renoir. The Germans had pillaged much of the collection in autumn 1944, but had not managed to take the paintings back to Germany. When the Russians entered Hungary, Soviet 'trophy brigades' got their hands on the works. But the Hatvanys managed to buy some of the pieces back from the Russians in 1947 and smuggle them to the West.

the very same family he had made friends with that morning ... the looting was not aimed at the 'fascist enemy' but caused simply by abject poverty. These Communist Russians were so impoverished, so miserably destitute, so completely stripped of everything ... that now, set loose after 30 years of privation and drudgery, they threw themselves hungrily on everything that fell into their hands.[9]

That included women. For more than four decades, until Soviet troops left Hungary in 1990, almost nobody dared mention the taboo subject of the rapes committed by Russian soldiers in 1945. Many victims would not talk about it in their own families or with friends, let alone in public. It is still not known exactly how many women were raped, but a report made by the Swiss Embassy at the time, kept secret for many years, made a rough estimate of around 150,000 (from a female population of about 4.5 million). As a direct result the abortion laws were liberalised so that women could terminate unwanted pregnancies.[10]

Women were attacked from day one of the liberation, as Christine Arnothy, a fifteen-year-old girl emerging with her sister Ilas from a Budapest cellar, recalled: 'The Russians were advancing and ... at each house, a group of soldiers left the main body ... One detachment entered our house. The officer who commanded it yelled at us to know if there were any Germans in the house. Several of us nodded in the direction of the staircase. The German was killed on the spot and Ilas, whom they had found close to this wounded man, was raped beside the still warm corpse. From the first instant we understood that what was happening was very different from what we had hoped.'[11]

Alaine Polcz, in her early twenties at the war's end, had been a prisoner of the Germans. When the Russians reached her village in eastern Hungary she was effectively held prisoner again. Soviet troops had seen a picture of her with her husband. He was an officer in the Hungarian army, so they arrested her. She was held with a group of other women in a church presbytery near the front line, where she could hear constant gunfire. Years later she remembered her ordeal. 'Earlier on in the war I had seen those posters in Budapest showing a Russian soldier tearing a crucifix off a woman's neck and I'd read pamphlets saying that the Russians did this and that. I didn't believe any of it. Propaganda I thought.' Soon she learned differently. She saw a young girl whose head was bleeding – a lock of her hair had been torn out. She was miserable and desperate.

'The Russians rode her,' said her mother. I didn't understand. 'With a bicycle?' I asked. The woman became angry. 'Are you a fool? Don't you know what they do to women?'

The next day Ms Polcz was in a room with her mother-in-law:

In came three Russians and told me to go with them. Now I knew exactly what they wanted. I put on my boots and tied my headscarf, then I untied it and tied it again, then I untied it once again to gain some time. As I stood there I heard something knocking on the door; it was the heels of my boots, I was trembling so much.

We stepped out into an L-shaped corridor. I started to attack them wildly ... kicked and hit them with all my strength, but the next moment I was on the ground. No one made a sound. We fought in silence. They took me to the kitchen at the back of the house and as I tried to defend myself they flung me down so that I hit my head against the corner of the rubbish bin. It was made of hard wood.

I came round in the priest's big room. The window panes were broken, the windows were boarded up. There was nothing on the bed but bare boards on which I was lying. A Russian was on top of me ... The feeling in my body hadn't returned with my consciousness; it was as if I was numb or gone cold ... In that windowless unheated room I was naked from the waist down. I don't know how many Russians used me after that, or how many there had been before. As dawn was breaking they left me. I got up. I could only move with great difficulty. My head and my whole body ached. I was bleeding profusely. Over the next few days new troops arrived and I was pestered a lot.[12]

She was infected with syphilis from the repeated rapes.

Men who tried to protect women were viciously brushed aside, or killed. The best-known case was Bishop Vilmos Apor, from the western Hungarian town of Győr, who had bravely opposed the persecution of the Jews. On Good Friday 1945 drunken Soviet soldiers entered his palace in search of a group of young women they had seen going in through a side entrance. When the soldiers went down to the cellar they saw the Bishop in full ceremonial regalia blocking the entrance to the room where the women had sought refuge. He tried to wrestle with the intruders, but they shot him three times. Bishop Apor died two days later on Easter Sunday.[13]

For many Hungarians 'official looting', as they referred to war reparations paid to Russia after the post-war peace settlements, seemed as bad as the pillaging by soldiers. 'We have had three great tragedies in Hungary – the Tartar conquest in the thirteenth century, the 150-year Turkish occupation – and the Soviet liberation,' a well-rehearsed saying of the time went. The division of Europe and the punitive damages awarded against Hungary in the Yalta and Potsdam agreements were resented almost as much as the Versailles and Trianon treaties had been a generation earlier after the First World War. 'The victorious country demands us to assert its rights for the reason that the vanquished country started war against it,' Vladimir Dekanozov, the Soviet Union's Foreign Affairs Deputy Commissar, explained bluntly on an early visit to Budapest.[14]

Russia was entitled to all German-owned property in Hungary; this was to compensate the USSR for some of the losses incurred at the hands of the Nazis. About a third of Hungarian industry had been controlled by German capital – worth around $1 billion (at 1945 prices). Two hundred complete factories, and the machinery from 300 more, were dismantled and sent to the Soviet Union.[15] Russia took over entire industries, setting up companies under joint Russian-Hungarian ownership. In this way the Soviets were able to profit from steel plants, railway construction, shipping on the Danube and transport, electricity coal and oil. István Ries, the first post-war Minister of Justice, a socialist, joked to a friend about the terms of the joint Soviet-Hungarian Shipping Company. 'You know, the agreement came about on the basis of perfect equality. The Russians have the right to ship up and down the river. We have the right to ship across.'*

A third of the gold and silver reserves were taken by the Russians. Two hundred million dollars had to be paid in official war reparations to the Soviet Union and $50 million each to the other neighbouring 'victorious nations', Yugoslavia and Czechoslovakia (at 1938 prices).

---

* A fatal joke as it turned out. His sense of humour often got him into trouble and was considered far too dangerous by the Communists. He was arrested, thrown into prison, and on 15 September 1950 beaten to death under police interrogation.

The Hungarian national budget for 1946–7 set aside as war reparations eight times the sum allotted for post-war reconstruction.[16] UN officials estimated three years after the war ended that the total material loss to Hungary of Soviet reparations, occupation and looting was 40 per cent of national income.[17]

Partly due to the pressure of paying the reparations, and partly due to successive years of poor harvest, the currency collapsed. Hungary faced record hyperinflation. A US dollar was worth 1,320 pengo in July 1945. By November that year the exchange rate was one to 296,000. In the summer of next year it was 4.6 quadrillion to the dollar (that is fourteen noughts, an unenviable record). Most Hungarians refused to be paid in money. The wallpaper in many Budapest rooms was decorated with large banknotes in fantastical denominations. The currency was stabilised, largely with the help of the Americans, who returned to the National Bank $40 million of gold reserves that had been taken to Germany in late 1944. Had the gold remained in Hungary at the moment of 'liberation' it would undoubtedly have been seized as booty by the Russians.[18]

Along with the Russian troops there came a group of Hungarian-born Communists, known as Muscovites. About 300-strong, they had spent long years in Russian exile, preparing for the day they would re-enter Budapest in triumph. Handpicked by Stalin, their purpose was to act as proconsuls in the Hungarian province of the Red Tsar's new imperium. They were chosen for one thing: unwavering loyalty to the USSR. Most of them were Soviet citizens and had spent fifteen or twenty years in Russia. They had lost contact with the land of their birth. The Soviet Union had given them shelter, a cause to believe in and a job. Most were professional Communist agitators who had never worked at anything else. Almost all of them had spent terms in jail of varying length under the Horthy regime. When they returned to Hungary after the war, they were not going home. Hungary had ceased to be home a long time ago for most of them. They returned as representatives of a foreign power, to serve the interests of the Soviet Union. They could have been sent anywhere and served their overlords in Moscow with equal fervour.

Life as an émigré in Soviet Russia was a dangerous business. Surviving the purges from the mid 1930s onwards was hard enough for a Russian. A foreigner who might be working as a Comintern agent, regularly in touch with other potentially dubious strangers, was always a mistrusted figure. Many lived in the seedy Hotel Lux in Moscow with other émigrés, constantly watchful of each other – and of their own backs. Several prominent Hungarian Communists had perished in Stalin's purges in the 1930s. The assassin's bullet had been the fate of Béla Kun, who had been head of the tragi-comic Communist republic in Hungary that lasted just 133 days in 1919. Even his status as a minor celebrity could not save him from being liquidated as a Trotskyite agent.

The Muscovite lived a life of slogans and – when the slogans changed, as they repeatedly did at the whim of Stalin – of grave danger.

> The Muscovite's life was by no means enviable. Its leitmotif was fear. A Muscovite ... was never safe wherever he went – least of all the Soviet Union. Neither his loyalty, nor his long Party membership would protect him. He knew that he did not even have to commit a mistake in order to be relieved of his job, or to be arrested and tried. Muscovites knew that no such thing as permanent truth existed – because no such thing ever existed in the Soviet Union. [A Muscovite] knew the truth has many faces and the only thing that concerned him was which face was on top just then. He was fully aware that at all times truth was what the Secretary General or the Supreme Body of the Party held to be truth and therefore it did not particularly bother him that yesterday's truth had changed, by today, into a lie.[19]

The Muscovites knew what was expected of them. They were to build a Soviet colony without the slightest deviation from the Stalinist model. But the plan was not to take over immediately. The order from their masters in the Kremlin was to wait until the time was right.

TWO

Budapest, 1945

The man Stalin chose as his viceroy in Budapest was Mátyás Rákosi. His crimes are little known outside Hungary. Had he acted on a bigger stage he would now be recognised as one of the greatest monsters of the twentieth century, despite competition from so many challengers. In nearly a decade of power he murdered and jailed as many Hungarians, proportionately, as his patron managed in the Soviet Union. He fascinated, repelled and terrified his subjects in equal measure.

Rákosi was born on 9 March 1892, in the small town of Ada Szabadka (now Subotica in Serbia). His father, József Rosenfeld, was a reasonably well-off grocer. The family Magyarised its surname in 1904, a common enough practice at the time for middle-class Jews who wished to assimilate into Hungarian society. The young Rákosi was extraordinarily precocious and at seventeen was awarded a place to study as a classicist at Budapest's Oriental Academy. But he wanted commercial experience, so he worked as a clerk in Hamburg in 1912 and for a few months in 1914 at a bank in London.

He returned to Hungary at the outbreak of the First World War and volunteered for the army. As a sergeant in an infantry battalion on the Eastern Front, he was taken prisoner by the Russians in 1915. He became a passionate convert to communism after the Bolsheviks took power while he was still a prisoner of war. Rákosi often used to say that one of the proudest moments of his life was when he briefly met Lenin in Petrograd in 1918. But as he was a supreme liar it is just as likely the meeting never happened. No record of it exists.[1]

He was one of the founding members of the Hungarian Communist Party. During the short but violent course of Béla Kun's Soviet Republic and Red Terror, Rákosi was the youngest Commissar, albeit in a junior post. He escaped the White Terror that followed Admiral Horthy's takeover; Hungary's history is one of extremes, especially in the last century. Rákosi fled to Austria, where he was briefly interned. Then

in 1920 he found his way to Russia, where the Soviets quickly recognised his abilities. He was a fabulously gifted linguist, an invaluable
asset in his chosen career of making world revolution. He spoke ten
languages fluently, including Turkish, which he had learned as a prisoner of war. As Secretary of the Comintern he travelled Europe on six
forged passports, helping to set up Communist Parties loyal to Moscow
in Czechoslovakia, Italy and Austria.

In 1925 he was sent back to Hungary, where the Communist Party
was banned. The next year he was arrested and sentenced to eight and
a half years in jail on charges of sedition. Rákosi became a well-known
figure of international standing when his jail term ended in 1935.
Instead of releasing him, the Horthy regime decided to make an example
of him and tried him again – this time for his activities in 1919. Protests
were made to the Regent from all over the world, but Horthy was deaf
to the pleas.

Rákosi conducted his own defence and, when sentenced to life
imprisonment, with little hope of seeing daylight again, he confronted
his fate with the bravery expected in Moscow of a revolutionary. He
defiantly declared in court, 'My personal fate is indifferent to me, but
the cause I live for will be triumphant.' Rákosi because a *cause célèbre*
on the left everywhere. The Hungarian battalion of the International
Brigade fighting in the Spanish Civil War was named after him. In 1940,
after the Hitler-Stalin Pact, Rákosi was allowed to leave for the USSR.*
He was given a hero's welcome in Moscow. Stalin gave Rákosi pride of
place on the dais at the Red Square celebrations on 7 November 1940
to celebrate the twenty-third anniversary of the Russian Revolution.

Rákosi had anything but heroic looks, though. Short, fat and bald,
he was, later, when dictator in Hungary, invariably called behind his
back 'Arsehead'. The Hungarian playwright Gyula Háy, who knew
Rákosi well in Soviet exile, described him: 'A short, squat body, as if
the creator had been unable to finish his work for abhorrence; the
head disproportionately large, topped by an enormous bald dome and
fronted by a pallid bloated face with a sweet-and-sour smile frozen on

---

* Rákosi was exchanged for two highly symbolic Hungarian battle flags that the
Russians had possessed for the last century. They were the banners of the revo-
lutionary Hungarian army fighting for liberation from Austria in 1848 under Kossuth.
The Hungarians' brave struggle had been bloodily crushed by the tsarist army of
Russia, in alliance with the Austrian emperor.

to it. Virtually no neck between the high shoulders, so that it was left more or less to the observer whether he called him a hunchback or not. Clumsy in movement, with a tendency to flatfootedness; short, stubby fingers . . .'[2]

His biographers suggest that he had no passions, except for power. He did not drink or philander. In sexual matters, he was a pillar of Bolshevik rectitude. Two years after his release from jail, at a rest home near Moscow, he met and married a lawyer from Yakutsk in Siberia. Fenya Fiodorovna Kornyilova was eleven years younger than he, equally fervent in Communist faith, and by all accounts they lived happily together until he died. Rákosi was formidably vain, and cruel to the point of sadism. He would never get blood on his own hands. Perhaps nearly a decade and a half in jail warped him. But he was fascinated by the mechanics of terror. Like Stalin he revelled in hearing from his thugs in grim detail how victims of his prisons reacted under torture or at the moment of execution.[3]

His cynicism was overwhelming. In 1952 Rákosi wanted to ban the word 'rape' in Hungarian literature after one writer, Tibor Déry, had written a story that dared to mention a women being violated by a Russian soldier after 1945. Rákosi furiously attacked the author: 'Can't you leave this idiocy alone?' he said. 'What is there to write about? In Hungary there are, say, 3,000 villages. Supposing the Russians have their way with, say, three women in each village that makes 9,000 in all. Is that so many?* You writers have no idea of the law of large numbers.'[4] He spoke about that law often. Once he explained how to keep Communist appraratchiks loyal. It was by 'calculating the law of large numbers . . . killing some and corrupting the rest'.[5]

Yet many people who met him were massively impressed. In some ways he was a man of remarkable ability and eloquence. He had phe-nomenal powers of memory. He had charm, wit, an exceptionally good brain and excellent manners when he chose to show them. He was a fine orator, who spoke in straightforward language. If he resorted to Marxist-Leninist jargon, he would leaven a speech with a few jokes. Rákosi was also blessed with luck. Stalin neither liked nor trusted him. For a start he was a Jew, and the Red Tsar in the Kremlin was a fervent anti-Semite. Stalin also knew that Rákosi was not the hero Communist

---

* Rákosi was not so brilliant with large numbers himself. He vastly underestimated how many Hungarian women were raped.

propaganda made him out to be. When Rákosi was arrested in 1925, under interrogation by Horthy's counter-intelligence service, he had given away some secrets about the operations of the Comintern which found their way to the espionage agencies in Britain and France. Many faithful Party workers, however long they had suffered in fascist prisons, perished for lesser offences. But instead of being 'purged' for such serious errors, all he received from the magnates in the Kremlin was a reprimand. Stalin said, in an untypically forgiving moment, that Rákosi had atoned in jail.[6]

Despite serious doubts, Stalin judged Rákosi to be useful and made him leader of the Hungarian Communists. When the Red Army completed its task of defeating the Germans, Rákosi was despatched to Hungary with specific instructions to turn the country into a model Soviet colony. They were orders Rákosi would obey in minute detail.

THREE

4 November 1945

This was polling day. Uniquely in its new European empire, the Soviet Union allowed genuinely free elections in Hungary. These were the first honest and fair elections the country had ever held (and the last for another forty-five years). Stalin always intended to take power in Hungary, but restrained himself from immediately installing puppet regimes as he had done in Poland, Bulgaria, Romania and his other fiefdoms. He was certain that time was on his side. More important than local considerations, big power politics dictated caution. He thought that a show of democracy somewhere in Central Europe might halt the tide of protests he was receiving from his erstwhile wartime allies about Russian behaviour elsewhere.[1]

Nevertheless, when late in the evening the results of the vote began coming in they were a profound shock to the returning Muscovites, and to Stalin's man on the spot, the preening sixty-four-year-old Marshal Kliment Voroshilov. He was not a man well known for his brains. As a military commander, he had been removed from any serious role in the war for decisively losing battle after battle. Yet, as a supreme syco-phant, he had not only survived, he was among the most prominent courtiers in Stalin's closest circle. Despite Voroshilov's great weakness for alcohol, Stalin had given him an important job in shaping Russia's western empire.

The Communists received just 17 per cent of the vote, the same as the leftist Social Democratic Party. The Smallholders Party, traditional representatives of the urban bourgeois and landed gentry, won a plur-ality of the vote. The results were even worse than the Budapest municipal election results six weeks earlier, when the Communist Party got 18 per cent of the vote and Voroshilov struck Rákosi in his anger.[2] The Russian had been led to believe the Communists would do much better: 'If we do them well they should show a colossal Communist/Social Democrat victory,' Rákosi wrote to Voroshilov in the summer. He predicted 'a majority of 70 per cent, perhaps more'.[3] 'The loss was heavily felt,' Gyula Háy, who had just returned to Hungary after years of exile, recalled. 'We couldn't believe that we would be so resoundingly defeated after all that the leading socialist nation in the world had achieved for Hungary.'

Rákosi, changing his tack, blamed the poor showing on the behaviour of the Russian liberators – one of the very few times he had anything critical to say of the Soviet Union. He wrote to Georgi Dimitrov, head of the Soviet Communist Party's International Department: 'Our position is made more difficult by the fact that the excesses of the Red Army are written on the Party's account. The cases of mass rapes of women, the looting, etc. were repeated with the liberation of each territory.'[4]

Voroshilov had already announced before the election that whatever the results would be, the coalition government which had been in place since the war ended would remain in office. The Communists had a share of power, three Ministries and a job for Rákosi as deputy Premier. The Russian Marshal, acting as chairman of the Allied Control Commission, made all the major decisions.* Technically, Voroshilov was supposed to run the ACC on behalf of the three Allies. But in practice at the weekly meetings he simply announced what he had decided to the American representative, Arthur Schoenfeld, and Britain's Alvary Gascoigne. As Schoenfeld wrote in a cable to the State Department: 'Orders have been given by the Soviet chairman of the ACC that communication between the representatives of the Western allies and the Hungarian authorities must be channelled through himself.'[5] The Western powers tolerated this with little complaint, tacit endorsement of Soviet control of the country that did serious harm to their prestige in the eyes of Hungarians. The small, lean, intense-looking Prime Minister, Ferenc Nagy, a forty-four-year-old Smallholder well known in liberal circles throughout Europe, described how he had to refer decisions to the Russian authorities. If he also told the Americans and the British, he was accused by Voroshilov of scheming.[6]

*

* Or rather his deputy Lieutenant-General Vladimir Sviridov took most of them. Voroshilov was a very heavy consumer of vodka, especially during his time in Budapest.

In the summer of 1945 the Communist Party moved into offices in central Budapest that had been occupied by the Gestapo. But at first the Communists behaved with propriety as coalition partners and even managed to look like model democrats. 'Unite all forces for reconstruction' was Rákosi's favourite slogan. To show their goodwill the Communists helped to repair bombed-out churches. Rákosi's sinister, cadaverous number two, Ernő Gerő, performed with superhuman effort the task of rebuilding the bridges over the Danube in Budapest.* The Communists were the driving force behind long-overdue land reforms that even leading figures on the right had urged over the last half-century. Hungary was still largely a peasant economy in 1945. For all Hungary's famed urban sophistication and the lively café society of its capital, it was also known between the wars as 'the land of a million beggars'. It was an aristocratic society where serfdom had been abolished less than a century earlier, in 1849. Almost half the arable land belonged to one per cent of landowners. The Esterházys for example owned 152,000 hectares, Count György Festetics 43,000, and Count Pallavicini 35,000. The Roman Catholic Church in Hungary was one of the biggest landowners in Europe, with 720,000 hectares of prime agricultural land.[7]

About two million hectares were now distributed among 600,000 peasants. Nobody was allowed to own more than twenty hectares. The plan was enthusiastically supported by all the parties in the coalition. But it was implemented by a Communist, a plump, cheerful, professional-looking forty-nine-year-old with a trademark walrus moustache called Imre Nagy who had become an expert in agronomy while in long exile in Moscow. He claimed the achievement as a victory for communism, earned the nickname 'Land Divider' and gained a large popularity he never lost.

Many Hungarians believed – with a strange optimism, and despite the evidence from elsewhere in the Soviet domains – that the Russians would allow this fledgling democracy to take root and prosper. The right-wing philosopher Oscar Jászi rejected the suggestion that 'what is taking place is simply a repetition of what has occurred in the Baltic States, in Bulgaria, in Romania. The demagogy of the Bolsheviks is absent. Communism has become respectable and gentlemanly. Even the criticism of certain governmental measures by the Roman Catholic

* Gerő, ironically as things turned out, earned the popular nickname 'Bridge Builder'.

hierarchy was listened to with respect ... and the rejoinder was moderate and tactful. Generally speaking there is not much talk about Communism today.' The atmosphere, rather, was 'of democracy with intensely patriotic overtones'.[8] Hugh Seton-Watson, a British academic expert on Eastern Europe in general and Hungary in particular, was hopeful for the future. 'A visitor to Hungary will be surprised by the vigorous intellectual activity displayed both in print and in con-versation. In comparison with the mental sterility and haunting fear prevalent in the Balkans, Hungary seemed an oasis of culture and liberty.'[9]

It could not last. Rákosi returned to Hungary with carefully cal-culated instruction from Stalin for a two- to three-year programme of capturing power step by step. The Soviet dictator wrote them down in a top-secret letter to his Hungarian satrap as early as 5 December 1944 while the battle for Budapest was still raging. He cautioned Rákosi against excessive speed and advised, 'Don't be grudging with words, don't scare anyone. But once you gain ground then move ahead. You must utilise as many people as possible who may be of use to us.'[10]

Stalin realised that Rákosi and the other Muscovites were returning to a country they barely knew or understood. Hungary would not be fertile ground, despite having endured a quarter of a century of fascism and a disastrous German occupation. There were hardly any Com-munists in Hungary. The underground Party leader inside the country during the last period of the war, the barely known thirty-two-year-old one-time mechanic János Kádár, estimated that there were perhaps 200 members when Hungary was 'liberated', a dozen of whom he knew personally. With such limited support, it was not going to be easy to take control. But there were still 75,000 Soviet troops in Hungary ready to lend a willing hand, and if the Communists had no training as democratic politicians they had plenty of experience in the arts of intrigue, bribery and intimidation.

The Muscovites had further major problems to overcome. They could bring no sweeteners with them from the Kremlin to make Hungary's defeat and occupation seem less bitter. The Soviets had swiftly made some border settlements after the war. Poland's western frontier was restored to pre-Hitler days. Romania was granted Tran-sylvania in perpetuity. Czechoslovakia was cleared of its German and Hungarian populations. These Slavic states seemed to win something at least, while Hungary, culturally totally apart, and allied to Germany, lost everything. The Muscovite leaders were aware of this. There was talk of what 'dowry' they could bring, but the Soviets were not prepared to discuss it. Rákosi and his clique had no national base, which made them even more dependent on the USSR, more keen to seek Stalin's favour and submit themselves to Soviet bidding, outdoing all other client states in their 'revolutionary vigilance' against the slightest deviation from the Russian model. The leading Muscovites – Rákosi and the trio closest to him of Gerő, the vicious Defence Minister Mihály Farkas and the urbane, brilliant and reptilian cultural tsar József Révai – were Jews. In a country where anti-Semitism ran so deep, this caused great resentment. Not to be outdone or outflanked, Rákosi, grotesquely, turned himself into one of the keenest anti-Semites in Hungary. 'You would think the Catholic Church was the largest centre of anti-state intelligence. But in reality, because Jews are everywhere, Zionism is the real centre of espionage,' he wrote in a private letter to a fellow Jewish Muscovite.[11]

There was little controversy about the early steps of the coalition government. Plenty of scores had to be settled from the war and the quarter-century of Horthy's dictatorship. After relatively fair trials, 279 war criminals, including four former Prime Ministers, Arrow Cross leaders, Hungarian volunteers with the SS and prominent fascists, were hanged. This was popular justice. A year after the war ended angry mobs stormed the gate of the Central Prison yard in Budapest when they heard that admission tickets would be required to witness the execution of war criminals. Until then such executions had been public spectacles.[12]

Some others, with good anti-fascist records, simply disappeared into the Gulag. István Bethlen, Prime Minister from 1921 to 1931 and a trusted adviser to Horthy, wanted a separate peace with the Soviet Union towards the end of the war. In the Cabinet he countered the objection that the Soviets would rape and loot with the answer, 'perhaps so, but they will do less if they came as friends'. He was arrested, deported to the USSR and never heard of again. In 1939 the distinguished monarchist politician Iván Lajos, a strong anti-Nazi, published the 'Grey Book' denouncing Hitler's preparation for war. The book was banned by Horthy following pressure from the Germans. He spent much of the war in Mauthausen concentration camp. After he returned home he proposed a Danubian confederation for Central

Europe that would include Hungary, Austria and Czechoslovakia. He was sent to Russia and disappeared.[13]

The Communists proceeded to fragment and eliminate the opposition using methods that Rákosi famously called 'salami tactics'. The initial target was the centre-right, bourgeois Smallholders Party which had gained by far the most votes at the election. Rákosi claimed to have uncovered a plot by a secret right-wing organisation called the Hungarian Community Movement which, he maintained, wanted to restore the pre-war regime. The charge was nonsense, but twenty-four Smallholder MPs were unmasked as members and forced to resign. The most impressive of the Smallholder leaders, Béla Kovács, was seen by the Communists as a threat. He was implicated in the so-called plot. He claimed an MP's privilege, which was supposed to give him immunity from arrest, but on 27 February 1947 Russian troops entered the Parliament building in Budapest, arrested him and deported him to the Soviet Union. He did not return to Hungary for nine years.

Prime Minister Ferenc Nagy was removed next. In the spring of 1947 he went on holiday. Rákosi called him in Switzerland and made him an offer he could not refuse to stay out of Hungary. Nagy would be unmasked as the ringleader of another plot if he returned. But if he stayed in the West his baby son would be sent to him. Nagy accepted the deal.[14]

Rákosi, speaking to trainee Party cadres later, was remarkably frank about the devious and duplicitous route the Communists took to power, boasting about the slow-motion putsch that gave them authority. He explained: 'Our demands were always modest at first – and were then increased ... For instance, first we demanded only "government control" of the banks; only later did we call for the outright nationalisation of the three largest banks. It was precision methods, salami tactics that enabled us to defeat the reactionaries.'[15]

Having decapitated his main political opponents, Rákosi led the Communists into new elections in the summer of 1947. All campaigning was overshadowed by the terms of the long-delayed Paris Peace Treaty. The details were a huge blow to Hungarian hopes that Soviet soldiers might soon leave. The Russians were allowed to keep their troops in the country in order to maintain lines of communication with their forces occupying a zone of Austria. Rákosi admitted that it was the continued 'presence of the Soviet troops that tipped the scales to set up the People's Democracy'. His fellow Muscovite, József Révai, explained it in simple terms, 'We were in a minority in Parliament and in the government but at the same time we represented the leading force. We had decisive control over the police . . . Our force was multiplied by the fact that the Soviet Union and the Soviet army were always there to support us with their assistance.'[16]

Despite the knowledge that Russian troops would stay for the foreseeable future, and the increasingly clear signs of the way Rákosi was moving, the voters still rejected the Communists. The 1947 election was much less honest than the poll two years earlier. Hundreds of thousands of people had mysteriously been disenfranchised in what was popularly known as the 'blue chit' election, because many absentee voters gave their proxies on blue paper to Communist activists, some of whom voted several times. Even so, the Communists received just 22 per cent of the vote.

From very early on the Communists had taken control of the trade unions, which they used as tools in their hands. They were definitely not in favour of strikes. As Rákosi said to Arthur Schoenfeld, 'strikes for the improvement of working conditions or higher wages were not permissible in Hungary. They were a luxury that only the American economy could afford.'[17]

Next the Social Democrats were destroyed. In the Horthy years Moscow encouraged Hungarian Communists and fellow travellers to join the (legal) Social Democrats. Now the party voted itself out of existence. It held a rigged internal referendum on merging with the Communists. As all those against the merger were barred from the party and banned from voting, only one result was allowed. In June 1948 the two parties united.* It had taken almost three years, the time frame Stalin had in mind, but now the Communists had untrammelled power.

---

* The merger formed the Hungarian Socialist Workers Party. Despite numerous name changes over the years, it never had the word Communist in the title. However, everyone knew it as the Communist Party and I shall call it such.

FOUR
1948

From mid 1948 the red star began appearing on public buildings and factories throughout the country. Rákosi was ready to perform the task for which his overlord in the Kremlin had selected him: to transform Hungary along Soviet lines into a People's Republic that would be the envy of the other satellites.

The banks had been expropriated in the autumn. On 28 December 1948, all companies with more than ten employees were nationalised. For a tantalisingly brief period of three years the peasants had been allowed to possess some of their own land. As a result, the shops were bulging with produce. Now farms were to be collectivised into huge, state-owned enterprises that would once more turn peasants into serfs.

Placards and posters on street corners displayed Rákosi's ugly features under the slogan 'Stalin's best pupil'. The most important lesson he had learned was that the simplest way to please his master in Moscow was to copy everything Stalin had done in the Soviet Union. In almost every walk of life Soviet 'advisers' were invited to show Hungarians how things should be done. Rákosi himself hardly moved a step without referring to his 'advisers'. The traditional, highly rigorous education system, based as elsewhere in Central Europe on 'gymnasium' schools, was altered to the Soviet model, with Russian taught to children as the only foreign language. The national flag was changed. It was still a red, white and green tricolour, but the emblem designed by the great nineteenth-century revolutionary hero Lajos Kossuth became a Soviet-style hammer and sickle. Public holidays now conformed to those in the USSR. The twentieth of August, the traditional Feast of St Stephen honouring Hungary's first king and patron saint, became Constitution Day. One of the first clauses in the new constitution itself, which took effect, with gross insensitivity, on 20 August 1949, contained profuse thanks to the 'glorious Soviet Union for its historic role in liberating our country'.[1] Christmas Day became 'Pine Needles Day'. The coffee house, so vital to the social and cultural life of Hungary, was denounced as the last vestige of a decadent lifestyle; so were the 'bourgeois' artists to whom the café was second home.

The army was reorganised. Standard issue weapons were Russian-made. Equipment included the Soviet T34 tank, but it could not fire shells. A vital component in the targeting mechanism was removed and held by the Russian adviser. It was smaller, everyday things that really annoyed officers, regular soldiers and conscripts, though. The main meal of the day in mess was changed from dinner in the evening to midday, for no obvious reason other than that was the way in the Soviet army. From 1946 the Hungarian army, the Honvéd, was clothed in Soviet uniforms, with Soviet lapel badges. This rankled with every-one who had been, was then, or would be in the army. In the country, even the name given to the loathed collective farm system gave offence. A collective was called a 'kolkhoz', a Russian, not a Magyar, word.

The Russification of the country burned as a profound national grievance. Becoming, in effect, a colony of another country was deeply wounding to a nation that had lost an empire of its own barely a generation earlier. 'That hurt the most,' Sándor Zsindely, a student at the time who later became a distinguished scientist in Hungary, recalls. 'Having communism thrust down our throats unwillingly was bad enough. Terrible. But having so many alien ways imposed on us, and being told they were superior, was a constant insult. Every day the Russians seemed to grind our noses in the fact that they were the masters. We couldn't forgive them.'

As usual, beneath the anger, a joke was invented by Hungarians to lessen the pain of what was happening to them. 'A Party Secretary is asked to make a tour of rural Hungary. Talking to an old farmer, he asks: "Tell me, who made the world?" The farmer knows there is only one answer, but knows also that it is the wrong answer. He hesitates before replying and the Party man looks at him in exasperation. "Wait, Comrade, I haven't finished," he says. "God made the world – with the help of Soviet experts."'

One replica of a Russian model that evolved into the most feared organisation in the country was the AVO.* Based on the Soviet Union's

---

* The AVO, 'Államvédelmi Osztály (State Security Department) became the AVH, 'Államvédelmi Hatóság' (State Security Authority) in 1948. Hungarians continued to call it the more easily pronounced AVO (Ah-voe).

KGB,* it became the engine of the most brutally efficient police state in Eastern Europe. Rákosi said: 'There was one position on which we [our Party] staked a claimed from the first minute – and here we considered no coalitionist compromise. This was the state security service . . . We took a tight grip on this organisation from the first day it was set up.'[2] The AVO's task was to eliminate opposition to the Party and for many years it was ruthlessly good at the job. There is a word in Hungarian that was widely used in the late 1940s and 1950s, 'csengőfrász', which translates as 'bell fever'. It meant the terror throughout the country of the ring at the door in the middle of the night – like most secret policemen throughout the world, the AVO operated best in the dark, in the small hours. AVO officers could be recognised by their blue uniforms with green epaulettes and their swagger.

The headquarters of the AVO was at 60 Stalin Avenue,† one of the smartest addresses in Budapest, which had been the base of the Arrow Cross. For eighteen months after 'liberation', on Rákosi's orders, the Communist Party recruited many former Arrow Cross members into the private security force it was organising for itself.[3] He once differentiated between the 'bourgeois Arrow Cross, the big fish', who were executed, and 'working-class fascists', the 'small fry' whom he welcomed into the fold. He cared less about their class consciousness, or their ideological commitment to communism. They were practised in brutal intimidation. He said they would remain thoroughly loyal out of self-interest, because they could easily be blackmailed later about their shady past. If they became a problem they could be disposed of when they were no longer needed.[4]

Outwardly, Number 60 looked like any of the avenue's other elegant office buildings. The AVOs' cars – always black-curtained Pobodas – decamped their prisoners along a side road, Csengory Street, through a gate into a courtyard that seemed innocuous enough at first sight. However, on one side of the yard the AVO had built a six-metre-high wall and placed a tower manned twenty-four hours a day by a machine-

---

* During parts of this story, Soviet intelligence also changed its name – from the NKVD, to the MGB to the KGB. I shall stick within the last, best-known, name, the KGB.

† The building is now a fascinating and very well-organised museum. Visitors should not be put off by its rather crass name, the House of Terror. Stalin Avenue, soon after 1958, became Avenue of the People and is now, as it was when it was built towards the end of the nineteenth century, Andrássy Avenue.

gunner. Inside this world were dank cells and torture rooms with
equipment ranging from whips, truncheons and nail presses to elec-
trodes. The basement housed the feared 'lefolyó', an acid bath where
victims' remains were sent into the city's main drainage system.

The boss of the AVO, Gábor Péter, was the most detested man in
Hungary after Rákosi. He had been born Gábor Auspitz in 1900, and
worked as a tailor's assistant before finding his true vocation of
thuggery. Arrested briefly by the Horthy police for Communist
agitation, he escaped to the Soviet Union and immediately began work
for the Russian secret police.* He was despatched as an enforcer
throughout Europe to keep local parties obedient to Moscow. When
he returned to Hungary with the other Muscovites he instantly set to
work building the AVO on strict Stalinist lines as a terror organisation.
The writer Paul Ignotus was interrogated by him, while the goon squad
of torturers looked on: Péter had 'a huge wood-panelled study, with a
big chandelier. Everything connected with him was on a big scale
except himself. He was a short man with rodent eyes and a Hitler
moustache ... His taste for good tailoring had never left him. He was
in an impeccable grey suit with a perfect silk tie, which he fingered all
the time.'[5]

His lifestyle was a real scandal. Most of the top Hungarian officials
led fairly humdrum lives of bourgeois propriety. Péter, on the other
hand, was a heavy drinker and kept a string of mistresses. He was
married to the beautiful and terrifying Jolán Simon, also a KGB agent,
who was Rákosi's personal secretary. They had an unconventional (for
the 1950s) 'open relationship' and lived in luxury, surrounded by
servants, in a large villa on Rózsadomb (Rose Hill) with a sweeping
view over the Danube below. He survived and prospered because
everyone knew he was one of the KGB's top men in Hungary, with a
direct line to the Lubyanka. In pride of place on Péter's office walls
was a picture of him clinking glasses with Stalin. He left deliberately
vague how close his relationship to the Glorious Teacher might be. He
was staggeringly cynical, even for a Communist executioner. When he
interrogated the poet György Faludy, who had returned in the late
1940s from the safety and comfort of America to live in Hungary, he

* Péter helped to 'turn' Kim Philby, one of Russia's most prominent spies and one of
Britain's notorious traitors, to the Communist cause. In the 1930s Péter recruited Litzi
Friedman, Philby's first wife, into working for Soviet Intelligence.

taunted his victim: 'We don't need such idiots as you ... You silly fool, returning from America to live in this filth.'[6]

Chief torturer was the notorious Lieutenant-Colonel Gyula Prinz, a coalman and a former member of the Arrow Cross, who had worked in the same building, doing the same job for the fascist dictatorship. He was a huge, pot-bellied, immensely strong man – bald on the top of his head but hirsute everywhere else – who, it was estimated, had personally tortured in his lifetime more than 25,000 people. He took much pride in his work. His task was to extract confessions and he insisted it had to be done 'correctly'. During his interrogation by Prinz, Ignotus was told to stand by the wall holding a pencil between his nose and his mouth. Of course, eventually the pencil fell. 'He beat me until my whole body was swollen with purple bruises and a couple of teeth were kicked out. He said to me: "Why don't you use a writer's imagination and write a confession?" The essence was not to write absurd things, but to tell "credible lies only".' Ignotus went on: 'The manufacture of outright lies, elevated to the status of truth through forced or forged confessions, was rationalised by the AVO inquisitors by various formulae. One sought to distinguish between ordinary "factual" proof and "political truth", with the latter of course taking precedence. The practical effect was that the moment anyone was placed on the regime's list of suspects, the crime of which he was suspected became a "political truth", justifying the invention of almost any "facts" needed to prove it.'[7]

Others had a different experience of the subtlety and sophisticated brainpower of the AVO's torturers. Faludy said:

They extracted a detailed confession from me in which I admitted that I had gone to France to join a Trotskyite group to engage in anti-Soviet activity while working for the post-war restoration of capitalism. I was handed over to an 'American expert' [in the AVO] who made me describe how I had engaged in subversive activity and, while in America, had joined the OSS, America's espionage agency ... I concluded they were preparing a Trotskyite spy trial of which I would be one of the principal accused. I therefore did my best to invent details of a kind to make foreign journalists guess what was going on. I told my interrogator, for instance, that I had been recruited to the OSS by two American agents: Captain Edgar Allan Poe and Major Walt Whitman, describing the two men in great detail. In case one of the investigators or the judge might discover my purpose, I invented a third American agent, the club-footed Z.E. Bubbel – an anagram of Beelzebub – whom I intended to unmask only at the trial. I talked at length about the wild orgies at the New York offices of the OSS from where – after we had got drunk to the gills ... – I had been carried home by Bubbel himself. When my interrogator asked me for the New York address of OSS HQ I was unable to answer because I had never been there, so I suggested he look it up in the NY phone book; upon which he gave me a beating and made me stand for two days and three nights with my nose pressed to the wall. By then he had put the address in my 'confession'.[8]

The most common form of AVO torture was the 'short iron' – agony on the back and knees. A prisoner's hands were fettered to his feet and he was told to stand for between four and sixteen hours. Another favourite, particularly of Gyula Prinz, was 'wolf's bandage'. This involved tying prisoners' wrists to their knees and hanging them on a pole, head downwards. In this position they would beat a (male) prisoner's testicles. A prisoner would then be ordered to drink salt water so his swollen tongue would almost strangle him. This could go on for days, or, more accurately, nights.[9] Béla Szász, a refugee who fled to Britain, was incarcerated for five years by the AVO and described a typical torture session: 'Somebody would sit on a man's backside and lift up his legs and another would hit him with a rubber truncheon with all his might ... This treatment consisted of twenty-five strokes on each leg. I was subjected to this more than thirty times. The soles of my feet looked like raw meat, the skin split, yet I had to stand on them.[10]

The AVO became a vast, inflated bureaucracy of terror that treated its own well. They were the élite in the system, handsomely rewarded. About 10 per cent of the AVO's total force of 48,000 were assigned simply to mundane duties as border patrols. They received average salaries. But senior officers involved in the grisly end of the work were paid roughly twenty times the national average, equivalent to a judge's salary.

They were aided by a vast number of informers, offering intelligence, obtained by intimidation, of varying degrees of reliability. It has been estimated that nearly a million Hungarians were regular informers of the AVO – 10 per cent of the population, which seems far-fetched. But a top-secret AVO 'State Security Review' that was smuggled out of the country after 1956 shows the thought that had gone into finding useful informers. 'Insurance agents, rent collectors, gas meter readers make excellent informers,' the document declared. 'Chimney sweeps are very useful. They can, as a rule, move about freely in people's houses. They are often left alone in various rooms; they can often engage in friendly conversations and no one suspects them.'

The AVO would not admit to mistakes. Gyula Fazekas was a vet from the south-western town of Pécs. He was arrested and interrogated about alleged friends he had never heard of. Interrogators beat and tortured him for three weeks. Then, one night, an AVO colonel came into his cell and told him that unfortunately it was a different Gyula Fazekas they were looking for. However, he said, in the state he was in it was impossible to set him free. He languished in a labour camp for several years.

János Cseri was arrested in a bar. Friends with whom he was drinking were singing a forbidden army song – 'I am Miklós Horthy's soldier . . .'. Cseri wasn't aware of this because he was drunk, under the table. His friends were taken to the local police station, beaten up and released. Cseri, however, was sent to Budapest AVO headquarters. His internment order was a masterpiece: 'János Cseri was arrested in a pub together with his friends who were singing anti-democratic songs. Although it was proven that, owing to the high degree of his intoxication, Cseri did not participate in the singing, it can be presumed that had he been sober he would have done so. On the basis of the above I intern Cseri for six months for state security reasons. Signed Lt.-Col. Márton Károlyi.' In fact, he served more than two years.[11]

FIVE

Christmas Day 1948, 3 p.m.

At the chapel on Gellért Hill, in the heart of Budapest, the city's faithful celebrated a special Christmas Mass. It was a bitterly cold day, but thousands of people braved the conditions to catch a glimpse of the tall, lanky, stern-looking cleric officiating at the service, Cardinal József Mindszenty, Archbishop of Esztergom and head of the Catholic Church in Hungary. The mood was sombre. As darkness fell the celebrants held candles, and offered prayers for their Archbishop as though in mourning. Sure enough, the next day he was arrested in his palace in the Castle District of Buda and was not seen again in public for eight years.

The new Communist masters in Hungary had destroyed political opposition by mid 1948 – 'the year of the takeover', as Rákosi called it. However, they still faced organised resistance in the form of the churches. Initially, during the coalition years, the Communists had co-operated with the churches. But it was always their intention to stamp out the influence of religion, principally the Roman Catholic religion, practised, at least nominally, by 70 per cent of Hungarians. The salami slicer was now to be used against the Catholic hierarchy.

The prime target was at the top. Mindszenty was born József Pehm in a small village in western Hungary near the Austrian border on 2 March 1896. After years in obscure backwater parishes, he rose to prominence in the last year of the war when, as Bishop of Veszprém, he was arrested by the Arrow Cross government. Generally the Catholic clergy in Hungary had done little to protect the Jews, either when vicious anti-Semitic laws were being passed between the wars or during the Holocaust. Mindszenty was never on record as speaking out against the transportation of Jews to Auschwitz. But, from nationalist sentiment, he called for Hungary to make a separate peace and sever the alliance with Germany. In full bishop's regalia, accompanied by twenty-four priests of his entourage, he was carried off by storm-troopers and jailed.

He was installed a Prince Primate on 7 October 1945. At first the Communists thought they might be able to make use of the brave Prelate who had stood up against the fascists. But they realised very soon that they had a serious opponent on their hands. Mindszenty was an unbending man who never believed in the separation of Church and state. In the 1945 elections he called on all Catholics to vote against the Communists. He preached regularly against the 'Marxist evil'. When Hungary was officially declared a republic in 1946 Mindszenty was one of a handful of prominent Hungarians who objected.[1] He had royalist views.

His virtues were a shining faith, admirable courage, fortitude and honesty. But he was neither wise, sophisticated nor clever. Though he was enormously popular among most of his flock, his abrasive style aroused misgivings among many Catholic intellectuals. The Jesuits, strong in Hungary at the time, urged him to be more subtle and flexible in his dealings with the Communists. The US State Department marked him down as a man bent on being a martyr, and bound to succeed.[2] The Pope, Pius XII, believed that in the Cold War in countries overrun by communism, the strength to face martyrdom was more important and valuable in a priest than intellectual brilliance.

The big battle was over Catholic schools. The Communists wanted to nationalise them all. They were bound to get their way ultimately, but Mindszenty's campaign against the plan prevented any compromise that might have saved a few. On 17 May 1948 he issued a Pastoral Letter threatening to excommunicate anyone associated with the secularisation of education. Initially he forbade Catholic teachers from working in nationalised schools altogether, which tested the fierce loyalty he commanded among the faithful. He relented a few weeks later.

Rákosi decided the time was now right to rid himself of this turbulent priest. The Communists felt they had to remove him from public life. That could have been done by sequestering Mindszenty away in a monastery, without subjecting him to humiliation, torture and imprisonment. They were determined not simply to render him powerless, but to show that any resistance to the regime was futile. On 19 November the Cardinal's secretary, András Zakar, was arrested. Mindszenty knew he would soon be next. He said in a sermon shortly before his arrest that if he was deprived of his freedom, his followers should not lose faith in him. They might be told he had admitted to committing seditious acts; these statements, he said, should be attributed to the frailty of human nature under duress. 'If you should read or hear it said that I have made admissions, or that I have resigned, or even that my signature is used to try to authenticate such confessions, this must be put down to my human weaknesses.'[3]

Mindszenty was tortured for days into making a confession that by any standards was unbelievable. Some of the evidence was later proved to have been forged, including claims of financial speculation. At his trial in January 1949, in front of a carefully selected audience, he received a sentence of life imprisonment. Hungarians would soon grow used to hearing accused defendants in show trials make wearily rehearsed admissions to trumped-up charges. The statements Mindszenty made in court, extensively quoted in Hungarian newspapers at the time, were ludicrous and entirely out of keeping with his voice and writing style. 'I am a Hungarian nobleman. My original surname was Pehm. The Pehm family was declared noble in 1732 ... My aim is the aim of the monarchist movement in Hungary; a federative, Central European monarchy with a personal union between Hungary and Austria and with other Catholic states. I only thought this possible by overthrowing the Hungarian republic with foreign and in the first place American aid.' It took the astounding cynicism of the Stalinists to imagine that any of it could possibly sound genuine.

The point, though, was not lost on the Hungarians: if this could happen to a Prince of the Church it could happen to anyone. Nobody who spoke out against the regime could feel safe. A few months after Mindszenty's humiliation, the number two in the Church hierarchy, Archbishop Károly Grosz, was arrested on sedition charges and sentenced to five years in jail. Next it was the turn of several 'liberal' Jesuits. Protestants, a sizeable minority of Hungary's population, were not left untouched. When the Lutheran Bishop, Lajos Ordass, was jailed it prefigured the persecution of all Christians. From 1949 priests of all denominations had to swear an oath to the constitution. Those who refused were jailed.

The most brutal treatment of all was meted out to the Greek Orthodox Bishop János Ödön Péterfalvy. He was arrested by the secret police and beaten up until his lower left jaw had no teeth. Three days later he was charged with being an American spy and thrown into a cell

filled with icy water. After three weeks he was turned over to the
Soviet KGB. He refused to sign a confession, even when his toenails
were ripped out. Finally his interrogator told him that they had arrested
his parents. 'Your father is old and infirm. Do you want to incon-
venience him too?' he was asked. The Bishop signed the confession and
was sentenced to twenty years in jail. He was deported to the Soviet
Union, where he spent nearly ten years in a labour camp in Siberia.[4]

The Communists found a powerful, physical way to emphasise their
point about religion. A year after Mindszenty was arrested, one of
Budapest's most beautiful churches, the Regnum Marianum, in the
city's magnificent Heroes' Square was pulled down. It was replaced by
a four-metre-high bronze statue of the Great Teacher Stalin, standing
on a plinth of red limestone. When it was unveiled officially in
September 1951 by the Hungarian Party's chief of ideology, József
Révai, even some hardline Communists were mystified by his
observation that 'this is a statue which springs from the soul of our
nation . . . It is a Hungarian statue.'[5]

SIX

15 October 1949, Budapest

At dawn Júlia Rajk was woken in her cell facing the courtyard of Budapest's Central Prison by the sound of boots on cobblestones. She was a tall woman, but the window in her cell was too high up for her to see anything. She had acute hearing, though, and instantly she realised she was about to hear a hanging – one of fifty-one she witnessed, or partially witnessed, that month. 'I heard the words "Géza, the execution can be carried out",' she said later. 'I heard the chair being taken away from beneath his feet. And in the great morning silence, I heard the doctor confirm that he was dead.' Only later in the day did she learn that in the morning she had heard the execution of her husband.[1]

The death of László Rajk marked the moment when, in the classic Bolshevik manner, the revolution began devouring its own children in an orgy of bloodletting. The AVO was at first directed at clearly defined opponents of the Communists and the Soviet puppet regime. The targets changed as the Soviet Union's international relations changed.

Between East and West, relations reached absolute freezing. Then, in the winter of 1948–9, a Cold War broke out within the socialist bloc. A leader in one of the 'liberated territories' dared to challenge the Red Tsar in the Kremlin. During the war, Josip Broz Tito had been a partisan hero in Yugoslavia's fight against Hitler, earning respect even among anti-Communists. He established a Marxist dictatorship in Belgrade, but resisted Yugoslavia's descent into the slave status of his Balkan neighbours. He said there were various paths towards socialism, declared himself a 'national Communist' and saw a future for Yugoslavia as 'non-aligned'. All this was heresy in the eyes of Stalin, who boasted, 'I could destroy Tito with a snap of my fingers.'[2]

It proved to be not quite so easy. Stalin thought he could afford to show no crack in Communist solidarity in case it was exploited by the West. Tito's defiance could not go unpunished and anyone in the Soviet bloc inclined to show sympathy with the Yugoslavs had to be stamped on hard. Stalin ordered a purge against the nest of 'Titoist Trotskyite spies' throughout his satellite states, which for the next few years convulsed all of Eastern Europe and shook Hungary hardest of all. Mátyás Rákosi, Stalin's best pupil, was predictably the most zealous among Russia's foreign vassals in following his overlord's commands. He volunteered several Hungarian battalions for a war against Tito, but Stalin vetoed that idea. So Rákosi had to be satisfied with organising the biggest and most dramatic show trial in the captive territories, implicating thousands of Communists in the Rajk Affair.[3]

László Rajk was one of the chief architects of Hungary's police state. As Interior Minister he had masterminded the trial of Cardinal Mindszenty and the suppression of the churches. Rajk was a hardline Stalinist, unforgiving of all opposition. 'Every man needs a compass and my compass is the Soviet Union,' he said. Rajk was tall, slim, arrestingly handsome and married to one of the great beauties in Budapest, Júlia Földi. They were the Communist glamour couple of the day. He was loathed by Rákosi, who used to quote Shakespeare to other magnates at Cabinet meetings with a warning about the danger of 'lean and hungry men'. Rajk's good looks and celebrity status gnawed at Rákosi. He saw Rajk as a potential leadership rival and, like most of the exiled Muscovites, he mistrusted the Communists who had stayed underground in Hungary during the Horthy years, as Rajk had done. For these reasons Rákosi chose Rajk as the principal target of the purge, though Stalin was consulted and approved the name.

Rajk was born in 1909 into a rich trader's family, originally from Transylvania. They moved to Hungary proper after the Treaty of Trianon. He became a passionate Communist at university. He organised an illegal Communist cell at Eötvös Loránd College, the élite training ground for Hungary's lawyers, civil servants and academics. He was betrayed by a fellow student and jailed. Unable to continue his law studies, he became a building worker and was deported after organising a big construction workers' strike in 1935. He fought in Spain in the Rákosi battalion of the International Brigade. Back in Hungary after the Spanish Civil War, he was the acknowledged leader of the illegal Communists until 1944. Arrested again, his life was saved by his brother Endre, a prominent Hungarian fascist, who was Secretary of State in the Arrow Cross government. The favour to his brother was returned when László Rajk emerged after the war as one of the leading Communist magnates in Hungary with a golden future.

Rajk may have had an intimation of his impending fall when he was replaced as Interior Minister soon after the Mindszenty trial began. However, he was appointed Foreign Minister, still a top job even in a country whose foreign policy was decided elsewhere. Rajk's arrest shook the country. On 10 May 1949 he and his wife were asked to lunch at Rákosi's villa. Júlia Rajk, at thirty-six, had recently given birth to a son and Rákosi told her he wanted to wet the baby's head. He was all smiles at the lunch – even though he had already signed the Rajks' arrest warrants. On their drive there a strange thing happened, recalled Péter Kende, then a young, eager Communist assistant to Rajk:

> I went to meet him outside his house . . . I was struck by the conspicuous number of guards at his gate and by the submachine gun that the guard who came in the car with us was carrying. As we were driving back, there was a huge thump. Something had hit the front of the car, making both the driver and the armed guard fall forward. We stopped and got out and saw that an eagle had flown into the front of the car . . . an ominous sign. If Rajk had been a statesman in classical times he'd have taken his own life after such a bad omen, or gathered his troops and left the country, because this was an unmistakable sign from the gods that some great danger was threatening him.[4]

The next day he was arrested by the AVO at his Budapest flat. He was under no illusions about the fate that awaited him. Initially, he refused to confess to trumped-up charges of espionage and treason. But the Soviets left nothing to chance. Stalin had despatched a team of thirty interrogators under the personal charge of the KGB's top official responsible for the satellite states, Fyodor Bielkin, to break Rajk and his thirteen co-defendants. After repeated torture Rajk and all the others confessed and, as was expected of them, played the role allotted to them in the trial. There were several rehearsals held, as if for a theatrical production. The defendants were not sure which of the 'performances' was the real trial – until the final one.[5]

The trial did not take place in a court, but in a large trade union hall which could hold a bigger audience. The charges were ridiculous. Rajk, the most loyal of Communists, was alleged to have worked for almost every foreign power, primarily Yugoslavia, but also for the US and Franco's Spain. People were not yet used to the language of Communist

show trials. They were bewildered to be told that a man who just a few
weeks earlier had been one of the top figures in the dictatorship had
all along planned 'a conspiracy against the state with the advanced
shock troops of international bourgeois reaction'. When sentence was
passed court officials and the entire audience alike showed their
approval by collective rhythmic clapping. Júlia Rajk, who had been
arrested with him, was sentenced to jail for six years. Her baby son,
also called László, was sent to a state orphanage under a different
name.[6]

The public seemed unsure how to react to the Communists settling
scores with each other. 'There was a rough justice in murderers turning
on their fellow murderers,' Sándor Zsindely, who was not a Communist,
recalls. 'But we had no time and not a lot of inclination to enjoy the
spectacle.' Nobody could remain indifferent to the message: in the new
Hungary, anyone, including top Party officials, could disappear from
one day to the next.[7]

The Great Terror following the Rajk case lasted more than three years.
The numbers, in a small country of less than 10 million people, were
staggering. Between 1950 and 1953, more than 1.3 million people were
prosecuted (and half of them jailed). This does not include the estimated
50,000 who were arrested on bogus charges and never faced trial.[8]
More than 2,350 were summarily executed – but many more rotted to
death in police cells. Three concentration camps – Recsk in the Tatra
Mountains, and Kistarcsa were the most notorious – held more than
40,000 inmates. Despite all this massive zeal by the AVO, Zoltán Biró,
Rákosi's half-brother, who was a senior official in the Communist
Party's propaganda and agitation division, reckoned that there were
'still around 500,000 hostile elements in the country'.[9]

Without any legal process, more than 13,000 'class enemies'
(aristocrats, high gentry, former officers, factory owners, senior civil
servants) were forced to leave Budapest and other towns and sent back
to work, under close supervision, in appalling conditions on farms.
The official reason was that this was inevitable 'at a time of imperialist
incitement and sharpening of the class struggle'. The real reason was
to satisfy the demand for suitable decent housing among the new
bureaucratic boss class.[10]

The élite were not always allowed long to enjoy their good fortune.
Of the 850,000 members of the Communist Party in 1950, almost exactly

half were in prison, in labour camps, exiled or dead three years later. Sometimes roles changed between victim and executioner with dramatic speed. In the summer of 1950 General Kálmán Révay, Commandant of the Military Academy, was executed. He was shot in the courtyard of the Military Police headquarters. Barely six months earlier he had commanded the firing squad that killed his old friend and comrade in arms György Pálffy, the great resistance fighter and former chief of military counter-intelligence.[11]

Within the Party, almost everyone was suspect. If you had left the country during the Horthy years, you might have been a spy for the West. If you had fought in Spain you were a Trotskyite. If you had stayed in Hungary, underground, you were a Horthyite informer. Péter Kende didn't believe the 'confessions' he heard, but as a loyal Communist, even if he had doubts, he kept them to himself. 'I listened to Rajk's confession,' he said. 'Although I didn't know the facts I had seen other "enemies" giving evidence in court. Enemies don't speak like people at a Party seminar telling the world how wonderful the People's Republic is while they, the enemies of the people, are terrible. On the contrary, enemies would either present their own world view or try to make the best possible impression. Something just didn't fit.'[12]

One of the most dangerous jobs to hold was Interior Minister, which was rather like being Lord Chancellor in England under Henry VIII. Rajk's predecessor ended up on the scaffold, and his three successors were all 'purged'. Perhaps the most tragic was Sándor Zöld, a distinguished doctor who had been a heroic figure in the wartime leftist underground. On 15 April 1951 he was criticised at a Cabinet meeting by Rákosi and fired from the government. He was convinced that he would be the third Interior Minister in a row to be arrested, tortured and tried. Terrified of the brutality that he knew awaited him, he became unhinged. He drove home, murdered his wife and two children and shot himself dead. He was found the next morning. The news spread like wildfire within the ranks of the Party. A top Party official at the time who knew Zöld well, Sándor Nógrádi, recalled: 'That event shattered a great many people. But there was no one with whom to discuss the tragedy; people were left alone with their doubts.'

Everyone felt fear. Miklós Vásárhelyi was a passionately committed Communist journalist in the terror years. 'I was terribly afraid,' he said. 'But I was in agreement with the campaign against Tito and the Rajk trial out of discipline, belief and opportunism ... I later lived in permanent fear, but I didn't tell anyone, not even my wife. If I had admitted my fear to her and possibly been arrested then she might have had doubts about me, because I was afraid. In a socialist system a person whose conscience is clear could have no reason for being afraid, so went the slogan of the time.'[13]

As the AVO became a law unto itself, a state within a state, the prisons and camps were brimming. György Páloczi-Horváth found himself in Vác jail among

> High church dignitaries, former Horthy generals and Spanish Civil War generals (on the Communist side, of course), the main war criminals, all the Rajkists, people like Prince Paul Esterházy and Zsedenyi, a former President of the Republic, a galaxy of former Ministers and Under Secretaries of State. On the first morning, when the convict orderlies came on their rounds, we discovered that our floor was served by a former Cabinet minister and a former Parachutist general. One of the gardeners was a count, the plumber of our wing was an old-guard Communist who had served as Under Secretary of State under Rajk. We met great names of the Hungarian, Romanian, Czech, French and Belgian Communist movements. In another wing Colonel Kálcsics was the orderly. He had fought through the Spanish Civil War and then the Belgian resistance and there is even a street named after him in one of the Belgian towns. In 1948 the Belgian Communist Party wanted him to stay. But Rákosi insisted. He pointed out that the great hero was of Hungarian origin and as such should help in rebuilding the Hungarian army ... He returned early in 1949 and was sentenced to life imprisonment as Rajk's accomplice.[14]

Innocence or guilt were irrelevant in a constant purge. Paul Ignotus was jailed for six years on entirely invented charges: 'To gauge the proportion of victims who had simply had bad luck, as against those who had really shown some spark of patriotism or human feeling, would be difficult. In general, those who had survived the purges unharmed were probably more sycophantic and barbarous than others who were murdered, imprisoned or at least pushed aside until Stalin's death. But some of the executed were chiefly sorry for not being amongst the executioners. The selection of criminals was based quite openly on assumptions about political deviation, rather than upon anything they had actually said or done.'[15]

The Szűcs brothers were faithful to the Communist cause all their

lives. Miklós Szücs, originally an engineer, who was jailed with Rákosi
in the 1920s, worked in London immediately after the war as a cor-
respondent for the Communist Party newspaper *A Free People* and the
Telegraph news agency. When the Communists took over, he repeatedly
said he wanted to go home to build socialism. Eventually he was
allowed to do so. He was given a job as an electrical engineer in
Budapest. He shared a flat with his brother Ernő, who was an AVO
officer and personal assistant to Gábor Péter. Ernő's position was
getting difficult. He was having a hard time with Péter. He thought to
reinforce his standing by denouncing his own brother, thereby proving
himself a reliable and loyal servant of the state. Miklós was arrested
for being a British spy. The arrest didn't help his brother. Ernő was
picked up by the AVO and put in the same cell.

One of the AVO's most brutal torturers, Vladimir Farkas, described
the end of the Szücs brothers in chilling detail later.

> Gyula Prinz and Gábor Péter's assistant József Kovács were in charge
> of softening them up. They were experts in beating people up, but to
> my knowledge had never beaten anyone to death before. Mihály Károlyi
> [who had interrogated the brothers and was convinced they were inno-
> cent, as Gábor Péter was also] and I were sitting in a room ... when
> after about an hour we were told that the two brothers weren't feeling
> well and needed a doctor. István Bálint, the chief doctor to the AVO,
> and his deputy Andor Köröso were still in the building. Bálint examined
> the two men. He came back and said 'I've given them an injection.
> Nothing serious. You can carry on beating them in an hour.' But the
> beating couldn't carry on, because less than half an hour later the thugs
> reported there was a real problem. I called Bálint and his deputy again.
> They confirmed that both of them were dead. Bálint reported that the
> cause of death was third-degree burning over the whole of their bodies.
> I couldn't understand that turn of events ... I couldn't understand
> either how they could have died in the hands of the professional
> torturers of the AVO.[16]

The grim joke was regularly told in Hungary: 'There are still three
classes in this country: those who have been in jail; those who are in
jail; and those who will be in jail.'

Rákosi, too, was afraid – of Stalin. He had every right to be. The
personality cult Rákosi had built around himself was becoming ever

more absurd – he ensured that by Party decree the word 'wise' (as in placards proclaiming him 'Wise Leader of the Working People') was reserved exclusively for him. He displayed his sadistic side more openly. On 24 April 1950 the head of state, Árpád Szakasits, formerly General Secretary of the Social Democratic Party, was invited to dine with the Party chief. Over coffee Rákosi leant over and said 'Szaki, I have something to show you.' It was his arrest warrant based on the evidence of forged documents 'proving' that he had been an informer for the Horthy secret police. He then handed the documents over to Szakasits, who was reading them when Gábor Péter, who had been waiting next door, arrested him. He was locked in the cellar of Rákosi's villa for several days before being carted off to prison.[17]

Rákosi was protective of his relationship with Stalin. He took all his holidays in the Crimea and not even his inner circle knew when – or if – they met. The squat Hungarian went nine times between 1948 and 1953 but there were no records of the visits. He communicated with Stalin in a series of letters to 'Comrade Fillipov', on a range of domestic subjects including the prosecution of Rajk. He asked for guidance personally on twenty-two occasions. But Stalin never bothered to reply to most of them. Silence was taken as assent. Rákosi had access to the Red Tsar largely through the good relationship he had built up with Alexander Poskrebyshev, Stalin's personal secretary and 'gatekeeper'. He, too, was an ugly man, with a triple roll of fat at the back of his neck and a shaved head. Perhaps their unfortunate appearance brought them together.

The access was resented by other Hungarian Communists. Also by some Russians, among them the Soviet Ambassador until 1954, Yevgeny Kisilev. The Hungarian diplomat György Zagar reported a conversation he had with Kisilev at a conference in the Middle East. 'He said that Rákosi was extremely stubborn and headstrong. He listened to nobody, neither to his associates, to him [Kisilev], or even the Soviet Party leaders apart from Stalin. Kisilev was never informed of the contents of his conversations with Stalin, which was a delicate problem, since he never knew whether Rákosi's actions were based on a private arrangement with Stalin.'[18]

Still, Stalin disliked Rákosi intensely and the Hungarian knew it. Frequently he brought up the issue of a famous picture taken in 1947 of Rákosi on the White House lawn on a visit to President Truman. While the other politicians in the picture, even the right-wing coalition members, looked uncomfortable or shifty or embarrassed near the President, Rákosi is at Truman's left chatting amiably and sharing a joke. The simple explanation was that Rákosi spoke fluent English and had met some of the officials before, during the Peace Treaty negotiations in Paris and London. Stalin looked on the scene as inappropriate – and said once that it suggested Rákosi was a spy for the West.[19] Rákosi was not a heavy drinker – unlike many of Stalin's circle. On one occasion, as a practical joke after dinner one night in the Crimea, Stalin forced Rákosi to drink so much vodka that he passed out. Some of the Soviet Politburo thought the Hungarian was dead, though he recovered. Rákosi told tales to his Hungarian cronies about the endless drinking bouts in Stalin's court. Mocking these was considered by the Soviet dictator very bad form.[20]

In a vicious circle, the more Stalin displayed his contempt for his Hungarian vassal, the more fear Rákosi showed, the more sycophantic he became to the man in the Kremlin – and the more he made Hungarians suffer.

SEVEN
31 December 1951

In offices and factories, for most Hungarians the normal working day began with a collective reading of *A Free People*. The daily ritual was considered by the regime a crucial propaganda weapon in the process of turning Hungary into a totalitarian state where the Party had control of everything – and most especially, or so they thought, of people's opinions. Workers would appear half an hour before their shifts. Beneath a picture of 'Our Wise Leader' Rákosi, the senior Communist official in each workplace would intone from the sacred text, in deathly Marxist-Leninist prose, the Party line of the day. Absence would be noted and very likely attract the attention of the AVO, a risk most workers were not prepared to take.

Most workers barely listened to these sessions. Like the regular organised marches they were required to attend in praise of the Party or the Soviet Union, the 'Nép [*A Free People*] hours' were resented as a waste of time and a constant reminder of how politics had intruded into every aspect of a citizen's life. In any case, few people believed anything that appeared in the Hungarian newspapers except perhaps the sports results. This particular morning, however, a front-page article in the paper caught the attention. Under the headline 'A Deadly blow in the face of the Imperialist and Western warmongers', the government announced a prices and wages 'reform' package. Prices – including some essential foods – rose between 11 and 20 per cent and pay was cut by roughly the same amount. Throughout Budapest that day wall posters displaying copies of the paper were daubed with the line: 'Another deadly blow at the imperialists and we will all starve.'[1]

That graffito was no joke. Since they began to redesign Hungary along Stalinist lines, the Communists had brought the Hungarian economy to the brink of ruin. In this workers' state, the workers suffered the most. On the land, forced collectivisation caused widespread famine. In the towns, the grind of daily living was an exhausting, dispiriting business. Even in some of the other countries behind the Iron Curtain, conditions were improving in the 1950s. In Hungary, they were getting worse. In the first four years after the Communist takeover, living standards fell by 20 per cent, while the average working week had lengthened. On an annual worker's salary it would cost a year and a half's pay for a man to buy a drab, ill-fitting suit – for there was no other kind to be had – or for one of Hungary's fashion-conscious women to find any sort of dress.[2]

Luxuries were for the very few: top Party officials, the secret police and a select number of black marketeers. In Hungary there were three kinds of shops. The first was where ordinary people queued, sometimes for several hours, for rationed goods; the second was for the Hungarian élite, which offered a far wider range of goods, some imported from the West, and where the basics were 25 per cent cheaper than at the regular stores. The third, most select of all, was for a handful of Russian 'advisers' and army officers where prices were about half those in the shops used by most Hungarians.

Hungary's economic tsar, and Rákosi's most powerful lieutenant, was a fellow Muscovite, Ernő Gerő. On a personal level, the two could not have been more different. While Rákosi presented an air around himself of bonhomie, false though it may have been, Gerő was utterly humourless. He had no life outside politics and seemed to have no interests other than the exercise of power. Tall, thick-lipped, with a mass of brown curly hair, he was almost skeletally thin. He suffered from an untreatable stomach ulcer, which gave him constant pain. Politically the pair were for all practical purposes identical, though Gerő managed to appear even more of a fanatical Stalinist and a tool of the Kremlin than Rákosi. Paul Ignotus, who knew Gerő, described him as a 'cross between an Inquisitor and a cash register'[3] and Miklós Nyarádi, who shared exile with him in Moscow, thought: 'Gerő looked like a modern-day Savonarola . . . one of those old-fashioned, ascetic Communists who accepted no money, no luxuries and took no joy in life.'[4]

His middle-class Jewish background was typical for a Hungarian Muscovite. Born Ernst Singer in 1899, he converted to communism as a student. From that moment he severed all contact with his parents and eight siblings. Jailed in 1922 for illegal Communist Party membership, he was allowed to leave Hungary for the USSR in 1924. Gerő went to the Lenin Academy in Moscow and trained as a Communist Party apparatchik, but was attracted to a life of intrigue. He joined the KGB and throughout the 1930s he was an agent for the Comintern. It was an open secret in Moscow émigré circles that it was Gerő who played recruiting sergeant into the Stalinist cause for Ramón Mercader, Trotsky's assassin.

Gerő earned his reputation for ruthlessness during the Spanish Civil War. He was the KGB chief in Catalonia – codenamed Pedro – where it was his job to enforce Communist orthodoxy among the Republicans and liquidate rival leftists and anarchists. He performed a thorough job and became known as 'the butcher of Barcelona'.[5]* Puritanical and incorruptible, he had serpentine ways. To the Soviet Ambassador, Kisilev, he confessed during the Rajk affair to being 'shocked that with Gábor Péter in charge of the AVO it did not matter if one was guilty or not'.[6] Around the same time he could say privately elsewhere: 'We know that Rajk conspired with Tito, but we have no proof of it. He must be liquidated, but to tell the entire truth to the public would be madness. They would not understand. They are not politically ripe enough. Whether he was actually a spy or not is irrelevant, for in its essence it comes to the same thing: committing treachery or being a spy. The crudeness of the charge is only the mechanical side of it and is of no importance.'[7]

To others still he could display a humble, honourable and decent side. As a young economist, Péter Kende – who left Hungary as a refugee after 1956 – was assigned to work for him. 'I was most impressed by Ernő Gerő. He was extremely reserved and polite, even shy. He showed great respect to anyone he talked to, regardless of rank or position. When a final verdict is reached on Gerő, it'll have to be considered that he was the least bloodthirsty person in the supreme leadership taking the crucial decisions in the 1950s. It is remarkable that nobody disappeared from his immediate environment. He wouldn't let his men be taken away.'[8]

That was an exaggeration. Gerő, too, could be callous. But he took no more delight in cruelty than he seemed to show for anything else in life.

Dogmatic, and inflexible, Gerő always wanted to be right and never

* No absolute proof exists, but it is almost certain that he aided and abetted the murder of Andres Nin, President of the Catalan Republic, in 1937.

knew the meaning of the term tactical retreat. He could be an efficient organiser, but in all his years in Russia he had been taught very little about economics, even Marxist-Leninist economics.[9]

Colonies exist to supply and profit their imperial masters. Hungary was no exception. Gerő and Rákosi saw it as the prime purpose of Hungary to serve the interests of the Soviet Union.

Reconstruction of the country after the devastation of war was relatively rapid, despite the Great Inflation of 1945–6. The Communists had played a part in rebuilding the nation. Gerő still basked in the sobriquet 'Bridge Builder'. But when he became boss of Hungary's economy he quickly undid the good that had been achieved. The new rulers made a catastrophic mistake. They attempted to turn a primarily agricultural country, with some light industry, almost overnight into a 'nation of coal and steel'. They did so because that is what Stalin had done in the USSR and the Soviet experience was dogma in all things.

Gerő's ruinous Five-Year Plans pushed the workers ever harder. In 1950, piece rates (being paid for each item a worker produces) became the basic system of pay in all factories. No system exploits workers more shamefully, A Free People had noted when the coalition government wanted to introduce a piece rate scheme, in 1947. A fair enough point for a socialist organ to make. When it became the state system, however, the same paper argued it was a 'blessing for the workers', who if they worked hard could make extra money.[10]

At the same time each worker was assigned a 'norm' – a personal production schedule he or she had to reach. The wages of workers who failed to meet the target were docked. Exceeding the 'norm' had its penalty, too. Workers found that the next month their 'norm' was increased – as they had proved they could produce more – so effectively their pay was cut.[11] For a while quantity rose, but at the expense of quality. There was a real problem with factory rejects. Even by East European standards at the time, Hungarian goods were notoriously shoddy. Russia cancelled dozens of contracts with Hungarian enterprises because the goods were inferior, leading to serious complaints from the Kremlin to their vassals in Budapest.[12]

Hardest to bear were the 'peace loans' extorted from workers each month, effectively an extra 12 per cent tax. Theoretically, these 'contributions in the fight against imperialism' were supposed to be voluntary, but anyone who refused to pay was publicly named and shamed or even fired – at a time when being unemployed was illegal. Changing jobs without authorisation was extremely hard, but not absolutely forbidden. In 1951, about 15,000 who tried to do so were charged with 'endangering the interest of the economic plan'. Most of them were jailed.[13] Theft from the workplace was very common. An acute observer, Ferenc Váli, thought that one of the worst effects of Hungarian communism was a new amorality: 'Many people believed embezzling the state, from big frauds to petty larceny, was OK. It was argued that it was even a way of fighting back, of resistance.'[14]

Most people simply accepted their lot, sullenly, grudgingly. They could do little about the chaotic mess the Communists were making of the economy. A prime example was the construction of Sztálinváros, a vast steel plant and new town fifty kilometres south-east of Budapest. It required large amounts of coke and iron ore, neither of which exist in Hungary and which had to be imported thousands of miles at vast expense from Soviet Central Asia. Of course, this made Sztálinváros hopelessly uneconomic and a drain on scarce resources. But such practical considerations did not concern Gerő. Sztálinváros had to be built because the plan said it would be built. Anyone who pointed out the craziness of these grandiose ventures was branded a saboteur.[15] Stalinist theory held that the system was perfect, the planners at the top of the Party were omniscient, and therefore if anything went wrong it had to be the fault of someone or some group – enemies of the state, terrorists, imperialist agents.

The Lengyeltóti oilfield, in eastern Hungary, the only reserves in the country, had production plans. Experts warned the managers and the politicians that too-hasty exploitation could result in flooding. The advice was rejected on the grounds that the plan was sacrosanct. They fulfilled the quotas. But the oilfield flooded. Simon Papp, something of a legend in the industry, worked hard to get the oilfield back into operation. In 1909, aged just twenty-three, he had been the first professor of petroleum geology in Hungary, but he was bored by academe. He became an oil prospector, one of those old-fashioned romantic figures, and in the 1920s travelled the world drilling for oil, even finding some in Yugoslavia, Turkey and the US. Back in Hungary in the 1930s he had been head geologist of the MAORT, Hungarian-American Oil Industry Ltd, a job he still held when the Communists took over. He warned on several occasions that a catastrophe would occur in the Hungarian oilfield unless production was limited. When the floods he had long predicted came, naturally someone had to be blamed and it was him. Papp and a group of other technicians were arrested. He was convicted of crimes against the democratic order and sentenced to life imprisonment.[16]

The pillaging of Hungarian resources was crude. The country's uranium reserves were mined to exhaustion, to serve the needs of the Soviets' nuclear weapons programme. The arrangement was classic colonial exploitation, the details of which emerged only in the 1990s after the collapse of communism. The deal was handled with immense secrecy; no mention of it appeared in either Soviet or Hungarian economic plans. Reserves of an estimated 15 million tons – one of the largest deposits in the world at that time – were found at Kővágószőllős, near the town of Pécs in southern Hungary. The Hungarians established a company codenamed Bauxite. The terms of the deal were immensely favourable to the USSR. Russia was in charge of exploration and extraction of the ore; Hungary was responsible for providing the infrastructure. Moscow was the sole buyer and set the price unilaterally. It also dictated the pace at which the ore would be exploited. The final agreement, made after exploitation had already begun, meant that Hungary would place the sites at the disposal of a Soviet 'geological expedition' free of charge and exempt the Russians who worked there from any tax. Housing installations for the workers were Hungarian responsibility. The Russians, in return, would provide all the scientific and technical equipment to refine the ore. Hungary made little from the deal.[17]

The distinguished physicist Professor Lajos Jánossi was the Hungarian scientist who worked most closely with the Soviets on extracting the uranium, but discovered on a visit to the USSR that he knew far less about the contract than his Russian colleagues. 'The Soviet authorities guarded everything concerning uranium jealously. No data came to light. The Hungarians were left completely in the dark. For example, as the Vice President of Hungary's Atomic Energy Commission I was not informed about the existence of uranium in Hungary. I learned about it only from newspapers. I don't even know what contracts we have with the Soviet Union.' The pillaging of Hungary's uranium became a major issue in the 1956 revolution.[18]

Rural Hungary was transformed utterly. Known between the wars as the breadbasket of Europe, vast swathes of Hungary's prime agricultural land now lay fallow. In just three years 300,000 peasants left the countryside and moved to the towns in Gerő's 'battle for industry'. Farming became a disastrous failure. Food rationing was tight in the early 1950s.[19]

Along with hunger went extreme fear. The post-war reforms that gave peasants land ownership for the first time lasted for a tantalisingly brief period. From December 1948 Rákosi and Gerő were bent on a rapid expansion of collective farms which brought the police state ruthlessly to the countryside. Peasants were forced to join the collectives – as they had in the Soviet Union during the 1920s. As in the USSR, unwilling farmers who loathed the loss of their independence faced repressive measures. Peasants were forced to sell their produce to the state, at prices fixed in Gerő's Five-Year Plan. The recalcitrant faced heavy fines, or worse. Refusal brought the AVO down on the family, or a prosecution for 'endangering public supply'. There were more than 400,000 cases of peasants charged with hoarding stocks. The 'sweeping of lofts' under AVO investigators was a daily feature of life on the land. In the darkest years of the early 1950s peasants' income fell by half. Some farmers preferred to kill their livestock rather than join the collective. They too were punished if caught for such resistance.[20]

Another Russian term entered the language: 'kulak', meaning well-off peasant. In the Soviet Union, Stalin had turned kulaks into class enemies who had to be liquidated. Rákosi and Gerő did likewise in Hungary. Any man (and it inevitably was a man) who possessed over eight to fifteen hectares, depending on the quality of the soil, was defined as a kulak. In every village 'kulak lists' were kept and published. Thousands were denounced – often by people they lived amongst for years – and sent to forced labour camps. Their children were debarred from university education. Their land was confiscated as a matter of course. So, very often, were their houses. Frequently they were removed by lorry, deposited miles away and found that their homes had been requisitioned during their absence. Rákosi declared that to beat up a kulak was a revolutionary deed.[21]

EIGHT

4 November 1952, Washington DC

The overwhelming victory of Dwight D. Eisenhower in the presidential election was hardly a surprise. 'Ike', at sixty-two, was hugely popular, a war hero who appeared to middle Americans as one of them. Both parties had wanted him as their presidential candidate for this election, not only because of his fame as a military commander, but also because of his personality. His face-splitting smile beamed optimism and an infectious contentment with life. Those who knew his true character understood better – privately he was prone to dark periods of gloom – but 'OK with Ike' the stump slogan went, and voters in their millions decided things probably would be. His pull alone ensured the Republican Party seized the presidency for the first time since 1928.[1]

Eisenhower was a master of political spin.[2] Few presidents have been so different in reality from the image they created. He presented himself as a folksy, homespun, unsophisticated figure, a man who preferred to play a round of golf with friends than spend time at the office. His avuncular style and slightly shambling gait almost hid the sharp intellect beneath, and his surprising breadth of knowledge. He was far cleverer than he seemed. Eisenhower invented the regular televised presidential press conference. He bumbled through words and seemed to be a stranger to syntax. However, read through his comments in cold print now and it is clear he always knew what he was saying. His carefully burnished image was of a soldier-statesman far above the political fray: almost a constitutional monarch. But he kept a shrewd eye on his popularity ratings and could be a partisan fixer of subtle skills.[3]

Eisenhower had fought an election campaign full of bellicose anti-Communist rhetoric. The worst of the McCarthyite witch hunts were over, but Eisenhower's team spoke frequently of the Red menace.[4] Ike's handpicked Vice President, Richard Milhous Nixon, cut his teeth as a hammer of the left on the House Un-American Activities Committee.

Americans appeared to think that if there were going to be new battles in the Cold War, they would be better off with a great general fighting them. Eisenhower said that his predecessor Harry Truman's policy of 'containment' of the Soviet Union was too 'passive'. He advocated 'rollback' of communism – not by war but by all means short of military conflict. He planned to raise the temperature of the ideological struggle against the Soviets and see how they would react.[5]

One of Eisenhower's affectations was to suggest that he left the hard work to others, while he merely turned up at the White House occasionally from the 18th fairway, to make the major decisions. Many diplomats and politicians – notably Anthony Eden[6] – were convinced that American foreign policy was directed by Eisenhower's Secretary of State, the stiff-backed puritan John Foster Dulles. As all the documents from the Eisenhower presidency have shown, Ike was far more interventionist than he wanted the public, or foreign leaders, to believe. He and Dulles were a formidable force, but the Secretary of State always remembered that he served at the President's pleasure.

Robert Bowie, a Foggy Bottom diplomat who in the 1950s advised Dulles on Eastern European policy, said:

> I have not the slightest doubt that it was Eisenhower who was setting policy. He was completely in charge. Dulles was a trusted advisor, he was frequently, he was always, listened to. He was frequently agreed with. But Eisenhower made his own decisions, without question. Everybody in the administration knew this. Dulles made a point of the people in the State Department understanding this. He would never make a big decision, he would never make a major speech, without clearing it with Ike. And Ike didn't just clear it by saying 'whatever you say, Foster'. He would write his comments on a document, or the text of a speech, and say I suggest that you would do this or say that . . .[7]

Dulles was a large, sombre man who looked like a stern Victorian father. His lips curved downwards and trembled when he felt angry, which was often. He almost always stood with his hands in his pockets. He was born into the State Department; his grandfather and uncle had been Secretary of State. 'Foster' Dulles had to wait until he was sixty-four before stepping into the office. He spoke in the unbending vocabulary used by a lay Presbyterian preacher, which he had been before becoming President of the World Council of Churches. For years, as head of a large New York legal firm, he had reportedly been the best-paid lawyer in the States.[8] An authoritarian figure, occasionally he showed some charm, though Churchill could not see it. After he met him for the first time in January 1953 in Washington the old man went to bed muttering that he wished to have no more to do with a man whose 'great slab of a face he disliked and distrusted'.[9] Six months later Churchill remarked to his doctor that Dulles was 'clever enough to be stupid on a rather large scale'.[10] Eden compared dealing with him unfavourably to dealing with Ribbentrop.[11]

Like the majority of Republicans, he had been an isolationist for much of the 1920s and 1930s. But passionate anti-communism changed his mind and gave him a heightened awareness of America's place as a superpower. Dulles invented the term 'liberation of the captive people' behind the Iron Curtain, which throughout the election campaign he had loftily declared would be a Republican administration's goal. Time and again[12] he said that the 'liberation policy of Eisenhower' would be 'activist', and would include steps by the CIA to supply and co-ordinate patriotic resistance movements in the Soviet satellites in Eastern Europe. His critics saw where the logic of 'rollback rhetoric' would lead. The former Ambassador to Moscow and Soviet expert Averell Harriman said on television in the summer of 1952, 'Foster, if you follow this policy you are going to have the death of some brave people on your conscience.' The prescient prophecy incurred an angry scowl from Dulles, for the doubts it cast on the Secretary of State's moral rectitude.

Hungary was not fertile territory for American espionage, as the CIA's station chief in Vienna in the early 1950s, Peer de Silva, would later acknowledge.[13] In the previous administration, the US had recruited Hungarian agents, but the AVO was surprisingly efficient at capturing them. Támás Pásztor, a Smallholders Party MP from 1945 to 1948, admitted after he escaped to the US from Hungary in 1956 that he had worked for the American Secret Service. 'Throughout the post-war years I had written weekly reports . . . upon the request of the [American] Legation in Budapest. I usually handed in these reports to a person from the Legation at a prearranged time and place in the street. Sometimes he didn't show up and then I was to meet the following week, at the same time and place . . . At one stage we missed two dates. So I had three reports when the political police arrested me. They had clear-cut evidence against me. I was handed over to the Military

Tribunal in Budapest, where I was tried ... and sentenced to life imprisonment.'[14] Another agent for the CIA, James McCargar, who was recruited to report on military movements by the Red Army in Hungary, managed to escape from the country just in time. 'The AVO were on to me and I had to get out. I think they had known quite early on.'[15]

The CIA despatched agents, but invariably their efforts amounted to little. The spy Gordon Mason was sent to the Transylvanian region of Romania, where he was ordered to contact ethnic Hungarian resistance movements who would be prepared to cross the border, infiltrate Hungary and work against the Rákosi regime. In late 1951 two of the agents he recruited were arrested with radio transmitting equipment, weapons and money.*

A year after taking office, the Eisenhower administration accepted that its spy network was of limited use in its 'liberation policy'. A secret National Security council document (NSC 174) prepared for the President recognised 'that the difficulties of conducting covert operations have steadily increased ... because of the growing effectiveness of the [Soviet] bloc-wide security apparatus ... In view of recent experience, it is of the utmost importance to proceed with extreme care in this field, with a view to solid accomplishments for the long run rather than to seek quick results in building up resistance capabilities ... at the greater risk of infiltration, detection and embarrassment of the United States political action and propaganda.'[16] In any case, the intelligence gained was of dubious value. A CIA report on Hungary in December 1953 stated unequivocally: 'There are no organised resistance groups. The population does not now, nor will they in the future, have the capacity to resist actively the present regime. But the Hungarian people will ... continue to resist passively.'[17]

In August 1953, eight months after entering the White House, Eisenhower was told by his defence experts that they were certain the Russians possessed the H-bomb. The news was no surprise, though it ensured that the President would act with extreme caution on the world stage. The President continued to talk tough about 'rolling back'

---

* A British businessman, Edgar Sanders, was arrested in 1949 and sentenced to thirteen years in jail in what came to be called in Hungary the Standard Electric Trial. The Rákosi regime used him as a bargaining chip to gain the release of some Communist activists in British Malaya, but no deal was ever made. Sanders was released in the summer of 1953, but two Hungarians tried with him on bogus charges were hanged.

communism and 'liberating enslaved people', while implementing a
practical policy of containment. In time, the contradiction at the heart
of the Eisenhower presidency would be exposed.

Eisenhower enthusiastically embraced the use of psychological
warfare. 'In the final analysis public opinion wins most of the wars and
always wins the peace,' he was fond of saying. The Cold Warriors
around the Oval Office were let off the leash as the administration
vastly expanded its propaganda budget and operations. More than
3,000 people were on the payroll of a propaganda department headed
in Washington by the inspiring, if erratic, Frank Wisner. The tall,
hard-living and hard-drinking Wisner, aged forty-two when Eisenhower was elected, had been a successful and well-connected Wall
Street lawyer in the 1930s. He was a legendary American Secret Service
operative during the war and served for most of the post-war years as
a spy in the front line of the espionage war in Berlin and Vienna. A
fervent anti-Communist, he became one of the founding fathers of the
CIA.

Wisner believed heart and soul in spreading the word of freedom
behind the Iron Curtain and keeping the flame of liberty alive. His
main, though by no means only, weapon was Radio Free Europe, which
had been launched by the Truman administration in 1949. Within
eighteen months of Eisenhower taking over it was broadcasting anti-
Communist propaganda and 'decadent' jazz, as the Stalinists described
it, twenty hours a day throughout most of the Soviet satellites.[18] In
Hungary RFE was immensely popular. Sophisticated jamming techniques used by the regime could not silence the émigré voices, speaking
to millions of Hungarians about America's mission to liberate Europe.
Domestic radio, run as an arm of the Communist Party, was entirely
distrusted. RFE had a far bigger audience and was eagerly believed by
its listeners.*[19]

The station was established as a CIA front, though it was vitally
important to the US that Washington could maintain 'plausible deni-
ability' and RFE could appear independent. 'RFE had to foster the
illusion of being a genuine private radio station,' explained its historian, Walter Hixson. It had never been. Launched by the National

* In a poll conducted by the Austrian Institute for Market Opinion and Research of
Hungarian refugees in Austria, 85 per cent of the respondents said they listened
regularly to RFE, compared to about 65 per cent who listened to Hungarian radio.

Committee for a Free Europe, its incorporation papers were handled by Foster Dulles's law firm, Sullivan and Cromwell. Dulles's younger brother, Allen, the pipe-smoking, bespectacled, cheerful-looking spy, was its first president until he became Eisenhower's CIA director, in 1953. RFE had an elaborate fund-raising structure. Crusade for Freedom rallies were held across America to raise 'Truth Dollars'. The meetings featured a replica of the Liberty Bell – symbol of the American War of Independence. There were 25 million contributors, but they did not raise enough even to pay for the Crusade rallies. The US government financed the rest through secret unattributed funds.

The CIA produced strict guidelines in the RFE handbook: 'Broadcasts should emphasise Western determination to undermine Communist regimes ... The station's purpose is to contribute to the liberation of the nations imprisoned behind the Iron Curtain by maintaining their morale and stimulating in them a spirit of non-cooperation with the Soviet-dominated regimes.'[20] Broadcasters were barred from using such words as 'peace' and 'disarmament' in relation to the Soviet bloc, as these might signal international acceptance of Russian control over Eastern Europe. No restraint was placed on RFE's anti-communism or its 'outspoken belligerence'.[21]

The station quickly earned a reputation for truth-telling by being first with news about the Soviet empire which the potentates in the Kremlin censored. In Hungary RFE broadcast regularly from a 'black book' that revealed the identities of police informers, particularly brutal AVO torturers and overbearing Party apparatchiks. Allen Dulles was especially proud that it told the story of a well-known smuggler who took money from anti-Communist Hungarians by promising to take them across the border to Austria but in fact delivered them to the AVO.

RFE launched Operation Red Sox and Operation Focus in Hungary. Balloons dropped millions of leaflets on the country bearing morale-lifting sentiments such as 'The regime is weaker than you think' and 'The hope lies with the people'. Others reported the creation of an (entirely fictitious) resistance movement run by a Colonel Bell of the CIA, who pledged that the day of liberation was at hand. Rákosi complained that the balloon bombardment incited the population to rebellion and subversion. Washington replied that the air drops were private RFE and Crusade for Freedom initiatives and had nothing to do with the US government.[22]

By 1953 Munich-based RFE employed 252 Americans and 1,526 Europeans in its new bureaux alone and its twenty-six transmitters provided 'saturation broadcasting' that was almost impossible to jam. Yet despite America's expensive and energetic propaganda campaign, the US was ill-prepared for rebellion in Eastern Europe. Lawrence de Neufville, an agent assigned to RFE in 1954, asked in his first month in Munich, 'What happens if a man in a raincoat comes here and says, "We've been listening to all this stuff and we're ready to start a revolution"? They discussed it in a special board meeting and they didn't know what to do ... They were all busy thinking they were doing good and nobody was doing any real plotting. And then events caught up on them.'[23]

NINE

3 January 1953, Budapest

At about five in the afternoon Gábor Péter, the sadistic chief of Hungary's secret police, was summoned to the luxurious villa of Mátyás Rákosi not far from his own in the Rózsadomb district. The stated purpose of the visit is unknown, but most of the business of running Hungary's gulag was conducted by this pair verbally. Little was put down on paper. Rákosi decided who in high positions should be purged. Péter and his bureaucrats of terror chose the other less well-known victims. Unusually, when Péter arrived at the Wise Leader's home a few minutes later, Hungary's Defence Minister, Mihály Farkas, was in Rákosi's office.

According to Farkas's son, Vladimir, one of the AVO's chief torturers and a favourite of Péter's, the formalities and courtesies were brief. 'We have evidence you are an enemy spy,' Rákosi shouted at him and rang the buzzer at his desk for Colonel Boda, commander of his personal guard, who placed Péter in shackles.[1] He was led by Farkas down the stairs to the basement of the villa, where he was later joined by his wife, Jolán, who had been arrested at her home. They were held in the damp cellar for a few days and fed on scraps from Rákosi's table, before being transferred to AVO headquarters in Stalin Avenue. They were kept in solitary confinement. Fellow prisoners could not see them. However, their identities became known immediately throughout the building's networks of dungeons and torture chambers, lifting morale to a surprising degree. 'Péter was quite brave after he was arrested,' said Paul Ignotus, another AVO detainee at the time. 'He declared so that everyone could hear, "Rákosi knew everything. It was his doing. Now he wants to smear all the dirt on me." He was treated a lot better than he treated others, though.' He was told to write a confession. He refused, but was never handed over to his erstwhile underling Gyula Prinz and the torturers. His attractive dark-haired wife was no less plucky. She would shout at the top of her voice, so all the other prisoners could hear, 'Justice for Jolán Simon'.[2]

Gábor Péter's arrest was not reported for a month, though it quickly became the talk of Budapest. By now the public had grown used to their masters' vicious internal feuding and Rákosi's continuous purges. Each twist and turn of events may have appeared incomprehensible; as Budapest's police chief, Sándor Kopácsi, said, at this stage 'who was a victim and who remained free was simply a matter of luck'.[3] Yet the fall of Péter was an earthquake. He had not foreseen it. He strutted arrogantly around the city as usual, visiting his retinue of young girlfriends, and felt confident that he was untouchable. He must have thought Rákosi could not afford to move against him, as he knew too much, and his friends in the Lubyanka would protect him.[4]

Domestic Hungarian politics played little part in his fall, which was rooted in Moscow intrigues. Péter was a victim of Stalin's last murderous crime. The Red Tsar in the Kremlin, now seventy-three, was after more than two decades in power, becoming increasingly paranoid. Also, his extreme lifelong anti-Semitism grew more pronounced as he got older. He mistrusted, above all, his doctors – 'murderers in white coats'. Stalin was convinced, or said he was convinced, that there was a vast conspiracy among Jewish doctors to murder him and other Kremlin leaders. The purge began with a roundup of scores of Jewish doctors in the Soviet Union. It quickly became apparent that Stalin's purpose was much more ambitious: he was bent on an anti-Jewish pogrom on a massive scale throughout his empire.

In Budapest, the Doctors' Plot foreshadowed a terrifying consequence for Rákosi and many of his fellow Muscovites – at least the Jews among them. It was only a matter of time, they were sure, before the spotlight would turn on the satellite states, and Jewish leaders in the Eastern bloc would disappear in a new Holocaust. Rákosi's method of survival was his tried and trusted one: slavish sycophancy and exact imitation of whatever the Great Teacher did. Rákosi tried to show that he could be as anti-Semitic as the next loyal Stalinist. In Budapest the AVO prepared lists of Jewish doctors who would be arrested and Rákosi increased his rhetoric against 'rootless cosmopolitans' – Soviet shorthand for Jews.

Then, on 5 March 1953, Stalin died.

TEN

13 June 1953, MOSCOW

In the Kremlin just before 11 a.m. a delegation of top Hungarian officials arrived for a highly secret meeting. It was so secret that the full details did not emerge until thirty years later. The Soviet magnates had ordered the Hungarians to appear before them, like liege lords demanding obeisance, for a dramatic confrontation. Rákosi was about to receive a body blow from which he would never entirely recover.

After Stalin's death, his heirs feuded bitterly amongst themselves. While the terrifying leader in the Kremlin lived, the personalities of his underlings were subsumed in his greatness. Disagreements were never aired in the open – and hardly ever in private. Their rival jealousies were concentrated on winning favours at court, or at least the grudging acceptance of Stalin. Now their ambitions, hatreds and conflicting lust for power came into the open. Moscow interfered in the satellite states just as much after Stalin died, but with far less consistency. 'In the absence of clear and unmistakable signals from Moscow the Eastern European Communists were ... confused,' said Ferenc Váli, who knew some of the top Hungarian Communists. 'The leaders curried favour with one or another faction in the Soviet Union ... Navigating political waters under Stalin was simple. All one had to do was turn one's political compass to Stalin's whims, kowtow to him in sycophantic adulation and all was well ... Under the new conditions, anticipating Moscow's pleasure became a complex art.'[1]

While they each groomed their various favourites in the satellites, the Kremlin potentates were agreed on one thing. They saw that maintaining the Communist empire which the Soviet Union had won less than a decade earlier was vitally important, for ideological and prestige reasons. At the same time they were instinctively aware of how easily the whole edifice could crumble unless they were constantly vigilant. In Hungary, correctly, they perceived a crisis brewing and they were determined to act decisively to prevent one.

The two sides sat opposite one another at a long table. All the Soviets there had taken a full and active part in mass murder. The burly, bald, bluff-looking fifty-nine-year-old Nikita Khrushchev had been named as First Secretary of the Soviet Communist Party. It was the position Stalin had held in name, but Khrushchev's position was tenuous. There genuinely was a collective leadership – of rivals. The Prime Minister was the obese, pasty-faced Georgii Malenkov, thought to be Stalin's favourite around the time of his death. The others included the gaunt Vyacheslav Molotov, long-time Soviet Foreign Minister and for many years effectively Stalin's number two; a neatly dressed Armenian with a discreet moustache, Anastas Mikoyan, and Lavrenti Beria, the head of the KGB, Stalin's most willing executioner.

The Hungarian team comprised Rákosi and Gerő, accompanied by a group of young Ministers who worked for them, including the thirty-five-year-old András Hegedüs, being groomed for greatness by Rákosi. The Russians, surprisingly, had demanded the presence of Imre Nagy, Hungary's first Agriculture Minister after the war, who had been in and out of Communist governments since then, in various relatively junior posts. Rákosi thought little about Nagy's presence, however. None of the Hungarians there had any idea why they had been called from Budapest at short notice.[2]

They soon found out that only one subject was on the agenda: the future of Rákosi. Beria got to the point straight away: 'Listen, Comrade Rákosi, we know that Hungary has had Habsburg emperors, Tartar khans, Polish princes, Turkish sultans and Austrian emperors. But as far as we know she has never yet had a Jewish king, and that is what you are trying to become. You can be sure we will never allow it.' Beria looked at the visibly sweating figure of Rákosi and began a list of complaints, beginning with a litany against the AVO, which he said had become a law unto itself and had committed far too many excesses. 'This is impermissible and will not be allowed,' Beria said. Coming from a murderer of Beria's accomplishments this must have sounded absurd, but Rákosi bit his lip.

Malenkov launched into the Hungarian leadership in general, but singled out Rákosi, whom he treated as an errant schoolboy. The Kremlin bosses were exceptionally well informed about affairs in Hungary. They had a thick file in front of them full of facts and figures, prepared by Moscow's Ambassador to Hungary, Yevgeny Kisilev. Malenkov said that under Rákosi's stewardship Hungary's economy was a disaster, unease was growing, the jails were full to overflowing, the courts were handing out sentences of a severity that could not be justified and Rákosi's personality cult was appearing more and more ridiculous. 'We, all of us here on our side, are deeply appalled at your high-handed and domineering style. It has led to ... countless mistakes and crimes and driven Hungary to the brink of catastrophe,' said Malenkov.

Mikoyan, an economics expert who had a reputation as a wheeler-dealer, brought up one specific error the Russians found it hard to forgive as it was costing the Soviet Union so dear in subsidies. The Hungarians were guilty of 'haphazard planning; for example, no one in Hungary had even tried to calculate the cost of producing steel'. Molotov weighed in. 'You have finally to understand that you cannot eternally govern with the support of Soviet bayonets.'[3]

Khrushchev warned the Hungarians that unless they were careful, their people 'will chase you away with pitchforks'. Then he announced the decision he and his fellow Kremlin bosses had reached. Rákosi had concentrated in his hands all the power. He was Party chief and Prime Minister, head of the government at the same time. This could not go on. If the Soviet Union, post-Stalin, could have a collective leadership, so too would Hungary. A month earlier the Russians had broached with Rákosi the issue of dividing the leadership, said Khrushchev. The Hungarian had agreed to do so, but he had objected to every name that had been suggested to him.

The visitors from Budapest were flabbergasted. It did not seem strange to the people around the table that the government of Hungary – supposedly an independent nation – should be decided by a group of a few men in Moscow. After all, most of the 'Hungarians' there were also citizens of the Soviet Union. It was the manner of the deed that appeared so brutal.

Rákosi crumpled and looked aghast. No one had spoken like this to him for years – not even Stalin. They were treating him now as though he was a servant they were about to dismiss. There were points he could have raised in his defence. But who could reply to Beria or Molotov that they too had enthusiastically worshipped a 'personality cult' – or to Khrushchev that the Hungarians were creating collective farms in the way that he had done in Ukraine during the 1930s? Rákosi tried to say something. He admitted that some of the criticisms of the Soviet comrades were no doubt valid, but they exaggerated in many ways. He was not allowed to finish. The Soviet leaders informed him that he had to give up the post of Prime Minister and would have to share power with a man he detested: Imre Nagy.[4]

ELEVEN

4 July 1953, Budapest

At about 2 p.m. in the Chamber of Hungary's enormous gothic-style Parliament building,* the portly new Prime Minister stood on his feet, carefully placed his pince-nez over his dark brown eyes and read from a text he had spent years preparing. Though delivered in the comforting burr of rural Hungary, the words at first sounded as if they could have been uttered by any Communist functionary. Imre Nagry was no great orator and he began in crabbed, stilted style, full of Marxist-Leninist jargon. He continued more simply and directly as he warmed to his theme.

Nagy promised a 'New Course'. He admitted that citizens had been treated 'unworthily' over the last five years of Communist dictatorship. Now, minor political offenders would be released, he pledged. The internment camps would be closed. Deportees – the so-called class enemies who had been forced out of the cities – would be allowed to return to their homes. All discrimination against kulaks would stop. In the factories, the hated norms system would be changed. On the land, the new government would allow farmers, if they wished, to leave the collective farms they had been forced to join. Small private enterprises would be allowed to set up in business.[1]

Hungarians seldom bothered to listen to their politicians talk. However, this speech was broadcast live on radio and his audience realised at once the significance of Nagy's words. None of this would have been allowed in Stalin's time. They knew Nagy as the 'Land Divider', a man of his word. However, he was still a Communist, a loyal apparatchik, a functionary of the system that had terrorised and

---

* The extraordinary late-nineteenth-century building on the banks of the Danube, partly modelled on the Houses of Parliament in London, is by some distance the biggest parliament building in Europe – quite an achievement for one of the continent's smallest countries, and one that had no real democracy until 1989.

pauperised them. Now Nagy was promising that 'The June Road', as he called it, would provide new hope for Hungary – and people needed hope. Even in the prisons, people heard the speech in amazement. György Páloczi-Horváth was listening in the punishment wing of the Central Prison in Budapest: 'A miracle happened – I heard the radio . . . from down below in the guards' duty room. It grew louder . . . so loud that the convicts could hear it. The guards had never done such a thing before. We listened with feverish attention. This was salvation. I thought the whole thing had been a hallucination . . . But next day, at noon, the punitive section [of the prison] was disbanded.'[2]

Imre Nagy did not look like one of the great tragic heroes of Hungarian history. He gave the appearance, rather, of the family grocer or village schoolmaster. He was never a firebrand revolutionary. For years he had loyally served tyranny.[3]

He was born on 12 June 1896 in Kaposvár, a small sleepy town in County Somogy, the rolling, fertile country in southern Hungary between Lake Balaton and the Serbian border. His parents had grown up in abject poverty as peasants, but had prospered. They were in service to the sheriff of the county. They brought up their only son and three daughters as Calvinists, who were a substantial minority in primarily Catholic Hungary.[4] Nagy gained a place at the gymnasium, rare at the time for a boy of such humble stock. A school report in 1908 noted that he showed no remarkable abilities of any kind, though one of his teachers instilled in him a love of music and literature that remained with him throughout his life. The school suggested he should leave the gymnasium course and his formal education ended there, at the age of twelve. He was apprenticed to an agricultural machinery manufacturer in Losoc (now in Slovakia), but he stayed for only a year. He had found work in the Mavag foundry, amidst the urban squalor of Budapest's industrial district, Angyalföld (Angel Fields).

When the First World War started he was conscripted into an infantry battalion and sent to the Italian Front, where he was wounded. Released from hospital, he was despatched to the Russian Front, where he was taken prisoner. By the time of the Bolshevik Revolution in 1917 he was in a prisoner of war camp in Siberia. Nagy had shown no interest in politics – even when he worked in grim conditions in Budapest. However, the war radicalised him. At twenty-two he became a Communist and found a faith he never lost.

Instead of returning to Hungary in 1918, Nagy volunteered for the Red Army in the Russian Civil War. He seemed to like soldiering, for the cause of international socialism. By all accounts he fought with courage. He was taken prisoner by White Guards but escaped and rejoined the Red Army. In 1921 he was sent back to Hungary to work, underground, for the Communist Party with a job to recruit members. His orders from Moscow were to infiltrate and subvert the legal leftist organisation, the Social Democratic Party. Four years later he married Mária Egetö, daughter of a prominent SDP politician in the district of his birthplace near Kaposvár. She was a pretty, brown-haired, brown-eyed, olive-complexioned girl a couple of years younger than him. Maria was a homely woman, utterly loyal as a wife and mother, but who never shared her husband's faith and would not join the Communist Party.

Like most of the Communists who were to take power in Hungary after 1945, Nagy spent time in Admiral Horthy's jails. He was arrested in February 1927 for illegal Communist activity and sentenced to two years in prison. He took to the cells with him a possession that proved valuable: a bowler hat that he used as a pillow. More important, he started learning, avidly, about agriculture.[5] After his release he was expelled from Hungary and lived in Vienna for a year, leaving behind his wife and two-year-old daughter, Erzsébet, born while he was in jail.

In 1930 Nagy went to Russia as a delegate for the Second Congress of the Hungarian Communist Party, held near Moscow. For the first time he stood out as a personality of political courage in the Communist movement. His first heresy was not to rise while the Internationale was played, which caused consternation among the ultra-orthodox Party apparatchiks around him. His second – more significant – was to argue that granting peasants their own land was a far better way of winning support in the countryside than forcing them onto collective farms, which is what Stalin was doing. This opinion, so different from the Party line, was to cause him trouble several times in his life. On this occasion, he was told he had to recant and go through that peculiar Communist rite of self-criticism. Despite occasional nonconformist gestures, Nagy was a disciplined Communist who believed the Party was right in all things. So he agreed to humble himself. The speech he was forced to make then – typical as a Bolshevik *mea culpa* of the time – was discovered only many years later. 'It is true that I said . . . I would not spring to attention when I heard the Internationale. I recognise that is an attitude unworthy of a Bolshevik. I do not want to justify myself but, believe me, I did not want to imply that I would not carry out unquestioningly the decisions [of the Party].'[6]

Nagy stayed in Russia for the next fifteen years. He and his family became Soviet citizens (his daughter could barely speak Hungarian when they all returned to Budapest in 1945). They did not, however, live at the Hotel Lux eternally plotting, like so many other exiles. He found a flat in central Moscow, with a shared bathroom. He worked in the Moscow Statistical Office and studied at the Agrarian Institute.

Nagy's years in Moscow exile are the most difficult to assess in his life. They still give rise to conjecture and spirited argument. We know he lived quietly throughout the purges which resulted in the deaths of half the intelligentsia of Moscow and many Hungarian émigrés. Historians disagree about how. One line of thought is that Nagy survived unscathed because he was an unimportant figure who kept his head well below the parapet. The other is that he somehow had protection. Throughout his years in Russia and during his period as a Communist Minister later, there had been rumours that Nagy had been a spy for the Soviet secret police. There is a set of documents that seem to incriminate him.[7]

According to these, Nagy, codenamed Volodya, had been recruited as an informer in 1933. 'Volodya', his handlers wrote, was 'a qualified agent' who shows 'great initiative' and an 'ability to approach people'. Of the total number of people against whom he informed, fifteen were either 'liquidated' or died in the Gulag. In 1939 Nagy, it is claimed, provided the names of thirty-eight Hungarian political exiles for 'cultivation' and in another document he listed 150 names, from elsewhere in Europe as well as Hungary.[8] It is important to be careful with these documents.* They do not prove anything and they surfaced, at the time the Berlin Wall fell, from KGB archives in suspicious circumstances. However, nobody has successfully argued that the documents are fakes and they probably tell part of the truth. Many times throughout his

---

* They were released by the then KGB boss Vladimir Kryuchkov (who in 1956 had been a very junior operative in the Hungarian Embassy) in 1989, when there was debate inside Hungary about rehabilitating Imre Nagy. Obviously Kryuchkov was keen to damage Nagy's reputation. On the other hand, though they tell a partial story, the documents appear genuine. Khryuchkov, later, was one of the ringleaders of the 'August coup' against Mikhail Gorbachev in 1991.

life people had wondered who in Moscow was Nagy's principal pro-
tector. The most recent evidence suggests it may have been the secret
policeman Beria, which gocs part of the way towards explaining why
Nagy was at first picked to share power with Rákosi in June 1953.*

It would not have been surprising if Nagy was close to the intelligence services in the 1930s. So many exiles felt it their duty, as well
as an act of self-preservation, to help 'the organs'. The reports on
'Volodya' suggest Nagy perhaps assisted more enthusiastically than
was strictly necessary. However, Nagy's brilliant biographer János
Rainer, who has examined the evidence in minute detail, says he may
have been an occasional informer about émigré activities, but he was
definitely not an agent. It's a moot point. All the émigré Muscovites
who saw their mission as bringing Soviet-style communism to their
homelands were to some extent 'agents' of Moscow, if not professional
espionage operatives.

During World War Two Nagy constantly asked Soviet army
command for permission to take some active part in the liberation of
Hungary. He even volunteered to join a proposed guerrilla group to
parachute behind Hitler and Horthy's lines. Instead, he was put to
work on a Hungarian-language radio station that had been set up under
the playwright Gyula Háy to beam Communist propaganda back to the
country. Nagy became a minor celebrity on Radio Kossuth, speaking
clearly and simply in his mellifluous voice with an appealing message
to the peasants: when the Russians brought peace, he said, they would,
for the first time, be given their own land. The philosopher György
Lukács, a Hotel Lux refugee who knew Nagy well in Moscow exile,
said that at that time 'I thought highly of his personal integrity and
intelligence and also of his expertise on the agrarian question. But I
did not regard him as a real politician.'[9]

Nevertheless, when the Muscovites returned to Hungary, Nagy was
the obvious choice to be Agriculture Minister in the coalition government. He delivered on his pledge of land for peasants. On the day
his division of the spoils began to be implemented, he described it as
'this glorious moment when the people of the Hungarian countryside
begin the final and definitive liquidation of feudal Hungary'. He took
land reform more seriously than Rákosi. He was fired as Agriculture

* János Kádár, towards the end of his life, was telling cronies and friends that he
knew Nagy was 'Beria's man' and received 'protection' from the KGB.

Minister after a year and made Interior Minister, but survived less than a year before he was dropped from the government altogether.

Nagy was different from the other Communists. He spoke in plain language, was fond of laughter and of telling jokes (a dangerous practice in those days, but he was prepared to take the risk). Most Sundays would find him as a 'man of the people' watching a football match. He was passionate about the game.

His daughter's marriage raised issues soon after his return to Hungary. In 1946 Erzsébet married Ferenc Jánosi. He had been a Protestant pastor, though later he joined the Soviet army, as well as the Communist Party, and he fought bravely as a partisan. The wedding, though, was celebrated in the main Calvinist church in Budapest. A Communist, especially a prominent one, needed permission to attend a church service. It was granted by Rákosi, but the entire incident was held against Nagy by Party conformists.

When the Communists took absolute power, Nagy was brought back into the fold and given the decorative but powerless role of President of Parliament. Again, he did not last long. When Rákosi and Gerő began to force peasants onto collective farms, Nagy bombarded the pair of them and their cronies with warnings of a disaster in the countryside if co-operatives were forced on the farmers too speedily. In August 1949 he was removed from office, and ordered to perform public self-criticism again for his heretical views. He had to make a humiliating speech, in the usual jargon of the time, confessing 'my rightist deviation ... Opportunism became apparent in my style of work.'[10]

Nagy might easily have been purged at this point, along with Rajk and thousands of others. However, he was allowed to return to academic life. Very few of the original Muscovites were jailed. The assumption was that each had friends in Russia who might watch out for them. Nagy taught at Karl Marx University in Budapest and at an agricultural college in the small country town of Gödöllo, fifty miles from the city, and seemed content with living quietly. Yet a year later he was back in politics. He was made Minister for crop collection, in the classic Bolshevik manner dating back from Lenin's time. As a test of loyalty, functionaries who did not believe in a policy were frequently required to implement that policy. Rákosi must also have seen it as a good way of destroying Nagy's popularity in the countryside. The 'Land Divider' was now responsible for the Communists' most hated and heavy-handed injustice: forcing farmers to deliver their crops at the state-controlled prices. However distasteful he must have found it, as a disciplined Communist Nagy again did his duty.

He was rewarded with the job of deputy Prime Minister. Within weeks of taking up the office Stalin died and Nagy had to make the eulogy in the Hungarian Parliament. 'My heart is heavy as I mount the speaker's platform to face our deeply mourning people,' he said. 'To express their deep love for our greatest friend and liberator and teacher, the Hungarian people are rallying around the Party, the government and our beloved Comrade Rákosi and they are devoting all their energies towards carrying Stalin's great cause to triumph in our country.'[11]

Three months later Nagy received the summons to appear at the Kremlin and was told to undo the damage Stalin had inflicted on Hungary.

The New Course failed to live up to expectations, let alone hopes. Life relaxed in some ways. Butter was available in shops, for the first time in a long while. In Budapest a few independent traders started working again – people could get a pair of shoes fixed by a cobbler, or a radio mended by an electrician. In September, some modest price cuts were announced on a range of goods. Books by Western writers could be read without fear of arrest. The AVO was still a threat, though no longer omnipresent. Detainees were no longer sent to the internment camps. But the release of political prisoners was painfully slow: in the first year no more than 250 well-known people, all of them former prominent Communist officials.[12] Nightclubs like the River Room opened offering American jazz until the small hours, at least for a few tantalising months. That was the main trouble, though. The effects were so short-lived and were felt by so few.

Rákosi never accepted demotion. Humiliatingly, it was now his turn to admit errors and perform 'self-criticism' in the time-honoured way expected of a good Bolshevik. How many Party members believed his apologies for creating a personality cult around himself is open to speculation. From the first day Rákosi worked tirelessly to sabotage Imre Nagy's premiership and take absolute power back for himself. He told a group of Stalinist toadies on 11 July 1953, just a week after Nagy's New Course speech: 'A kulak is still a kulak, with or without a list.'[13] He was still Party boss, a powerful position which he used to ensure that apparatchiks loyal to him would not co-operate with the government. Nagy was unwilling – or lacked the tactical ability –

to bypass the Party machine to manoeuvre his own supporters into positions of influence. Gerő remained the second most important government official, a glowering presence, deeply ambitious, enraged, as the acknowledged number two in Hungary, to be overlooked in favour of Nagy.

From Moscow's perspective, splitting the leadership in this way was one of the big errors that led to the convulsions in Hungary later. If the Soviet magnates had removed Rákosi entirely at this point – and clearly backed Nagy's New Course – the revolution in 1956 might have been averted. Instead, they played off two leaders against each other to see who would emerge on top and encouraged a rivalry that poisoned Hungarian politics for years. Khrushchev admitted the mistake later and railed against Rákosi for 'ruining' things in Hungary. However, he said that at the time they thought Rákosi was not merely clever, but the only Hungarian leader who was 'absolutely trustworthy'.

Why had the Kremlin leaders plucked Nagy from relative obscurity and placed him in the vipers' den opposite Rákosi? That he was not a Jew played a part in the decision, but only a very small part. They were prepared to leave Hungary's other Jewish leaders in place.[14] They opted for Nagy because of his reputation as an honest man. As a Muscovite who had shown absolute loyalty to the USSR, he would, they reckoned, be reliable enough. His job was to remove the excesses of Stalinism but keep the foundations of the edifice solid. The Soviet leaders had approved every part of his New Course and Nagy expected Moscow's full support in carrying it through. He never received it. Largely because of the splits among themselves in Moscow, they began the experiment in Hungary half-heartedly.[15] They gave their choice as Prime Minister less than eighteen months to prove himself. Each cautious, halting step Nagy took to de-Stalinise was watched by Rákosi, the leading Stalinist left in the Eastern bloc, who launched guerrilla raids against him. The result was paralysis.

Every major decision had to be taken in the Kremlin, as both sides in Budapest appealed to Moscow for an adjudication from the top. The Soviet leadership was careful not to come down unequivocally on one side or the other in the dispute they had created. A prime example occurred in May 1954. Rákosi had consistently been blocking the release of political detainees. He had managed to place his own nominees on all the review bodies that decided which prisoners would be

freed, much to the indignation of Nagy. Khrushchev called both Prime
Minister and Party boss to Moscow to arbitrate between them. Even
on this issue Khrushchev appeared to back both sides. 'Rákosi is responsible for these arrests. Therefore he does not want to release these
people,' the Russian said. 'He knows he is guilty and will compromise
himself . . . It is not permissible to denounce men and to throw suspicion
on them.' But then he swung round 180 degrees. 'The rehabilitations
should be carried out so as not to destroy Rákosi's authority,' he
insisted, and the releases proceeded slowly.

Over time the determined intriguer Rákosi became clear favourite to
win the battle. He spent several weeks in Russia, ostensibly on a rest
cure for his high blood pressure, but in fact to take his cause direct to
Moscow, bombarding the Kremlin with ceaseless complaints about the
'kulak' Nagy. Disenchantment with Nagy was growing in Moscow.
Undoubtedly sincere in his wishes, Nagy was failing to deliver on his
pledges and Hungary still seemed to the Kremlin a potential crisis
waiting to happen. Surrounded by enemies, a naive plotter compared
to them, he was increasingly isolated. His friends and supporters were
writers, journalists and a few intellectuals. He had plenty of admirers
within the Communist Party, but they were too afraid of Rákosi to
show themselves publicly.

On 21 December 1954, in the ancient provincial town of Debrecen,
a moment revealed to anyone watching how acute was the split among
Hungary's leaders. Both Nagy and Rákosi were there to celebrate the
tenth anniversary of the start of the Red Army's liberation campaign
in eastern Hungary. Nagy made a speech that he doubtless meant at
the time: 'The victorious battles of the glorious Soviet army . . . brought
about the historic moment . . . when we could unfurl our national
standard, the symbol of our freedom and independence. What would
have become of our country and culture and of civilisation the world
over without the Soviet army? One sorry chapter that has occurred all
too frequently in our country's history shows it being subjected to a
foreign oppression that thwarts . . . progress for generations . . . Ten
years ago, for the first time in Hungary's history, things took a different
turn: because the Soviet army entered our country not as a conqueror,
but as a liberator.'

Rákosi made a similar rousing speech. Afterwards the parties retired
for a meal at the Arany Bika (Golden Bull) restaurant. Two large trestle
tables were placed in the main dining room. At one sat the Prime

Minister, looking depressed and deflated, with a few writers and friends. At the other sat Rákosi, cheerful and elated, surrounded by assorted Party apparatchiks. Diners at the two tables eyed each other warily, never exchanging a single word – the symbol of a dangerous split.

TWELVE

7 January 1955, MOSCOW

Again the overlords in the Kremlin demanded into their presence the provincial satraps from Hungary. At the same long table as eighteen months previously, the Russians once more demanded the head of a prime minister – only this time it was the head of Imre Nagy. In a mirror image of the encounter in 1953, the Soviet Union decided who would comprise the government in Budapest.

The cast list saw a few changes. For the Russians, Beria was no longer there. Eighteen months earlier the collective leadership in Moscow had decided collectively to execute him. The wiry, energetic, intense Lazar Kaganovich, an ardent Stalinist, had become a power in the land over the last year and a half. He sat directly opposite Rákosi, looking him in the eye.[1] The ruddy-faced Kliment Voroshilov, a great survivor, remained powerful. It was assumed, mainly by himself, that because of his post – 1945 position in Budapest he had some valuable knowledge of Hungary and its Communist officials. Rákosi's plotting to unsteady Nagy had worked.

Once again the chief prosecuting counsel was Georgii Malenkov, a key Nagy supporter in June 1953 but now in a precarious position himself in the Kremlin pecking order. He referred to another large dossier about conditions in Hungary, prepared this time by Moscow's new envoy to the country, the suave Yuri Andropov.[2] The documents purported to prove that Nagy's New Course had been a miserable failure. Malenkov gave Nagy, his former friend, treatment as hard as he had previously meted out to Rákosi. He accused the Hungarian of economic incompetence, naivety and 'bourgeois nationalism'. Nagy was even blamed for a small anti-Soviet demonstration during a Hungary v. Soviet Union water polo match in Budapest the previous summer, which had attracted comment in the Russian press. Malenkov slapped down the dossier on the table and bellowed: 'This is not what we told you to do.'

Nagy tried to answer back: 'If it's true there are still problems in Hungary, these are the inevitable heritage of the previous policy of my predecessors.' But he was grumpily interrupted by Malenkov and told that in agriculture 'he had not kept before his eyes the magnificent example of the Soviet kolkhozy [collective farms]'. Nagy, hurt and angry, could not entirely control himself. He blurted out: 'You made not a few mistakes of your own when you formed your kolkhozy.' Now the Russians were startled. They were not used to underlings whom they had ordered to the Kremlin for a dressing-down daring to stand up to them. This remark probably did more harm to Nagy than all the intrigues of Rákosi. Immediately after the meeting, Khrushchev said angrily to Mikoyan and Malenkov: 'Nagy should be careful. In former days I had better men than him put to death.' The icy atmosphere didn't deter Voroshilov from placing his own spin on the proceedings. Rounding up the discussion, he said that he regarded this 'friendly interference in Hungary . . . provided a model for our relations with all the People's Democracies'.[3]

The Soviets desisted from firing Nagy on the spot, but they left his position untenable. Rákosi could strike at him now at any time he wanted. Before he did, though, Nagy suffered a mild heart attack.

THIRTEEN

2 March 1955, Budapest

Nagy was barely out of hospital when the coup against him was mounted. Rákosi called together the leading Communist Party officials in Hungary. The only item of business was to begin the process of removing the Prime Minister from office. Nagy was unable to appear to defend himself. He remained convalescing at his home – an elegant two-storey villa in Orsó Street, a desirable address* – under strict doctor's orders not to go out. Over the next few weeks he was axed from every position, however minor, that he held in the Party or the government. On 18 April his replacement as Premier was named: András Hegedüs, the young cypher of Rákosi, who meekly followed whatever orders his master gave him.

Nagy was told, not for the first time in his life, to recant his heretical views, confess to the errors in his New Course, don his hair shirt and submit to the ritual of self-criticism. He refused. Nagy considered himself a disciplined Communist, as loyal to the cause as ever, but this time felt he had nothing to be self-critical about. 'The June Road is the way – the only way – to save communism in Hungary,' he told supporters. 'I will not say it is an error.'[1] From this moment his popularity rocketed. 'If he had done what was required of him, he would probably have been given a sinecure somewhere, an office, maybe even a car and allowed to perform minor services for the Party. But the people would never have given him a second thought afterwards. He salvaged his reputation, his honour and his pride, said Eva Walko, an anti-Communist but an admirer of Nagy.[2]

Rákosi could now brand Nagy as a troublemaker and he was

---

* In the Buda Hills, fifteen minutes from the centre of Budapest and one of the smartest and most expensive parts of the city. Nagy was granted the house for his Communist Party work. It is now a small museum of his life, immaculately kept exactly as it was in 1956.

determined to destroy the rebel. Nagy was unable to return to academic life as a teacher, or find any sort of wage-earning job. Finally, in a move that pained him deeply, he was expelled from the Communist Party which he had served faithfully for nearly forty years. In official life he was a nobody. However, with each new humiliation Rákosi inflicted on him his reputation grew, among ordinary Hungarians and particularly among Party members fearful of a slide back to Stalinism. Nagy did not seem like a charismatic figure, but he could inspire astonishing loyalty through the power of his apparent integrity. Jenő Széll joined the Communists in early 1945 during the siege of Budapest. Between 1948 and 1950 he had been Ambassador to Romania, then, back in Budapest, head of the Party's propaganda department. He was typical of a group of reform-minded Communists who started to form an unofficial group around Nagy. 'My opinion of Imre Nagy was that he was a thoroughly decent person, almost too honourable for me to ... consider him a politician. By the time Rákosi's counter-attack on him began I'd have followed Nagy through fire and water.'[3]

The nucleus of the group was formed among political prisoners who had been released over the previous eighteen months. Most prominent Communists – especially the brightest and the best – had at one time been jailed or interned since the Rajk trial and the purges. The closest to Nagy was Géza Losonczy, who joined the Party in 1938 aged twenty-one. During the war he worked with distinct courage for the anti-fascist resistance. A short, slim figure with wavy brown hair, he wore horn-rimmed spectacles and was what he looked: serious-minded, sophisticated, highly intelligent. He edited the Communist Party news-paper from 1945, 'a fiercely dedicated Communist to the last breath of his body' according to Gyula Háy. But he was too outspoken to survive under Rákosi. In 1951 he was jailed for twelve years following a show trial. He suffered appallingly in prison – his TB could be cured quickly, but the experience left him with mental scars that took a long while to heal.[4]

Losonczy's great friend, Ferenc Donáth, emerged from jail in 1954 aged forty-one around the same time, grotesquely thin and gap-toothed, having been tall and lean when he went inside. He too had been an underground Communist in the Horthy years. After the war he practised and taught law, and as a Party activist proved a shrewd political tactician. Journalist Sándor Haraszti had been a deeply committed Party member for thirty years and one of the most popular figures in what was left of Budapest café society for his wit and constant fund of information. He had been jailed by the fascists, but in 1951, aged fifty-five, he was sentenced to death on trumped-up charges. He waited for nearly two years on death row, thinking every day might be his last, before a jailer eventually told him his sentence had been commuted to life imprisonment.[5]

Rákosi seemed to be back in control but he found that things had changed. His absolute power had gone. He reversed Nagy's economic policies, but his overlords in Moscow no longer allowed him to run Hungary as his personal fiefdom. The Kremlin bosses told him they would sanction no new purges against Communists, nor a revival of the Rákosi personality cult.[6] The AVO could still fill the jails with workers who complained about their production targets, or peasants who refused to rejoin the collective farms which they had left under Nagy's New Course. However, prominent figures were to be left alone. In Hungary the Soviets in effect allowed a semi-official opposition to exist – heavily circumscribed, and free to operate within strict limits only in Budapest. Nevertheless, here was an experiment – the only one of its kind in the Soviet satellites – that had fateful consequences.

Meanwhile, Nagy lived quietly. A Communist to the core, he insisted that no political activity in Hungary must be taken outside the Party.[7] Yet he had a powerful sense of mission and was convinced that one day he would be called back to complete the task he had begun – to show there was such a thing as communism with a human face. Being a politician, however, he was also deeply interested in his approval ratings. He made sure he was highly visible on the streets of Budapest. 'He travelled by bus, always cheerful and with a pleasant word to say, always approachable. At weekends he was regularly seen at Gerbeaud's* feeding ice cream to his grandson. He just seemed so ordinary. We were not used to politicians like him. Yes he was a Communist, but we knew, everybody knew, he had stood up to Rákosi.'[8]

'If ten or so Hungarian writers had been shot at the right moment, the revolution would never have occurred,' said Khrushchev, some years later.[9] The right time, from his perspective, would probably have been now, when writers and intellectuals of all kinds began to flock to

---

* Budapest's most famous café, then as now.

support 'the old man', as the group around Nagy referred to him. Writers in Hungary, with a few famed exceptions, had always played an overtly political role. The traditional story has it that the national poet, Sándor Petőfi, began a revolution (in 1848, against the Austrians) with a public reading of one of his verses. He died on the battlefield a year later when Russian soldiers under Tsar Nicholas I brutally crushed the rebellion.

Under communism, writers existed to serve the Party as, in Stalin's term, 'engineers of the mind'. Naturally, no anti-Communist voices were published. They left the country, like the novelist Sándor Márai, or went into hibernation, hid their writing, and earned a living some other way. However, writers willing and able to serve the Communist masters were pampered, treated like celebrities and granted huge rewards. Many, who had opposed fascism, were socialists by conviction. Others co-operated out of ambition or survival instinct, while a large, sprawling bureaucracy of literature was created as an adjunct to the Party.

The Communist writer was a peculiar phenomenon – a creator of imaginative works but also a functionary following instructions. 'Any young man with a gift of phraseology, who could learn to master the simple techniques of Party literature was assured of becoming a prominent person, a socially important figure, very unlike the ... writers of the old order – or in the West, who although they were sometimes buried with national honours, were seldom treated as important in their lifetimes. To receive a high income from the State for writing poems was unheard of in pre-Communist Hungary.'[10] Producing odes in praise of Rákosi – or for Party hack journalists, reporting the latest Central Committee speeches of the Wise Leader – struck many of the writers as an acceptable means of living. Their complacency was shaken when, under Nagy's premiership, people like themselves, friends they had known and admired, began returning to Budapest looking haggard and telling of the tortures they had endured as political prisoners.

Works started to appear that pushed at the boundaries set by the Party censors. One poem by a small, bespectacled, wiry young man few Hungarians had previously heard of, László Benjámin, seemed to sum up the sense of shame felt by the Communist writers who had turned a blind eye to the injustices. Addressing his friend Sándor Haraszti, who had just been released after years in jail, he wrote: 'It was my crime to have believed in *yours*.'[11] Daring articles began appearing in the Writers' Union magazine, *Literary Gazette* (*Irodalmi Újság*). The fiery socialist realist novelist Tamás Aczél, a passionately committed Communist who had won the Hungarian Party's Kossuth Literary Prize and the Soviet Union's Stalin Prize, wrote a story revealing details of a secret that Party functionaries wanted hidden: the existence of a holiday village for senior Communist officials on the shores of Lake Balaton, separated from the prying eyes of ordinary mortals by high walls and barbed wire.

'There is one question which arises in relation to this intellectual revolt,' the *Literary Gazette*'s editor, Miklós Molnár, said. 'One wonders why this group, reputed to have more insight than the man in the street, needed such brutal shocks before they could recognise the true nature of the system and perceive what a simple peasant or train conductor had known for years.'[12] Nevertheless readers, fed nothing but Stalinist propaganda for years, at last wanted to know what the best of these writers had to say. The *Literary Gazette* printed 40,000 copies a week. It always sold out within an hour of hitting the bookstalls and afterwards changed hands for three times its cover price. 'There was a desperate hunger for decent writing that told the truth. That is a deep need in Hungary and always has been. One of the reasons we hated the Soviets so much was that they took our literature away from us.'[13] People were astonished when little retaliation was taken by the once almighty Rákosi against the rebel writers. Molnár was fired and given a menial job, but in former days he would certainly have been tortured by the AVO, jailed and probably executed. 'That was the point when anger replaced fear amongst so many of us.'[14]

In October 1955 fifty-nine prominent writers and artists signed a manifesto protesting against 'administrative methods' used against intellectuals and demanding more freedom of expression. Nothing like it had been seen anywhere in the Communist world. On 3 December Rákosi summoned the ringleaders of the Writers' Revolt to a show-down. He insisted they retract the petition and toe the Party line. 'We do not give writers a free pass,' he said. When they refused he barely looked surprised. Rákosi brooded and waited and prepared a list of a dozen writers he would arrest when the time was right. The time never came. Before he could strike at his enemies a drama unfolded in Moscow that left him politically crippled.

FOURTEEN

25 February 1956, Moscow

During the Cold War, most of the decisions that had an effect on Hungary were taken outside the country. This day's events in the Kremlin were no exception. At 6 p.m. in the Great Hall of the People, Nikita Khrushchev began one of the most dramatic speeches ever made in the Soviet Union. By the time he finished, six hours later, he had sparked off a series of bloody upheavals in the Soviet empire.

At the 20th Congress of the Soviet Communist Party, in front of hundreds of top Communists who owed their positions of power to Joseph Stalin, Khrushchev unmasked the late dictator as a mass murderer. Most of the audience revered the memory of Stalin and barely knew how to react when they were told about the old monster's purges, the millions of executions over nearly two decades, the untold numbers of deaths in the Gulag.[1]

During the last three years Khrushchev had emerged from the Kremlin power struggles as the most influential of the magnates, though he was by no means the tsar. His so-called 'secret speech', which he knew would not remain secret for long, was one battle in a continuous fight against his principal opponents in the 'collective leadership', hardline Stalinists who wanted to row back from the tentative package of cautious reforms he initiated – especially his efforts to reach a 'peaceful coexistence' with the West. The speech did not mention the Soviet satellites once, yet, without Khrushchev foreseeing them, the consequences were felt more immediately in the slave states of Eastern Europe than in Russia itself.[2]

Radio Free Europe reported the speech in detail within a few weeks. As none of the newspapers in the Communist world had said a word about Khrushchev's bombshell, the scoop obtained by RFE boosted the station's reputation for providing accurate news from behind the Iron Curtain. Immediately it became apparent that Khrushchev had created a problem for all the satellite states, but especially for Hungary.

If Stalin had been a criminal, then what about Rákosi, 'Stalin's best pupil', who had been his willing creature and copied him with devotion in all things? Rákosi told his friends and supporters to keep calm. 'In a few months Khrushchev will be the traitor and everything will be back to normal,' he advised.[3] The prophecy sounded plausible enough for the nervous Kremlin-watchers around him, but this time the 'Wise Leader' was wrong.

For the last decade, criticism of Rákosi in public had been unimaginable inside Hungary. Now, within the Communist Party circles, at least in sophisticated Budapest, open mockery of him was widespread. Rákosi seemed powerless to reassert his authority. 'There's nothing so impotent as a dictatorship that's weakening before your eyes,' said the writer Stephen Vizinczey, who was a student in Budapest at the time. 'It seemed from then as if change was really possible. For one thing, the AVO were not the force they had been; we were not so scared.[4] The head of the 'regular' police force in Budapest, Sándor Kopácsi, noted that senior AVO men began to worry seriously that they might be denounced. The fear that they could soon face long spells in their own jails, like their former boss Gábor Péter, 'concentrated their minds and made them act properly'.

Rákosi repeatedly made speeches during early 1956 attacking the 'cult of personality', but as the personality that attracted the cult was his, the comments were not entirely convincing. For many years stage performances of *Richard III* had been banned. Now, in a new production at the National Theatre, there was no hiding who the ugly, hunchbacked tyrant brooding menacingly on the stage represented. On the first night, the applause was deafening. Other long-suppressed classic works by Hungarian and foreign writers were now freely available. Concerts were performed of pieces by Zoltán Kodály, the great Hungarian composer whose works fell out of favour with the Stalinists because of their alleged 'chauvinism'. When, at the public meeting in March, a young, almost entirely unknown schoolteacher, György Litván, interrupted a speech by Rákosi to say 'You have lost the trust of the people: resign', it caused a stir. Much more significant, there was no retaliation against the hot-headed historian by Rákosi or his henchmen.[5]

FIFTEEN

27 June 1956, Budapest, 7 p.m.

On a swelteringly hot night, the main meeting room of the neo-classical Officers' Club, in the centre of the city, was packed with everyone of significance in the intellectual and social life of Budapest. Word of mouth had spread a rumour that a dramatic event would take place that evening to strike a knockout blow against Mátyás Rákosi.

An imposing, curly-haired woman aged forty-four strode to the lectern. Immediately she was recognised as Júlia Rajk, released six months earlier from a jail sentence which had not been kind to her looks. Holding back tears, she spoke with a firm, steady voice:

> I stand before you deeply moved after five years of prison and humili-ation. Let me tell you this: as far as prisons are concerned, Horthy's jails were far better, even for Communists, than Rákosi's prisons. Not only was my husband killed, but my little baby was torn from me. For years I received no letters and no information about the fate of my son. These criminals have not only murdered László Rajk. They have trampled underfoot all sentiment and honesty in this country. Mur-derers should not be criticised. They should be punished. I shall never rest until those who have ruined this country, corrupted the Party, killed thousands and driven millions into despair receive their just punishment. Comrades, help me in this struggle.

The audience rose to their feet to applaud. In a further painfully humiliating punishment her name had been changed, against her will, to Lászlóné Gyork – part of the campaign to turn her late husband into a 'non-person' – but she was still known as Júlia. Mention of the Rajk case proved disastrous for Rákosi, not only because of the injustice done to one former Communist Minister, but also because the case was a symbol for all the others. If Rajk was innocent, what of the thousands of others? Rákosi tried to lay the blame for the Rajk prosecution on the terror tactics of Gábor Péter, now himself in prison, but he was not believed.[1]

With every day during the spring and summer pressure mounted on Rákosi, who in Budapest was now being openly called a murderer. A new opposition group had been established in March. The Petőfi Circle (named after the poet) was a debating group, formed by the Communist youth organisation DISZ, and run by enthusiastic Communists, which did more to destabilise Hungary's Communist Party than any other single force. Its meetings became huge public events, unique in the Soviet bloc, where for the first time since 1948 politics could be freely discussed. Júlia Rajk's devastating intervention was at a Petőfi Circle debate on 'socialist legality', otherwise known as the police state. In a debate on 'socialist science', part of the story about Russia's exploitation of Hungarian uranium was revealed to waves of fury. At a debate on philosophy, the Marxist thinker and literary critic György Lukács bitterly attacked socialist realism as third-rate literature produced by Party hacks.

The climax of the Petőfi Circle's campaign came on 7 July, when Hungary's most prominent writers and journalists debated a free press. More than 6,000 people queued in the streets outside the hall until 4 a.m. listening on loudspeakers. The final speaker was Géza Losonczy, Imre Nagy's great friend and confidant, who was still recuperating from the psychological breakdown he had suffered at the hands of the AVO. Quietly, he explained in detail how the former Prime Minister had been sacked, disgraced and never allowed to defend himself. At the mention of Nagy's name the audience rose and chanted 'Imre, Imre'.

SIXTEEN

12 July 1956, Washington DC

For a reluctant politician, President Eisenhower gave a good impression of enjoying the role – and the exercise of power. In his re-election campaign he fought the same opponent as four years earlier, the Democrats' charming, intelligent but uncharismatic liberal intellectual, Adlai Stevenson. The Republicans' aggressive Cold War rhetoric also sounded familiar from 1952. The President's spin doctors still spoke of bringing freedom and democracy to the whole of Europe. However, inside the White House, the mood shifted. The President made it clear to his advisers that in reality his aims were more modest and limited. A National Security Committee paper of a few months earlier, which Eisenhower mentioned regularly, said clearly that 'the detachment of any major European satellites from the Soviet bloc does not now appear feasible except by Soviet acquiescence or by war'.[1] As the Russians rejected the former option and the President flatly ruled out the latter, that meant that Eisenhower in reality accepted the status quo behind the Iron Curtain, although nobody in the administration was allowed to say so publicly.

Secrecry was paramount to the administration, as newly released accounts of an extraordinary conversation held on that day between the President's key advisers make clear. Officials were aware they could look like hypocrites if their true position was known. Secretary of State John Foster Dulles read out the text of a highly confidential new policy paper the NSC was preparing. He quoted from the draft text: 'The US should encourage the satellite peoples in passive resistance to their Soviet-dominated regimes when this will contribute to minimizing satellite contribution to Soviet power or to increasing pressure for desirable change. In general, [we] do not discourage, by public utterances or otherwise, spontaneous manifestations of discontent and opposition to the Communist regime ... [in the satellite states], despite risk to individuals, when the net results will exert pressures for their release from Soviet domination.'[2] Dulles then explained the meaning of the policy in starker terms. He said: 'Sometimes unrest and uprisings are an important part of the way we have to play the game in the present situation we are confronting with the Soviet Union.' Vice President Richard Nixon was blunter still, suggesting that a failed uprising somewhere in the Eastern bloc crushed by the Russians would, in public relations terms, help America: 'It wouldn't be an unmixed evil, from the point of view of the US interest, if the Soviet iron fist were to come down hard again on the Soviet bloc.'[3]

The administration agreed that without 'rollback' as a serious goal, the new US policy should be to accept the development of 'national Communist' governments like Tito's in Yugoslavia throughout Eastern Europe. This was a radical step. National Communists were still Communists and during an election year in the Cold War, showing any sort of approval to a Communist government, even lukewarm support, could appear weak. Nor should people in the Eastern bloc be told that the US had, in effect, agreed to abandon them. Said Nixon: 'I can think of nothing which would, from the point of view of domestic politics or of our international relations, be worse than a leak tending to indicate that we at the highest levels were agreeing on a policy of national communism under any circumstances. I hope everybody, from those present here all the way down the line, will keep their mouths shut on this subject.' The Treasury Secretary, George Humphrey, agreed. 'Imagine what would happen if . . . this appeared in the newspapers? The effect on the administration would be murderous. We must do our best to minimise the possibility of a leak.' The administration was worried about American voters, but also concerned about European anti-Communists knowing how far rhetoric had moved from reality in the White House.[4]

US and Western intelligence about Hungary was pitifully poor. A National Intelligence Estimate prepared by the CIA at the end of 1955 predicted that 'Passive resistance inside the country will grow. It takes the form of absenteeism, job-hopping, shoddy work, waste, frauds and often culminates in deliberate sabotage. In Hungary there was no tradition or history of active resistance, and all the evidence indicates that this tradition has not been broken. During World War Two there was some, but these exploits were probably best described as feats of individual heroism. Most of the resistance in Hungary is of a passive character ... there are few potential underground leaders.' The CIA noted that

> much of the underground activity reported seems to have been inspired by the regime itself. If one were to believe the claims of émigré organisations and reports of the Communist press there has been considerable organised active resistance. However, an analysis of available information leads to the conclusion that there is really no underground movement ... and that the Communist regime itself was either the sponsor of some of the organisations reported, or invented them for the purpose of building up a case against individuals whose removal from positions of public influence was desirable. The Communists promote 'resistance groups' with names like White Hand, Black Eagle etc. to apprehend disloyal citizens.[5]

American diplomats seemed almost deliberately to cut themselves off from life in Hungary. When in June 1956 Eric Johnston, President of the Motion Picture Association of the US, arrived in Hungary on a semi-official visit, diplomats wanted to give him a cocktail party. Johnston gave the Legation a list of leading artists, writers, actors, academics and politicians he would like to invite. Legation officials were shocked: 'But Mr Johnston, we never meet with these people socially,' he was told.[6] Neither America's spies nor diplomats sent back to Washington accurate accounts of the pressure building inside Hungary. When journalists on the spot were predicting imminent change the intelligence agencies discounted their reports as sensation-seeking.

Nor were the British much better informed. Their Ambassador to Hungary was Sir Leslie 'Bunny' Fry, ex-Sandhurst, ex-Indian Army, formerly a First Secretary in Lisbon and an official at the East European department of the Foreign Office. At the start of the year he sent a despatch to the Foreign Secretary, Selwyn Lloyd, with the confident assertion that 'the national genius [of the Hungarians] is for survival rather than successful revolt. Even if courage were among the more notable Hungarian qualities, the geographical features necessary for a Resistance movement – mountains, forests or seaboard – are lacking ... There will, accordingly, be no hurtful kicking against the pricks ... It is highly improbable that a bold hazard will be attempted. Apathetic resignation, the compromise of "go slow but don't strike" sums up the general attitude.'[7]

In the middle of April Fry was convinced that, despite Mátyás

Rákosi's problems, 'he will be with us for some time to come'.[8] On 15 June Fry reported to the Foreign Office: 'There is a strong sense of expectancy here ... but any idea that Rákosi will not remain the most powerful single figure may ... safely be discounted.'[9]

SEVENTEEN

13 July 1956, Budapest

The magnates in the Kremlin were now seriously worried about affairs in their Hungarian colony. They had been kept well informed about events by the Soviet Union's clever young Ambassador on the spot, Yuri Andropov, who for the last few months had been sending back to Moscow disturbing reports about 'hostile elements' destabilising the country. They despatched to Budapest their chief troubleshooter, Anastas Ivanovich Mikoyan, with orders to 'lance the boil'. The elegant, sharp-suited sixty-one-year-old was a vastly experienced operator, intimately involved in running the satellite states, who had been at the top inside the Kremlin for decades. It is misleading to talk of hardliners and moderates in Stalin's court; everyone in his circle was implicated in ghastly crimes. Mikoyan, a canny survivor, was anything but an innocent bystander during the purges.* However, he had occasionally stood up to Stalin, after whose death he emerged as a kingmaker – and also as a man with a sense of humour. He was a close ally of Khrushchev, who had enthusiastically encouraged him to attack Stalin's memory. On the Hungarian question, he was convinced Rákosi's time was up and he seemed to relish the prospect of personally delivering the *coup de grâce*.[1]

According to András Hegedüs, the young Prime Minister, early in the morning 'Rákosi and I went to meet him [Mikoyan] at the airport and took him back to the city by car. We were almost at the government guest house when Mikoyan turned to Rákosi and said "The Soviet leadership has decided you are ill". Rákosi didn't think he was ill, but of course in those days illness was a political decision. Mikoyan continued: "You will need treatment in Moscow."'[2] Rákosi had been

---

* Mikoyan lasted in the highest circles of Soviet politics for nearly five decades. He was there, at a place of honour as a leading Communist, at the funeral of Lenin in 1924, and represented the USSR at John F. Kennedy's funeral in 1963.

warned of his fate but he still fought back. At 11 a.m. Mikoyan met the Hungarian satraps at the Communist Party headquarters at Academy Street. The 'Wise Leader' outlined the steps he was planning to take which he assured his Russian overlord would restore his and the Party's authority. He produced a list of 400 names, with Imre Nagy's at the top, of prominent opposition figures he would arrest 'at once'. The wily Armenian interrupted him:

> 'Tell me, Comrade Rákosi, what do you think of the Petőfi Circle?'
> 'A movement organised by enemies of the Party,' replied Rákosi.
> Mikoyan continued: 'That's interesting. In Moscow we have heard that the Party has been repeatedly acclaimed at Petőfi Circle meetings. That sounds like a remarkable bunch of enemies of the Party.'[3]

All the Hungarians remained silent. Then Gerő, in his vulpine way, seized his opportunity. For years he had resented playing second fiddle to Rákosi – whom in private, towards the end, he used to describe as 'discredited and senile'. Gerő was not at all the loyal lieutenant he depicted himself. He said: 'Might I suggest to our beloved and wise father of the people that mass arrests are not reconcilable with our new brand of social legality.' Mikoyan 'suggested' that Rákosi resign on grounds of ill health. Rákosi would not believe what he was hearing. He left the room and placed a call to Khrushchev in Moscow, who confirmed the decision.[4]

In a secret cable back to the Kremlin the next day Mikoyan reported the scene to Khrushchev and warned that even with Rákosi out of the picture Hungary remained at crisis point.

> I emphasised that . . . it was impermissible that anything unexpected and unpleasant should happen in Hungary . . . One can see how, day after day, the comrades are further losing their grip on power. Nothing is being done. The comrades prepare reports . . . while enemy elements act among the masses and in the country unpunished. A parallel centre is forming from enemy elements operating actively, decisively and self-confidently . . . The press and radio are not under [Party] control any more. Every day the influence of the hostile, opposition mood . . . is expanding.
>
> Everything came down to the question of Rákosi, but none of them could raise it. All of them were waiting for us to raise the issue because

they feel bound by our line on this matter . . . When I raised the question of whether it would be better for Rákosi to resign on his own, it was clear that the Comrades . . . breathed easier . . .

As far as Imre Nagy is concerned . . . we believed previously, and we believe now, that it was a mistake to expel him from the Party, even though he deserved it with his behaviour. Had Nagy remained . . . he would have had to obey Party discipline and carry out Party will. By expelling him . . . it has complicated its own struggle with him. It is necessary to explain to Nagy very directly that he cannot return to the Party by fighting against it. The path of fighting against the Party is one that will inevitably lead him to prison.[5]

That afternoon, the newspapers were warned to hold the front page for an important statement. Some of the editors thought the news would be the announcement that Nagy and various other leading opposition figures were being arrested. Some were partly right and predicted that the breaking news was the downfall of Rákosi. Nobody appeared to foresee the name of the man set to replace him – Ernő Gerő. 'It was scarcely conceivable. An absolutely foolish absurd choice to replace Rákosi with an equally inflexible Stalinist, implicated in all the crimes during the terror.'[6] Within hours Budapest had made its analysis of the development. The saying went around: 'They have replaced a bald Rákosi with a thin one.'[7]

Along with Mikoyan, there had gone from Moscow to Budapest a group of military men whose uniforms were covered in medals and braid. The delegation was led by General Mikhail Malinin, first deputy Chief of Staff in the Soviet army, who arrived with two sets of orders. The first was to make a general review of the Russian formations based in Hungary. The Austrian Peace Treaty had finally been signed on 15 May 1955, and the Soviet Union agreed to take its troops out of the country. Technically that would have meant that Russian soldiers were no longer allowed to stay in Hungary. But the previous day Hungary had become a member of the Warsaw Pact, which authorised Soviet soldiers to stay. About 75,000 Russian troops and airmen – the Special Corps – were stationed in Hungary in three divisions.

Malinin's second mission was to issue a tough reprimand to the Special Corps' commander, Lieutenant-General Piotr Laschenko. After the East German disturbances in 1953, when Russian troops fired on strikers near Berlin, all Soviet forces in Eastern Europe had been ordered to devise anti-riot and counter-insurgency operations in case of large-scale disturbances in the satellites. Laschenko had not produced any. When this lapse was reported to Marshal Georgi Zhukov, the Soviet Defence Minister, at the end of June, he was livid and ordered that the document must be produced immediately.[8] Within two weeks Operation Volna ('Wave') was prepared and Malinin was instructed to assess it. The plan envisaged the use of tens of thousands of Soviet troops at very short notice, within three to six hours, 'to uphold and restore public order' in Hungary. The formulation of Volna in such double-quick time suggested just one thing: the Russians needed a fall-back option in case Mikoyan's political efforts failed and more robust measures were needed to bring troublesome Hungary in line.

Lieutenant-General Yevgeny Malaschenko, thirty-two, second in command of the Special Corps, worked night and day setting the plan down on paper. He had doubts from the first about whether it would be effective. He told one of Malinin's aides, General Mikhail Tikhonov, the top Soviet adviser to the Hungarian army, that 'due to lack of troops, our men could only assume the defence of main targets and could not take part in maintaining order if there were protests or gatherings'. Tikhonov told him not to worry. 'The Hungarians have a strong state security service and army, so they can maintain order themselves quite easily. Our help won't be necessary.' Malaschenko replied, 'Just as well that the plan will remain a plan on paper only.'[9]

EIGHTEEN
6 October 1956, Budapest

On a miserably cold, wet and windy day more than 100,000 people lined the streets of Budapest to witness one of the most bizarre events in modern Hungarian history: the reburial of László Rajk and four of the men who had been hanged with him nearly seven years earlier. While he lived, Rajk had been a hated figure in Hungary. He had been chief among the fanatics who installed the murderous and rotten system on the country, notorious as an architect of the police state. But as one of the most prominent victims of the Terror, he had been transformed into a patriot, deserving of a state funeral at the Kerepesi cemetery, last resting place for Hungarian heroes. 'Having had a show trial, he now had a show burial.'[1]

Gerő, enjoying the power he thought should always have been his, had reluctantly agreed to the reinterment soon after his masters in Moscow had made him the new proconsul in Budapest. Following several direct appeals from an impassioned Júlia Rajk for the public rehabilitation of her husband, he agreed. She had been offered 200,000 forint in 'compensation' – a fortune which an average working Hungarian would not see in half a lifetime. She refused, declaring she wanted no money, she wanted justice. Gerő's first instinct was to reject the idea of a reburial, which would be politically risky. Later he was persuaded that it could be turned into an anti-Rákosi event to show how the new government had made a fresh start. The date set was carefully chosen: 6 October is a symbolic anniversary, the day that thirteen Hungarian generals were executed by the Austrians after the failed 1848 revolution. Gerő should have stuck with his first judgment, that any mention of Rajk would strike the regime at a vulnerable spot. The funeral became a dress rehearsal for events three weeks later.[2]

The two separated groups of mourners barely acknowledged each other's presence. The official Party functionaries who had been ordered to attend, most of them survivors from the Stalin era, looked edgy and uncomfortable. Ferenc Münnich, an old Muscovite who had fought with Rajk in the Spanish Civil War, was charged with the task of explaining the Rajk Affair and apologising on behalf of the Communist Party. When he reached a passage describing the 'criminals who had emerged from a quagmire' to kill the brave revolutionary hero Rajk, he was almost drowned out in catcalls. Some of those criminals were there on the rostrum still representing the Communist Party.[3]

Júlia Rajk, in a plastic cape clutching her seven-year-old son, Laci, to herself, was surrounded by all the leading opposition figures, none of whom were allowed to make speeches.* She stood alongside Imre Nagy, who looked sombre, 'but was telling them that soon it would be Stalinism that will finally be buried'.[4] Jenő Széll, who would soon take a job in Nagy's private office, described the reburial as though it were carefully scripted and stage-managed. 'The funeral was ghastly. It started pouring with rain – not a cloudburst but enough to get us all thoroughly soaked. And beforehand, what a huge streaming crowd of people with grim faces! That sort of thing was very rare in Budapest. People came, acquaintances looked at each other and greeted one another, but they didn't as usual form little groups to gossip . . . Everyone here was looking to see who would be in the leadership from now on. The expression "Comrades, never again" was heard all the time, which sounded like a bad joke.'

A finale to the afternoon's macabre show followed in the early evening: Budapest's first unofficial political demonstration since the Communists took power. A group of 500 or so students marched to the Batthany monument in Buda – a memorial to the first constitutional Prime Minister of Hungary, who had been executed by the Austrians in 1849 – and began shouting anti-Communist slogans. The police broke up the demonstration quickly and peacefully, but it was a warning sign the Hungarian Communist élite failed to comprehend.

Khrushchev quickly became disappointed in Ernő Gerő. His puppet seemed not to understand the urgency of the crisis as it appeared from the Kremlin. Vladimir Burlatsky, who briefly worked as one of his speech-writers, claims that Khrushchev recognised later how profound

---

* The younger László Rajk became one of Hungary's best-known architects and was a leading figure in dissident circles of Budapest during the early 1980s.

an error he had made in over-promoting the vain, inflexible and at the same time complacent Hungarian.[5] The appointment of Gerő, one avoidable step that led directly to the tragedy to come, was a typical example of the enigmatic Khrushchev's contradictory leadership style. His efforts to modernise the Soviet Union and abandon Stalinism were laudable as far as they went, but erratic and hesitant. 'Yes Khrushchev walked on two legs,' his great rival in the Communist world, Mao Zedong, observed, 'one is boldly striding into a new era, the other is hopelessly stuck in the mire of the past.'[6]

The Kremlin, however, was far better informed about Hungary than the USSR's viceroy in Budapest appeared to be. Yuri Andropov, Russia's highly ambitious Ambassador, was deluging his superiors back in Moscow with worrying reports of how tension in Hungary was mounting alarmingly throughout the summer and Gerő seemed incapable of dealing with it. In a top secret telegram on 29 August he said: 'the political situation in Hungary ... requires constant attention. Of most concern to us is the fact that the Hungarian Comrades have so far achieved insignificant results in the struggle to strengthen their power in the country.'[7] Vladimir Kryuchkov, a junior diplomat at the Embassy at the time, who later stepped into Andropov's shoes as KGB chief, said: 'Andropov sensed the danger and warned Moscow. He sent ... telegrams, made phone calls and even went to Moscow himself. He tried to warn everybody but it was all in vain. Khrushchev thought he could cope with the situation.'[8]

As did Gerő. Andropov saw the Hungarian leader regularly and from the despatches he sent back to the Kremlin, he despaired of Gerő's complacency. According to Andropov, by early September Gerő privately acknowledged that he 'was finding it enormously difficult to foster unity within the Party leadership ... The disunity was exacerbating the dangerous and unstable position in the country as a whole.'[9] If Gerő was being serious it is hard to see why he was willing to absent himself from Hungary for so long over the next few weeks. During much of September and the first week of October he was in the Crimea, occasionally holding talks with his Russian overlords but mostly taking a holiday. He saw Andropov shortly before he left. 'Gerő openly acknowledged when he set out on the trip that he was not at all sure whether "things would be OK" while he was gone,' Andropov reported.[10] When he returned 'he told me that "now I am back in Hungary I can see that the situation has become much worse and more turbulent than I had imagined when I was in the USSR. Acute discontent has spread throughout the country.'"[11]

He was away for the Rajk reburial, though he admitted to Andropov that he had not anticipated its profound effect. As soon as he returned, he realised the implications of what he had done. On 12 October he confided to the Ambassador: 'The reburial of Rajk has dealt a massive blow to the Party leadership, whose authority was not all that high to begin with.' Despite these misgivings, Gerő left the country again. From 15 to 22 October he was in Yugoslavia. The main purpose was to hold talks with Tito, but he extended his stay to take a holiday on the Croatian coast. Gerő insisted that he could feel the build-up of pressure in Hungary, yet he felt no compunction about leaving the country. The Russians, Khrushchev in particular, would not forget his irresponsibility.

As autumn approached, Khrushchev was simultaneously dealing with another crisis in the Soviet empire. The Poles had not endured a regime anything like as brutal or unforgiving as Hungary's after World War Two. Comparisons between the two countries are odious; post-war differences between them were as great as the similarities. Yet the day-to-day tyranny and poverty, the imposed conformity and bland dullness of totalitarian communism were equally hated in Poland – as was slave status as a colony of the Soviet Union. National pride burned strong in Polish hearts. At the end of June, riots broke out in Poznan, an industrial town on the Baltic coast. They were easily crushed within a day by Soviet troops. However, the disturbances prompted a display of rare courage among Communist apparatchiks. As in Hungary, Polish Communists had split between a Stalinist old guard and a group of 'reformers', which had widened since Khrushchev's 'secret speech' earlier in the year.

On 19 October the top leaders of the Polish Communist Party met in Warsaw amid high drama. They chose as Party boss the once-discredited Wladislaw Gomulka, who had been jailed between 1951 and 1954, during Stalin's anti-Titoist purges, but had been rehabilitated and now presented himself as a 'national Communist'. Gomulka's elevation alarmed the Soviets.[12] Khrushchev ordered Red Army units to encircle Warsaw and flew there himself for a confrontation with his Polish vassals. He deeply mistrusted the suave and subtle Gomulka. After a two-day standoff, when Khrushchev said the Soviets would not recognise Gomulka's leadership and the Poles called Moscow's bluff, they finally reached a peaceful compromise. The Russians withdrew their soldiers, accepted Gomulka and acknowledged his right to seek 'a Polish road to socialism'. The Poles, on their side, guaranteed that their reforms would not threaten local Communist Party rule or the unity of the Soviet bloc.[13]

The Nagy group was inspired by Gomulka's transformation from outcast to saviour of the nation. The 'old man', as his supporters referred to him, was surrounded by radical voices who advised him to increase the pressure on Gerő and loudly demand a place in the leadership. Nagy, however, was cautious and instinctively a loyal Party man. He had spent the past few months writing a secret manifesto, which was eventually smuggled out of the country. It is an eloquent attack on how the Communists under Rákosi and Gerő had almost destroyed Hungary:

> It is not compatible with public morality to have still in leading positions the directors and stage managers of fabricated mass trials, people responsible for torturing and killing innocent men ... economic saboteurs and squanderers of national resources who through the abuse of power have either perpetrated or procured serious acts against the people. The public, the Party and the state must be purged of these elements.
>
> The abuse of power and the use of illegal devices has reached alarming proportions ... and has exceeded even the worst practices of the period between 1950–52. Most of the workers have come to believe that they are at the mercy of illegalities and that there are no laws guaranteeing their rights as human beings and as citizens; that a people's democracy is synonymous with anarchy; that such a democracy leaves plenty of room for violations of the law; then in such a democracy the life of the individual is overshadowed by constant insecurity and fear.[14]

Party functionaries who owed their allegiance to leaders like Gerő, he said, were careerists and bootlickers. 'They have no principles or opinions of their own. They will declare without compunction that black is white. In every case they curry favour with those in a position to assure them a better place in Party or state affairs, greater prestige, more income, broader authority and – above all – a limousine.'[15]

Nagy understood the shortcomings of the system all too well. Yet the knowledge never shook his faith. Instead of leading an opposition –

The ninth anniversary of the Liberation of Hungary. Accepting the cheers of a grateful nation, Mátyás Rákosi (centre), whose personality cult labelled him 'our wise leader' and 'Stalin's Best Pupil', is flanked by two colonial overlords from the Soviet Union, the bibulous old Stalinist, Marshal Kliment Voroshilov (right), and the stern, unbending Communist Party ideologist, Mikhail Suslov (left).

Cardinal József Mindszenty, spiritual leader of Hungary's Roman Catholics, at his enthronement as Primate in 1945 (left), and at his trial on trumped-up treason and corruption charges in 1949 (below). The Cardinal bravely kept alive the flame of opposition to Communism as long as he could, though some of his critics thought him an inflexible man with a martyr's complex.

László (right) and Julia Rajk were the golden couple of Hungarian Communism until, in 1949, he was arrested, starred in a show trial and was executed. Himself an ardent Stalinist, his fall marked the beginning of a brutal purge that saw the torture, imprisonment and murder of tens of thousands of innocent Hungarians.

In 1956, just a fortnight before the Revolution broke out, he was rehabilitated and reburied in an extraordinary funeral in Budapest attended by Mrs Rajk, her son László (below), and around 200,000 others.

The clever and supremely ambitious Soviet Ambassador to Hungary, Yuri Andropov (centre), was a pillar of Marxist orthodoxy and a firm supporter of Communist hard-liners in the Hungarian regime like the cold, calculating Party leader Ernö Gerö (right).

Imre Nagy was one of the few genuinely popular Communist politicians in Hungary. He was widely respected as an honest and sincere man of the people. In the few days immediately before the Revolution began he was in good spirits as a guest at a wine festival in the agricultural region of Badacsony.

A characteristically belligerent Nikita Khruschev, Soviet Communist Party leader, whose tentative reforms and anti-Stalin campaign unleashed forces in Hungary which the Russians could not control without resorting to traditional methods of the 'iron fist'.

President Dwight D. Eisenhower (right) and his Secretary of State, John Foster Dulles (left), were cold warriors whose rhetoric about 'rolling back Communism' and 'liberating captive people' never matched their actions. The Hungarian Revolution co-incided with the last few days of 'Ike's' second-term re-election campaign and another international crisis, in the Middle East, when British and French forces attacked Egypt and tried to occupy the Suez Canal.

More than a quarter of a million people massed into Budapest's Parliament Square on the evening of 23 October 1956 in a show of 'People Power' that terrified Hungary's Communist leaders and their masters in the Kremlin. The spontaneous, unplanned demonstration was entirely peaceful. Violence flared only when the secret police fired shots at demonstrators nearby and, in response, protestors found ways to gain possession of small arms.

The toppling of the 'Great Dictator' was the first big symbolic moment of the Revolution. The 12-metre high bronze statue of Stalin, a gift to Hungary from the Soviet Union, was placed on a plinth in Heroes' Square in 1951, on a prominent site formerly occupied by one of Budapest's most beautiful churches. Demolition was not easy. Cheered on by enthusiastic crowds, it took industrial workers some hours using blow torches to bring down the tyrant's head.

let alone a revolution – he was desperate to rejoin the Party that had expelled him. Finally, on 13 October, he was admitted back into the fold. He instructed all his supporters to do nothing that could again damage his status in the Party, the only organisation in Hungary, he argued again and again, that was in a moral or a practical position to change the country. 'Everything will fall into place, if we wait,' he advised a friend who wanted to work outside the Party to restore him to power.[16]

Then on 21 October, at the height of the tension in Budapest, Nagy left the city. He went to Badacsony, on the shores of Lake Balaton, in the heart of Hungary's wine-growing district. A great lover of food and wine, as his hefty stomach testified, he was guest of honour at the local wine festival. He said he would leave Budapest to 'cool down'.

In Székesfehérvár, forty kilometres south-west of Budapest, at the headquarters of Soviet military forces in Hungary, the senior officers were tense. Lieutenant-General Yevgeny Malaschenko had noticed over the last few months a big change in the Hungarian population's attitude to his presence. 'Our officers, soldiers and their families in Hungary, as elsewhere abroad, lived somewhat isolated lives,' he said. Mainly his officers and men dealt 'with the leaders of the local Party and state organisations and with commanders of the Hungarian military formations and units. We were regularly invited to official occasions . . . Our meetings were limited; we did not know the lives and feelings of the Hungarian citizens.[17]

'Until the summer of 1956 we had good relations with the Hungarian population. But there were signs of a change. For example previously [many] people could not get into the concerts we put on. We always had full houses. But now we hardly saw anyone . . . and those who did come behaved in a way that they never had before. Among the population anti-Soviet remarks became common and false stories were spread . . . the atmosphere in the country was becoming increasingly acrimonious.[18] Malaschenko said they were well aware of the political situation. 'We prepared a report early October to Moscow warning of the possibility of "isolated" armed action in the near future. The Commander in Chief of the Special Corps, Piotr Laschenko, crossed out the word "isolated", making our report an objective mirror of subsequent events . . . We had a good idea of the events taking shape.

But what actually took place went far beyond our imaginings and expectations.'

The General Staff in the Soviet Union was taking no chances. On 19 October Laschenko was ordered to make some of his units battle-ready in case they were needed for action in Budapest.[19]

Students were a pampered group in Hungary. To the Communists' credit they had made big strides in education, raising literacy standards in the countryside and massively increasing the number of places at colleges and universities for the children of peasants and workers. By 1956, most of the students had known nothing but Communist education and Communist indoctrination. By Marxist-Leninist theory, they ought to have been loyal to the Party and the system which had given them so many benefits; yet they felt anything but gratitude. Students set the fuse for the revolution. They shared the whole nation's fury – at domination by the Soviets, at Hungary's squalor and poverty, at the absence of freedom – but had specific complaints, too, about conditions at colleges and universities. Life on campus was dominated by the Communist student organisation, DISZ. In early October, near the start of the new academic year, students at universities throughout the country began forming their own independent groups. The Party bosses were furious.

Students had learned their own lessons from the dramas in Warsaw. Patience and caution were not among them. At 3 p.m. on Monday, 22 October more than 5,000 students packed into the main lecture hall at the Budapest Technological University, where most of the country's leading scientists and engineers had been trained. No single event had ever previously brought half the student body and the faculty together. Initially, the meeting was called for Budapest students to decide whether to leave DISZ and launch their own organisation, which was overwhelmingly agreed within minutes. By the time the meeting ended at around midnight one of Hungary's most historic documents had been written, by a committee of young authors with names unremembered – The Sixteen Points. It became the manifesto for the revolution.*[20]

The meeting started out as total chaos, according to several who

* Still one of the most straightforward and simple statements of the Hungarians' grievances at the time (see Appendix, p. 303).

were there.²¹ 'But then, strangely, we were overcome by a sense of the gravity of the occasion and without any real leaders taking over it was all very orderly. The list of demands just seemed to emerge.'²² Halfway through the meeting a suggestion was made – by whom was never recorded, though many have since claimed the credit – to call a demonstration the next day, using the excuse that they were showing sympathy for the Poles. The plan was to march to the statue of József Bem, a Polish general who fought on the side of the Hungarians in the failed revolution of 1848 and was executed by the Austrians. On the other side of the Danube, the arts and humanities students of Budapest University spontaneously held a mass meeting of their own. They also agreed to demonstrate. The two marches would set out simultaneously at 3 p.m., one from Buda and one from Pest, and meet at Bem Square.

The students wanted their manifesto to be read over the radio. A faculty member of the Technological University, István Pribeky, volunteered to drive them. As he scanned the text, he looked doubtful whether the Communists in charge of the radio would allow the Sixteen Points to be broadcast. He drove them back to the polytechnic where students, teachers and sympathetic secretaries hastily typed up and printed flysheets of the demands which overnight they plastered on walls and trees throughout the city.

Like so much that happened over the next days, this opening move of the revolution was haphazard, spontaneous, rudderless.

PART TWO
REVOLUTION

NINETEEN
Tuesday, 23 October 1956

It was a glorious, crisp autumn day. The 6 a.m. news on the radio included a straightforward announcement about the demonstration planned for the afternoon, but went into no details. The Communist Party newspaper looked forward to the march with a front-page editorial headlined 'New Spring Parade'. Educated readers would have picked up the reference to a famous revolutionary poem from 1911. However, *A Free People* these days was caught up in the radical fever of the times and was no longer a reliable guide to the thinking of the Hungarian Communist Party leaders.[1] It was unclear how they would react to the unprecedented challenge facing them.

At around 8.30 a.m., at Budapest's Eastern Railway Station, Gerő and his entourage arrived by train from Belgrade. The Hungarian Party boss started the day in good spirits. He regarded his visit to Yugoslavia as an important diplomatic breakthrough, and told an interviewer on the platform that his meetings with President Tito would help to restore vital unity in the socialist camp. He stepped into a Zis limousine and was taken to Communist Party headquarters.

His mood darkened during the drive as the officials he had left in charge told him of the disarray in the country. At first Gerő, always inclined towards complacency, told them they were exaggerating. However, back at the Party building he flew into a rage at Lajos Ács, the ranking consul in Hungary during his absence, who painted a gloomy picture of events in Budapest. Throughout the morning a stream of delegations met Gerő, all with a familiar story: Budapest was a tinderbox.[2] Balázs Nagy, Secretary of the Petőfi Circle,* was at one of the meetings. 'There was total chaos,' he said. 'Nearly all the leaders [of the Party] were gathered together, in a turmoil of confusion, fear

* Not to be confused with Imre Nagy.

and hesitation. Gerő at one point left the meeting in exasperation while the others, pale and restless, hesitated.'

At about 11.30 Gerő saw a group from the Party organ. Márton Horváth, director of the editorial committee, argued that Gerő should welcome the march and embrace it as a Communist cause. 'Nonsense,' muttered Gerő. Horváth then said in blunt terms that 'you will have to give more consideration to the 16 points and the demonstrators' demands'.[3] The short-fused Gerő lost his temper, as he was to do again many times that day. 'You've all lost your heads. We have all the means we need to control troublemakers. We can just ban the demonstration. And if there's no demonstration, there can't be trouble.'[4] Horváth pointed out that by now, nearly midday, there would already be students milling around the city in their thousands: 'It might be too late to ban the march. What if the students ignore the ban?'

The former cultural tsar and chief ideologist József Révai still retained influence as an unreconstructed Stalinist and supporter of Gerő. In a thunderous voice, almost a scream, he declared: 'We would fire. We would open fire.'[5]

The decision was made. At 12.53 the gypsy music on the radio was interrupted by an announcement that all public gatherings in Budapest had been banned.

The mood at Imre Nagy's villa on Orsó Street was sombre. Since he returned home from the wine festival early in the morning, his supporters had been drifting in and out. One of his most imaginative, gifted and radical advisers, the polyglot forty-one-year-old journalist Miklós Gimes, among the most inspiring voices of opposition in Hungary, urged Nagy to stand at the head of the demonstration and 'seize the moment'.[6] Nagy was against the student protest on principle and appalled by the idea of taking any part in it, let alone leading it. He disagreed with many of the Sixteen Points – the evacuation of Soviet troops from Hungary, for example – and he opposed the idea of holding free elections as 'bourgeois democracy'. The Party was the leading political force in the country and the Party should make the decisions, not a mob on the streets, he said.[7] The students' demands went far further than Nagy wanted. He hoped for a return to power so that he could implement the reform programme of 1953, the June Road. He did not want a revolution.

There was another reason for his hesitancy. One of his oldest

Communist friends and supporters, the Spanish Civil War veteran Imre
Mező, had warned Nagy in September that the dangerous Gerő was
planning a plot to inflict a final defeat on him from which he could
never recover. In Spain, Gerő had specialised in terrorist outrages,
'provocations' designed to eliminate opponents. The plan now, according to Mező, was for Gerő to provoke a big demonstration, ensure
that it became violent, and implicate Nagy in an alleged attempt to
overthrow the government by force. Such methods had worked in
Barcelona; why not in Budapest, said Mező. Nagy had grounds for
suspicion that the demonstration could be an elaborately planned trap.[8]

At about 1.30 p.m. the thirty-six-year-old Interior Minister, László
Piros, a former butcher's assistant, summoned Sándor Kopácsi into his
presence. The Minister, a Gerő loyalist of firm Stalinist views, wanted
to know how the police would enforce the ban on demonstrations.
Kopácsi commanded a force of 1,200 regular officers, but he had no
mounted units and his men were ill-equipped with anti-riot gear. They
were not even issued with truncheons. He said that if the students
were intent on marching, it would be very difficult to stop them. Piros
replied gruffly, 'But rifles have butts, don't they?' Kopácsi noted, to
the indignation of his immediate boss, that the basic error of the leadership 'was to have turned a political problem into a police problem'.[9]
    Kopácsi, a former lathe operator at a factory, who became a partisan
war hero, had been appointed to his job by Rákosi in 1949 aged
just twenty-nine. A man of rare bravery, he gained respect and wide
admiration for an incident early in his police career when he single-
handedly faced a mob of angry and drunken miners who were determined to lynch an overbearing Communist official, saving the man's
life. However, Kopácsi was never a Rákosi supporter and was lucky to
have survived the Terror. He not only lived through the purges, he
did what he could to protect others from them. On a brief tour of duty
as an inspector at the Kistarcsa internment camp he managed to ensure
the release of some innocent prisoners. One of the few popular Communist officials, Kopácsi was secretly a sympathiser of Nagy's reformist
ideas. He detested Piros and the other careerists around the stiff-necked
Gerő but was used to obeying orders. He determined now that
this time he would disobey if it meant using force against peaceful
demonstrators.
    His unsatisfactory meeting with Kopácsi gave Piros second thoughts,

even though he was never an original man. He knew that at least 10,000 students had gathered at the courtyard of the Technological University, preparing to defy the government. He called Gerő for further instructions. If the police were not going to impose the ban, it would make the government look weak. Gerő fumed that 'Party discipline has broken down'. But, with extreme reluctance, he changed his mind about the march.[10]

At 2.23 music was again interrupted on the radio with an announcement that the demonstration could proceed after all.

The demonstrations set off smoothly at 3 p.m. in afternoon sunshine. At the bigger of the two, on the Pest side of the river, there were about 12,000 people at the Petőfi statue when the procession began. They were sent on their way with a poem. One of Hungary's best-known young actors, Imre Sinkovits, declaimed Petőfi's hymn to nationhood which the Communists had once tried to ban:

> Arise Hungarians, your country calls you.
> Meet this hour, whate'er befalls you.
> Shall we free men be or slaves?
> Choose the lot your spirit craves.[11]

The students were buoyed by the uncertainty shown by Gerő and his flunkies. They were made to look indecisive rather than statesmanlike by banning the march and then at the eleventh hour permitting it to go ahead. At first the slogans and banners were moderate: 'Friendship with Poland', 'Long Live the Youth of Warsaw' and 'Poland Shows us the Way'. As the demonstrators gained confidence, marching ten abreast across Margaret Bridge, the shouts grew more raucous: 'Gerő into the Danube'.

Nothing like this had been seen in Budapest for decades. Károly Makk, then at film school, was working with a newsreel crew that kept its cameras running for the next few days. 'The first few moments of the marches were maybe the most extraordinary. The pent-up emotions, the feeling that at last after years people could show what they felt, was so liberating. Nobody thought that in a few hours' time there was going to be a revolution and this was the start of it. But people felt – I felt – a huge weight being lifted from our shoulders. All kinds of people, not just students, joined the march the whole time. Older people you could see were crying tears of joy that at last they could find a way to speak.'[12] It took an hour and a half for the

Pest protesters to complete the journey of two kilometres to the Bem statue.

At the other march, about 8,000 students gathered at the Technological University. Their route was three kilometres along the Buda Embankment, past offices and apartment blocks, where they were cheered from thousands of windows. It is from one of these that the most potent symbol of the revolution made its first appearance. Someone had cut out the hammer and sickle emblem from the green, white and red Hungarian tricolour. The new flag, with a hole at its heart, was passed down to the marchers below and borne aloft at the front of the procession. The entirely peaceful protesters were still shouting cautious slogans about Hungarian-Polish friendship. The biggest roar was heard when they were joined, an hour or so into the march, by 700 cadets from the élite Petőfi Military School, supposedly sons of the most loyal Communists in the land.

By 4.30 there were already 25,000 people crammed into Bem Square and thousands more had spilled over onto the adjoining embankment. The protest had been hastily called and spontaneous. Nothing had been organised to take place when the demonstrators reached their destination, so nobody knew what would happen now. The march was over but people did not want to leave. The head of the Writers' Union, the novelist and Party hack Péter Veres, rose on a platform and called for moderate reforms that fell far short of the revolutionary Sixteen Points. Just as the boos for his speech reached a crescendo, hundreds of voices cried 'To Parliament'.

The route from the Bem statue to Parliament Square is across the Danube, two kilometres into the heart of Pest, through some of the city's principal residential and commercial districts. All of Budapest had heard of the demonstration, but now its nature changed utterly. Workers who had finished their morning shifts went to see if everything they had heard could possibly be true – that the Communists were being challenged. People stepped out of their offices and swelled the numbers. When the crowd reached St Stephen's Boulevard, one of the chief arteries of the city, people were marching forty abreast, and the mood was getting angrier. The huge cry that bellowed throughout the centre of Budapest was 'Russkik haza' ('Russians go home'). On the streets the unity was forming between the workers and intellectuals that Lenin prescribed as essential for revolution.[13]

*

During the afternoon, as Gerő realised the size of the demonstration, he began to panic. The old Stalinist was not used to seeing spontaneous, unscripted reaction on the streets of Budapest by his subjects. Shortly before 5 p.m. (7 p.m. Moscow time) Gerő spoke by phone to the Soviet Ambassador, Andropov, who was equally worried. Andropov had earlier been driven around the city in his black, dark-curtained Zil limousine displaying Soviet pennants. He was jeered at, and could judge for himself the mood of the crowds. Gerő asked the diplomat if the Russians would send troops to halt the demonstrations. Andropov agreed they should be despatched at once and said he would do what he could to persuade Moscow. Immediately afterwards Gerő called the Soviet military attaché and senior adviser to the Hungarian army, Mikhail Tikhonov. He made the same request and received a similar answer.[14]

Curiously, Gerő waited until after he made those calls to speak to any of his overlords in the Kremlin. Khrushchev had been hearing regular reports from Budapest throughout the day, but had been in no direct contact with his Hungarian consuls until now. 'You must come to Moscow urgently for talks,' he brusquely demanded. Gerő begged to be excused. 'The situation in Budapest is serious,' he told Khrushchev. 'I would rather not go to Moscow at this time.' However, he was evasive when Khrushchev asked him how serious. Nor – as an odd omission – did he mention that he had already requested Andropov and Tikhonov to send Soviet soldiers to Budapest.[15]

Khrushchev broke off the conversation after barely three minutes. He had received an urgent message from his Minister of Defence, the sixty-year-old World War Two hero of the Soviet Union Marshal Zhukov, who had been speaking to the Russian Embassy in Budapest. Zhukov told him Gerő had asked the Soviet military attaché to send troops to halt a demonstration 'that was taking on unprecedented dimensions'. At the same time a call came through to Khrushchev from Andropov. The Ambassador said the position in Budapest was 'extremely dangerous and the intervention of troops is necessary'.[16] Khrushchev did not commit himself to sending in the army but indicated to both that he probably would. The 'collective leadership' would have to decide.

The Ambassador, meanwhile, had already assumed that Russian intervention was inevitable. Shortly after talking to Gerő he spoke on the military telephone link direct to Lieutenant-General Laschenko of the Soviet Special Corps. The conversation was frosty. Laschenko did not favour military action, for which he knew the Russian troops were ill-prepared. Andropov told the tall, forty-five-year-old soldier, who had commanded an infantry division during the war with notable gallantry, how serious things were looking in Budapest. He asked Laschenko to 'send troops to help liquidate the disorder in the capital'. Laschenko refused to comply, addressing Andropov with extreme formality: 'It is a task for the Hungarian police, state security and Hungarian soldiers,' he said. 'For one thing, intervention is beyond my authority and for another it is not desirable to bring Soviet troops into something like this. Comrade Ambassador, our troops can only be ordered into action by the Minister of Defence and Chief of Staff, by a decree of the Soviet government.'

Laschenko's reluctance made no difference. At around 7.45 p.m. an order arrived at the Soviet command in Hungary from Marshal Zhukov for the Special Corps to prepare for combat.[17]

As the numbers on the street grew, Imre Nagy remained at his villa, firmly convinced that the demonstration was a mistake which could end in disaster. Most of his friends and supporters, however, joined the march and heard how regularly Nagy's name was shouted by demonstrators, along with the phrase repeated again and again: 'Russkik haza'.

At dusk, the protesters reached Parliament. While the square was filling with people, all the lights suddenly went out, as if the entire event was being choreographed. Thinking it would dampen the fervour of the crowds, or send them home, two minor Communist functionaries, István Hidas and József Mekits, ordered a switch to be flicked in the Parliament building and briefly all was darkness. But their move merely heightened the drama. First one person rolled up a copy of *A Free People* and lit it with a match. Soon hundreds, thousands of people were holding flaming lanterns improvised from the Communist organ and the flysheet copies of the students' Sixteen Points. 'It was a beautiful and moving sight that added to the knowledge that something exceptional was happening,' one eyewitness remembered.[18]

A loud roar went up through the square. 'The crowds began angrily demanding the appearance of Nagy who, in a way certainly unusual for a Communist, had really become the great hope of the population,' recalls the ardent anti-socialist law student George Gábori.[19] Two of

Nagy's closest friends, Losonczy and the journalist Miklós Vásárhelyi, were standing next to each other. A group of demonstrators recognised Losonczy.

> 'Where is Imre Nagy?' he was asked.
>   'At his home.'
>   'Isn't he coming?'
>   'Certainly not.'
>   'But why not?'
>   'Because, if he came his presence would be used against him.'[20]

Neither Losonczy nor Vásárhelyi, who had been Imre Nagy's press secretary when he was Prime Minister, believed what they were saying. They rushed back to Orsó Street to try, again, to persuade Nagy to go to the Parliament building and speak to the crowds. They were not alone. The house was full of friends and sympathisers telling him the same thing. Tamás Aczél, who had driven from central Budapest earlier, told Nagy:

> 'You have to go immediately. There is not a minute to lose.'
>   Nagy was slumped in an armchair and looked tired. But, for the first time he seemed irresolute, as if he was wavering and might change his mind. He asked Aczél: 'You have come from the Square?'
>   'Yes,' the writer, always a bundle of nervous energy but now highly charged with the events of the day, replied. 'Uncle Imre, the crowd is calling you. For God's sake, why do you wait? If you do not start immediately something awful is going to happen.'
>   Vásárhelyi said it might already be too late. Nagy answered irritably, 'How can I be late? Late for what?'
>   At about 7.30 p.m. he rose slowly and deliberately to his feet. 'Very well,' he said. 'I shall go. But I doubt that it will do any good. Aczél, will you take me in your car?'[21]

Aczél took the wheel of the white Skoda he had bought with the money from his Stalin Prize for Literature. For the first part of the twenty-minute drive, while the car was descending from the Buda Hills towards the centre of the city, Nagy was silent. Finally he asked:
'How big is the crowd?'
'Tremendous. Perhaps 200,000. Maybe more.'
Nagy fell silent again. When they crossed the Danube and began to see the teeming streets of downtown Pest, Nagy looked mystified.

Peering out of the car he suddenly exclaimed, 'Look. Look at that
flag in the window.' For the first time he had seen the flag with the
hated emblem cut out of the centre. Nagy twisted in the back seat
of the car and looked at other windows. 'But all the flags are like
that. What can be happening?' They arrived at Parliament Square a
few minutes before eight, just in time to hear Gerő make an address
to the nation on the radio.[22]

Throughout the afternoon some demonstrators broke off from the
march and headed towards the radio station. Students were determined
that the Sixteen Points and news of the unprecedented protest in
Budapest during the day should be broadcast. Budapest Radio occupied
a large compound, one whole block in the centre of the city. Its main
entrance was in an old, narrow, cobbled street, Sándor Bródy Street,
barely wide enough for two cars to pass each other. It had a rear garage
entrance on another small road and high walls, with just one gate,
separating it from the garden of the Hungarian National Museum. The
main building was a four-storey rococo house of grey stone, with ornate
mouldings of cherubs on the roof, a wide portico supporting a balcony
and a huge oak front door. A warren of makeshift buildings – studios,
equipment storage depots – had mushroomed around the main office
complex.

Trouble at the radio station had been anticipated. The security
authorities had prepared for a demonstration. The previous night,
between 9 and 10 p.m., a group of half a dozen students stood outside
the building shouting a few slogans. AVO Colonel Miklós Orbán, head
of the secret service's security department in Budapest, ordered an
extra platoon to reinforce the building's defences. They had arrived
just before midnight, when the students decamped. That morning
Orbán led two more platoons to the radio station, one of them equipped
with heavy machine-guns, a large store of ammunition and fifty can-
isters of tear gas. Altogether between 260 and 280 men guarded the
building, including soldiers and AVO. They thought they were impreg-
nable against students.[23]

By around 6.00 p.m. thousands of young people had managed to
cram themselves into Sándor Bródy Street and more were arriving the
whole time. The excited crowd was noisy but peaceful, continually
chanting: 'A microphone in the street'. Upstairs, through net curtains
from a first-floor office window, Valéria Benke, director of Budapest

Radio, watched the mass of people below. A plain-looking, dark-haired
woman aged forty-three, married to her job, dressed in no-nonsense
fashion, she had briefly been Education Minister under Rákosi – a loyal
Party official of long standing. Although in her sensitive job as one of
the Party's chief propagandists she never went public about her views,
she was a sympathiser of Nagy's reform agenda. 'But I could never
abide a mob,' she said.[24] It was obvious to her that the radio could
not broadcast the students' demands, certainly not those about the
evacuation of Soviet troops or the call for free elections. Nevertheless,
the gathering crowds looked menacing. In a series of phone calls to
Party bosses, she was told to negotiate. Her staff were offering the same
advice. She allowed twenty of the demonstrators into the building –
but refused to open the locked doors. They had to climb up onto the
balcony from the street below.

In her office, a dozen armed AVO men under the command of Major
Lajos Fehér stared ominously at the protesters. When they were all
seated at the long table Benke got down to business and asked coldly,
'Well, what do you want with the radio?' The deputation had been
formed hastily from various different groups and they did not know
each other. They did not give their names, presumably because of the
presence of the AVO officers. They looked 'a quaint mixture of bravado
and apprehension, not unlike schoolboys confronting their head-
master', according to one of the radio station staff who was in Benke's
room.[25] One of them blurted out:

'We want the radio to belong to the people . . . and what's more we
are not going to leave here until we obtain satisfaction for our demands.'

Benke sneered: 'But you are not the people . . . And what do you
mean by "the radio must belong to the people" anyway? How could
"the people" run it? Where are the technicians, the announcers? Don't
be fools. The radio is for experts, not schoolboys.'

'We want microphones set up in the street so that the people can
express their opinions,' another student demanded.

Benke now was struck by an idea that for a clever, logical woman
seems idiotic. She halted the meeting briefly, and from her desk called
the manager of the radio's main transmitting station at Lakihegy,
about fifteen kilometres north of Budapest. 'If you hear any unusual
voices or programmes, cut off all transmissions,' she ordered. The
demonstrators outside were becoming more noisy and frustrated. The
talks had gone on for nearly half an hour and a rumour was spreading

that the students' delegation was being held hostage by the AVO.

Then, at about seven, the demonstrators let out a cheer. Few of them noticed a vehicle at the fringe of the crowd at the corner of Sándor Bródy Street and the main Museum Boulevard. This was a truck carrying a score of well-armed AVO reinforcements, who entered the rear of the building. However, everybody spotted a second vehicle, a mobile radio van, which was accompanied by a crew of five technicians guarded by a policeman. A blonde woman announcer in a burgundy-coloured dress stood on the roof of the van and shouted through a loudhailer that Valéria Benke had agreed to let the students' demands be broadcast. If the demonstrators would stay silent the manifesto would be read out now, live. Slowly the woman began reading.

But quickly the crowd realised something was wrong. People in the flats above, with their radio sets on, were not hearing the Sixteen Points. They were listening to music. The whole operation had been an elaborate hoax by Benke. From everywhere in the street and the flats above shouts of furious rage erupted. The plan had been Benke's alone.[26] She discussed the idea with nobody above her in the government, only a few technicians among her own staff, and the AVO man Colonel Orbán. Within minutes the tragic folly of her attempt became clear. The radio van had been left in the street. The students began to use it as a ram to batter down the doors as they laid siege to the building.

On the radio, instead of hearing a declaration of the Sixteen Points, listeners were treated to a vicious public scolding from the Party boss, Ernő Gerő. While the demonstrators imagined they were making history, the inflexible Stalinist was determined to drag time backwards. He made a snarling, aggressive speech – a string of Communist clichés – that might have been designed to inflame tempers, not to calm them. He called the young students 'a mob attempting to make trouble, cause "provocation" and 'national subversion'. But they would not succeed, he insisted: 'We condemn those who seek to instil in our youth the poison of chauvinism and to take advantage of democratic liberties that our state guarantees to the workers to organise a national demonstration.' There would be no concessions to 'hostile elements', he declared. The speech was typical Gerő – uncompromising, unimaginative, ill-judged. 'The mood changed as soon as he had finished. You could sense it at once,' Mátyás Sárközi, a young reporter who was at the radio building demonstration, recalls. 'The speech was . . . the fuse that set off the explosion.'[27]

As darkness descended another spontaneous demonstration formed in a prominent part of Budapest. Heroes' Square, at one of the main entrances to the City Park, was, as the name suggests, designed to be a memorial to great Hungarians. For the last four years it had been dominated by a giant bronze statue of Stalin, made especially hideous because the subject was depicted with a benevolent smile on his face. During the day there had been isolated attacks on Soviet targets. Horizont, the Russian bookshop and publisher on the main Boulevard, was gutted. Its contents – texts by Marx, Lenin, Stalin et al. – were piled in the street outside and burned. The Hungarian-Soviet Friendship Society building had been set on fire and scores of red stars on public buildings had been smashed to pieces.

Now a huge crowd amassed to see if the ultimate symbol of Hungary's slavery could be destroyed. Tearing down this Russian icon would be no easy task. Twelve metres high and on a solid marble plinth, it was built to last. Students tried to shimmy up the dictator's torso, place a noose round his neck and connect it to a lorry. But instantly the rope snapped. More industrial methods were required. Colonel Sándor Kopácsi sent a detachment of men under eager young Communist Lieutenant Kiss, but there was little he or his officers could do. When he arrived, Kiss called his superior.

'Comrade Colonel, people are pulling down the statue. Please send us orders immediately.'

Kopácsi: 'OK Comrade Lieutenant, tell me about this pulling down.'

Kiss: 'There are about 100,000 people around the statue.'

Kopácsi: 'Are you sure there as many as that?'

Kiss: 'Comrade Colonel . . . All of Heroes' Square, all the edge of the woods is thick with people. What shall I do?'

Kopácsi: 'OK. How many men have you got?'

Kiss: 'Well, twenty-five, Comrade Colonel.'

Kopácsi told him it was useless and to leave the crowd to get on with it. 'You are willing to sacrifice your life for the Party, but for the Stalin statue?'[28]

After several more attempts with ropes, finally a group of workers arrived armed with heavier machinery. Engineer Dániel Szegő began using metal-burning equipment and the statue was attached to three cranes commandeered from the tram system. It was a laborious process but after about thirty minutes the great statue began to totter and finally, at exactly 9.37 p.m., Stalin fell. Stephen Vizinczey, a student at the time, recalled: 'It was such an eerie sound; several thousand people sighing with joy. I think we all had a sense of making history. We thought the whole world is looking at us and the whole world is happy.'[29] The other sound heard nearby was a constant hammering at the bronze. The crowd were all trying to take a piece of Stalin. The head was dragged along busy Üllői Avenue and left outside the National Theatre.

All that remained of the statue was the Great Dictator's jackboots, and everyone in Budapest referred to Boot Square.

The response of the crowd at Parliament Square to Gerő's speech was instant: boos and catcalls and fresh demands for Nagy to speak. At about 8.45 p.m. the street lights came on and Nagy made an appearance. As soon as he showed himself the crowd let out a great cheer – then they fell silent. Nagy was waiting for someone to find a megaphone. As it never occurred to the Communist government to communicate with the population directly, there had not been a public address system on the balcony for several years. 'Comrades,' he began. 'No,' the crowd roared back in protest, and people began shouting, 'we are not Comrades.'[30] Nagy was staggered, visibly shaken by this rejection of a term he had used as a matter of course all his life, at first unable to grasp what was happening. Thousands of people started whistling and saying, 'We do not whistle at you but at your word.'

He hesitated, uncertain, and tried again. 'Citizens,' he began to an ironic cheer. No official record was kept of his short speech and, surprisingly, none of the newspapers bothered to report it. But a journalist took notes, publishing them later. 'I affectionately salute those who are present here. All my esteem goes out to you young, democratic Hungarians who, by your enthusiasm, would help to remove the obstacles that stand in the way of democratic socialism. It is in negotiations in the bosom of the Party and by discussion of the problems that we will travel the road that leads to the settlement of our conflicts. We want to safeguard constitutional order and

discipline. The government will not delay at arriving at its decisions.'
When he finished, 200,000 people stood silent. Then he appealed for
them to leave the square and go home, but he was heckled. 'We'll stay.
YOU go home.' Instead of appeasing the crowd, this short address, so
out of sympathy with the moment, prompted angry mutterings across
the square. In desperation, Nagy started singing the national anthem.[31]

Even his greatest supporters concede that Nagy disastrously mis-
judged the mood of the crowd and failed to rise to the occasion. He
was never the most inspired orator, but he fumbled this opportunity
disastrously. 'At this instant of matchless opportunity, with Budapest
waiting for a signal, Imre Nagy made the wrong speech,' Aczél said
later. 'He could have saved the situation. All he had to say was "Hungarians, go to your factories and occupy them. Take the leadership in
your own hands, I am ordering your army to supply you with
weapons." That was what Gomulka had done only a few days before
in Warsaw, though under less desperate circumstances. Instead, Imre
Nagy said, "My friends, go home now and leave everything to us."
Much as he loathed Stalinism, Nagy was irretrievably a Communist.
He was a Communist talking, he hoped, to other Communists ... a
mistake.'[32]

Young, eager Péter Kende, who was entirely under the old man's
spell and would later become head of the Imre Nagy Institute, described
it simply as 'a miserable performance'.[33]

In Moscow, Khrushchev summoned a gathering of Soviet magnates for
9 p.m. During the day there had been many moments when bloody
revolution could have been avoided. The half-hour meeting at the
Kremlin now was one of the main turning points. The mood was grim.
Zhukov began by saying that as they were talking, 'The radio station
in Budapest is on fire. There is a difference between this and Poland.
Troops must be sent. Martial law must be declared in the country and
a curfew introduced.' Khrushchev agreed. 'There's no alternative but
to send in soldiers without delay.' He was supported by the hardliners.
Molotov said, 'Hungary is coming apart' and Kaganovich warned,
'The government is being overthrown.' Only one dissenting voice was
heard: Anastas Mikoyan, who was heard as one of the main experts on
Hungary. He put forward a political solution, 'like the Polish deal'.
The wily Armenian suggested: 'We should get Imre Nagy into the
Hungarian leadership and let him try to restore order. It's cheaper for

us that way. What are we losing? If our troops go in, we will ruin things for ourselves. The Hungarians will restore order on their own. We should try political measures and only if they fail then send troops.'

Khrushchev agreed that Nagy should be brought back, given a senior position and instructed above all to maintain order, but insisted that Soviet soldiers should help him. At the same time he despatched Mikoyan to Budapest to oversee events on the ground, along with Mikhail Suslov, the Party's chief ideologist, an ultra-orthodox fifty-four-year-old apparatchik with a stern look that never left his face. The inflexible Russian could not have been more different from the smooth Armenian, but it was a classic Bolshevik method to assign a task to two functionaries with sharply opposing viewpoints who would keep a wary eye on each other. Khrushchev sent two other senior figures with them, incognito. One was the army Chief of Staff General Malinin, placed in overall command of the troops. The other was Ivan Serov, head of the KGB, a rare foreign mission for a Soviet Intelligence chief, which indicated how seriously the bosses in the Kremlin were taking the Hungarian crisis. Straight away Khrushchev placed a call to Gerő and told him the troops would be on their way. 'Your request will be fulfilled, provided that the Hungarian government puts it in writing.'[34]

With the one exception of Mikoyan, the Soviet leaders regarded it as an obvious step to send the Red Army to the streets of Budapest. Yet they could have hesitated. The decision turned an internal dispute that might have been settled by Hungarians into a national freedom struggle against a foreign oppressor.

At the radio station the mood was growing uglier. Infuriated by Valéria Benke's attempted trickery, demonstrators were spurred on further by the insults they had just heard from a ranting Gerő. The efforts to batter down the front door of the building failed, but the crowd had broken half the windows when they threw bricks and cobblestones. The AVO men inside at first hurled tear gas at the crowd, a risky tactic in such a narrow street. The fumes swept back into the building through the broken windows. The air inside and out was acrid with smoke. Water hoses were tried, with warning shots above the demonstrators' heads. For a few minutes the people dispersed and the street was almost deserted. But the crowd regrouped and surged back to the front of the building.

At around 8.30 p.m. the duplicitous Benke and the senior AVO officer in the building, Major Lajos Fehér, called their superiors in a panic. They had already seen that the regular police were powerless to act, even if they had wanted to. It was clear, however, they had no intention of becoming involved. The police captain in command at the scene, Károly Lasso, said he had only a handful of men available and the orders he had given were neither to shoot nor be shot in the mêlée. As a matter of routine his men tried 'to address the crowd and ask them to disperse'. But when it became obvious they would not leave, 'the officers were withdrawn'. The Defence Ministry assured Benke that troops would be on their way. But the AVO was not prepared to wait. Fehér ordered his men to clear Sándor Bródy Street. They fixed bayonets and forced the demonstrators along two lines a dozen metres from the entrance to the building where they established a cordon. That was when death came to Budapest. It is not known who fired the initial shots – almost certainly a trigger-happy AVO recruit – but the first demonstrators to fall were students, Géza Julis and Jenő Borth. Another volley of shots rang out, hitting one young eighteen-year-old girl in the head and two young men in the back legs as they were trying to run away.

Within minutes an ambulance, clearly marked with a giant red cross, arrived at the side entrance to the National Museum garden. Demonstrators began to rush the wounded towards it, but a dozen heavily armed AVOs jumped from the vehicle and entered the building. At around the same time Hungarian army units began to arrive. The Defence Minister, István Báta, and the unpopular deputy Chief of Staff, Major-General László Hegyi, both hardline Stalinists and trusted Gerő supporters, had issued orders for the soldiers to relieve the radio station, restore order and crush the demonstration. The troops did precisely the opposite.

The first to appear was a company of infantry under Colonel László Zolomy, who had recently been appointed to his first senior command position. He saw the AVO attacking the crowds, realised there were already several casualties, and ordered his men to do nothing. 'I did not experience any armed resistance from the protesters,' Zolomy, who was later jailed for his part in the 'Battle for Budapest Radio', said. 'Since no orders had been given ... to use arms against the demonstrators I forbade [shooting] against the crowd. I would only allow ... firing if the protesters entered the radio building.'[35]

Soon new units arrived on the scene. Fourteen tanks from the Pilicsaba Tank Regiment and seventeen lorryloads of infantry were commanded by the tall, sandy-haired, forty-year-old Lieutenant-Colonel János Solymosi. He took a few minutes to size up the moment. Then he steered his own tank into Sándor Bródy Street, stopped, stood on the turret and declared that under no circumstances would his soldiers fire on the protesters. A massive cheer went up, from the demonstrators and from Solymosi's men.

Some soldiers joined with the crowd and fought against the AVO – at least one senior officer was killed. 'Soldiers anywhere with a universal draft are nothing but young people in uniforms,' Béla Király, shortly to assume command of Hungary's armed forces, said. 'The troops who went to the radio building on 23 October had sentiments no different from the other youngsters in civilian clothes, lining the streets and chanting revolutionary slogans. At the very first confrontation ... the young men under arms refused to fire on their compatriots. The People's Army proved its prime loyalty was to the people – not the Party.'[36] Most of the troops did not fight on either side. They returned to barracks. But their contribution shifted the balance in favour of the rebels. They handed their weapons and ammunition to the citizens – anybody who asked was handed a rifle. Guns were also arriving from elsewhere. After wrestling with his conscience for much of the evening, Sándor Kopácsi decided he would no longer try to remain neutral. He enthusiastically went over to the revolution and opened police weapons' stores.[37]

The news of shooting at the radio station swept through Budapest. One of the city's main ammunition depots, at Soroksári Street was raided at around 10 p.m. The city's two military academies, the Zrinyi and the Petőfi, many of whose students had gone on the demonstration, sent weapons. The United Lamp Factory on Csepel Island, Budapest's biggest industrial area, was well known as a cover for an arms factory. Late in the evening workers removed at least 1,000 rifles from the plant and loaded them onto lorries bound for the radio station.

A protest had turned into an armed insurrection. The battle raged half the night. Benke and a dozen aides and technicians managed to escape from a rear entrance. Fehér and four of his AVO men were killed, a score were wounded and sixty were captured. Sixteen of the revolutionaries were shot and sixty were wounded, mostly before they obtained arms. Finally, just before dawn the radio building, aflame and heavily damaged by gunfire, fell to the insurgents. However, the victory was pyrrhic. There was a duplicate transmitter at the Interior Ministry nearby so the freedom fighters could not gain control of the airwaves.

Nagy did not look deflated after his faltering display in front of the crowds. When he stepped from the balcony back into the Parliament building Aczél told him about the violence at the radio station and he frowned. He remained chatting to some of the organisers of the student march for a few minutes, but then told everyone to go home. At a few minutes after ten, he strode the 400 metres to the Communist Party headquarters in Academy Street, accompanied by his tall son-in-law Ferenc Jánosi, a stern-looking forty-two-year-old of military bearing who was the 'old man's' closest adviser. When they arrived at the steps Jánosi left him.[38]

The scene awaiting Nagy was confusion and chaos. The Hungarian Communist proconsuls were used to lording it over Hungarians – even as they were craven towards the Russians. Now they were visibly frightened and arguing amongst themselves. In former days all Party matters had been decided by Rákosi and Gerő. Now, as things were falling apart, the Politburo met and acted 'as though paralysed by a stroke', András Hegedüs said: 'Somebody proposed a measure, it was unanimously adopted. Then an hour later they would convene again and adopt a totally different measure.'[39] They still barely understood the enormity of their failure or how they had been overwhelmed by people's power. Within a few hours, the police, the army, even some of the privileged AVO had abandoned them. 'Ten years of the most thorough indoctrination could not buy them four hours' precious loyalty.'[40]

When Nagy made an appearance Gerő launched a tirade against him 'You instigated the riots . . . Now you can stew in your own juice,' he shouted.

Nagy was equally angry. For months he had been trying to warn about unrest in the country, but he was never heeded. He had always insisted on working within the Party, not against it. 'I have instigated nothing and you know it.'

Gerő was still seething. 'You have no position within the Party or the government, no authority. How did you dare to go to Parliament and incite the crowds by speaking from the balcony?'

Nagy retorted, accurately: 'Everything that is happening now could have been prevented if you had handled the situation better during the day.'[41]

However much he despised Nagy, Gerő knew he could not afford to lose his temper and cause an irretrievable breakdown in relations with him. He needed Nagy. First, Khrushchev had told him that he must bring Nagy into a top position, in order to appease the public. The devious Gerő could see the sense of it. He hoped, also, that he could use Nagy as a figleaf. He reckoned that if the real power was still in the hands of the hardliners, a naive Nagy could be tainted by association and his popularity would disappear. The tactic nearly worked.

At midnight Nagy was informed that he had been appointed Prime Minister again. He accepted without a moment's hesitation. He was also told to sign a formal invitation to the Soviet government to send Red Army troops into Budapest to restore order. Nagy may have been naive, but he was not a fool. He knew this was a trap and he refused to sign.[42] Who actually asked for the troops to be sent has been a contentious issue for fifty years. Over the next few days Nagy's enemies – and US propaganda – successfully spread the story that he made the request and the claim caused him enormous trouble. We now know Nagy did not invite the Soviet military into Budapest. He did, however, as his first act, sign a martial law declaration giving almost unlimited powers to Hungarian troops to impose curfews and to order summary executions.

Gerő was convinced, as he tried to catch a few hours' sleep after midnight, that although he faced plenty of political problems, events on the streets the next day would take care of themselves. There were troublemakers, but he thought 'Soviet troops would mop them up without difficulty in a few hours'.[43]

TWENTY

Wednesday, 24 October

Soviet troops entered Budapest between 2 and 3 a.m. They were expecting to meet little real resistance in a police operation to crush rioting students. Straight away they found themselves in an urban guerrilla war against a determined and inventive enemy.

On the first day the Russians sent 6,000 men and 700 tanks into the city from two mechanised Guards Divisions (the 2nd and the 17th) based at Soviet military headquarters in Székesfehérvár. A similar force had been despatched at 9 p.m. the previous evening to seal the border with Austria. On high alert in reserve, already mobilised inside Hungary, the Soviets had placed a further 20,000 infantry, 1,100 tanks and 185 heavy guns. Two Soviet fighter divisions totalling 159 planes could provide air support for the ground forces and two Soviet bomber divisions were on standby at four airfields in Hungary and the Transcarpathian Military District to the east.[1]

For the first task they faced, however, all this massive firepower was largely irrelevant. The Russians did not know what had hit them, the senior Soviet generals admitted. The moment their troops were spotted in Budapest, 'We were greeted by a hail of gunfire and bullets' from an ill-organised band of rebels, many of them in their teens, armed with a few rifles and some hastily prepared Molotov cocktails.[2]

The character of the fighting was established on the first morning. Rebels relied on local knowledge to harry the Soviets where they could with hit-and-run tactics that the Russians found hard to counter. The lumbering Soviet T34 tanks could capture the city's bridges or large traffic intersections. But they could not follow freedom fighters down Budapest's alleyways or penetrate behind apartment blocks that faced inwards towards a central courtyard – most of the homes in the city. These were perfectly suited for the kind of urban warfare the rebels were conducting. The Russians were not prepared to risk major casualties by sending infantry into the streets for hand-to-hand combat.

It was the least-organised revolution in history. There were no leaders, no plans. Groups of armed men and women (most of them young) spontaneously formed in places that offered a vantage point to strike a swift blow, and then hide. Sometimes a group of a dozen or so would come together for one firefight; when that was over they would split up and never see each other again. Battles were isolated, small-scale. Guns would be blazing along one street, while around the corner a grocery shop would remain open and people would be queuing for bread. The freedom fighters' aims, at first, were moderate: to keep the flame of rebellion alive. 'We fed off each other's enthusiasm and excitement. Even those of us who didn't do any of the fighting,' the poet Ágnes Gergely, a student teacher in 1956, said. The real success of the rebels was not so much to capture a building and keep it for a few hours, but to raise people's hopes by holding out even for a while against such a superior force.[3]

At 4.30 a.m. Budapest Radio wished listeners a good morning and then gave its version of the news: 'Fascist and reactionary elements have launched an armed attack against our public buildings and against the forces of law and order. In the interests of re-establishing law and order, all assemblies, meetings and demonstrations are forbidden. Police units have been instructed to deal severely with troublemakers and to apply the law in all its force.'[4] The message was repeated at half-hourly intervals and from 6 a.m. accompanied by a further announcement from the Stalinists who retained control of the radio wavelength: 'The Soviet soldiers are risking their lives to protect the peaceful citizens of Budapest and the tranquillity of the nation . . . Workers of Budapest, receive our friends and allies with affection.'[5]

The exhortation was ignored. Rebel groups had obtained weapons from police stations throughout the city, raided lightly protected armaments stores and had surreptitiously been handed arms from barracks. At this point only a few hundred people had decided to take the fight to the Russians, but thousands of rifles and a few light machine-guns were already in their hands. Overnight, as the words 'revolution' and 'freedom fighter' began to be used for the first time, insurgents had captured two telephone exchanges, the Budapest Radio building, the offices of A Free People and the Eastern Railway Station, all on the Pest side of the Danube. Across the river, a small group had built barricades to fortify Széna Square, a busy transport terminus. There were no major clashes until just after 8.30 a.m. when two Soviet tanks near

Marx Square opened fire, killing two passers-by. Near the Western Station, along Budapest's main Boulevard, a tank killed an unarmed soldier talking to a civilian – and then opened fire on a student who rushed to the soldier's assistance. Tanks were opening fire in the People's Park, where a crowd had formed to see what was left of the Stalin statue.

In Moscow, Khrushchev was woken with the encouraging news, for him, that 'things are not as dire as we thought in Budapest'. According to his son Sergei he had been relatively optimistic the previous evening that the crisis in Hungary would be settled swiftly. He said he had confidence in Nagy. 'Hungary needs a strong person capable of taking events into his own hands,' he said. 'Nagy is the man to cope with the storm – all the more so as the demonstrators had demanded his appointment.' Khrushchev had been reluctant to send in Soviet troops, but he was told that now the soldiers were there, they were mopping up 'pockets of bandits' and would soon have the city under control.[6]

   If he was misinformed about the military situation in Budapest, Khrushchev's intelligence was better about politics. He had lost faith in Gerő and his cronies, whose lacklustre performance and indolence he blamed for getting the USSR into 'a mess'. He raged at a meeting with Molotov, Malenkov and other magnates early in the morning. 'I can't understand what Gerő, Hegedüs and the others are doing. There were signs that the situation in Hungary was extremely serious . . . That did not prevent them from spending time by the sea, in the Crimea in September. And as soon as they returned home they left on a "trip" to Yugoslavia.' However, he decided to wait and see what happened in Hungary. The team the Kremlin had despatched to Budapest had only just left Moscow and he would do nothing until he heard from them.[7]

Overnight, the Hungarian one-party monolith collapsed. The government could not control the streets of the capital. The ruling party which had decided everything in the country for the last eight years, had all but ceased to function. A general strike called by the insurgents at midnight swelled the rebels' numbers. The top brass in the army were still loyal to the old regime, but were unsure if the lower ranks would obey their orders. Nevertheless, they could not afford to look completely inactive against an uprising aimed at overthrowing the system to which they owed everything.

During the morning armed groups of freedom fighters formed in four main strongholds. Széna Square was the first in Buda. In central Pest, the commercial centre of the city, they held key points at Tompa Street, near the National Theatre and in Báross Square, near the Eastern Railway Station. By far the most important and best-known was the Corvin Cinema, which quickly became the chief symbol of civilian resistance to the Soviets. An ugly mud-brown building, in the brutal Stalinist style, it was one of the largest cinemas in Budapest. The Corvin was set back slightly from the main Boulevard encircling the inner city, and Üllői Avenue, one of the main roads heading east; the Russians needed a route past it if they were to gain easy access through Budapest to the Parliament building, the Communist Party headquarters, the Russian Embassy and the bridges over the Danube.

The Corvin was equally important for the freedom fighters. Each hour they could hold it and maintain resistance raised the spirits of the city. It turned out to be perfectly positioned for a guerrilla band. On the ground floor of a solid, four-storey block of flats, its sturdy front entrance could be blockaded quite easily. Russian tanks could not get close. Tactically, its main bonus was the narrow Corvin Passage alongside the cinema complex. It was connected to a warren of underground alleyways and secret corridors linked to dozens of roads and other buildings in the vicinity. Rebel fighters could appear for a few minutes, as if from nowhere, make a swift attack and then, just as they were spotted by the Russians, hide back where they could not be found. They always had an element of surprise. The Corvin had two other big advantages: right behind the cinema was a fuel pump with enough petrol to make thousands of Molotov cocktails. And on the opposite side of the street there was a solid old military barracks that could be turned into a mini-fortress in the heart of the city, the Kilián Barracks.

Formerly the Maria Theresa Barracks, the Kilián had been built, with thick walls, in the 1850s as a base for the Austrian army. By now it had little real military significance and housed only about 900 conscript recruits to the engineering corps. Reports that the civilian freedom fighters were in touch with the rebels infuriated the senior figures of the army – Defence Minister István Báta and his Chief of Staff László Tóth. They feared a mutiny. When at around 11 a.m. they heard that scores of revolutionaries had been allowed into the barracks by the conscripts, they decided to send a senior officer there to ensure the

Kilián did not fall into rebel hands. Tóth called the duty officer of the day and ordered him to send a detachment of tanks to the Kilián to stiffen the backbone of the soldiers there. Tóth had a reputation as a poorly informed and unlucky general. He was about to prove both observations true. He thought he was helping to crush the uprising. In fact he called the most flamboyant and inspiring personality to emerge from the revolution.[8]

Colonel Pál Maléter was an immense man, more than two metres tall, with thick black wavy hair, blue-grey eyes, a wide mouth and a prominent chin. Aged thirty-nine, his appearance was that of a hero, born to command, and his men looked up to him for instant guidance. He had barely slept all night – shots were ringing through the city and he held an anguished debate within himself to decide how he would act in the coming liberation struggle. To any of his juniors who asked what they should do about army desertions all around them he replied simply: 'Your loyalties are to the army, the country and to the legal government.'[9]

Maléter found some tanks. He marched 400 metres from the Defence Ministry to a unit of the Aszod armoured regiment in Mari Jaszai Square guarding an AVO building and ordered the commander, Major Ferenc Pallos, to give him five tanks. He stepped into one and the others followed him slowly along Üllői Avenue towards the Kilián Barracks. At this point he was still unsure, he said, exactly what he would do when he got there. As he approached he saw a furious fight between insurgents around the Corvin Cinema and Soviet tanks. He heard the rattle of gunfire from the freedom fighters and shells exploding from the Soviets. His path was blocked by two disabled Russian tanks. He did not at that stage want to engage the Russians so he stopped his patrol. 'I was horrified and deeply upset by what I saw ... It didn't seem to me that these were fascists or counter-revolutionaries. All I saw were the bodies of kids lying in the street – and tanks being shot up by rifle fire,' he said later.[10]

He sent two of his men on reconnaissance. 'Within half an hour they were back and the first thing they told me was that the only civilians in the barracks were students, many of them teenagers, and some policemen. He ordered his men to follow him and placed his own tank directly in front of the main doors of the barracks, blocking its entrance. The remaining Russian tanks withdrew. Maléter got out and looked 'at a scene that might have been the end of a battle in a major war. Bodies lay all over the place, the wounded were screaming and I ordered my men to improvise stretchers out of house doors and carry them inside.' In his report of the incident back to his superiors he wrote simply: 'As a result I informed the Minister of Defence that I was going over to the insurgents.'[11]

Many criticised Maléter; some thought he was an opportunist. But his personal courage was undoubted. He became a Communist – perhaps from ambition. Now he supported the revolution – out of conviction. 'This was the moment I knew I would have to make a decision that would change my life. Once in the barracks, it was clear to me that those fighting for their freedom were not bandits but loyal sons of Hungary.' He had five tanks and two anti-tank guns. It was a modest arsenal. But he built a huge reputation. In one morning, the socialist soldier-turned-revolutionary had become a national hero.[12]

Maléter was born in the Slovakian town of Eperjes, from solid bourgeois stock. His father was a law lecturer who wanted him to go into one of the professions and he trained briefly to be a doctor. But he had always longed for a military career. In 1940 he enrolled as a cadet in the Ludovika Military Academy, then Hungary's finest, and passed near the top of his class. He was commissioned as a lieutenant into a tank division. In May 1944, with the Second Hungarian Army on the Eastern Front, he was one of the few survivors when his unit was overrun by the Russians. He was taken prisoner but somehow came to the attention of one of the leading Hungarian Communists, a 'Muscovite', Zoltán Vas, who offered to trade his prisoner of war existence for a new commission fighting Nazis. He was parachuted over Transylvania and fought an outstanding guerrilla campaign alongside the Red Army. He was awarded a decoration for valour personally by the commander of Soviet forces in Hungary, Marshal Malinowsky. He prospered in the coalition years and, with the rank of Major, became head of the Presidential Guard.[13]

Maléter joined the Communist Party – a requirement among senior officers – yet his real politics have remained a mystery. He was one of the very few soldiers to wear his old medal from the Horthyite army as well his Soviet award – a brave thing, but possibly an indication of his ability to trim. Many of his men appreciated the gesture. He inspired loyalty among his juniors, but the Party brass never entirely trusted him. Repeatedly, in the Terror years when many army officers were purged, he was tested. One morning a contemporary from his military academy days knocked on his door and, after a friendly conversation about old times, began a political discussion. 'We know your feelings. We all want to live in a free world. You must help us to get rid of the Russians.' Maléter pulled out his revolver and marched his old friend to the police. The man turned up a short while later in an AVO uniform and congratulated him for spotting a trap.[14]

Nevertheless, his career did not progress as he would have liked. More politically correct officers were promoted above him and he languished in dull desk jobs. His first marriage, to an artist, Maria, split up amid acrimony. He married again, a woman eighteen years younger than he, Judith Gyenes. He was discontented with his own lot, and during the last few months had barely bothered to conceal his exasperation at the state of the country. He yearned for action, and for change. When the opportunity came he seized it.

Imre Nagy spoke live on radio at midday. His words were ignored by the majority of people, and deeply disappointed some of his closest friends and supporters. Again he failed to rise to the occasion.

> People of Budapest, I announce that all those who cease fighting before
> 14.00 today and lay down their arms in the interests of avoiding
> further bloodshed will be exempted from martial law . . . As soon as
> possible, and by all means at our disposal, we shall realise the
> systematic democratisation of our country in every sphere of Party,
> state, political and economic life. Heed our appeal. Cease fighting and
> secure the restoration of calm and order. The hostile elements that
> joined the ranks of peacefully demonstrating Hungarian youth misled
> many well-meaning workers and turned against the people's
> democracy . . . Hungarians, Comrades, my friends. I speak to you in a
> moment filled with responsibility. Resist provocation, help restore
> order. Together we must prevent bloodshed . . . Stand behind the Party,
> stand behind the government. Trust that we have learned from the
> mistakes of the past and that we shall find the correct road for the
> prosperity of our country.[15]

There was no mention of the Russian troops in Budapest; no mention of the demands of the students; no mention of the Stalinist hardliners still in the government. Nagy was already twenty-four hours behind the revolution – where he was to remain for the next few days. A well-intentioned, decent man of moderation, he hoped to return to June

1953 and start afresh on a modest programme of reforms. He had no idea of taking part in a revolt against the Russians and communism. Many of his admirers have tried to argue over the years that Nagy was a prisoner in Academy Street at this time, guarded by AVO officers and held as Gerő's stool-pigeon. There are various colourful accounts that he was forced at gunpoint to make the speech, with its reference to 'hostile elements'. There is no evidence for that. Nagy was a free agent in the sense that he could come and go as he pleased and say what he wanted. But he was a prisoner of his own mind, unable to understand the mood in the country or keep pace with the speed of the drama.[16]

When Nagy was made Prime Minister his two friends and advisers, Géza Losonczy and Ferenc Donáth, were given senior positions in the Communist Party. They refused and told the newly installed Prime Minister why. They were furious about the martial law declaration; they were appalled that in the streets young people were being shot by the AVO. They said that Nagy should have insisted he would not join a government that contained Gerő and his clique of Stalinists. Like the freedom fighters, they harboured hopes that the Russians would leave Hungary. Along with Miklós Gimes and others they pressed Nagy to move closer to the revolutionaries, or at least separate himself from the hardline Communists, but he would not listen. Nagy chose to isolate himself in the Party headquarters where he could not hear the growing hostility of the public, or the advice of his friends.

His supporters were nonplussed. Péter Kende had been on the phone to members of the Nagy group all morning and most had the same sense of foreboding: 'I was in despair. I thought it was terrible that Nagy should come back to power like that.'[17] Vásárhelyi, a perceptive analyst, said he knew the moment Nagy had accepted the premiership that 'everything was lost' for the reform Communists like himself. 'We had accumulated over the years a measure of moral and political capital; but now Nagy had accepted the role of Prime Minister in a government which was otherwise the same as two days earlier – the government against which we had been fighting.'[18]

The gun-wielding revolutionaries, in a less sophisticated fashion, felt the same. They were indifferent to Nagy while he opposed the principal demand 'Russkik haza' – and ignored his amnesty call. Deadlines came and went and not a single freedom fighter handed over a weapon.

*

Around 2 p.m. two Soviet armoured cars, sandwiched between a brace of tanks, appeared in front of the Hungarian Communist Party head-quarters. From the first there stepped a stocky Armenian with a mous-tache and a permanent sly half-smile on his face. He was Anastas Mikoyan. From the other appeared the stern Mikhail Suslov, wearing a muffler and an astrakhan cap. Their aeroplane was forced to land fifty kilometres from Budapest, because of temporary banks of fog. On the drive into the city they could see conditions for themselves. 'In Pest there was continuous shooting between isolated groups of provocateurs and our machine-gunners ... our men did more of the shooting. To single shots we replied with salvoes,' they said in the first of a series of telegrams – sometimes two a day – that they sent to the Kremlin while they remained in Budapest.[19]

Yet, despite the evidence of their eyes and ears, they seemed remark-ably sanguine. In phone conversations with Khrushchev, and in a later telegram they said that things were not as bad as they seemed. 'The preliminary reports from the Soviet military command and the Hun-garian military command were exaggerated in a rather negative way. We had the impression that Gerő especially, but other comrades as well, are exaggerating the opponents' strength and underestimating their own ...'[20] They said they had come to take control, but they seemed inclined to let the Hungarians make the decisions. Nagy told them that it would be far better if Hungarian units were sent on more operations 'to lighten the burden on the Soviet troops'. Mikoyan and Suslov agreed – as long as they stayed loyal and did not go over to the insurgents. At 3 p.m. they told Khrushchev in plain terms: 'All the hotbeds of insurgency have been crushed.'[21]

That was not the impression two other senior Russians who had just arrived from Moscow were receiving. When Mikoyan and Suslov were meeting the Hungarian politicians, the Soviet chief of Intelligence Ivan Serov, fifty-one, one of Khrushchev's best friends, and the Staff Officer General Malinin, fifty-seven, a hero of Stalingrad, went to Russian military headquarters, which had been set up at the Ministry of Defence. According to Malaschenko they both arrived in a temper. They too had heard gunshots on their way into the capital and were far more concerned by the sound than their political masters had been. 'Without waiting to hear our reports they expressed their dissatisfaction with the indecisiveness of the Soviet operations,' said Malaschenko.[22]

Serov was a frightening figure when roused to anger. He had piercing eyes of an intense blue, a short attention span and a habit of snapping his fingers loudly in irritation. He taunted the officers: 'Useless. You have proved incapable of dealing with student groups.' Malaschenko defended himself and his men. He interjected – bravely, as Serov was one of the most powerful men in the Soviet Union who could send people to the Gulag on a whim – 'Ivan Alexandrovich, you are not familiar with the situation. There is fighting going on all over town; we need more force to take decisive steps. We have one division. Let us go now and take a tour of the city in tanks and armoured vehicles.' Serov agreed. They went and, according to Malaschenko, within a few minutes, 'We were twice fired on with machine-guns and several times our path was blocked. Then we returned to the Ministry of Defence. We realised that in a big city with more than a million and a half inhabitants our military force was not even enough to maintain order.'

That was the last time Serov left the protected areas in the centre of the city – and his reports, which are now available, contained no more criticism of Russian troops.[23]

Washington was entirely unprepared for revolution in Hungary. It took the Americans by surprise, even more so than the Polish crisis had done a few days earlier. The US did not have in place a head of its diplomatic mission in Budapest. A new man, Tom Wailes, was expected in a few days, but meanwhile the Legation had to rely on a chargé d'affaires, Spencer Barnes, who was experienced, but of low rank to handle, potentially, a major Cold War crisis. President Eisenhower was reaching the final crucial stage of his re-election campaign. He wanted nothing to derail his chances for another thumping victory and specifically nothing that would involve the US in a foreign adventure. Recent news from the Middle East was disturbing. There was a threat of war over the Suez Canal, though his intelligence agency was not warning that conflict was imminent. The last thing he wanted was violent instability in Central Europe, which would expose the weakness of his expressed policy of rolling back communism.

At 12.07 in Budapest – just past six in the evening Washington time – John Foster Dulles in the State Department placed a call to Henry Cabot Lodge, the US Ambassador to the UN in New York. Dulles had already spoken to the President twice about Hungary. They had decided to do nothing and wait for more information before the administration made any public response. Now Dulles told Lodge: 'Apparently the fighting is developing in quite a big way and there is clear evidence of considerable Soviet military activity in the area to repress it. We are thinking of the possibility of bringing it to the UN Security Council. I am worried that it will be said that here are the great moments [in history], these [Hungarian] fellows are ready to stand and die and we are caught napping and doing nothing.' Lodge suggested that the Americans should call for a ceasefire. Dulles told him to think about what can be done at the UN. 'The British and the French should join in. They may be reluctant, though I think they would vote with us.' Lodge said, 'I'll go to work on it and wait for word from you.'[24]

As night descended, Budapest grew quieter. Russian tanks fell back into secure, protected formations and ceased patrolling the streets. There was sporadic shooting. Fire burned down part of the natural history section of the National Museum. The blaze at the radio building had been put out early in the morning. A few hours later the Russians tried, unsuccessfully, to recapture it, but fire was raging for a second night. In Budapest an estimated 3,000 freedom fighters had taken up arms during the day, around eighty had died and 450 were wounded.[25]

The revolution was spreading beyond the city. Events in the capital, with about a fifth of Hungary's population, determined the shape of the uprising. However, throughout the country, people were inspired by the fervour of Budapest. In many towns and villages, without the Soviet army to back them up, the Party and government handed over to insurgents. In Debrecen, the next-biggest city with 140,000 people, about a third of the population came out to demonstrate. The most worrying thing for the Communists was that in the industrial towns, the workers, assumed to be pillars of Communist Party support, were the most determined to join the rebellion. Transport, electricity and gas still functioned, but the general strike halted practically everything else. In the socialist stronghold of Csepel, the island south of Budapest known as 'Red' Csepel, the workers took over their factories. In Miskolc, the big industrial city near the border with Czechoslovakia, the Communist Party boss, Rudolf Földvári, went over to the revolutionaries. Everywhere, given half a chance, people turned their backs on communism.[26]

*

In Moscow, Khrushchev, who had been hearing optimistic forecasts for much of the day, was now being told the bad news. The Russians had lost twenty dead and forty wounded throughout the day. Four tanks and four armoured vehicles had been shot to pieces. There was no sign of 'order' being restored and Khrushchev was not in a mood for compromise. Towards midnight he asked to see the amusing, literate, sophisticated Yugoslav Ambassador to the USSR, Veljko Micunovic. There was a message he wanted to send urgently to Marshal Tito. Micunovic was an inveterate gossip and Khrushchev knew the message would be delivered to many other places as well. The Soviet leader was a worried man and he wanted others to know it. 'Blood has been shed in Budapest,' he said. 'The West and anti-Soviet elements in Hungary have taken up arms against the Socialist camp and the Soviet Union. The West is seeking a revision of the results of World War Two. It has started in Hungary, and will then go on to crush each socialist state in Europe one by one. But the West has miscalculated. The Soviet Union is ready to answer force with force. The Soviet Union is completely unanimous on this.' He said the Russians would support a political solution in Hungary if possible. But late that night he was losing faith in political solutions.[27]

TWENTY-ONE
Thursday, 25 October

At 6.23 a.m. Budapest Radio started the day as it had done the previous morning – with a big lie: 'The army, the state security forces, the armed workers' guards and Soviet troops liquidated the counter-revolutionary putsch attempt on the night of October 24. The counter-revolutionary forces are totally scattered . . .'[1]

As soon as the curfew was lifted at 7 a.m. and people poured out of their homes, gunfire was heard across the city. Soviet tanks had resumed patrols at dawn and fighting flared again, not as heavily as twenty-four hours earlier, but persistently. The rebels had not been 'liquidated'. On the contrary, they were buoyed by the knowledge that they had survived against the armed strength of a superpower for a day and a night. There was no central command of the freedom fighters, no formulated plan, just one principal aim on which all the separate groups agreed: forcing the Russian army to withdraw. 'It was a flea against an elephant in military terms,' Gergely Pongrácz, one of the leaders of the fighters at the Corvin group, said. 'The idea was that if we could keep the Soviets fighting for longer and fighting badly, that would raise the spirits of the Hungarians, we would gain sympathy around the world and the Russians would negotiate – or just leave. The whole thing was so spontaneous we didn't really think things through. We just took a gun and acted.'[2]

Russian tactics were mystifying. Reinforcements had been sent to Budapest overnight. Around 14,000 extra troops and 250 more tanks arrived – units from the 128th Rifle Division, part of the Soviets' standing army in Hungary, and from the 33rd Mechanised Division despatched from bases in Romania. The Russians occupied the gutted remains of the radio station – fought over pointlessly, as nothing was being broadcast from there, but symbolically important. The Russians seemed to have learned little from the previous day's action. Soviet troops had been trained for urban fighting in towns and cities; but against enemy armies, not insurgent bands. During the war, their armour would wreak maximum destruction on whole city blocks, and later, amid the rubble, the infantry would mop up in hand-to-hand fighting. It was ugly and cost vast numbers of casualties. However, it had been effective. These options were closed to the Russians now. The military were under instructions, at this stage, to bring order to Budapest, but not destroy the city. 'They may have had much more firepower, but unless they were prepared to use it, their men were like sitting ducks,' said Pongrácz.[3]

President Eisenhower had decided almost at once that he would not interfere in Hungary. From the moment he heard that an armed uprising had begun in Budapest, the President's main anxiety was to reassure the Soviet Union that the United States had no interest in the satellite states. He was sure that Americans were not prepared to risk a war on behalf of 10 million or so Hungarians. Ike was exceedingly cautious. He wanted to give the Russians no excuse to accuse him of meddling in their affairs. Besides, he thought that he would soon be embroiled in a crisis in the Middle East and did not want to be sidetracked by events he could not influence in Eastern Europe.

The President was in New York preparing to deliver a campaign speech at Madison Square Garden in the afternoon. Earlier he had seen an intelligence briefing telling him that British and French forces had reinforced their air bases in the Mediterranean and their fleets were readying themselves for sea.[4] Ike intended to take no action, but to wait and see what happened in Budapest. He realised, though, that he had to say something. Just before 1 p.m. he was on the telephone to his Secretary of State in Washington. John Foster Dulles, arch Cold Warrior, was as careful as his boss. He said he was unsure whether this was a good opportunity for American diplomacy or not and agreed that it would be best to play for time.[5]

They talked about devoting a passage in Eisenhower's forthcoming speech to the battles in Budapest. Dulles suggested making a comparison between Hungary's fight for freedom now and its struggle for independence from Austria in 1848, which had also been crushed by Russian troops. Then the Austrians invited the Russians into Hungary. Now the Russians invited themselves. Eisenhower read from the script provided. 'The employment of Soviet troops to shoot down Hungarian people breaks every moral law and demonstrates that Hungary to

Soviet Russia is merely a colonial possession, the demand of whose people for democratic liberty warrants the use of naked force.'[6] The line was banal and, apart from stating the obvious, was inelegant for a good writer like Dulles. The President interrupted with an observation: 'I think it might be a good thing to add a final sentence about how the people of America feel about this situation.' Dulles quickly came up with a neat, non-committal line that would not worry the Russians, would make a good soundbite for the home market, and had the quint-essential ring of Eisenhower. 'At this moment the heart of America goes out to the people of Hungary.'

At about 1.30 p.m. the President called Dulles back to discuss what, if anything, could be done at the United Nations. Eisenhower said: 'I don't think we should walk into this alone. It would look as if we were doing it for internal . . .' The sentence remained unfinished, but it was clear he was thinking how his actions would be perceived. Ike thought that the Nato countries should join in and they should act together. Dulles said they 'would be reluctant . . . they'll interpret it as an election move'.[7] Eisenhower, however, made it clear he did not want the US to act unilaterally. 'I'd like to hear from our allies – even a grudging assent. I'll be back in Washington first thing tomorrow, let's talk then. The worst thing would be to be thought of as guilty of [taking] spurious interest here.'[8]

The two Soviet troubleshooters Mikoyan and Suslov heard sporadic gunfire overnight. They were listening to the sound of shells exploding in the distance when they arrived at the Communist Party headquarters at about 9 a.m. They had spoken earlier to Khrushchev in Moscow and to the Russian officers in command of the faltering military operation in Budapest. The Hungarian government had lost power; the Communist Party, almost a million strong, had all but collapsed; the Soviet Union, in an attempt to prop up the Hungarian Communists, had been sucked into a series of bloody battles and, who knew, maybe a war. The Kremlin's emissaries were now determined to show their Hungarian vassals who was in command. Mikoyan was usually a man of subtle inflexions. This morning he tore into Ernő Gerő, the Soviet Union's most slavish puppet, as the author of all their troubles. Gerő, 'a poor politician', was mostly to blame, declared Mikoyan. 'You stampeded us into an ill-advised commitment of Soviet troops through an exaggerated and distorted picture of the situation.'[9] Suslov butted in and 'suggested' that a shattered-looking Gerő should resign at once. The Hungarian tried clinging to straws. He said Khrushchev himself, barely a few weeks earlier, had told him he was needed to hold the Party in Hungary together. Mikoyan replied: 'The Party has already fallen apart thanks to your incredible blunders.'

Gerő was replaced by a tall, brown-eyed forty-four-year-old with a self-effacing smile called János Kádár. An ascetic, quiet man who rarely raised his voice, Kádár was among the second rank of Hungarian Communists when the revolution broke out. He was chosen by the Soviets because he was neither an old-style Stalinist – he loathed Rákosi – nor was he associated with Nagy. He was known as an up-and-coming personality within the Party, but he was too careful a man to give away anything significant about his opinions, and he was barely recognised at all outside Communist circles. He had a dry sense of humour, but was too circumspect to show it often in public. The Soviets knew little about him, but he had always been loyal to Russian interests, and seemed a figure of common sense, unlikely to panic. He had a deceptively open and frank look, an intense gaze. He was an exceptionally disciplined man who hardly drank, was not interested in food, had no affairs with women and whose only real hobby was chess.

János Czermanik was born, illegitimate, on 25 May 1912 in the port town of Fiume, now Rijeka in Croatia. His mother was a Slovak servant girl, Borbala. His father* was a soldier who abandoned them both at his birth. Unlike most of the leading Hungarian Communists he was brought up in abject poverty, in the working class that they all claimed to represent. His mother could find only occasional work as a washerwoman. Kádár left school at fourteen and trained as an apprentice toolmaker. He became a Communist at nineteen, while the Party was illegal. When, as a temporary tactic under Stalin, Moscow ordered national Communist Parties to infiltrate other leftist organisations, Kádár joined the Social Democrats, and soon sat on the party's Budapest

* Kádár's father was a soldier called János Kressinger. When Kádár was sixteen he found a letter his mother had hidden carelessly: 'My dear Boriska, I can't send you any more money because I have to support my other children. But please keep our child and try to educate him.' This was the nearest he had ever come to finding out who his father was – his mother had never discussed it with him. Kádár met his father, and his three half-brothers, for the first time only in 1960. It was then that he discovered that his father was a small landowner and could have supported him fairly easily.

branch committee. His cover was soon blown, however, and he was arrested by the Horthy regime in 1937. He spent nearly three years in prison.[10]

On his release, unlike so many other Communists, he did not go to Russia to emerge later as a 'Muscovite' Party panjandrum. He stayed in Hungary and, with his mentor and close friend László Rajk, he ran the underground Party during the war, under a new pseudonym, János Kádár. He escaped death, narrowly, in 1944 after he was arrested trying to cross the border into Yugoslavia to make secret contact with Tito's partisans. He was despatched with a trainful of Jews to Mauthausen concentration camp in Austria. They were offloaded at Komarno, in north-western Hungary, and transferred to the town's prison. But he managed to escape and return to Budapest.[11]

After 'liberation' he became Budapest's deputy head of police and he succeeded Rajk as Interior Minister in 1948. His reputation for deceit and untrustworthiness dated from his role in the Rajk trial. Many people denounced and betrayed their friends in the Terror years. But there was a macabre touch to Kádár's treachery that chills the blood. In 1949 Kádár was made godfather of Rajk's son, László. The two families were intimately connected. Kádár was close to Júlia Rajk, as was his wife, Maria, an elegant, shrewd brunette a couple of years younger than her husband whose commitment to communism matched his own. A few weeks after the ceremony – and the day after the two men had a long game of chess – Rajk was arrested.[12] Kádár, scared for his own life, was despatched to see the prisoner by the sadistic Rákosi to bully Rajk into making a confession at a show trial. The interview was secretly recorded and the transcript released recently makes gruesome reading. Kádár knew Rajk was innocent, yet as Interior Minister made speech after speech accusing him of all manner of crimes. He was forced to attend Rajk's execution, which left a searing impression on him always. His friend 'died praising Stalin's name', Kádár recorded later.[13]

Inevitably, he became a victim of the purges. He could see his downfall coming. Just before the May Day celebrations in 1951 an edict went out to all 13,750 Party organisations not to carry pictures of Kádár on their march. He was arrested shortly afterwards. Altogether he spent seven years of his life in jail; the worst were the three in solitary confinement under the Rákosi dictatorship. At a secret trial in November 1951 he was sentenced to life imprisonment, charged with being a spy for the Horthy police in 1943. His ordeal began a few days after he was arrested. The notorious torturer Vladimir Farkas, a colonel in the AVO, questioned him. He and another AVO thug began to beat Kádár. He was writhing on the floor when a newcomer arrived, Vladimir's father, the venomous Defence Minister, Mihály Farkas. Kádár was raised from the ground. Vladimir Farkas stepped close. Two henchmen prised Kádár's teeth apart and the Colonel urinated in his mouth. Everybody laughed. A little while later, the telephone rang on the table. Mihály Farkas picked up the receiver. It was Rákosi. The 'Wise Father' and 'Great Leader' of the people was nervously enquiring whether Kádár had confessed. 'No,' said Farkas. 'He has not confessed yet.' Kádár heard an angry rumbling at the other end of the line. Rákosi was giving his orders. 'Beat him. Beat him until he talks. These are my orders.' They did. Kádár eventually 'confessed'.[14]

He was released in 1954 during Imre Nagy's first term as Prime Minister. He went to meet Rákosi, who received him kindly, asked after his welfare, told him how pleased he was to see him and appointed him head of the biggest Party branch in Budapest, the industrial working-class district of Angyalföld.[15]

Kádár had two other potentially awkward encounters soon after he came out of jail. He went to see Nagy, who tried to win him over and gain his support in his clash with Rákosi. Kádár was cautious. 'Rákosi is the leader of our Party and the Hungarian worker cannot imagine life or the history of Hungary without him,' he parroted out wearily. But as they parted Kádár put out his hand. 'I'd like to thank you for securing my release.' Nagy replied, 'I hope that when my turn comes you would do the same for me.'[16] He called on Júlia Rajk, who had just been freed from jail herself. He told her what she already knew – that he had seen her husband in jail, tried to force a confession out of him and had witnessed his hanging. 'Can you forgive me?' he asked. 'I forgive you. My husband would have been murdered anyway. But can you forgive yourself? If you want to live as a decent person you should inform Hungary about the secrets of the Rajk trial.' He left and did nothing.[17]

If the good news about Gerő had been made public immediately, the single bloodiest atrocity of the revolution might never have happened. A peaceful and speedy end to the uprising might even have been found. Around the time Gerő was being fired, some 3,000 protesters carrying 'Get Lost Gerő' banners were marching along the main Boulevard.

They were planning to join another group protesting in front of the Parliament building. As they neared the Astoria Hotel, the base for a unit of Russian soldiers, their way was barred by three Soviet tanks. There was a tense standoff for a few minutes. The tanks did not fire. The students, uneasily, stood their ground. Then a strange thing happened in the middle of a revolutionary battleground, according to an eyewitness, József Kővágó, one-time Smallholder Mayor of Budapest.

Some students who spoke Russian clambered onto one of the Soviet tanks and began speaking to the Soviet troops. They started handing out leaflets they had printed, in Russian, overnight. 'Russian friends. Do not shoot! They have tricked you. You are not fighting against counter-revolutionaries. We Hungarians want an independent, demo-cratic Hungary. You are not shooting at fascists but at workers, peasants and university students.'[18] The soldiers got out of their tanks, began reading the flyers and talking to the demonstrators. The Russians were persuaded. The officer in command agreed they would not shoot and for the next few minutes there was a friendly discussion. Amazingly, 'the crew of one tank said that they felt that the demands of the demonstrators were justified and they should go to Parliament together'.[19]

A few students climbed aboard the tanks and, in a line, they all headed off along the wide Bajcsy-Zsilinsky Avenue, past Budapest's central police station at Deák Square, watched by bemused onlookers. The soldiers had placed Hungarian flags in the turrets of the tanks – one of the most curious sights of the revolution. When the procession arrived at the square, there were already about 5,000 other dem-onstrators there calling for Gerő's dismissal, the removal of other Stalinists from the government and another appearance by Nagy.

Though demonstrations were still banned, and martial law was still in force, none of the protesters seemed concerned, either by an AVO colonel who through a loudhailer ordered the crowd to disperse, or by the presence of AVO sharpshooters on the roof of the Ministry of Agriculture building which occupied one side of the square. Opposite, a guard of half a dozen Soviet tanks defended Parliament itself. For half an hour the demonstration was allowed to continue. 'The atmosphere was light, celebratory, almost like a carnival.' Then, without any warning, the shooting started, amid scenes of total confusion.[20]

Survivors tell two different versions of the massacre. Some say categorically that the shooting came from above. AVO officers on the rooftops of the neo-classical Agriculture Ministry opened fire on the protesters unprovoked, or because they feared the building they had occupied might come under attack. There was a burst of machine-gun fire on the demonstrators below – many children among them, according to some eyewitnesses. Then, as people were vainly seeking shelter in the open space or trying to run into side streets, the shooting began again.[21]

Other witnesses say Russian tanks in front of the Parliament building were the first to shoot and many of the dead were victims of shellfire and weaponry the AVO did not possess. There is some documentary evidence to back that up. One account pins the blame directly on the malign head of the KGB, Ivan Serov. The Intelligence chief was a few hundred metres away at the Communist Party headquarters in Academy Street when the demonstration reached its noisiest. He had been holding talks with Mikoyan, Suslov and Hungarian officials. A reliable Russian account from Soviet security officers in Budapest at the time records that in the middle of the meeting a messenger arrived and told Serov about the scenes at Parliament Square. He left to see for himself. 'Serov was particularly annoyed about reports of fraternisation between Hungarian students and Russian troops,' according to these reports. That, he declared, was not the kind of thing that should happen in a counter-revolution. 'He issued orders to the commander of the tank company guarding the Parliament building to "clear the square" – which meant firing on the protesters.'[22] They began with warning fire and the demonstrators panicked. Both versions are likely to be true. In the revolution, the Russians and the AVO were on the same side, so they fired on the protesters too. Amidst the mêlée the chaos became worse when a Hungarian army unit which had been despatched to investigate started shooting at the Soviets. The Russians fired first, however.

For more than thirty years the Hungarian government never mentioned the atrocity. Officially it never happened. But a report prepared at the time by the Chief of Staff of the Hungarian army, László Tóth, recently made public, declared: 'The Soviet troops received the order to liquidate the protest in front of Parliament. This they did ... Soviet soldiers opened fire on the rebels.' Most of Serov's reports to the Kremlin during the period he was in Budapest have been available – but not the one covering the Parliament Square massacre that left 75 dead and 282 wounded. Half an hour after the slaughter the news was finally announced over the radio that Gerő had been removed.[23]

Word of the massacre spread throughout Budapest. It changed the nature of the uprising and the mood of the people 'from exhilaration and excitement to bitterness and desperation'.[24] Rumours circulated that hundreds of people – including children – had been deliberately rounded up, herded into Parliament Square and slaughtered in cold blood. Many of the survivors went straight to the nearest armed rebel group, took a weapon and began fighting the Russians and the AVO as soon as possible. Others marched to protest elsewhere. A few hundred quickly formed outside the American Legation two blocks from Parliament Square, begging for aid by the US, some arms and ammunition, and some support.

During the slaughter, Spencer Barnes, a greying, nervous-looking man of fifty who seemed a decade older, had been lying prone on the floor sending a dramatic account of the mayhem on a telex line back to Washington. 'At noon dead and dying Hungarian women and men lay everywhere on the square in front of Parliament . . . then massacre happened after a few hundred protesters arrived there on top of vans, armoured vehicles, even Soviet tanks . . . The Russians say they do not want to shoot Hungarian workers . . . the guys on the Russian tanks smiled and waved . . . But this love was short-lived and had tragic consequences.'[25]

Now Barnes was reporting to the State Department that a 'large crowd is in front of the Legation shouting for help, etc.'. American officials assured the crowd, behind firmly locked gates and solid iron railings, that they saw the massacre, knew all about it and had sent full reports to Washington. But the crowd would not be quietened. Barnes, through an interpreter, told them: 'We understand the situation. It has been reported to our Government as fully as we are able. You will understand that we ourselves can take no decisions. This is a matter between ourselves and the United Nations.' Some of the protesters, as they were leaving, shouted 'Give us guns, we'll do the fighting' – and 'Why is the UN doing nothing? Make them send troops.'[26]

A few hundred metres across Budapest, near fashionable Vörösmarty Square and within eyesight of the city's main police station, another crowd grew outside the British Embassy. Leslie 'Bunny' Fry allowed a small delegation inside. They demanded that Britain raise in the UN the presence of Soviet troops in Budapest.[27]

The crowds would have left the embassies even more angry and disheartened if they had known the contents of traffic between the State Department and Henry Cabot Lodge at 1 p.m. Washington time. Dulles's aides produced a document recommending a joint rather than unilateral approach to the UN, which would take more time. Lodge agreed with the strategy and explained his rationale: 'Even if final action blocked by Soviet veto, initiative would, in addition to increasing US prestige, add to prestige of UN in eyes of satellite peoples who now hold organisation in low esteem because of its past failure to note their plight.' The Russians would naturally veto any UN resolution that called for the withdrawal of Soviet troops. So there was nothing, in practice, that the Americans were able to do. But the US was left with an opportunity: America could suggest sending UN observers to Hungary. Again the Russians would reject the suggestion out of hand. But 'this could be done with a great show of reasonableness and sincerity ... We will get maximum support if we strike while the iron is hot.'[28]

The rebel groups went on the offensive, swelled since the Parliament Square massacre by many new recruits. The freedom fighters' tactics did not change – hit, run and hide – but they increased their attacks on the Russians and devised new methods to combat tanks with Molotov cocktails. The revolutionaries had captured new strongholds, usually a small square or transport terminus they could defend, like Zsigmond Móricz Square in Buda, or a dense concentration of narrow roads that were hard for tanks to penetrate, like Tűzoltó Street. The strongest resistance remained at the Corvin Passage and the Kilián Barracks. The rebel freedom fighters now numbered a little over 1,500 and Maléter commanded 600 at the Kilián Barracks. A big banner was displayed in front of the cinema entrance: 'There are three Great Powers – the US, the USSR and the Corvin group.' Between them they symbolised the armed wing of the revolution. They had an uneasy alliance. Maléter always maintained he was a socialist, was used to giving orders and having them obeyed. The freedom fighters were mostly very young and unused to military-style discipline. The leaders were on the whole viscerally anti-Communist. During the previous evening and earlier that morning Maléter's men and the Corvin group had, for brief periods, exchanged fire in an internecine struggle over who was to make decisions about joint operations. But all the differences were put aside when the news came through about the slaughter earlier that morning.

Gergely Pongrácz, who was to became the Corvin group's leader, joined the fighters with his four brothers late the previous night. Aged twenty-three, an agricultural engineer, he had left his farm eighty kilometres from Budapest when he heard that fighting against the Russians and against communism had broken out. He spent all the previous day driving to the capital on a tractor in a state that fluctuated between wild excitement and deep solemnity. The Parliament Square massacre, he said, had changed everything. The Soviets and the AVO had shown no mercy; the rebels had to prove, immediately, that they would not be intimidated into giving up the struggle. The morale of the city depended on it. Maléter's tanks defended their own stronghold. They believed themselves safe. From 2 p.m. the freedom fighters began attacks on Soviet tanks within a kilometre radius of the Corvin complex, using the underground passageways for swift movement. They knocked out three tanks within a couple of hours and captured another two, along with an armoured car.

The Soviets moved their tanks along the Boulevard towards the Corvin for the biggest battle of the uprising so far. Almost none of the freedom fighters had used weapons in anger before. 'We saw them off, held the position, and fought them to a standstill,' said Pongrácz, nicknamed 'Bájusz' ('Whiskers') because of his elaborate Edwardian handlebar moustache. 'That was the first action I saw. I had a couple of years' military training, most of the men my age had a bit, but I had not seen fighting. When the Soviets were coming towards us I saw the head of a Russian looking out from behind a tank. I had a Mauser rifle and I saw the Russian head looking out ... I aimed and pulled the trigger and I saw the Russian soldier fall on the sidewalk. I started to cry.'[29] When the Soviets withdrew 'in defeat' the Corvin group were left with heavy armour and equipment they had captured, a permanent supply of fuel and a proven defensible position. Most important, they had raised hopes in the city, where people were beginning to believe in themselves, and in the possibility, however remote, of a victory.

TWENTY-TWO
Friday, 26 October

Soon after dawn, a fifty-nine-year-old man with huge side-whiskers, wearing a gunbelt and a wide-brimmed hat, presented himself before the barricades at Széna Square. He was János Szabó, who quickly became known throughout Budapest as 'Uncle' Szabó, the most popular of the insurgent chieftains. Among the freedom fighters, leaders simply emerged – either by example because they had performed impressively in a particular skirmish, or because they spoke well. Szabó may have looked somewhat bizarre with his hooked nose and unkempt features, but he had an uncanny flair for guerrilla fighting, a modest demeanour and a natural air of authority. There was no challenge for leadership of the group, according to one of the fighters. 'Uncle Szabó stood out as the obvious choice among all of us. He was totally uneducated, was not very articulate, but he possessed the clearest vision and recognised most fully what was going on. He had amazing leadership qualities.'[1]

János Szabó was born to a poor peasant family in Zaruzseny, now in Romania. He left school at twelve, before training to be a fitter. He was conscripted into the army in 1914 and served throughout the First World War. He fought as a company commander in the Red Army during the short-lived Soviet Republic under Béla Kun. He stayed in Romania, among the Hungarian minority in Transylvania, working as a maintenance man on the railways. He moved to Hungary in 1944 and found a job as a chauffeur at the Agriculture Ministry. For a while he was Imre Nagy's personal driver when the 'Land Divider' was in the coalition government. Never a great believer in communism, he nevertheless joined the Party in 1945. It was a sensible thing to do. But he left the year after Rákosi took dictatorial power. In 1949 he was jailed for three months after he tried to leave the country illegally. After his release he found another job as a driver with the national Food Delivery Enterprise, but he was arrested in 1953 on trumped-up spying charges. He was lucky to avoid torture, and to get out of jail after nine months without facing prosecution.[2]

Széna Square in 1956 was a busy transport hub in the heart of the Buda side of the river, linking the Danube bridges to routes heading to the north of the city. A group of insurgents had fought there since the first morning of the revolution, occupying it for short periods using overturned tramcars as barricades. They were repeatedly dispersed but managed, albeit uneasily, to regroup. After Szabó became leader the fighters, never numbering more than 500, built a strong defensive position around a drilling tower that was being used for construction of the metro system. 'We fought with few weapons at first, infantry rifles and a few machine-pistols we got from the Hungarian army. Later we captured tommy-guns from the Soviets. Then we got hold of a Russian armoured car with a heavy machine-gun. In the early phase of the fighting it was the most important weapon we had. We were organised, but democratic and chaotic in some ways. If a man wanted to fight, he simply got hold of a gun, went to Széna Square, stopped at one of the street corners and fought. Nobody questioned him or tried to hamper him in any way.'[3]

After he secured the base, Szabó sent his fighters out on missions to harass the Russians. He improvised unconventional methods that had the Soviets mystified. For several days they could find no answer to the original and creative tactics he devised against their lumbering old-style World War Two T34 tanks, with rubber caterpillar tracks. One revolutionary with Szabó's group explained a frequently used trick: 'Ordinary saucepans or frying pans were filled with water, balanced on cables and stretched across the road. When we heard the Soviets coming along we lowered the pans slowly until they were about a metre above the ground. At first the Soviet tanks would hesitate. That hesitation would give fighters placed in apartments or offices above the time to hurl Molotov cocktails and grenades from the windows.'[4]

Another, equally effective method was to place bricks across the road covered by wooden paving. From a distance these looked as though they could be landmines. When the tanks halted, they were open to attack from above. Szabó reminded all his rebels that, once disabled, the tanks made good barricades for the next skirmish so that each Soviet loss benefited the rebels twice over. In Buda, built on a series of hills, Szabó's group came up with the idea of covering some of the roads with silk and pouring soapy water over the material.

Cumbersome T34s would slip and slide, leaving them unable to manoeuvre, crashing into each other.[5]

Very often children built the roadblocks and threw the Molotov cocktails. In many parts of Budapest the revolution was a schoolkids' war. In Széna Square the vast majority of the fighters were teenagers.[6] Szabó is a Hungarian hero, widely revered. Like some of the other resistance leaders he had no qualms about sending twelve- or thirteen-year-olds into battle against Russian tanks. 'If they want to fight, they are old enough,' he is said to have told relatives of his fighters.[7] People respected him. 'He cared for his men – and was the father of the kids fighting with him, scolding and praising them by turns.'[8]

Gergely Pongrácz, one of the leaders of the Corvin Passage fighters on the other side of the city, said he agonised over the child fighters:

> The average age didn't reach eighteen. We had children at the Corvin as young as twelve. They didn't want to leave. At first I think it was excitement, they were there because they had a gun, it was a thrill. Yes I do accept that. But things changed when a few people got killed or wounded around them. The ones who stayed, it was patriotism and ideals that kept them there. That's why they stayed with us and it was impossible to send them home. We had a few older fighters – but there were perhaps only a dozen older than me. I was twenty-four. The rest were younger.
>
> Quite a few times I wanted to go home. Maybe the next bullet is going to be mine, I thought. And I did start to go. But when I saw children, dead, I couldn't. I was in the services for two years. I knew how to handle a gun. Am I going to leave these kids to die? The shame kept me there.[9]

Children were brought up in schools to read a famous Soviet book about partisan fighting, *The Young Guardsman*, by Alexander Fadeyev. Some of the freedom fighters thought it very useful for the guerilla battles in Budapest in 1956. Not everyone. Anikó Vajda, fourteen at the time, said: 'Obviously I had no idea how guns worked. But an older man, Pista Baczi, said: "Don't worry about it. I am going to teach you." Then I looked again at the gun – it was bigger than me. They explained to me how to use it and showed me a couple of times. The first time I used it I just closed my eyes, because I was so scared. There were some [Hungarian] soldiers where we were fighting near the Corvin. They had torn off the red stars on their uniforms. One of them said "Don't worry about it, little girl, we will show you." And they did.'[10]

Some people were appalled by the butchery of children in the name of revolutionary fervour. A different Szabó, György, who was one of the leaders of the revolution in Győr, said: 'Once I refused to let five truckloads of young boys go to Budapest to get killed there. Enough was enough. They were very angry with me in Győr, but I stuck to the decision. I did not want it on my conscience that I allowed youngsters to go to their deaths. One truck did go, though. It came back empty, but with a black flag inside it.'[11]

The story of Péter Mansfeld, a young rebel at Széna Square, is one of the saddest. He was fifteen and had a particularly immature look with blond curly hair and blue eyes. He took part in some of the bitter fighting, but his main role was to smuggle weapons to other guerrilla bands. He was active with the insurgents for a few days, then drifted away. After the revolution he got into trouble with the police for a series of petty crimes. Then he was recognised as a freedom fighter and was arrested for his relatively minor role in the uprising. Originally he received a long jail term. But then, on 21 March 1959, eleven days after his eighteenth birthday, he was hanged.[12]

For the last three nights Imre Nagy had managed to catch a few fitful hours of sleep on a camp bed in an office of the Communist Party headquarters. Hour by hour he was seeing his dream of Hungary embarking on a peaceful, moderate course of reform communism – under him as a legitimate leader – smashed. He was surrounded by enemies among the old guard of Party apparatchiks, who were urging the Russians on to a final showdown with the freedom fighters, whatever the cost in lives. Gerő had been removed from any official position, but he still had a room in the building and was spreading poison against Nagy. Gerő's placeman Hegedüs remained a deputy Prime Minister, and hardliners like István Bata and the discredited Interior Minister László Piros, who mishandled Tuesday's demonstrations so disastrously, were still in the government. Nagy was determined now that the Stalinists had to be removed and he would bring 'liberal' Communists in his image, as well as a few non-Communists, into a new government.[13]

First he had to square the idea with the Soviet emissaries. The unbending Suslov and the more wily Mikoyan had been given plenipotentiary powers by the Kremlin. They were fast losing patience with the squabbling among the Hungarian Comrades, while Budapest burned. On the other hand they were too wary of the 'kulak' Nagy to give him a free hand. When the Russian pair saw him at about 9.30 a.m. Mikoyan challenged Nagy about his reference on radio the previous night to the withdrawal of Soviet forces. 'You should not have said anything like that,' Mikoyan told him. 'Especially without telling us first. Who gave you the authority to say it?'[14] Nagy argued that after the Parliament Square massacre the government had to 'take the initiative or be beaten'. The Soviet magnates were eventually per-suaded. Even Suslov admitted that the slaughter had made 'the position of our troops here very bad'. They reluctantly agreed to let Nagy choose the government he wanted, but told him 'not to go too far'.

Mikoyan wrote a personal note to Khrushchev during the morning explaining the agreement: 'There are two possible paths before us: first to reject all of those demands ... for change and rely on the Soviet army to continue the struggle. But in that case they will lose all contact with the peaceful population, there would be more deaths which will widen the chasm between the government and the population. If we follow that path, we will lose.'[15] Mikoyan loathed the idea of bringing non-Communists into the government but justified it in Hungarian circumstances: 'In response to our warning that the path of appealing to bourgeois democrats is a slippery one, that one had to be careful otherwise one could slip ... Nagy responded that they are doing this out of the utmost necessity in order not to lose the government's rudder and as the minimum required measure.'

Nagy was warned by his friends and supporters that the modest proposals he had made to the Russians would not satisfy the revo-lutionaries on the streets or the endless delegations that came to visit him from factories, towns and villages making fresh demands. The passionate Losonczy, utterly loyal to 'Uncle Imre', told Nagy at a mid-morning meeting that revolutions happen at vast speed and people who cannot keep up are left behind. Nagy invariably looked 'impatient and displeased' when he heard criticism, according to Miklós Vásárhelyi, a great but not blind admirer.[16] Now he was beginning, for the first time, to listen more carefully to the voices who had supported him for many years – even when he did not like what he was hearing. He stopped calling the rebel fighters 'counter-revolutionaries' – a big step for him to make. When the astute tactician Ferenc Donáth sug-gested the government should negotiate directly with the freedom-fighting groups, he expected Nagy to reject the idea out of hand and snap a reply. The Prime Minister simply returned one of his typical cheerful-looking smiles and said he would seriously think about it.[17]

Inspired by Budapest, the revolution spread. Throughout Hungary, provincial towns were taken over by the rebels after barely a fight. Most of the Russian troops in the country were bogged down in Budapest or guarding the borders. Elsewhere the Soviet army was barely visible, in isolated garrisons or training barracks, where local commanders wisely sought peace terms rather than risk the possibility of defeat. The other enemy, the AVO, often simply disappeared after a show of resistance.[18] By mid-morning Pécs, the main town in the south of Hungary and centre of a mining area near the Yugoslav border, was in the hands of a 'National Committee' chaired by a professor of military science from the town's University. At dawn the Pécs AVO chief, Colonel Bradács, tried to impose a curfew, but when it was ignored he handed over the headquarters to a youth brigade and he skipped the country. In Debrecen, on the eastern border with Romania, there had been demonstrations at around the same time the big march began in Budapest on Tuesday. Protests had continued since. By midday on Friday there were hardly any red stars left on public buildings and a 'Revolutionary Socialist Committee' declared it had taken over the local administration.[19]

A major figure of the revolution emerged in Győr, an elegant town of 60,000 people two hours due west of Budapest on the main road to Vienna. Attila Szigetthy, thirty-eight, a huge, heavy, sprawling man with a flaming-red moustache, aristocratic antecedents he made no effort to hide and relentless energy, had installed himself as the insurgents' chief power-broker in Transdanubia (the entire region between Budapest and the border with Austria). Szigetthy ran a state farm, but was used to a much bigger stage. The revolution gave him one. A good personal friend of Imre Nagy, he had been a well-known MP for the National Peasants Party in the coalition years. Everybody knew he was a Communist fellow traveller, yet he always commanded respect for his wit and for displaying as independent a mind as possible. He was too unorthodox to stay long in national politics. He was exiled from Budapest and despatched to Győr. Szigetthy had a flair for the dramatic and understood the whirlwind excitement of revolution. Meetings of his National Revolutionary Committee went on for days amid an air of breathless enthusiasm. He set up a loudspeaker system at Győr town hall which played Beethoven's *Eroica* Symphony for many hours a day.[20]

In some areas outside the capital the old guard fought, and lost. In Miskolc, the main industrial town in north-eastern Hungary, a crowd of a few hundred demonstrators appeared at 10 a.m. outside the main police headquarters. They were protesting about the arrest the previous day of a dozen or so young people as they left on lorries to join the freedom fighters in Budapest. They had been brought back to Miskolc and locked up in the cells overnight. The local police were ready to let them go, but the building was protected by the AVO, whose captain, László Csürke, insisted on keeping the youngsters jailed. The demonstrators besieged the building. Csürke ordered his men to fire into the crowd. They dispersed, but returned minutes later, doubled in size, with a contingent of armed miners from nearby Szukahalló. There were no Soviet units anywhere close, so Csürke rang the Hungarian garrison and pleaded for them to intervene. Soldiers arrived – and promptly joined the rebels. They sent an ultimatum to the AVO: surrender or the army will attack. Csürke ran up a white flag. The insurgents ransacked the building and massacred the two AVOs, including Csürke.

From then Miskolc became one of the main provincial centres of the revolution under a Borsod County National Committee. Among its first acts was to issue a statement about the police headquarters riot. 'Stalinist provocateurs have felt the just punishment of the people.'[21] The other was to confirm, in direct elections, Rudolf Földvári as leader of the revolution in Miskolc. Like many of the emerging rebel chiefs, forty-five-year-old Földvári was a Communist who had played a significant role in national politics until falling foul of Rákosi and Gerő. He had been a senior figure in the Party's agitprop department, represented the Hungarian Communists at Stalin's funeral and was destined for political stardom. However, he publicly backed Nagy against Rákosi and Gerő after 1953 and was sent to internal Party exile in Miskolc.

For a few days these 'councils' had real power and influence. 'The Workers' Councils and Revolutionary Councils were a direct and very immediate form of democracy that typified the Revolution. Respected figures were elected and it didn't always matter if they were Communists. You could say that "good" Communists got in and "bad" ones didn't but it wasn't always as simple as that. Sometimes people who had never shown any obvious distaste for Stalinism or for any kind of communism were elected because of their personal qualities.'[22]

Földvári was a stooping, professorial-looking man, though he only finished elementary school before becoming a tool-fitter in a factory. He supported the revolution from the start and helped to shape it. He was in regular contact with Nagy. They had a long conversation the previous evening. Földvári, like the intellectuals around the Prime Minister, begged the cautious Nagy to toughen his negotiating position with the Soviets. They should be told they had to leave Hungary by 1 January at the latest, Földvári said. He backed up the demand with a threat: the strike in Miskolc would continue until the Russians agreed to withdraw their troops.[23]

At about midday in Mosonmagyaróvár, a small town of 5,000 or so people twelve kilometres east of the Austrian border, a demonstration began similar to dozens that had taken place over the last few days in Hungary. Half the town's inhabitants were there, including old men and women, girls who worked at the local bauxite factory, young mothers with babies in their arms and schoolchildren. It proceeded in relatively good humour. They marched, shouted the ubiquitous slogan 'Russkik haza', sang the national anthem and ceremonially cut out the Communist emblem from the tricolour. When they reached the AVO headquarters near the central town square, where a huge red star stood out against the sky, they stopped. The AVO commander, Lieutenant József Stefko, called out, 'Halt, what do you want?', and the people at the front of the crowd shouted, 'Take down the red star.' An eyewitness records what happened next:

> The reply was a hoarse word of command, the rattle of machine-gun fire, the mowing down of those in the front ranks; then the screams of the wounded. No warning was given ... There was not even an initial burst of firing into the air, or over the people's heads. At the command of Lieutenant Stefko, two machine-guns hidden behind the windows of the headquarters pumped bullets into the thickest part of the crowd. AVO men also threw hand grenades. The firing went on for four minutes, and some of those wounded were shot again in the back as they tried to crawl away. Men and women, students and workers, children and even an 18-months-old baby were among the victims.

Fifty-two were killed and eighty-six injured.[24]

The crowd fled in disarray, as did most of the two dozen secret police responsible for the slaughter. When the demonstrators returned a few minutes later they brought with them a few weapons and laid siege to the AVO building. The local soldiers would give them arms but no help, so some of the protesters drove to Győr, fifteen kilometres away. A company of men arrived, and tried to prevent further bloodshed. A strange, heroic young man was despatched with them as the representative of the Győr Revolutionary Committee. Gábor Földes, a handsome thirty-three-year-old actor, director of the Kisfaludy Theatre in Budapest, was an idealist who sized up the situation instantly. The crowd had formed a lynch mob to get their hands on the four AVO officers still inside. A passionate but sensible revolutionary, he knew that Mosonmagyaróvár was one of the first towns in Hungary that Western journalists reached on their way from Vienna. Instant justice witnessed by reporters would do the image of the uprising no good at all. He and the company of soldiers from Győr did their best to save the AVOs, but could only reach two, one of whom was Stefko. They were both badly injured and were taken to hospital. The other pair were captured by a furious mob. 'The crowd threw itself upon them. They were beaten until their bodies were bloody objects. Then they were split into pieces as if this had been the work of wild animals.'[25]

In Washington, where it was 9 a.m., President Eisenhower's most senior intelligence and foreign policy advisers were meeting in the White House at a National Security Council briefing. On the Hungarian crisis, Ike had moved overnight from simply a cautious wait-and-see response to 'active non-involvement'. He made it abundantly clear to all his advisers that he was determined to do nothing which could be misunderstood in Moscow as an intention to interfere in the Soviet sphere of influence. 'I doubt that the Russian leaders genuinely fear an invasion by the West,' he said. 'But with the deterioration of the USSR's hold over its satellites might not the Soviet Union be tempted to resort to very extreme measures, even to precipitate global war? This possibility we must watch with the utmost caution. After all, Hitler had known well, from the 1st of February 1945, that he was licked. Yet he carried on until the very last and pulled down Europe with him in his defeat. The Soviets might develop some desperate mood such as this.'[26]

CIA director Allen Dulles did not predict the revolution or that

Russian tanks would be engaged in street battles with Hungarian schoolchildren, yet he was already learning some lessons from the uprising:

> The Hungarian revolt may demonstrate the inability of a moderate national Communist regime to survive in any of the satellites ... it constitutes the most serious threat yet posed to continued Soviet control in the satellites. The revolt confronts Moscow with a very harsh dilemma: either to revert to a harsh Stalinist policy or to permit democratisation to develop ... to a point which risks the complete loss of Soviet control of the satellites.
>
> The current Soviet leadership is certainly on the defensive and Khrushchev is probably being held responsible for what has happened. Khrushchev's days may well be numbered. It is quite possible that Marshal Zhukov will decide who Khrushchev's successor would be. Indeed it was even possible that Zhukov himself may be the successor.*[27]

Eisenhower was intrigued by a suggestion from his chief adviser on disarmament, the former Governor of Minnesota, Harold Stassen, which was entirely in keeping with the President's hand-wringing strategy. He wanted to send a clear message to Zhukov and others in the Kremlin saying unequivocally that the achievement of freedom in the satellite countries should not be considered by the Soviet Union as posing any threat to their national security. When the NSC meeting ended at 10.40, Stassen went straight to his office in the White House and wrote Ike a letter putting flesh on the idea. He said: 'The Soviet Union may calculate that if they lose control of Hungary that country would be taken into Nato by the United States and this would be a great threat in Soviet eyes to their security. May it not be wise for the United States in some manner to make it clear that we are willing to have Hungary be established on the Austrian basis – and not affiliated with NATO?'[28] Ike had his doubts about the existence of neutral states in Europe. However, he was enthusiastic about sending the Russians reassurances that they would not misunderstand.

Eisenhower turned down the frantic requests from Cold Warriors in

---

* Not as numbered as Dulles's own days. Khrushchev remained leader of the Soviet Union until 1964, when he was finally removed by his enemies in the Kremlin. Allen Dulles was fired by President John F. Kennedy after the Bay of Pigs fiasco in 1961.

the CIA for permission to fly over Hungary and airdrop supplies to the freedom fighters, including weapons. As William Colby, then a junior intelligence officer, later the Agency's director, said: 'This was exactly the end for which the Agency's paramilitary capability was designed. But Eisenhower said a loud and clear no. Whatever doubts may have existed in the Agency about Washington's policy in matters like this vanished ... It was established once and for all that the United States, while firmly committed to the containment of the Soviets ... was not going to attempt to liberate any of the states within the sphere'.[29]

At 4 p.m., insurgents declared a symbolic victory when, without a fight, they occupied the police headquarters in the industrial heartland of Hungary, 'Red Csepel'. At the same time Mikoyan and Suslov were meeting the remnants of the Hungarian Communist Party's leadership. The two Soviets noticed a shift in the Prime Minister's demeanour. They were still prepared to go along with Nagy's list of new Ministers. They approved the proposals he was making to them – measures like pay rises for workers, and other economic concessions. However, for the first time they expressed serious doubts about Nagy in their reports back to the Kremlin. In a jointly signed telegram in the afternoon they said that they again warned Nagy not to say publicly that Soviet troops will withdraw: 'We said we consider this a grave error, since withdrawing Soviet troops would inevitably bring the entry of American troops ... We must keep an eye on Imre Nagy's swings of mood. Because of his opportunistic behaviour he does not know where to draw the line ... For our part we warned the Hungarian leaders that no other concessions must be made, otherwise it will lead to the fall of the authorities.'[30]

In Washington, President Eisenhower was thinking again of ways to allay possible Soviet fears that the US would interfere in Hungary. At 5.50 p.m., nearly midnight in Budapest, he called his Secretary of State. He had been mulling over the suggestion Harold Stassen had made a few hours earlier about the 'border states' in the Soviet bloc, like Hungary. 'They need have no fear that we might make an effort to incorporate them into NATO or to make them part of our alliances. We want to see them have a free choice. All we hope is that they have the same likes as Austria.' Dulles was due to give a campaign speech in

Dallas, Texas, the next night. 'I think you should put something like this in your speech,' Ike said.

Dulles did not like the idea of a neutral Hungary. He thought it did not maximise possible gains the US could make. He also did not want to negotiate directly with the Russians about Hungary 'without going through the UN Security Council ... We could have some backstage talks going on during the Council session which would be more or less legitimate.' The British, he said, wanted a delay in discussing Hungary altogether, until the General Assembly met in mid November. Half an hour later Dulles called Lodge in New York suggesting informal talks at the UN with the Russians. 'It looks bad all along the line,' he said, referring to the crisis brewing in the Middle East. 'We do not know what the British and French have agreed to, and I think they may be going in to fight.' On Hungary Lodge told Dulles that 'We'll lose a good deal if we do nothing'.

Just after 7 p.m. Ike and the Secretary of State spoke again. Dulles said: 'I've been thinking over your thought and wonder if you would approve my saying something to the effect that all we want is their [the satellite states'] genuine independence and that if they once had it that would alter the whole aspect of the European scene and the whole problem of European security would be altered.' 'Yes,' said Eisenhower. 'The whole European and world security would seem to be on the road to achievement ... From the evening paper it looks as though it is spreading in Hungary.' Dulles said he was sending a telegram to Selwyn Lloyd, the British Foreign Secretary, suggesting Hungary be raised at the next Security Council meeting 'so the Russians will not commit vast reprisals and give us a chance to talk privately with them there'. Eisenhower said: 'Tell Lloyd that it is so terrible we would be remiss if we don't do something.'[31]

TWENTY-THREE
Saturday, 27 October

Budapest Radio was still reporting its incredible version of the news. The Soviets were continuing to 'liquidate the counter-revolution'. However, it opened broadcasts at dawn in untypically lyrical style: 'Enough bloodshed. Enough ramshackle streets. We would love to know whether our children, whether our relatives, are still alive. We would love to be together again . . . We would love to enjoy life again. We would like not to fear death any longer . . . In Hungary, after order has been restored, life will be more beautiful, more human, more Hungarian, than it was before.'[1]

Though it was another sunny morning, all those hopes seemed pious on the fourth day of the revolution. Bloody fighting had left parts of central Budapest in ruins. Károly Makk, the film student who had been recording the uprising for a movie crew since Tuesday's demonstration, saw some of the devastation from above in a balloon:

> The city was terribly scarred. In some sections along the Körút, the main boulevard, there hardly seemed a single building that hadn't been damaged or totally destroyed. There were huge holes in the main roads from shellfire and you could hardly move along them. People had ripped up so many cobblestones in some of the smaller roads that it was difficult to get through those too. We had moved from a demonstration, to a riot into a war in practically no time. People's mood changed by the Saturday. There was nothing much to be confident about, for sure, but people did feel pride, even those of us who watched what was going on and didn't take a direct part. We were proud that we stood up and were not beaten.[2]

Overnight, Budapest had been quiet, while Russian tanks moved to their protected positions. On the last three mornings, fighting flared up as soon as the tanks began patrolling the streets at dawn. Now only a few isolated shots rang out on the edge of the city. The curfew had been lifted so that people could buy food. The revolution had hardly penetrated rural Hungary. In some places unpopular collective farm officials had been thrown out, or chose to leave from fear. There had been almost no fighting. However, produce was not being collected and delivered in the normal way through the central state distribution system. Farmers brought food direct to Budapest, and many showed support for the uprising by simply handing food out free. 'They would say it was their contribution to the revolution. This was another spontaneous thing about the uprising – totally unheard of. Peasants bringing in lorryloads of fresh food and giving it away was like a dream come true for city dwellers. Many people in Budapest had never eaten so well as during the revolution. Strange, when all that fighting was going on, to remember that, yet it was so.'[3]

There was hunger, also, for news. The old newspapers began publishing again, revolutionised. The Communist organ *A Free People* was filled with leading articles and columns from Party members supporting the uprising. The trade union paper *People's Voice* (*Népszava*) revealed details about the privileges afforded to Party leaders – free villas in the best parts of town, free nannies for their children, a warehouse full of the choicest foods allocated only for them. New independent papers appeared each day following the launch of the first one, the previous day, called *Truth* (*Igazsag*). The police paper *Magyar Randor*, in its first revolutionary issue this morning, headlined its front page: 'With the people through fire and water'. An army newspaper was launched, a couple of professionally produced student publications, and a paper from the workers at 'Red' Csepel.[4]

'People thirsted for the printed word as though they had crossed a desert,' said Dora Scarlett, an employee of Hungarian Radio during the Revolution, a passionate Communist whose commitment to the cause was shaken by years of living under Rákosi. Often the new papers comprised just two broadsheet pages. Distribution was a problem so they were pasted on walls throughout the centre of the city. The main shopping arcade on the Boulevard was 'like a public reading room'. Each copy was shared by dozens of readers. 'The walls and shop windows were plastered with notices, poems, caricatures and jokes.'[5]

In Mosonmagyaróvár, scene of terrible atrocities the previous day, there was unfinished business to settle. At about 10 a.m. another demonstration began. A vast crowd gathered outside the town's only hospital demanding that the AVO officers taken there under army guard after the massacre be handed over to them for summary justice. One of the two had died of his wounds overnight, but the lieutenant in command of the AVO detachment, József Stefko, was still alive and the demonstrators clamoured insistently for him to be brought out to them. Badly injured, he had received surgery the night before. For a while the surgeon, his wife, and a young factory worker who had volunteered to help with nursing at the small hospital, Flora Polz, tried to reason with the crowd. But they would not listen. Finally, the doctor gave in, shrugged his shoulders and, despite the entreaties of Flora Polz, handed his patient over to the crowd.

> A few minutes later . . . a stretcher carried by four men appeared out of a hut in the hospital grounds. On it lay Stefko, wearing a blue shirt. His legs were covered by a blanket. His head was bandaged. He was carried close enough for me to have touched him. He was fully conscious, and he knew quite well what was going to happen to him. His head turned wildly from side to side and there was spittle round his mouth. As the crowd saw the stretcher approaching they sent up a howl of derision and anger and hatred. They climbed the wire fence and spat at him and shouted 'murderer'. They pushed with all their might at the double gates, burst them open and surged in. The stretcher was flung to the ground, and the crowd was upon him, kicking and trampling him. Relations of those he had murdered were . . . foremost in this lynching. It was soon over. They took the body and hanged it by the ankles for a short time from one of the trees in Lenin Street. Ten minutes afterwards only a few people were left outside the hospital.[6]

Imre Nagy was still lagging at least twenty-four hours behind the revolution and his efforts to catch up were failing. At 11.18 a.m. he announced his new Cabinet. Out went some of the old guard – the young Hegedüs, the incompetent Piros and the ruthless Báta, who had wanted Hungarian troops to fire on demonstrators. They were replaced by Party hacks whose faces were less well known, but whose first loyalties would always be to toe Moscow's line. In came some reform-minded Communists, the respected philosopher György Lukács, for example, as Minister of Culture. The news that Imre Nagy, somewhat naively, hoped would stun the nation was the appointment of four non-Communists, two of them well-known figures from the past. If any of these names had been announced on the first day of the revolution, the public might have shown a modicum of interest. Now it was far too little, far too late.[7]

With 350 Soviet tanks on the Budapest streets, more than 325 Hungarian civilians dead and 2,200 already wounded in fighting against the Soviets, the public did not really care about a Cabinet reshuffle or that a former Social Democrat, József Bognár, had been made Minister for Foreign Trade.[8] The new government was stillborn. The list was too cautious, it still had too many *ancien régime* Communists, and its coalition aspect hardly looked convincing. Zoltán Tildy, the new Minister of State brought in as, effectively, Nagy's deputy, was the best-known figure, but not necessarily for the right reason. He did not possess the prestige and political weight that the Communists thought.

A former Calvinist pastor, aged sixty-seven, the shrewd, slim, elegant, silver-haired Tildy had been one of the leaders of the Smallholders Party after the war. He was President of Hungary between 1946 and 1948 while Rákosi was implementing the 'salami tactics' that brought the Communists to power. Tildy was remembered as a weak, indecisive man who did little to stand up to the Communists. While Tildy was President his son, Endre, a junior diplomat in Egypt, was recalled to the Foreign Ministry, arrested on bogus spying charges and executed, without, as far as anyone can establish, Tildy senior protesting against a murder in his own family. Tildy had been placed under house arrest in 1948 – the gentler side of Rákosi emerging with a comment that he had been so useful to the Communists that it seemed a pity to jail him. An impeccably dressed man who looked after his handsome appearance carefully, he had been freed just a few weeks previously. Nagy's reliance on Tildy, which would be revealed in coming days, was curious. József Kővagó, the former Mayor of Budapest who knew Tildy and his wife Maria well, met them at the Parliament building soon after he was named as a member of the new government. 'While we talked I wondered whether the two of them realised how unpopular they were with the people. Did they know that people were almost unanimous in disliking them and regarded Tildy as one of the traitors of the nation? I wondered if there was any way of telling them this and warning him that this time he should seize the helm of history with a firm hand otherwise the nation would never forgive him.'[9]

The other well-known name on the list was the only respected figure who the public could be sure was not compromised. Named as the new Agriculture Minister was Béla Kovács, the courageous and civilised Smallholder General Secretary who nine years earlier had been seized by Soviet soldiers, abducted and deported to a Siberian labour camp. He had returned to Hungary and been released from AVO imprisonment the previous April. Seriously ill with a heart condition, he had kept a low profile in Pécs, where he said the air was cleaner. His appointment was not what it seemed. When the bibulous and treacherous President, István Dobi, rang him to offer the job, Kovács initially accepted. Then, when he discovered the Communist Party hacks and has-beens who would be in the Cabinet with him, he called Nagy back, resigned and said he wanted nothing to do with the new government.[10]

The Interior Minister, Ferenc Münnich, was the most intriguing of the old Communists Nagy had brought back. Münnich was a plump sixty-nine-year-old who on the surface seemed like a grey, orthodox Marxist of the old school. In fact he was cheerful, witty, charming, a great raconteur in several languages, a heavy drinker, and a womaniser. A great survivor, his story paralleled the cause of communism in Europe in the twentieth century. 'I just have the good luck to be standing on the piece of soil where the bullets aren't landing,' he used to say.[11] In his early twenties he had been Béla Kun's personal secretary. He managed to escape with his boss to Russia when Horthy took over in 1919. He fought in Spain, and, with some bravery, on the Stalingrad Front. He had been in a battle unit with Khrushchev and he survived the purges unscathed. Without a doubt he was a KGB agent. After the war Münnich returned to Hungary with the other 'Muscovites' and was head of the Budapest police. Unlike most of the prudish Communist leaders of the country he caused a scandal by leaving his Russian wife for his secretary, thirty years his junior. Münnich had been a good friend of Nagy in their exile years in Moscow. Until two months earlier, the sharp, cigar-chomping Münnich had been Hungary's Ambassador to Moscow, and until ten days previously he was envoy to Yugoslavia. Nagy wanted him by his side helping to negotiate with the Russians and, in particular, dealing with the KGB's man on the spot, General Ivan Serov.[12]

Far from regaining the confidence of the public, let alone the bands of freedom fighters who believed they now had the power in Budapest, the new government was welcomed with jeers, a fresh wave of civil disobedience, a firmer strike call, and hundreds of protest telegrams.

The rebel radios in the provinces rejected Nagy's proffered compromises. In Miskolc, Földvári backed a statement rejecting the new government: 'We workers of Borsod County will continue with our strike until our demands are met.' From Pécs, from Győr, and in the afternoon again from Miskolc the rebels were saying the same thing: 'No, No, a thousand times No ... Imre Nagy should have the courage to get rid of politicians who can only lead with weapons used to suppress people.'[13]

The morning's calm was shattered at midday when a column of Soviet tanks and artillery moved towards the Kilián Barracks and the Corvin Passage. The Russians may have made some political concessions; they were now mounting a display to show that their military would make none at all. Maléter had organised a solid defence of the barracks. He had sent nearly all the 900 conscript engineers who were at the Kilián when he had arrived on Wednesday to other duties elsewhere in Budapest. Now he was left with fewer than 150 men, but they were all regular, trained soldiers. He had reinforcements among the insurgents at the Corvin Passage who were dotted around the neighbourhood ready to operate as snipers or to throw Molotov cocktails. He was in command of a few tanks – including one that was placed at the vast main gate of the building. Maléter could not believe, at first, that an assault against his stronghold was imminent. He rang the new Defence Minister, Károly Janza, a Stalinist like his predecessor. 'Is this how the government tries to make political concessions?' he said. 'If that's so I'll be forced to fire on the Russians.'[14]

The battle was the most furious of the revolution. It left both sides damaged. Russian shellfire destroyed most of the windows in the barracks, killed a score of Maléter's men and Corvin rebels and destroyed at least six buildings along the Boulevard and on Üllői Avenue. Maletér's gunners destroyed four tanks. The Corvin freedom fighters set fire to a lorry with supplies and disabled an armoured car. Half a dozen Russians were killed. The Soviets withdrew. Neither side emerged the winner, though, as always in the first few days of the revolution, each skirmish that the rebels survived was a victory of sorts that kept the Hungarians' morale alive. The battle left Maléter more committed to the revolution than ever. He said afterwards: 'For us, there is no choice. Either we win or we fall. There is no third possibility. We have confidence in Imre Nagy but we will not give up our arms except to Hungarian troops, and we will put ourselves immediately at the disposal of the new government if there is one truly worthy of the name.'[15]

The Russians were left licking their wounds. They were facing immense difficulties defeating the rebels in Budapest. The Soviet forces' second in command, Malaschenko, admitted later that 'doing our duty, maintaining order in Budapest, was beyond our power' at that stage. Like most military men explaining failure, he blamed the politicians. They tried to make his men fight with one hand behind their backs, he suggested. Nonetheless he did concede that not all his soldiers had the stomach for a fight in Hungary.[16]

Western journalists covering the revolution continually reported that there were mass Soviet desertions and Radio Free Europe repeatedly claimed that Soviet soldiers 'were showing what they think of communism, and of their Kremlin masters by defecting to the freedom fighters'. The Italian Ambassador to Hungary, Fabrizio Franco, wrote in his diary: 'The shelling and rifle fire in the streets reached a climax at 10.30 a.m. when it turned into a full-scale battle. We learned ... that Soviet tanks began fraternising with the rebels and a battle broke out between Russians on the Chain Bridge.'[17]

Bishop Péterfalvy, the Greek Orthodox prelate who had recently returned to Budapest after years of detention in a Siberian labour camp, said: 'I talked to a Soviet soldier who went over to the Hungarians. He sold his truck for three bottles of rum. Many Russians would have been happy to stay on in Hungary; many came to like it.'[18] The Bishop no doubt knew what he saw but there were hardly any defections. General Sharatin in the central Hungarian town of Kecskemét declared the neutrality of his men, as long as they were not attacked. He was one of very few officers to be disciplined on the Soviet side.[19] A Russian conscript of Hungarian origin, Matvey Janovich Lukacs, of the 32nd Mechanised Guard Division based in Békéscsaba, went absent without leave. However, he returned three days later, without boots or greatcoat and wearing Hungarian army trousers, and was sentenced to jail by a court martial.[20] Just fifty-nine Russian soldiers were reported missing after the revolution, a small figure for a military operation of such a size. It turned out later that nearly all of them had been killed.[21]

From the CIA station in Vienna, Peer de Silva reported back to the US his doubts about large-scale Soviet desertions, but his bosses did not like to hear. 'Headquarters was caught up in the fever of the times and became avid fans of this school of creative journalism. They bombarded me for information. When I explained in ... detail why there were no Soviet defectors I received peevish replies that I wasn't being aggressive enough.'[22]

Mikoyan and Suslov used the same phrases repeatedly in their telegrams back to the Kremlin. 'The soldiers' behaviour is impeccable; the mood is good.' However, Soviet officers were aware that their men were exhausted, tired, demoralised and hungry. Tank crews were supposed to 'live off the land', which was a real problem in a city where that meant getting food from shops and thereby becoming a target for urban guerrillas. Russian troops were seriously low on supplies, which partly explains their poor performance on the streets of Budapest. 'It is difficult to overestimate the part which the Russians' food shortage played in undermining their own morale and raising the hopes of the Hungarians,' said one military expert.[23]

The Hungarian army played a confusing role in the first few days of the revolution. There was still an ultra-hardliner at the top who wanted to join the Russians in crushing the rebellion. Mikoyan and Suslov insisted there had to be someone 'trustworthy', as they saw it, in charge.[24] The new Minister, the corpulent Lieutenant-General Károly Janza, continued to issue orders to his officers to 'liquidate the troublemakers' and threatened court martial to anyone who did not. But he knew he could not rely on his troops. Many, like Maléter, joined the insurgents, fought bravely and built reputations as heroes. 'Most of the army stayed in barracks,' as Béla Király, who later became Commander in Chief, said. 'On the whole it was left to each officer to make up his own mind what they would do, and usually they would carry their men with them. The army's attitude towards the revolution was a reflection of general popular sentiment in Hungary ... the army shared the anti-Communist and anti-Soviet feeling that dominated the country.'[25]

Not every soldier, though. The most senior Hungarian officer to fight against the rebels was a curious forty-four-year-old Moscow-trained Communist fanatic who during the revolution killed dozens of his own people in a consistent battle to restore the old order. Colonel-General Lajos Gyurkó commanded the 3rd Army Corps battalion based in Kecskemét. On the first day of the uprising he told Communist Party headquarters that he pledged to fight with full force 'to ensure that White Terror which followed the 1919 Soviet republic is not repeated'.

He threatened to execute any of the men under his command if they refused to obey orders. He was ruthless in trying to suppress the revolt. Two days earlier he had sent 150 troops onto the streets with orders to shoot at demonstrators planning a march. The protest was called off. A strikingly tall, good-looking figure, he was a popular leader, inspirational in his way, who commanded loyalty among his men, despite his politics. His men respected his decisive, straightforward character. That afternoon, at around 4 p.m., a crowd of 500 or so young people marched to the centre of a small township in central Hungary, Tisza-kecscke. They unfurled the new revolutionary flag, sang the national anthem and tore down any red stars they could see. Just as they reached the open ground in the main square a MiG fighter plane from the Hungarian army, under the orders of Colonel-General Gyurkó, strafed the demonstrators killing 17 and wounding 110. Later in the afternoon, he ordered low-altitude aerial attacks on two other towns when he heard trouble was brewing.*[26]

The US chargé d'affaires, Spencer Barnes, saw and heard much of the fighting. He had to face angry demonstrators outside the American Legation demanding some action from Washington. His deepest sympathies lay with the revolutionaries, and his assessment of America's interests was that the US should be much firmer in support of the insurgents. He wrote to his superiors in Washington urging a more visible policy. 'The Legation strongly believes ... that the US government should lead the case in the UN and use all its influence to mobilise world opinion.' He recommended considering giving material help to the Hungarian rebels. 'Some risk is warranted by the emergence of this tremendous revulsion against Soviet domination.'[27]

Eisenhower was averse to the risk. At 1 p.m. in New York the US, Britain and France formally asked the UN Security Council to discuss Hungary, where Soviet forces 'were violently repressing the rights of the people'. However, he was not intending to go further. He and Dulles spoke on the phone during the morning and agreed they still

* He might have expected a better career for himself after 1956, considering his loyalty. Early in 1957 he was appointed head of the training division at the Ministry of Defence, and from late 1957 until his dismissal in 1960, commander of the border guards. After that he was appointed manager of the Pig Fattening Station at Nagy-tétény and then worked in a filling station. He died in 1979.

knew too little about what was really happening in Hungary and could only guess at what the outcome of the uprising would be. Dulles warned the President against showing any enthusiastic support for Nagy. 'The Nagy government . . . contains a number of bad people, associated with the Molotov school,' he said. This was an important point. Nagy had a poor reputation in the US and the Americans never backed him. They viewed him as a Moscow-trained Communist, which he was. However, they failed to see beyond his rotund exterior or his apparent Party orthodoxy.[28]

The Secretary of State was about to fly to Dallas for his biggest campaign speech of the election and the President and Dulles went over the text. In particular, Eisenhower approved the crucial part of the speech on relations with the Soviet Union. 'Let me make this clear beyond a possibility of doubt,' Dulles would tell the Republican faithful in Texas later, in a passage that was clearly directed at the Soviet leaders in the Kremlin. 'The US has no ulterior purpose in desiring the independence of the satellite countries. Our unadulterated wish is that these people from whom so much of our national life derives, should have sovereignty restored to them and that they should have governments of their own choosing. We do not look upon these nations as potential military allies. We see them as friends and as part of a newly friendly and no longer divided Europe. We are confident that their independence . . . will contribute immensely to stabilize peace throughout all of Europe, West and East.' That was the most important message that Eisenhower wanted to send to Moscow. Over the next few days exactly the same words would be used by others in the administration so the Kremlin bosses could not misunderstand.[29]

Late into the evening Nagy was debating in his Academy Street office with his closest advisers, Losonczy, Donáth, his secretary József Szilágyi and some of the journalists who had been in his opposition group during his time in the wilderness. Tildy was there too as a newcomer, but a figure whom Nagy seemed instinctively to trust. Nagy had finally made up his mind that trying to steer the middle course, his plan for the last five days, was not working. He had tried, as he kept putting it, to be a 'bridge' between the revolutionary groups and the various Party factions. They walked right over him but never met on the same side.

He had persuaded some of his supporters to try to campaign for the new government. The line they were encouraged to take was this: now the Nagy Cabinet was in place there was no reason to continue fighting. Gyula Háy, a popular figure among young people and one of the intellectual inspirations of the revolution, said on radio in the evening: 'There must be a changeover to peaceful methods without the slightest delay. The armed struggle must stop immediately. Even peaceful demonstrations are not suitable at this time because they can be mis-construed.'[30] It became obvious within hours that the time had long passed for appeals for restraint. Háy was ignored, like others. 'Writers and intellectuals became irrelevant during the revolution at the moment the first shots were fired.'[31]

From Győr, the increasingly influential Szigetthy was garnering more radical backing. He said that evening: 'Though Nagy has the nation's support, that is not enough. Soviet guns are still active in Budapest. The people have spoken their judgment with arms in hand and the Soviet troops should be sent home.'[32] Other rebels increased their demands further. Some were already calling for Hungarian withdrawal from the Warsaw Pact and an immediate declaration of neutrality. Nagy's hope was to persuade Mikoyan and Suslov to agree to a ceasefire. Without that, he could not convince the freedom fighters that the Soviets would at least withdraw their troops from frontline action as a first step. He thought that at least he had a good chance of pulling that off. Far more difficult would be to explain his more significant decision. Nagy, the loyal Communist, had decided to accept nearly all the insur-gents' demands. He was not going to follow the revolution any longer. He would try to lead it.[33]

Towards midnight Nagy met the two Soviet emissaries, who had now been in Budapest for four days with little to show for their efforts. They had reached a stalemate in political and military operations. Nagy, however, had acquired an ally, or at least an apparent ally. For the first time, the previously unassuming Party chief, János Kádár, emerged as a significant player in the events. In and out of various governments and Party roles, Kádár was best known as an organised and efficient apparatchik who had survived through the tactful method of keeping silent as often as possible. Nagy used to say 'Kádár was born sitting on the fence'.[34] But now Kádár began to impress the two Soviets, par-ticularly Mikoyan. Kádár, like Nagy, made a forceful plea for a ceasefire but then he argued with vigour for a political deal that he thought might work if the extremists from both sides were effectively sidelined.

Once the fighting was over, he wanted to disband the loathed AVO. He wanted to discuss the long-term future of the Soviet troops in Hungary. He proposed an amnesty for all the revolutionaries who had fought over the last few days. For Nagy this seemed like vital support at a vital time. They were not friends; but the main thing from Nagy's point of view was that a sensible and credible voice, from a senior position in the Hungarian Party, was calling for a moderate arrangement that it would humiliate neither side to accept.

It took just a few minutes, and Kádár did most of the talking, but the bones of a deal were agreed shortly after midnight. There were two hurdles. One, which Kádár and Nagy were told about, was that Khrushchev had to agree. They would get a reply from the Kremlin midway through the following morning. The other was not mentioned to the two Hungarians. The Soviets had a plan to try one large assault against the armed rebels first in an attempt to gain a military victory.

TWENTY-FOUR
Sunday, 28 October

Imre Nagy was woken just before 6 a.m. by a frantic telephone call from Géza Losonczy. He was told that the Soviets, along with a few elements of the Hungarian army still loyal to the old order, were planning a massive attack on the main rebel strongholds to crush the revolution once and for all. 'It would be disaster, ruin, if this happened,' the emotional Losonczy said. It would mean the end of everything that they had worked for over the last years, not just the past days. 'Uncle Imre, you must stop it.'[1] For a man who survived so long among the Stalinist snake-pits, Imre Nagy could on occasion be extraordinarily credulous. He knew that a possible assault on the insurgents had been discussed by senior Red Army officers and the Hungarian 'military committee' of discredited generals thought loyal to Moscow. However, he thought − as did Kádár − that just a few hours earlier, at their late-night summit, he had reached a political deal with the Kremlin representatives and the planned attack had been called off.

Then he had the news confirmed. A column of more than fifty Russian tanks was moving into position along the Boulevard, with additional field guns and extra ammunition, in a show of force through the centre of Budapest. The idea was to wipe out the resistance at the two fortresses of national independence, at the Kilián Barracks and the Corvin Passage. There were also secondary targets planned for other small pockets of rebel fighters at Boráros Square, near the Western Railway Station, and at Tüzoltó Street, near the National Museum. The Russians were convinced that if one or two of these strongholds fell, the Hungarians' spirit would wilt, they would abandon hope, and the rebellion would simply melt away.[2]

Moments after speaking to Losonczy, the Defence Minister Janza sought Nagy's approval for the attack. Janza, who had spent long years at military training schools in the Soviet Union, said it was important that Hungarian soldiers took an active part in 'restoring order' in

Budapest.[3] Nagy was appalled. 'I forbid this absolutely,' he said. 'Do not shoot at the apartment blocks as it would create a very difficult situation. Do not carry the plan out in this way. Avoid mass bloodshed. I'm afraid of the consequences. I will resign as Prime Minister if this idea goes ahead. I will not act as political cover for a massacre. Uncounted numbers of civilians could die. Other methods must be used.'[4]

The Hungarian soldiers were unwilling to take part in the operation, but at dawn, under extreme pressure from their superior officers, it looked at first as though they might be forced to obey. Janza told his Chief of Staff, László Tóth, at least to try to get as many of his men as possible to join in the assault. Tóth had always been a loyalist of the old regime. He was convinced that eventually the Russians would prevail against any real challenge posed by the rebels. Yet even he raised serious doubts now. He told the Minister: 'This is a completely unprepared operation which risks the lives of the men at stake and has no hope of success.'[5] Colonel András Márton, head of the élite Zrinyi Military Academy and one of the most skilled officers in the Hungarian army, was ordered to comply instead. He too refused: 'I will not lead units to the slaughterhouse even if they string me up,' he said. 'This type of operation, involving the destruction of soldiers and civilians, would mean a massacre and has to be avoided at all costs.' No Hungarian troops took part.[6]

The Russians were left in a dilemma, which they made worse for themselves by vacillating. Their tanks were almost within shooting distance of their main targets, but the guns remained silent while desperate negotiations began. Nagy spoke to the Russian Ambassador, Andropov, at about 6.30 a.m. and soon afterwards to Mikoyan. Then, a few minutes later, he spoke to Khrushchev. Nagy repeated his threats to resign if a major attack on the insurgents was launched.[7] He said he would not be responsible for the slaughter that could ensue if the attack went ahead.[8] Khrushchev was cmollient and assured the Hungarian that there was no need for a dramatic gesture like resignation, 'which would make matters worse'.[9] The Soviets could not afford to lose Nagy. He was their only hope for any kind of peaceful settlement, and they knew it. The Russians, however, had no clear strategy and continually sent contradictory and confusing signals. They knew they were not prepared to let Hungary leave the Soviet camp, but they had no idea how far they were willing to go to reach a compromise.

Mikoyan and Khrushchev wanted to devise a Polish-style deal that would keep the essence of Soviet rule, allow a little more independence for Hungary and would hold out the prospect at some point of Russian troops withdrawing. Suslov was immediately ordered back to Moscow, at dawn, to provide a first-hand report from the Budapest front line.[10]

Along with the talk of political compromise the soldiers were making odd moves that were difficult to explain in military terms. They did not, as expected, call a complete halt to the blitz they were planning. But they withdrew more than a third of their force, launched a half-hearted attack, and in a furious two-hour battle with Maléter's men lost three tanks and a huge amount of prestige. Beaten, they withdrew and agreed to the ceasefire. Suing for peace came hard to the Russians. Laschenko, the commander of the Soviets' Special Corps in Hungary, and his number two, Lieutenant-General Malaschenko, blamed the Hungarian army for refusing to fight and the Hungarian Communists for lacking the will to stay in control. They did not have enough force on the ground, said Malaschenko. 'The Hungarian government gave us many contradictory requests, essentially asking that our troops not shoot, not pursue active operations yet carry out the task at hand,' he said.[11]

There were good reasons for the Russian failure to crush the revolution. The main one was that they did not have a clear aim beyond policing a city of more than 1.5 million inhabitants, almost every one of whom wanted to see the Soviets leave.[12] No excuses could hide the embarrassment of the Russian military commanders, relieved though the soldiers were by the ceasefire. The troops had been through an ordeal. By now around 500 had been killed.[13] They were exhausted and hungry and needed a rest. The first chill of winter had arrived and they were cold. As the Soviets retreated, they couldn't even risk burying their dead, as snipers aimed at any Russian soldier who dared put his head out of a tank's turret. The bodies of Soviet soldiers simply lay where they had fallen and were later covered with lime.

The Hungarians, on this Sunday, were taking part in moving funerals throughout the day which swelled the emotion of the uprising, giving the rebels renewed impetus. Just a few days earlier it would have seemed inconceivable that the world's second superpower could be so completely humbled by bands of ill-armed, untrained amateur fighters, many of them in their teens. The revolution caught the imagination of the world. Throughout the Western capitals there were demonstrations in support of the plucky Hungarians who had the courage to challenge the Soviet Union.

The Soviet magnates needed a way out of the Hungarian impasse. The uprising was the biggest threat they had yet faced to the empire they had won little more than a decade earlier. The air of crisis in the Kremlin was palpable. True to form, their first instinct was to squabble amongst themselves and blame each other for 'a capitulation' in Budapest.

Khrushchev had told Nagy early in the morning, in his cheery, expansive style, full of bonhomie, not to worry. The ceasefire would hold from the Russian side, he insisted, and he issued an order to the military commanders to make sure that it did. Despite the commitment he had given, though, he needed the other Soviet leaders to agree, which was not a foregone conclusion. The serious splits and personal rivalries in Moscow made decision-making a protracted business of elaborate horse-trading. The Soviet potentates finally agreed to the ceasefire in Budapest after a bruising encounter of several hours – starting at noon and interrupted by calls to Mikoyan in Budapest.

The divisions that initially emerged the day Stalin died had deepened and with the stakes so high the discussions grew bitter. The hardliners began the attack. Voroshilov, invariably still dressed in a uniform covered with medals, blamed the two emissaries who had been sent five days earlier to Budapest – but particularly his sworn enemy Mikoyan – for the 'bad situation' in Hungary. 'They are poorly informed. Mikoyan cannot carry out his work ... We acted correctly when we sent in the troops. We should be in no hurry to pull them out. We should not withdraw but act decisively.'[14] Molotov brooded and was itching to make a move to destabilise Khrushchev at the first available opportunity: 'Things are falling apart in Hungary,' he said. 'Mikoyan and Suslov are providing calm and reassurances while things have deteriorated badly. Nagy is actually speaking against us.' Kaganovich was simple, direct and predictably unimaginative: 'Firm action is needed against the centres of resistance. We cannot retreat.'

Then the moderates weighed in. Marshal Zhukov, who was all in favour of sending in troops a few days earlier, was now far more conciliatory. 'It's unfair to criticise Mikoyan right now. The situation has unfolded quite differently than we thought when we decided to send in the troops. We must display political flexibility. We should

keep the troops on full readiness . . . but [also] the question of a troop
withdrawal from Hungary must be considered. In Budapest we must
pull troops off the streets in some areas.' At this Voroshilov flared up.
His criticism became harsher: 'The American secret services are more
active in Hungary than comrades Suslov and Mikoyan are. We sent
them there for nothing.'

Khrushchev quietened him down and reminded him that they should
focus on what to do next, rather than make recriminations about the
past. But he continued to bristle. Nikolai Bulganin, dapper with a
goatee beard, saw himself as the 'moderate' candidate to take over if
Khrushchev fell. He wondered what would happen if they allowed the
new Hungarian government to crumble. For the time being, he said,
they should support Nagy and Kádár: 'Otherwise we'll have to undertake an occupation. This will drag us into a dubious enterprise.'

Suslov, summoned back urgently from Budapest, arrived direct from
the airport halfway through the agonised discussion. His voice, as an
inflexible Stalinist who knew Hungary and the other satellite states
well, was highly influential. He surprised everybody by pleading
strongly to give Nagy more time to form a stable government, as long
as it remained essentially a Communist government. 'The popular view
of our troops now is bad and has got worse' because of the Parliament
Square massacre, he said. 'There is no alternative to supporting Nagy.
We must.'

Khrushchev had gnawing second thoughts about having intervened
with troops in the first place and wanted to avoid doing so again. 'We
will have a lot to answer for if we don't face facts. Will we have a
government in Hungary that is with us, or one that . . . is against us,
and will ask us to pull the troops out of Hungary altogether. What
then? . . . Capitulation? There is no firm leadership there in Budapest.
The uprising has spread into the provinces. Their troops may go over
to the rebels.' He said they faced a series of grim choices but as long as
they did not make too many concessions there was a chance of 'holding
the line'. 'They must not go too far. We will go along with the ceasefire,
but we must not foster illusions. We are saving face.'

He ended with an intriguing comment. He seemed to know about an
imminent attack on Egypt and could see an opportunity in it. 'Politically this is beneficial to us. The English and French are in a real mess
in Egypt. We shouldn't get caught in the same company.'[15]

*

The ceasefire was announced on the radio at 1.20 p.m. – to muted celebrations at first. People were unsure if the truce would hold. Yet this was the day when the revolution became far more straightforward and Nagy's role, confused and opaque over the last five days, much clearer. Again he acted at least a day too late, but now Nagy embraced the revolution. He was a reluctant hero, but his reputation as an inspirational leader who would sacrifice all for the cause of freedom rested on his actions from now onwards.

Nagy met Mikoyan at about the time the truce was declared. He demanded from the Armenian a much freer hand to deal with the Stalinist leftovers still hanging around the Academy Street head-quarters of the Communist Party. Mikoyan agreed. Within a few hours the detested and most compromised members of the old regime – including Ernő Gerő, the one-time Interior Minister László Piros and the former Defence Minister István Bata – were put on a plane to Moscow, with barely enough time to pack. That was a sweet victory for Nagy.[16] Then the two of them went over the details of the address Nagy was planning to make later in the evening, which he described as the most important speech of his life. Again Mikoyan seemed content and assured the Hungarian leader that Moscow had confidence in him and the Kremlin leaders would back him.

The Soviets were careful to tie up another important loose end. When on 23 October Gerő had asked for Russian troops to be sent to Budapest, Khrushchev agreed on condition that the Hungarians for-mally put the request in writing. Nothing had been received by the Soviet government, which now wanted the matter settled. The full details of who signed the letter were only recently clarified when Soviet archives were opened.[17] The Russians were being careful about the issue of who asked for the troops to be despatched – and when – because the UN Security Council was due to discuss Hungary soon. If there was no formal request, the Soviets were acting illegally as an aggressor. This was more than a legal nicety. It could have been highly embarrassing to the Soviets in public relations terms. The steely Soviet Ambassador, Andropov, was beginning to play a vital role in sup-pressing the revolution. He was ordered to deal with the relatively minor, but potentially tricky, matter of the missing letter.

The tall, silver-haired, piercingly blue-eyed Andropov, who seemed to shuffle rather than walk, was an enigmatic figure who elicited widely mixed responses. He was picked out from his early teens as a high-flying functionary and educated at the most élite Communist Party schools and colleges. At first, diplomatic work, especially in a satellite country like Hungary, seemed a backwater to an ambitious, fast-tracked apparatchik. However, he was working his way back upwards after an uncomfortable obstacle had briefly blocked his path. He had been Second Secretary at the Karelian Finnish Republic in Petrozavodsk, and all was looking good in his career trajectory. Then in 1950 his immediate boss and mentor Gennady Krupnarev was arrested and charged with financial mismanagement and incompetence. Andropov was tainted by association. He was moved to a junior job at the Central Committee secretariat in Moscow and slowly earned rehabilitation. Despatched to Budapest in 1954, initially as First Secretary, he took over as Ambassador within a few months.[18]

He and his wife Tatiana were fairly popular in Budapest. Andropov learned Hungarian, his son Igor and daughter Irma went to local schools and they made friends with Hungarian children. He travelled widely in the country. The family took holidays in the Hungarian 'Riviera' at Lake Balaton. He cut quite a dash as Ambassador. The head of Budapest's police force, Sándor Kopácsi, recalled that at formal receptions Andropov would summon the police band's gypsy orchestra and would sing in a good tenor. He liked nostalgic songs – his favourite Hungarian tune was a ballad about a crane that lost its lifelong mate and flew off, wandering above distant lands. He enjoyed flirting with women, including Kopácsi's beautiful, raven-haired wife, Ibolya.[19]

Andropov seemed to present himself as a reformer, yet it was hard to understand on what basis. Unlike his predecessor, Kisilev, and apparently contrary to instructions from Moscow, he backed Rákosi against Imre Nagy. He respected Nagy neither politically nor personally.

The first thing most people noticed about him was that his face wore a permanent smile that made it even more inscrutable. He was a sharp dresser, a considerate host, and had impeccable manners. 'He was not a Russian bumpkin but a Soviet dandy.'[20] He never appeared to raise his voice. He seemed tolerant and liberal-minded, a new breed of Soviet official, not a hardliner, nor a harsh colonialist, entirely different from the type that Hungarians had been accustomed to receiving. Even some Hungarian radicals came away believing Andropov was on their side.[21] However, Miklós Vásárhelyi, who would soon regain his old job as Imre Nagy's press adviser, was not fooled. To him Andropov seemed a brooding presence. 'Andropov was taciturn and reserved. He was very disciplined and not talkative at all, not like his predecessor Kisilev who was very much a man of the world. He did not gossip, in a very gossipy town.'[22]

In the last days of the uprising, he was the Kremlin's eyes and ears. As Khrushchev said later, for a short period after the ceasefire, Andropov was the man who single-handedly replaced the Soviet army as the gatherer of intelligence on Budapest.[23] Andropov began his delicate mission about the request for Soviet military help by trying to persuade Nagy to sign a backdated letter asking the USSR 'to send Soviet troops in order to put an end to the riots . . . in Budapest . . . and to restore order as soon as possible'. Nagy refused firmly. He said he had not been Prime Minister when the request was made. Andropov found a willing accomplice, however. He convinced the hated Hegedüs, the minion of Gerő and Rákosi, to sign the letter, five days after the first Soviet troops arrived in Budapest, but dated 24 October.[24]*

President Eisenhower went to elaborate lengths to avoid a confrontation with the Soviets over Hungary. If Ike had ever believed in 'rolling back communism' or 'liberating captive peoples' – which was doubtful – he had lost faith some time earlier. John Foster Dulles had been a believer, but he was absolutely loyal to the President and would never have intrigued for a more muscular approach against Ike's wishes.

There was nothing dishonourable about the Eisenhower policy. Quite the opposite; it was eminently sensible and the President would have followed the same path if the Hungarian crisis had begun a few days after the election, not a few days before. Yet the administration stood accused of deep cynicism. One of Ike's great admirers recognised it as a blot on his fine reputation:

> The spontaneous events in Hungary were unpredictable but nevertheless they had long been expected. At least from the rhetoric. In the administration it had been an article of faith that sooner or later the captive people would rise up against their masters. The US had antici-

---

* After fifteen years as head of the KGB, Andropov finally made it to the top in November 1982 when he succeeded Brezhnev as general secretary of the Soviet Communist Party. He was already an ill man with serious kidney disease and survived a mere fifteen months in absolute power.

pated a revolt, and encouraged it, but when the revolt came they had no plans prepared. There was nothing they could do – look at the map, there was no trade to speak of between Russia and the US, so they couldn't use that to bargain with. There was nothing except appealing to the court of world opinion that Eisenhower could bring to bear on the USSR in Hungary. The President knew it, had known it all along which made all the Republican talk over the last four years of 'liberation' so hypocritical.[25]

The President and his men remained for ever in denial about their role in the Hungarian Revolution. But there can be no doubt that official America cheered on the revolutionaries to continue fighting – and to trust in US backing – when it was well known in Washington that the Hungarians would receive no material help.

Much of the encouragement came from Radio Free Europe, heard regularly during the uprising by upwards of 80 per cent of the Hungarian population. Each day the CIA controllers of the station in Park Avenue, New York, sent a series of instructions, 'policy lines to follow', to the editorial offices in Munich. For the first few days of the revolution Washington was trying to find out exactly what was happening in Budapest. RFE's broadcasts stuck on the whole to factual reporting and moderate, carefully worded commentaries. That changed from early on the day of the ceasefire, almost as though the broadcasters did not want the truce to hold. Very few recordings of RFE broadcasts during the revolution exist – and even fewer transcripts. But some that survive show a bellicose tone that urges the freedom fighters on.[26]

The most incendiary were talks by two Hungarian émigrés, calling themselves 'military advisers', providing detailed hints on partisan fighting. One, by a former Hungarian soldier, Gyula Litterati-Lootz, explained exactly how to make a Molotov cocktail, recommended ways to disable Soviet T34 tanks by throwing grenades into their turrets, and provided a guide for designing home-grown landmines with small amounts of explosives.[27] The other, by Julian Borsanyi, could not have been a clearer rallying cry for the freedom fighters to ignore the ceasefire. He said there were fewer Soviet troops in Hungary than most people in the country supposed and the rebels had a better chance of 'victory' than expected. 'Two Soviet divisions and a part of a third were stationed in Hungary, altogether approximately 25,000 men. It is true that these are armoured divisions, but we cannot talk about overpowering force. The Hungarian People's Army had about 100,000 soldiers on active duty two weeks ago. If only a third of them take an active part in the fighting, numerical equality would be re-established.' He went on to describe fighting against partisans as a regular army officer during the war. 'They [the guerrillas] made us believe they were in places they were not, that they were strong where they had no strength at all and attacked ... where they were not expected. That was the secret of their success. It was not by a supremacy of arms or numbers.'[28]

All these talks received the approval of senior CIA officers who were monitoring Radio Free Europe. The station did its best to undermine Nagy. Listeners were reminded of his background as a loyal Comrade who had spoken the eulogy in the Hungarian Parliament on Stalin's death. To the CIA he did not seem a 'national' Communist like Tito, who had managed to follow a line of his own for several years, or even Gomulka in Poland, who maintained as much independence as he could while staying firmly in the Communist bloc. Washington remembered that Nagy spoke and wrote often like an orthodox Marxist against 'American imperialism'. On 14 November 1954, during his first term as Prime Minister, he denounced the CIA's propaganda campaign of dropping balloons on Hungary bearing uplifting messages: 'Neither news without foundation, nor the balloons that constitute the subject of humour and jokes have been able to mislead our people. Of course our enemies have not buried the war hatchet, and we must be on the alert, because, as the saying goes, the Devil never sleeps.'

Washington saw no reason to give political aid and succour to Imre Nagy, which was a political decision with major consequences for Hungary. If his political fortunes had been bolstered by a few even vaguely supportive signs from the Eisenhower administration, the revolution might have travelled along a different path.

During the evening an RFE commentary piece specifically denounced the truce: 'Imre Nagy and his supporters want to revise the Trojan horse episode. They need a ceasefire so that the present government in power in Budapest can maintain its position as long as possible. Those who are fighting for liberty must not lose sight even for a minute of the plans of the government opposing them. Otherwise there will be a repetition of the Trojan horse tragedy.'[29] Another commentary ratcheted up the tension: 'Now is the time to concentrate every effort on ensuring that the victory in war continues as a victory in peace as well. The sacrifice of so many of our brave young men in rising against Soviet tyranny must not have been in vain. A political victory must follow an armed victory.'[30]

If the insurgents thought they had the US on their side, they might have acted differently had they heard the telephone conversation between Ike and his Secretary of State at 8 a.m. Washington time. Dulles, in optimistic mood, called the President. He was pleased with the way his speech had gone down in Texas the night before; and overnight the news from Budapest and the Middle East was better than he had expected. 'On Hungary and on Suez at least we have gained twenty-four hours,' he said. Eisenhower was far less sanguine. He was by now sure that an attack on Suez was imminent, although he did not know exactly when, and he wanted more substantial achievements in Hungary.

'The Russians might be willing to talk sense now, more than at any time since this Administration has been in power,' the President said. 'We could say that things are not going the way any of us wants, better have a meeting that recognises these points.'

Dulles suggested there was confusion in the Kremlin: 'Undoubtedly there's a battle on in the Presidium ... some of the people probably want to go back to the old Stalinist policies ... but it's now too late. They are up against a tough problem.'

Eisenhower said: 'I agree. We should take advantage of it. Now is the time to talk more [with them] about reducing tensions in the world.'

Dulles ended with a prescient point about talking to the Russians at this stage: 'We would have to be very careful not to do anything that would look to the satellite world as though we were selling them out.'[31]

TWENTY-FIVE

Monday, 29 October

The ceasefire held – more or less. There was minor skirmishing in the city, but nothing of the intensity of the last five days. At dawn the Russians announced that their troops would withdraw from Budapest. The belief spread throughout the city that the Hungarians had won a victory. It had been expensive. By the time the ceasefire was declared around 1,000 Hungarians and more than 500 Soviet soldiers had died. The devastation was overwhelming in small and confined parts of central Budapest, but elsewhere the capital looked unaffected, as though a violent revolution had never happened. People could walk the streets safely, the food shops were open. One of the first things the new government did, under the direction of the moustached Marxist economist Zoltán Vas, was to halt food exports. The shops in Budapest were bulging with meat and fresh vegetables that most people in Budapest had not seen for years. Aid flights with medical supplies, especially blood plasma, were arriving regularly, initially from the Eastern bloc countries, but now the Soviets allowed aid from the West.[1]

One of the miracles of the city over the last week was the efficiency and capacity of the telephone exchanges. Most people had been restricted to their homes, and, emboldened by the belief that the secret police had other things on their minds and were too busy to monitor phone traffic, the population spent their time on the phone. The lines never went dead. A study among refugees later suggested that on average people had made between 300 and 400 calls in thirteen days – 'Did you hear that explosion at the City Park', 'Can it be true the Russians are going?', 'They have goose liver at the közert' (grocery), 'Do you still love me?'. Life had been lived holding a telephone. Now, on a cool but bright morning, friends and acquaintances met at the eszpressos to discuss news.[2] 'This period was completely unreal,' recalled Ágnes Gergely, then a twenty-two-year-old student teacher, who became one of Hungary's most distinguished poets. 'I was young and politically naive, I know that. But more experienced people, even those who thought they really knew what was going on, felt the same. We really thought we had got away with it, at least for a while.'[3]

At 9 a.m. Imre Nagy left the Communist Party headquarters for the first time in six days. In a symbolic gesture he moved his office into the Parliament building. Nagy had not abandoned communism, but as his great supporter, Tibor Meray, explained, he was trying to show Hungarians that he was making a fresh start. He told his chauffeur to drive on ahead and he began to walk the 400 metres or so through the streets of Budapest. He frowned as he picked his way through the rubble and shards of broken glass, but he wore his usual smile and appeared his calm, avuncular self when he was recognised by passers-by near Kossuth Bridge. He smiled through a barrage of questions about the future and when the Russians would leave. Then a woman addressed him: 'It is good to see you Comrade Nagy. Everyone was saying you are a prisoner.' He smiled more broadly and opened his arms wide. 'You see how much I am a prisoner.' A man in working clothes asked what was going to happen. 'Go back to your work, Comrade, and have no fear,' he said. 'Return to your work . . . everything will be arranged in the end.'[4]

The most urgent task in Nagy's eyes was to restore order as soon as possible. There were thousands of guns in the hands of the revolutionaries. As the morning wore on a few isolated shots were heard across the city − nothing compared to the ferocity of the fighting over the last few days, but the danger was that the Soviet troops could again become engaged and Budapest would erupt once more. Mikoyan, still in Budapest, was constantly reminding Nagy that the Soviets would not stand for any continued fighting from the rebels or by the Hungarian army. The only way Nagy could maintain Kremlin support was for the ceasefire to be tightly enforced. The revolutionaries had to be persuaded to lay down their arms and the workers to return to work. Otherwise the Soviets would not believe the concessions they had made were worthwhile and the Red Army would come back in force.[5]

His strategy was to entice the rebels themselves into peacekeeping. Sándor Kopácsi, who joined the revolutionaries on the first day, was put in charge of setting up a new, unified 'National Guard' of police, insurgents and the army, who in theory all had a stake in making sure that fighting would not start again. He chose as commander a dynamic soldier, Major-General Béla Király.

Tall, fair-haired, with wide, generous lips, Király, forty-three, had the brooding good looks of a war hero. He had been one of Hungary's best-known officers after the war, but he had disappeared into Rákosi's gulag and most people had assumed that he was dead.[6] He had a meteoric career. A Colonel aged just thirty-two, he was aide-de-camp to one of the last of the fascist Defence Ministers. He had married the foster daughter of Gyula Gömbös, one of Admiral Horthy's Prime Ministers, but the marriage did not last long. Towards the end of the war he deserted to the Russians with 8,000 troops utterly loyal to him and offered to fight the Germans. He and his men performed with outstanding valour. Promotion followed swiftly after the war ended. He was Commander in Chief of Hungary's land forces before 1946. Although he became a member of the Communist Party, he joined simply out of expediency. Király was never convincing as a member, though. At the end of 1948, he was given a less visible job as commandant of the Army Academy.

It came as no surprise when he was arrested in August 1951, at the height of the purges in the army. He was sentenced to death on the usual trumped-up treason charges, but the sentence was commuted to life imprisonment. He was not released when Nagy was Prime Minister for the first time. If that rankled with him he did not show it. When he was finally released, in the middle of August 1956, after a tough ordeal in prison he had sustained a serious leg wound and required urgent medical treatment.[7] Király had met Nagy a few times before he was jailed, although they did not know each other well. He was friendly, however, with Nagy's son-in-law and most trusted confidant, the former army officer Ferenc Jánosi, and he knew some of the other figures in Nagy's circle. At the Rajk funeral in early October, Király briefly spoke to Nagy, whose parting words to him were: 'I know you are undergoing treatment in hospital now. After you have recovered get in touch with me. You are needed.'[8]

From his hospital bed on the morning of 29 October, still in some pain, he wrote to Jánosi: 'I am overwhelmed with bitterness when I think that I should stay out of work like this which is so close to my heart. Through you I offer my strength, my enthusiasm and my sympathy to Imre Nagy and his government. I believe you know that it is not the position or the glory that I crave but the task ... I believe that my place is on the Ministry of Defence chief's General Staff.'[9] Before Jánosi had received the letter, Király had already been asked by Kopácsi to take charge of the National Guard. He was met at the hospital by an escort of three armed revolutionaries, donned one of his old uniforms and was driven to Budapest police head-quarters.

Between them, the stocky policeman and the lean soldier had to find ways of persuading the freedom fighters to throw in their lot with Nagy and the government. That would be no easy task. Kopácsi had already met some leaders of the rebel groups and was worried. Far from talking peace, they were maximising their demands. To complicate matters further, just as the Russians promised to leave, the revo-lutionaries split into rival groups, arguing, and in some extreme cases fighting, amongst themselves.[10]

There was some good news, however. Maléter placed his immense reputation unequivocally behind the government. 'We trust the pro-visional government,' he declared to the bruised and battered Prime Minister's relief. 'And we shall support it to the hilt because it is trying to restore peace and order in our country. We know Imre Nagy and Zoltán Tildy ... represent the people. The freedom fighters, heroes of the armed struggle, will keep calm. I appeal to the people of Budapest to keep calm too and not permit anyone to foment trouble. Do not think we are not socialists, because we are. This is not a rising by capitalists bent on restoring the old order of things. Its purpose is to liberate Hungary, and to restore to the Hungarian people their freedom.'[11]

Some bizarre characters played significant parts in the uprising, for a short while. The most curious was undoubtedly József Dudás, who early on Monday afternoon led a group of around 150 insurgents into the offices of *A Free People* and occupied it until the end of the revolu-tion. His flame flickered, brightly, before burning out dramatically. Short, chubby, and with a jutting jaw, he did not look a prepossessing figure, yet he was a man of extraordinary chutzpah.[12]

Unlike his associate 'Uncle' Szabó, forty-three-year-old Dudás did not take part in much fighting, yet he had a reputation as a warrior. He appointed himself head of a body he called the National Revolutionary Committee, although he represented nobody except his own group of followers. His great ability was an enormous flair for publicity and for making grand theatrical gestures. He was eccentric. He wore an old-fashioned Tyrolean hat with a feather in it, and a coat draped over himself like a cloak. He always had a gun in his belt, but there is no evidence that he used it in the revolution.

Western journalists who interviewed Dudás presented him as one of the main rebel leaders guiding and inspiring the uprising. He had tremendous braggadocio, but his real influence was debatable. He published a newspaper, *Hungarian Independence (Magyar Függetlenség)*, a four-page sheet with snippets of news but mostly containing the thoughts, often contradictory, of József Dudás. He was articulate in a simple, direct way and people took him at his own estimation. He was made for stirring times and caused enormous trouble for Nagy as his noisiest revolutionary opponent. The Russians believed the legends around him as one of the 'chief counter-revolutionary fascist villains'. It was the government's inability to silence Dudás and the other rebel leaders and strip them of their arms which made the Russians lose faith in any kind of 'Polish-style' solution for Hungary.[13]

Dudás, born in Transylvania, spent nearly a quarter of his life in various prisons. He trained as a tool-fitter and was jailed for seven years in Romania for illegal membership of the Communist Party in the 1930s. He spent two years in manacles and chains after an attempted escape. He arrived in Hungary in 1941 and joined the anti-fascist underground. In 1944 he took part, as a member of the resistance, in the abortive talks between the Soviets and the Horthy administration which had tried to bring an early armistice.[14]

After 1945 he vociferously opposed Moscow's domination of the Hungarian Communist Party. Typically, this was a hopeless cause. There could have been only one result from a conflict with the 'Muscovites'. Dudás quit the Communist Party and the next year, 1949, was jailed for organising 'a counter-revolutionary plot to overthrow the regime'. He was sent to the Recsk penal colony, where survival was hard. He enjoyed tremendous popularity amongst the inmates, for his personal qualities of courage and spirit. He was released in 1954 and went back to work as a fitter in a factory. When the revolution began he led a small band of rebels – most of whom worked with him – to the barricades at Széna Square, along with 'Uncle' Szabó, and later at nearby Zsigmond Móricz Square.[15] He became known for his revolutionary exploits, however, only when he took over the offices of *A Free People*.

He was described by Tamás Aczél, who met him, as 'just a petty *condottiere*'. Another witness claimed that Dudás, 'an adventurer', had a room at his headquarters specially for torturing AVO officers; yet another, that Dudás sat behind a desk piled with heaps of cash his followers had robbed from a bank. But all these legends were discounted by members of his rebel band. He made a lot of noise but was moderate in action and handed over any prisoners he took to the police under Sándor Kopácsi.[16]

His friend, former cellmate and 'political adviser' for a few days, the young lawyer George Gábori, said there was much debate about Dudás's views. He quotes him as saying: 'I've been everything politically, a Communist, a Smallholder, you name it. I don't think in those terms any more. So I'm shooting the bastards and trying to defend the decent people. We're likelier to get somewhere that way.'[17] Dudás was aware that there were some accusations of anti-Semitism within the insurgents. He wanted to stop it wherever it surfaced among his men: 'In a situation like this one doesn't have the time to screen recruits,' he said. 'Some of these bandits may be raving anti-Semites ... The first case I see I'll blow the bastard's brains out.'[18]

Dudás was in many ways preposterous, but he was not totally mad. It was said that he saw the revolution as an opportunity to take personal power; but he kept his delusions of grandeur under control: 'There must be elections and the Communists must take part,' he said. 'We are people with our feet on the ground. We know that Russia is the world's second power and this country of 200 million borders our country of about nine million. We want no Danubian Korea. The leaders of the revolutionary forces must have faith in Imre Nagy even if the people have lost it. This is for the good of the country.'[19]

Jenő Széll, who ran Nagy's secretariat for four days during the revolution, had a disturbing encounter with him. On the day Dudás occupied the newspaper building he marched to Nagy's office demanding an audience with the Prime Minister. 'There were some pretty ardent lads who turned up, all of them with a "gimme guitar" [colourful slang for a tommy-gun] around the neck. Usually I said "I'll pass on your request. But you can see how things are here ..." They then went away. It was completely different with Dudás and co. His men appeared and stood round the table. Then Dudás made his entrance, picked up the "gimme guitar", kissed it and put it down on the table. Dudás made my flesh creep. He gave an impression of fishing in troubled waters.'[20]

People celebrated their first hours of freedom in various unusual ways. During the afternoon a group of 'Uncle' Szabó's youngsters from Széna Square gained entry into the compound of luxurious villas on Rose Hill, where their Communist rulers used to live. The security guards simply lifted up the gates, allowed them in and left. They could not believe the ostentatious display of privilege they were seeing. Rákosi's gracious house, with a pretty garden, had been empty since he left, evidently in a hurry, in July. It had hardly been touched since, and there was a film of dust in most of the twelve rooms. On his desk was his Party membership card – a touch that amused the rebels who first entered the room. His subscription was just 160 forints a month, roughly the same as an ordinary worker would have paid, from a monthly salary huge by the standards of the time of 40,000 forints. He had a swimming pool, and two luxurious bathrooms were fitted out with gymnastics equipment. There were drawers full of imported vitamin pills. He had a shining new American-style kitchen, with the most up-to-date appliances. He had a brand new radio-phonograph, two pianos and brilliant white phones in every room. A button from the drawing room could call the AVO guard, instantly. Another summoned the servants. There were thick pile carpets, boxes full of Dutch cigars. A bar was filled with decent French wine, champagne and liqueurs. An immense portrait of Stalin dominated the main room, and, like the Great Teacher himself, a thick, padded door separated his office from his living quarters.

Another important release valve was the discovery of thousands of secret police documents. The AVO had destroyed vast amounts of incriminating paperwork over the last few days, but only a fraction of the total. Now their files were opened. Long queues formed of people desperate to know what had been written about them, and who had been the informers. Many of the things Hungarians learned about their compatriots were deeply disturbing. At the start of the uprising, György Szabó had become president of Győr Revolutionary Council – effectively number two to the swashbuckling rebel leader in the west of

Hungary, Attila Szigetthy. Szabó was in charge of releasing Communist Party and secret police documents. As he was sifting through them he saw one file that related to him in a painful way. He learned that an old friend of his was a police spy. The informer was a highly respected teacher in a gymnasium school by the name of János Gyimesi, who had been a senior Social Democrat leader. 'Under the pseudonym of Gyarmati he had also been an AVO agent throughout the past decade,' Szabó said. 'He received 1,500 forints a month fee, just a little more than his salary from teaching. Unfortunately, Gyimesi was my best friend in the early 1950s.'

Szabó discovered the truth in a ghastly way, which briefly put the spotlight on him as the likely informer. Another old friend of his, Udvaros, was jailed. 'Udvaros was an elderly man, who had been Mayor of Győr in the late 1940s. He told me a lot of information, SDP material, Party secrets. As a much younger man, he thought I should know. I kept everything to myself until, in 1952, I told Gyimesi. I thought that he . . . as a leading SDP member, should have the information too.' Udvaros was arrested, imprisoned and released only during the revolution. Szabó had not seen Udvaros since his arrest. It was only when he read the documents that the truth struck him. 'He thought I was the informer because the details he had given me came up in his AVO interrogation. There was no doubt he was convinced I had betrayed him.' In fact the traitor had been his own best friend: 'That was the type of place Hungary was at the time.'[21]

In Moscow, the Soviet leaders tried to put on an air of business as usual. Early in the evening Khrushchev, Molotov, Bulganin and the faceless Foreign Minister Shepilov made brief appearances at two functions on the diplomatic circuit, at the Turkish and Afghan Embassies. Khrushchev looked more cheerful than he had for days as he spoke cordially with the suave and experienced British Ambassador in Moscow, Sir William Hayter, and his American counterpart, Charles 'Chip' Bohlen, who gave the appearance of an Ivy League professor.[22]

At the second reception Bohlen had a long talk about Hungary with Marshal Zhukov, weighted down as always with medals on his uniform. Unusually for a senior Soviet soldier he was a man with a highly developed sense of humour, but he was in sombre mood as Bohlen, under orders from Foster Dulles, repeated word for word the carefully worked-out American response to the Hungarian crisis – 'we do not see these states as potential military allies'. Zhukov understood the point and said he was optimistic about a peaceful settlement in Hungary. 'A government has been formed that enjoys our support and the support of the Hungarian people,' the Marshal said. However, Bohlen – unlike many other Western diplomats in Moscow at the time, and unlike the policy-makers in the State Department – had an uneasy feeling about Soviet intentions. He noted that Zhukov, while looking emollient, had been careful to say that in Nagy's broadcast the previous day he had not announced an 'immediate' withdrawal from Budapest. Russian soldiers could stay until Nagy asked for them to go or 'until they had restored order'.[23] Bohlen sounded a warning that the Russians may have no real intention to withdraw and the announcement might have been a 'trick . . . to cause the insurgents to cease fire'.[24]

From the American Legation in Budapest, at roughly the same time, Spencer Barnes was sending an urgent telegram desperately requesting Washington to send significant, practical assistance to the insurgents. They needed Western military aid and high-level moral support 'to give them better bargaining strength and fighting potential if the conflict is kept alive'.[25] His pleas were in vain. The Eisenhower administration would not provide such support. In Washington, the Secretary of State effectively parked the issue of Hungary. Dulles told Lodge that he would draft a UN Security Council resolution calling on Soviet armed forces, secret police and military advisers to leave the country. However, there would be no vote on the resolution when it was debated in four days. Dulles stated clearly that the object was for the meeting to be adjourned. It was a waste of time, he thought, ritually to cast votes when everybody in the room knew the Soviets would use their veto.[26] The political purpose of the State Department was simply that America should be seen to raise the matter. By the time the debate began in New York, the US, Britain and France had other business they thought was more pressing, in Egypt.

For Nagy it had been another day of chasing events. He could chalk up a few minor victories. A radio transmitter had been moved into the Parliament building, directly below his own office, so he had a propaganda tool. True, he acquired it far too late to make a significant difference, but he had a weapon at last. With the Stalinists gone, more of the old man's friends and allies went to work for him. His faithful secretary, the passionate József Szilágyi, tried his best to began efficient door-keeper; his chief political strategists, Géza Losonczy and Ferenc Donáth, were with him constantly and Miklós Vásárhelyi would soon become his chief publicist. He had a team around him that he could trust. But Nagy was deeply frustrated.

His great failure was that he could not bring the revolutionaries to see that they would never win an absolute victory against the USSR or persuade them that half a loaf was better than nothing at all.[27] Nagy thought that the deal he had made with the Russians was the best Hungary was going to get. But many of the rebels saw the compromises he had already made as just the start of further negotiations. Why should they back down at a time of victory? Arms and the strike had brought them the gains they had made: they were their best hope for winning more.

The central image of the Hungarian Revolution was fighting on the streets of Budapest; the grainy black and white pictures of children stopping Russian tanks with handguns and petrol bombs are unforgettable. But the revolution was characterised equally by talk – endless talking among people who had not been allowed to say what they thought for decades. When at last they were free to speak, they could not stop. After the fighting in Budapest ceased the long revolutionary meetings began where the words were full of idealism and liberty and hope, but where the endlessly debated resolutions became increasingly unrealistic. 'We thought for a while that anything might be possible,' Ágnes Gergely said. 'The mood was intoxicating – and that was the trouble. Many people were so drunk with the joy of the present, so full of euphoria, that they couldn't see what was really happening, or what was going to happen. A few sceptical people were dubious and thought that it was too good to be true but they were drowned out by the wild optimism.'[28]

Nagy's door seemed open to almost everybody. For hours each day he was seeing representatives of newly created Revolutionary Councils, or Workers' Councils, pressing him to make increasingly impossible demands that he knew the Soviets would not accept. Finally, on this day, he snapped, in front of the three-day-old Revolutionary Committee of Hungarian Intellectuals, a body comprising many of his friends – writers, leaders of the Petőfi circle and others who had inspired the revolution and supported him through his ideological and personal battles with the Stalinists. A small delegation presented him with a list of fresh concessions they said he must make that included holding free elections. They insisted that Soviet troops must leave Hungary. Nagy was a polite and mild-mannered man who seldom lost his temper, but his frustration got the better of him now. He looked at his visitors and sneered a response. He would not accept their demands:

> In any case, there must be an end. Neither you ... nor any others can keep coming to the government with constantly changing demands. A truce on your demands. They are worthy only of hotheads ... The Government has its own programme, which I made known last night on the radio. We will go just that far, and no further. You are writers, journalists, Party men. Your task is to apply and popularise the programme. That is what I demand of you. I repeat, the time for hotheads has ended. If you do not agree with me we are no longer friends ... It is intolerable that the authority of the government should be sapped by demands that are constantly changing.[29]

At a midnight meeting, General Király and the police chief Kopácsi prepared detailed plans to set up the National Guard. It would oversee the Ministries of Defence and the Police, replace the AVO, unite the various student militia groups and rebel freedom fighting bands into a revolutionary army, in effect the freedom fighters' army. 'We thought the success or failure of the revolution depended on this,' Kopácsi said. 'We had to find a way to stop the troublemakers from ruining everything. That was the crucial thing. If we couldn't keep them under control, it would be all over for us.'[30]

There were problems from the start. The top brass in the army, some of them still loyal to the old regime, hated the idea of turning the ad hoc freedom-fighting groups, factory guards and 'kids in the streets' into a security force responsible for keeping the peace. Even Maléter, who supported the revolution, was dubious about the idea. He never thought it would work. 'From the very first moment I was against using the insurgents to raise units of the public force,' he said.[31]

Király and Kopácsi proposed raising two divisions of 26,000 men who would guard Budapest's strategic buildings: Parliament, the railway stations, key road intersections. Rebels who volunteered to join were automatically handed a weapon if they did not already have one and given an armband to show they were 'officially' a National Guard member. It was designed as a symbol to signify that they were part of the revolution. They wanted people, said Kopácsi, 'suitable for ridding Budapest in a few days of all the dubious elements, the *déclassés*, and other power-hungry adventurers'.[32]

They began the task of persuading the various rebel groups – there were now about two dozen of them – to disband and join the new National Guard. The tumult in Hungary had lasted almost a week. To many Hungarians it seemed as though the revolution had been successful; the Russian troops promised to leave the capital, the rest of the world was looking at Budapest with new-found admiration and respect, and Communist power had collapsed.

Now the revolutionaries seemed to be very different from those who had taken up arms on the first day. Kopácsi and many others noticed the change as they went round negotiating with rebel leaders. For a start there were fewer students and intellectuals. Most of them had given up their weapons and returned to writing resolutions and proclamations. There were still many in their early teens, children really, who should have been at school; except the schools had closed.[33] There was no such thing as a typical freedom fighter. But a survey conducted later among thousands of refugees by an American university gave the only detailed study that exists. More than three-quarters of them were under thirty and most were factory workers and apprentices from the industrial areas of Budapest. 'They were amongst the poorest of Hungarians – the ones communism was supposed to have helped the most but did not. On the whole they were the young people who had the worst jobs, the worst education and the least hope. They wanted an end to communism . . . not reforms to a system they despised. They had less to lose by rebelling so spectacularly than any other group in the country.'[34]

From their first talks with the insurgent bands, Kopácsi and Király could see difficulties. In the first week of the Revolution, in the guerrilla fighting against the Russians, it had not mattered that the rebel groups did not know each other. In many ways it was an advantage – the more loosely knit they were, the easier it was to mount one-off operations, disappear for a while and quickly regroup. But now the lack of any central command among the rebels was a handicap for the uprising. Negotiations were hampered by mistrust. The leaders of the groups could not guarantee that anything they agreed with Király, Kopácsi or Nagy would be accepted by their members. The various groups disagreed with each other. There was no single rebel commander or chief of authority with whom Nagy could negotiate directly.

The Corvin Passage group had influence in a part of central Pest, 'Uncle' Szabó was boss in Széna Square and a small section of Buda. Dudás had power within his own supporters, but no authority anywhere else. Some groups decided to join the National Guard; others opted to have nothing to do with it and to stay on their own in opposition. It was difficult, for example, to see many similarities between the colourful, loud-mouthed Gergely Pongrácz of the Corvin fighters, and the thoughtful, quiet, ascetic former inmate of Auschwitz, the twenty-six-year-old István Angyal, who led the Tűzoltó Street insurgents, a band that knocked out half a dozen Soviet tanks in a week of fighting.[35] Pongrácz wanted an end to communism, refused to join the National Guard and vowed to keep fighting until the last Soviet troops had left Hungary. He said once, 'Yes I made a lot of mistakes. The biggest was not to allow executions of the AVO men we captured. There were some lynched by others, but not by us.' Angyal remained a Communist of the Nagy brand, wanted to take out the red flag to battle along with the Hungarian tricolour and was appalled by the instant justice that was 'defiling the revolution'.

He was not alone. Nothing did so much harm to the revolution as the well-publicised cases of mob revenge meted out to AVO officers. The explosion of anger against the secret police never abated and had tragic consequences well beyond a few dozen barbaric deaths. The murders seemed to emphasise that nobody in Budapest had control of the streets. Along main roads, amidst the rubble, the gaping holes where buildings had once been and the burned-out tanks, it was fairly common for passers-by to see corpses left to rot on a makeshift scaffold. Often victims were hanged by the legs, beaten until they were nearly dead and then burned. A peculiarly Hungarian feature was that often under the body lay a pile of cash, sometimes in significant amounts and always untouched, which indicated that the dead AVO had been in possession of blood money no Hungarian should keep.

Instant justice was usually just that, the work of a moment. 'A crowd would form spontaneously, as if from nowhere – men, women, even children. They would lift up a terrified, shaking figure, shout "killer, torturer, spy" and then hang him on a post or a tree. There would be a small cheer and then people would disperse very quickly, not looking at each other.'[36] Nobody knows exactly how many AVO officers were murdered in revenge attacks during the uprising. The propaganda White Books, published in 1957 by the government that smashed the revolution, said that 289 security officers died; but most of them were killed in fighting between the rebels and the AVO and were not murdered in cold blood. The best estimate is that somewhere between 90 and 100 were lynched.

Some of them were entirely innocent. The socialist newspaper *People's Voice* published a vivid description of a mob that almost got the wrong man:

> The slip knot was tightening around the man's neck. His head fell back and the ... wind set his body swaying. Death was imminent. At this point someone in the crowd called out 'quick, let him down. He's not an AVO. His name is Kelemen and he lives in Kobanya.' By good fortune it was in time. Kelemen, still alive, was taken to hospital. There were other incidents in which the anger of the people was vented against innocent victims who were accused in error. Members of the air force and of the entertainment branch of the Honvéd [people's army] were attacked by fanatics who took them for members of the AVO because they too wore blue collars on their uniforms. Frequently there were 'people's trials', followed by lynchings, in which the identities, much less the activities, of the victims were never verified.[37]

General Király deplored the lynchings but maintained that 'The Hungarian Revolution was not characterised by brutality. Quite the opposite. It was characterised by moderation, mainly. If you think of the thousands who perished under the Rákosi regime, the hundreds of thousands who were interned or imprisoned, there was really very little violence against the oppressors. The Hungarian Revolution was moderate compared to the regime it was attempting to topple.'

By now all the responsible voices in the revolution had spoken out against the lynch mobs. József Szilágyi was speaking for the Prime Minister when he wrote: 'All honest people should resolutely oppose the troublemakers. The lynchings should cease immediately. There is no mercy for the criminals, but they should be responsible for their crimes in the orthodox way, before the courts.' Miklós Gimes, pillar of intellectual support for Nagy, who would be executed with him, said: 'We should not allow the purity of our revolution to be violated ... We are speaking of the so-called "popular judgments" of the lynchings ... whose spirit is foreign to our revolution. There should be judgments, but not on the streets, not in the passion of the moment.'

Yet there were voices ready to explain and justify the murders. Zoltán Szántó, formerly a senior diplomat under the Rákosi-Gerő governments, would say of the lynch mob victims at the height of the revolution: 'We are not sadists but we cannot manage to feel sorry for those Hungarians. Crimes have been committed against the people. The Communists have heaped the guilt on themselves.'

TWENTY-SIX
Tuesday, 30 October

Russian troops were continuing to leave Budapest. Intermittent shots had rung out overnight in the city centre around the Corvin Passage, but not enough to shatter the ceasefire. At dawn on another fine day, Soviet tanks guarding Parliament, the national Communist Party head-quarters, the bridges across the Danube and other strategic points began to be replaced by Hungarians. Celebrations and euphoria were muted. Anger and bitterness were not. As the columns of Russian soldiers left, 'carrying their dead with them', they were booed and jeered.[1] 'A Hungarian peasant spat on one T34 tank as it passed him an arm's length away. The Russian crew did not notice. Hatred literally oozed from the Hungarians who silently lined the roadsides watching the Soviets evacuate Budapest. The Russians were alert. They manned their 100-millimetre tank cannon which were zeroed at the horizontal for firing straight ahead if necessary.'[2]

The real intentions of the Soviets were deliberately shrouded in mystery. Early in the morning the Russian leaders seemed content with their decision to make a dignified tactical retreat. They warned that it would be thirty-six hours before all the soldiers left the city. But to any Hungarians who doubted their sincerity, the persuasive Mikoyan referred to an extraordinary statement the magnates in the Kremlin had agreed and signed first thing in the day 'On Friendship and Co-operation between the USSR and other Socialist States'. It promised again that Russian troops would leave Budapest. It said the Soviets would negotiate 'with the Hungarian . . . government and other sig-natories of the Warsaw Pact on the question of the presence of Soviet troops elsewhere in the territory of Hungary'. The declaration went much further. It admitted 'violations and mistakes which infringe the principles of equality between sovereign states'. It talked about creating a kind of 'commonwealth' of independent socialist states, recognised the right of Hungary and all the other satellites to national sovereignty and was the most liberal, progressive manifesto for a loosely based grouping of states with shared ideas ever produced by Moscow. We now know that the statement, a carefully phrased list of pieties that committed Moscow to nothing specific, was originally drafted earlier in the summer following the troubles in Poznan and simply adapted for use in Hungary when the need arose. However, there is evidence that some of the leaders in the Kremlin took it seriously, if only for a while.[3]

Khrushchev said later that he and the other Soviet leaders vacillated on Hungary.[4] That was a major understatement. The Soviet potentates met at the Kremlin around 9 a.m. and showed uncertainty, indecision and confusion on how to proceed with the crisis in Budapest. Khrushchev arrived late. He had been negotiating with a delegation of Chinese officials led by Liu Shao-chi. Relations between Russia and China were deteriorating but the views of Chairman Mao were still considered important in Moscow. Khrushchev was told that Mao, at this stage, wanted the Soviets to make a deal with the Hungarians and that there was no reason for panic measures to crush the rebellion.[5] Khrushchev said he agreed and parted with the Chinese on good terms. He then joined in the strangest conversation his colleagues in the Kremlin had during the crisis.

For a few fleeting moments even the hardliners seemed prepared to look for a face-saving formula that would remove Russian soldiers – as long as Hungary remained firmly in the Soviet bloc and retained the Communist system. Zhukov said gnomically that 'there is a military political lesson for us in this. Anti-Soviet sentiments are widespread. We should withdraw our troops from Budapest and from Hungary if that is demanded.' None of the Stalinists seemed to disagree – or at least could say so. All reports suggest that Khrushchev, at this point during the day, meant his summing-up: 'We are unanimous. There are two paths, a military path, one of occupation and a peaceful path – the withdrawal of troops, negotiations. We should take the second path.'[6]

The government press was authorised to give Imre Nagy the Soviets' seal of approval and welcome the turn of events in Budapest. 'The Nagy government has won the support of the people,' declared *Pravda* that day. 'Reports pouring in from all over Hungary show that the workers support the government's new programme.'

*

Republic Square, near the Eastern Railway Station, was one of the largest open spaces in the central commercial district of Pest. On one corner stood the graceful early-twentieth-century Erkel Theatre, famous for productions of light opera. Directly opposite was one of the ugliest buildings in the city, a concrete and glass slab that was the headquarters of the Greater Budapest Communist Party. There had been a few small demonstrations there over the last few days, but unlike several other Party buildings throughout the country, it had not, at least so far, been a target for takeover by the rebels. The atmosphere inside was extremely tense, however. A contingent of forty-seven secret police had been despatched there a week earlier on the first day of the revolution.[7] Most of them were new, young conscripted recruits, with no choice but to join up, and too scared to let themselves be seen outside after reports that AVOs were being lynched. They were joined by a few hardened, well-trained 'old guard' AVOs, like the commander of their unit, Colonel József Papp. Even though the AVO had been disbanded, the officers stayed at their posts. They did not believe assurances from the regular police in Budapest that they would be safe and looked after if they handed themselves over, though Kopácsi kept several hundred AVOs under protection.[8]

Despite the tension inside the building, work was going on. The Budapest Party's boss, the plump, cheerful, forty-eight-year-old Imre Mező, was meeting soldiers from the newly formed National Guard about how factories could best be defended if they came under attack. Mező was a respected figure who had fought in the Spanish Civil War and in the French resistance to the Nazis, was a great supporter of Imre Nagy's reform agenda and was one of János Kádár's closest personal friends. He was a loyal Communist, widely admired outside Party circles. The previous night Kádár had visited him. Mező said he had a few worries about his safety, but was confident that he would be protected if Republic Square was attacked.[9]

At about 9.30 a.m. two things happened. First, the Russian and Hungarian soldiers who had been guarding the building withdrew, as part of the ceasefire agreement, and the Party headquarters were left defenceless. Then a truck drew up outside the building and a large consignment of fresh meat was delivered inside. Food was easily available in Budapest now, but the sight of special deliveries made to Communist Party apparatchiks infuriated a group of shoppers queuing patiently at a 'közert' nearby. They told a group of freedom fighters what had happened. The insurgents went into the building demanding to know why Communists should be so favoured, and they immediately recognised AVO officers in the building. A furious exchange of gunfire followed that escalated into a brutal three-hour siege and the most notorious battle of the revolution.

The first insurgents in the Party building retreated when they realised how badly outnumbered they were. But they quickly returned to Republic Square with heavy reinforcements. The rebels tried to negotiate a surrender of the building – but instead of talks the shooting became heavier. The civilians inside the building rang every government office they could contact to plead for some protection. Eventually, the Ministry of Defence sent five tanks from the 33rd Tank Regiment, commanded by Colonel Ede Virágh, to Republic Square. He did not lead the men himself, which may explain the confusion and tragedy that followed.

Two of the tanks failed to arrive and when the others did get there they encountered a separate group of Hungarian soldiers on the rebel side firing at the building with a tank of their own. So they began bombarding it too. By then every window had been smashed and a gaping hole could be seen in the middle storey. Some Western journalists reached the scene. The gifted *Paris-Match* photographer Jean-Pierre Pedrazzini, twenty-nine, on one of his earliest war zone assignments, stepped from behind the cover of a tank for a split second to take a picture. He was caught in the crossfire – from which side nobody knows – and was shot in the stomach. He died of his wounds a few days later in Paris.

With shards of masonry falling through the building, it was obvious it would soon be stormed. The terrified Mező, a decent and generous man, tied a white sheet to a stick, walked outside as confidently as he could, shouted at the top of his voice 'Stop, please don't fire, I surrender' and was promptly shot in the chest and legs. He was rushed to hospital but died two days later. Another photo-journalist, the American John Sadovy from *Life* magazine, described the final gruesome episode:[10]

Suddenly there was a noise of people running . . . They were closing in fast. I went in with the first group. We met another group led by a man carrying a huge flag. 'Come on, come on, we made it. It's ours,' he was saying. Other . . . rebels were coming in from the side, screaming and going into the building . . . Now there was only occasional machine-gun fire from the top floor. The tanks were still shooting and bricks fell from the building when the tanks blasted it. People were still being careful. There were two burned-out lorries in front of the building with seven burned bodies under them. The people had crawled there for shelter and been caught. It was a mess . . .

Now you could feel confidence sweeping the crowd. They advanced right to the main door of the building. The AVO men began to come out. The first man to emerge was an officer, alone. It was the fastest killing I ever saw. He came out laughing and the next thing I knew he was flat on the ground, his legs spread, dead as anyone could be. For a while it didn't dawn on me that this man was shot. He just fell down, I thought. Then the first group, the bravest of the lot, decided to go inside the building. They brought out a good-looking officer, his face white as chalk. He got five yards, retreated, argued. Folded up. It was over with him. They went back again and two came out together. There was a scuffle. An array of rifle butts, punching, kicking. Suddenly there was a shot. The two just dropped.

Six young officers came out, one very good-looking. Their shoulder boards were torn off. They wore no hats. They had a quick argument. 'We're not as bad as you think we are. Give us a chance,' they were saying. I was three feet from that group. Suddenly one began to fold. I hardly heard a shot. They must have been so close that the man's body acted as a silencer. They all went down like corn that had been cut. Very gracefully. They folded up smoothly, in slow motion. And when they were on the ground the rebels were still loading lead into them.

Another came out, running. He saw his friends dead, turned, headed into the crowd. The rebels dragged him out. Then my nerves went. I had spent three years in the war, but nothing I saw could compare with the horror of this. They brought out a woman and a man from the building. Her face was white. She looked . . . at the bodies that were spread all over. Suddenly a man came up and walloped her with a rifle butt. Another pulled her hair, kicked her. She fell down. They kicked her some more. I thought that's the end of her. But in a few moments she was up, pleading. She said she was not an AVO member. There were shouts of No prisoners, No prisoners, but she was put on a bus standing by . . . more came out, one a high-ranking officer. His bleeding body was hung by his feet from a tree and women came up to spit on him.'[11]

Altogether twenty-three AVO officers were killed through 'instant justice' at Republic Square. The rebels were convinced there were underground dungeons in the building and they conducted a fruitless search for several hours to find them. Six had been wounded and taken to hospital before the building fell to the rebels. The rest managed, somehow, to escape. Among the dead, it was the picture of László Elek, an AVO conscript barely out of his teens, hung upside down with rebels kicking him, that most shocked the world. Colonel Papp was strung up by his feet with cable wire, soaked in petrol and his face and torso were burned. The acrid stench filled the Square.

At about midday Cardinal József Mindszenty, the Prince Primate of Hungary, gained his freedom in dramatic fashion. After his torture and trial, he had spent most of the last eight years in solitary confinement. During Imre Nagy's first term as Prime Minister the troublesome Cardinal was not released, though the harsh conditions under which he had been held were improved. Under house arrest for the last two years, in the medieval castle of Felsopeteny, around sixty-five kilometres north of Budapest, he had been out of Hungarian public life for so long that his real significance now was debatable. Yet to the faithful he was still a martyr.

From the summer of 1956 he had been allowed a radio and to read newspapers. Abruptly, with no explanation, on 24 October those privileges were withdrawn and once again he was isolated. He had heard vaguely about a few disturbances in Budapest but not that a revolution had broken out. 'The tension could be felt every time I saw one of the guards,' he said. 'Then they broke their silence.'[12] Early in the morning the guards told him to pack a bag and leave. 'They said my life was threatened.'

'But who threatens me?' I asked.

The AVO officer replied: 'The mob.'

But Mindszenty refused to leave the castle. 'I won't go. If . . . I should die here, I will die. But I will not move,' he said.

'The AVO were puzzled,' the Cardinal continued. 'They spoke briefly amongst themselves. Then one of them asked, almost timidly, "Would you go if we used force, just token force? For example, we could touch your arm as a symbol of force. Then would you go?"' He said no.

A Russian armoured car drew up to the castle gates and out stepped János Horváth, the Communist chief of the Hungarian Office of Church

Affairs. He told Mindszenty, 'Your life is not safe in this place. I have orders to move you.' Mindszenty refused again. 'I will not go, you have taken from me everything there is to take, you can take nothing else,' he said. Horváth was reluctant to use force against the prelate – especially as hundreds of farmers had now gathered outside the castle, carrying pitchforks, spades and hoes and shouting 'Freedom for Mindszenty'.[13]

Horváth consulted his superiors in Budapest, but he did not realise that all calls from the castle were being tapped by the insurgents. Sensing an opportunity, an army unit with two tanks and an armoured car commanded by a dashing officer, Major Antál Pálinkás, based at a military training camp at Rétság, twenty kilometres away, rushed to Felsopeteny to rescue the Cardinal. By the time he got there, though, Mindszenty was free. The AVOs panicked in the face of the farmers' demonstration. The officer in command approached the Cardinal 'with humility and respect' and to the old man's astonishment declared they had 'formed a Revolutionary Committee', that he had been wrongfully imprisoned and was free to go. Clearly it was a way for the AVOs to save their own skins, but it worked.

A few minutes later the tall, lanky, gap-toothed Pálinkás arrived, went into the great hall of the castle and disarmed the AVO officers. The meeting of the Cardinal and the thirty-four-year-old soldier was fateful. For the first time in six years he used his real name as he knelt to kiss the prelate's ring. He was born Antál Pallavicini, scion of one of Hungary's oldest and richest aristocratic families. He volunteered for the army and was commissioned as a lieutenant in the Armoured Corps in 1943. But he joined the anti-Nazi resistance after the Germans occupied Hungary the next year and went over to the Russians, commanding a battalion of troops. He returned to Hungary in 1946, a decorated war hero, a member of the Communist Party and the commanding officer of a tank brigade. He had changed his name to a more proletarian-sounding one in 1950 and seemed to be a rising star of the People's Army. But he fell foul of the Party during the repeated army purges. In 1954 he was demoted on the usual fictitious charges, and was lucky to escape with his life. In July 1955 he was sent to train NCOs in Rétság, effectively an internal military exile. When the revolution began he took the side of the insurgents, but he might have survived that, as many of his colleagues did. His fate was sealed when he chose to make the rescue mission to free Mindszenty. He would never be forgiven by the Soviets.*[14]

The Cardinal wanted to head straight for Budapest with his military escort and enter the city in a triumphal procession. He had been preparing for a grand occasion when he declared to the crowd as he left the castle, 'My sons, I shall carry on where I left eight years ago.' But a ceremonial event was the last thing Imre Nagy or János Kádár wanted. They knew the sight would goad the Russians, thought it could easily turn into a massive violent protest and wanted the release to be handled with the minimum fuss possible. Pálinkás was ordered to take the Cardinal to the garrison at tiny Rétság and escort him to his baroque palace at Úri Street, in Budapest's Castle District, early the next morning.[15] The Primate arrived with Pálinkás and a company of men just after dawn – 'for his own safety, because the streets would be safer at that time', according to the radio. There were no crowds outside, as nobody had been informed when Hungary's most famous prisoner would finally reach his home a free man.

Between 7,500 and 8,000 other political prisoners were released from jails throughout the country. One of the principal aims of the revolution was achieved when Vác was liberated, the notorious fortress jail on the Danube about fifty kilometres north of Budapest where dozens of inmates had died from neglect over the years. Many managed to escape Hungary afterwards, including some foreign prisoners the Hungarians had always refused to acknowledge existed. Among them was the British doctor Edith Bone, who had been arrested in 1949, on the personal orders of Rákosi, as she was at Budapest airport about to board a plane back to England. She was in solitary confinement for years and was almost overlooked by the revolutionaries when they entered Budapest Central Prison. They did not, at first, believe who she was.†

---

* After the revolution, Pálinkás/Pallavicini surrendered without a fight to the Soviets. He was arrested on 25 December 1956. After his release, he was demobilised. At first he was sentenced to life imprisonment, but two months later, after the prosecution appealed, he was sentenced to death. He was hanged on 10 December 1957 at the National Prison in Budapest.

† Edith Bone was an extraordinary woman. The daughter of a Hungarian lawyer, she qualified as a doctor in 1914 and was appalled by hospital conditions for 'other ranks' in the First World War. She turned her back on Hungary and travelled Europe as a Communist Party activist, finally settling in Britain in 1933. She became disillusioned by Stalinism. She returned to Hungary after the Second World War and worked as a translator, but wanted to leave soon after Rákosi took absolute power. Arrested at the departure gate at Ferihegy airport, she was thrown into Vác and left to rot,

*

Around the time the Communist official Imre Mező was fatally wounded, at 2.30 p.m., Imre Nagy made his biggest concession so far. 'The tremendous force of the democratic movement has brought our country to a crossroads,' he declared on radio.[16] 'The government has decided to take a step vital for the future of the nation. The Cabinet abolishes the one-party system and places the country's government on a basis of democratic co-operation between coalition parties.' He formed a new streamlined Cabinet of six members – three Communists, two Smallholders and one from the Peasants Party – and begged people to halt the violence: 'We have to establish order first of all,' he said. The elderly, fastidious Tildy took the microphone immediately afterwards and made a similar passionate appeal.

Nagy's announcement about multi-party democracy was a giant step – which he almost certainly knew the Russians would never accept. He had himself found it hard, as a loyal Communist of forty years. He struggled with his conscience for a long time, he said. But he also realised he had to catch up with the revolutionaries – or be swept away by them. As the Hungarian émigré Paul Zinner put it, Nagy was similar to other tragic figures 'caught in the swirl of revolution and horribly mistreated by it'.[17] At times it was a visible ordeal. Within an hour of making 'this historic statement' he was besieged with more and increasingly impossible demands.

The final straw came at about 4 p.m. in his office at the Parliament building when he met a five-man delegation from Győr. It was, again, led by the huge, bristling, ruddy figure of Attila Szigetthy, who was beginning to see himself as a possible alternative leader of the country. He made clear a threat that he had hinted at two days before. Szigetthy warned that unless a date was set for free elections within three months 'Győr might break with the Nagy government'.[18] Nagy replied that that would be unfortunate and hoped they would understand that the

charged with espionage. She vanished, without an identity, not even a prison number. British protests met with the response that she was not in the country. She flew out in 1949 and had not been back in Hungary since, they said. She spent years in solitary confinement. She had no writing materials, but she made letters out of the alphabet with the bread. She made an abacus so she could count, and a calendar. She was a woman of indomitable spirit. Later she was allowed books and a pen and studied Greek and mathematics. After her eventual release by the revolutionaries she returned to Britain where she died in 1976, aged eighty-nine.

most important thing was to prevent further bloodshed. Hecklers
demanded loudly that Nagy abrogate the Warsaw Pact. Nagy flared up
in frustration and anger, threatening to resign. From the back of the
room one of the delegates was heard muttering 'Fine. That would be
wonderful.' Nagy was ushered out of his office, red-eyed, deflated and
practically in tears by Géza Losonczy. He returned a few minutes later.[19]

The national radio station, finally, had been prised from the hands of
the Stalinists. It was now controlled by the government, directly by
Nagy's long-time trusted supporter, the stern intellectual Ferenc
Donáth, but was promised the kind of freedom no Communist broadcaster had ever been permitted. Renamed Free Radio Kossuth, it carried
at 3.06 p.m. the most extraordinary statement ever heard on a
Hungarian frequency:

> Dear Listeners. We are beginning a new chapter in the history of
> Hungarian radio. For many years our radio has been an instrument of
> lies; it merely carried out orders. It lied by night and by day; it lied on
> all wavelengths. Not even in the hour of our country's rebirth did it
> cease its campaign of lies. But the struggle which succeeded in securing
> the nation's freedom and independence in the streets has spread to the
> radio as well. Those who were the mouthpieces of lies are, from this
> moment, no longer on our staff. We who are before the microphone now
> are new men. In future you will hear new voices on old wavelengths. As
> the old saying has it, we shall tell the truth, the whole truth, and
> nothing but the truth.[20]

In America President Eisenhower had a week to wait until election
day. He was confident of an easy victory, but he wanted to take nothing
for granted. His major concern now was the yawning crack in the
Western alliance and a conflict in the Middle East that he feared could
extend the Cold War to another continent. Ike made it clear that from
now on the most pressing issue for his administration was the Suez
crisis. Over the next few days he had dozens of meetings and telephone
calls about the Middle East and very few about Hungary.[21]

The US had known for months that the British and the French, in
collusion with Israel, were planning to attack Egypt. It looked certain
from the day the Egyptian President, Colonel Gamal Abdel Nasser,
nationalised the Suez Canal in July. Yet when it happened Washington
seemed unprepared. The President hoped that at the last moment

France and the UK would draw back. As a military man he could see no strategic value for his Western allies to launch the attack. It would not, as they claimed, protect their oil supplies, which were under no threat. The war would make the world a more dangerous place and risk a potential conflict with the Soviet Union. Politically, the Suez invasion made even less sense to the American President. It seemed an outdated Anglo-French imperial adventure that was doomed to failure. Eisenhower, in fact, set about *ensuring* it would fail, and as an inevitable consequence, bring down the British Prime Minister, Sir Anthony Eden.

Israeli paratroopers landed on the Sinai Peninsula the previous day and reached their military objectives within a few hours. The attack was followed by an ultimatum by Eden and the French Prime Minister, Guy Mollet, for both sides to cease fighting, knowing that Egypt would not. That would provide a pretext for Britain and France to launch their own invasion. 'It is about as crude and brutal as anything I have ever seen,' John Foster Dulles told Ike at a White House briefing session at about 10 a.m. Washington time (4 p.m. in Budapest). Eisenhower was furious that despite the 'special relationship', Eden had given him no warning of the attacks. The President would never forgive the Prime Minister, who was already a sick man. He fired off a 'Dear Anthony' telegram warning him that if the British and French went ahead with their threat, America would publicly disassociate itself from an invasion that was endangering the unity of the West. Dulles, by telephone later in the day, agreed with Ike, and thought one point should be added. 'There is another thing: it is a tragedy that just when the whole Soviet fabric is collapsing, the British and the French are going to be doing just the same thing in the Arab world.'[22]

For years after the Suez debacle it was alleged by some conspiracy theorists that the British and French timed their attack to coincide with the crisis in Budapest. The invasion of Egypt, the argument ran, would seem less brazen and shocking after pictures came out of Hungarian civilians fighting Russian tanks with petrol bombs. We now know this was not true. The date of the attack was decided at a secret conference in Sèvres, near Paris, on 22 October, before the revolution in Hungary began. But, as an accident of history, Suez had an effect on Hungary. The world's attention drifted away from Budapest, and the fate of 10 million people imprisoned behind the Iron Curtain suddenly seemed less significant than it had a few days earlier.

*

The savagery of the violence at Republic Square horrified the Russian emissaries, Mikoyan and Suslov. They heard about it soon after meeting Imre Nagy to discuss the Soviets' 'friendship' declaration. Immediately, they telegrammed Moscow with the most alarming yet of their reports back to the Kremlin, where in the morning Khrushchev had appeared to cherish hopes of a peaceful deal. They wrote:

> The political situation in the country and in Budapest . . . is getting worse . . . There is a feeling of helplessness. Hooligan elements have become more insolent, seizing Party committees, killing Communists . . . The factories are stalled. The people are sitting at home . . . Hooligan students and other resistance elements have changed their tactics and are displaying greater activity. Now they are hardly shooting at all, but instead are seizing institutions. The Hungarian army has adopted a wait and see position. Our military advisers say that relations between Hungarian officers and generals and Soviet officers have deteriorated in the past few days.[23]

They warned that soon the Hungarian army might go over en masse to the insurgents and 'then it would be necessary for Soviet units to undertake military operations once more'. They concluded with a desperate plea which indicated how close the Soviets were to the brink: 'We think it is essential that Comrade Konyev come to Budapest immediately,' they said. Marshal Ivan Konyev was Commander in Chief of all Warsaw Pact forces. His arrival, if the Kremlin agreed, could mean only one thing: that the Soviet army, which publicly had agreed to retreat, was readying itself again for battle.[24]

What of the 'friendship' document signed just a few hours earlier in Moscow? There are two schools of thought. The first is that at the time it was a genuine attempt by the Russians to reach a compromise that would prevent a full-scale invasion and military occupation of the country. Mikoyan definitely thought so, as all his subsequent actions seem to establish beyond doubt. He still wanted a Polish-type agreement. Others have argued that the declaration had always been a cynical sham, designed to buy Moscow time and to deceive the Hungarians. The evidence suggests, though, that the Soviets were uncertain what to do and revised decisions, not daily but hourly.[25]

Sir William Hayter, the British Ambassador, was usually well informed and never misty-eyed about communism or Soviet intentions. After a reception that evening at the Syrian Embassy he reported back to the Foreign Office that he believed in the sincerity of the declaration. 'The Soviet government has of course made many theoretical statements about the independence of the People's Democracies. But the present Declaration is far more important as the Soviet Union now proposes to take practical and concrete steps to abandon its authority over those countries.' The US Ambassador, 'Chip' Bohlen, was more prescient: 'Soviet leaders including Khrushchev, Bulganin, Molotov, Kaganovich were noticeably more glum than yesterday,' he cabled the State Department. Soviet policy could shift, he predicted, 'for example if the Nagy government has completely lost control and what is termed in the Declaration "black reaction and counter-revolution" has taken hold, their position on troop withdrawal may well be reversed'. Both he and the CIA reported the same observation that evening: if Moscow had the choice to accept the situation and allow Hungary to become independent, or to restore their power by force of arms, the Russians would certainly opt for the latter.[26]

Democracy was reborn. Or at least the old political parties of the post-war coalition began legally operating again – apparently with the consent of the Soviets. Zoltán Tildy, the former Smallholders' leader, was Imre Nagy's influential deputy. Within a few days the revolution had brought them close together. Béla Kovács, the most impressive of the post-war democratic politicians, after initially refusing to join Nagy's government, finally accepted a place in the 'inner Cabinet' of six which had been created earlier in the morning. He would not leave his home in Pécs for a further two days, however, Nagy saw the Smallholders as a crucial part of the coalition he was trying to create and was prepared to give them a helping hand. He returned the Party to their old headquarters, a fine turn-of-the-century building in Semmelweis Street that until a few days earlier had been occupied by the Hungarian-Soviet Friendship Society. Kovács reciprocated in the spirit of compromise. The Smallholders were historically a right-wing party representing bourgeois traditionalists, yet Kovács declared: 'No one should dream of going back to the world of aristocrats, bankers and capitalists. That world is definitely gone. We . . . cannot think along the lines of 1939 or 1945.' The witty József Kővágó, who had been released from jail a few days before the revolution began, was given back his old post as Mayor of Budapest.[27]

Most of the Social Democrats who returned to active political life had spent time in jail. Their leader was the earnest and passionate feminist, sixty-seven-year-old Anna Kéthly, who was one of Hungary's first women MPs. She was arrested in Rákosi's purges in 1950 and was close to death when she was released from the brutal conditions in Vác prison four years later. Nagy ensured her release, soon after he became Prime Minister for the first time. Kéthly trusted Nagy. But inside her party the same debate raged now as eight years earlier when the Social Democrats were sliced to pieces in Rákosi's salami tactics: should they co-operate with the Communists? Finally, after hours of talks with Nagy – and after the Party was given back control of its old newspaper *People's Voice* – they agreed. Kéthly took a job in the government, but was promptly despatched by Nagy to Vienna for a meeting of the Socialist International.[28]

The National Peasants Party, a fellow traveller of the Communists after 1945, changed its name to the Petőfi Party. Among its leaders was the brilliant writer and one-time doctor László Németh, fifty-five, who swiftly grew disillusioned by the 'squabbling among politicians which was destroying the revolution'. But that was not the typical reaction of most people. A return to democratic bickering was one of the causes for which so many Hungarians had been fighting for the last week. The first days of the formation of new parties were heady and exciting. At the Social Democratic headquarters, so many recruits wanted to join that by late in the evening the queue outside it blocked part of Rákóczi Avenue, one of Budapest's main roads.[29] At the Smallholders Party the enthusiasm was the same. 'There was a long row of cars outside . . . Everything went well until 10 p.m. but after that there was such a rush that one could not avoid the impression that the whole city wanted to get inside the house . . . People were flocking in from every direction.'[30]

János Kádár's job was to reinvent the Communist Party. A week earlier it had been the only political force allowed to exist in the country; it had 800,000 members and dominated every Hungarian's life from cradle to grave. Or at least so the Party thought. Now it had disintegrated. Nobody knew how many sincere Communists existed in the country. One supreme victory for the revolution had been won: people no longer had to pretend to be true believers when they were not.

The calculating Kádár at this point was hedging his bets. He was not sure what the Russians were going to do, or how he should act. He was appalled by the attack on his friend Imre Mező, who was struggling for his life in hospital. But while the Soviets still supported Nagy, Kádár had no incentive to make an enemy of him. Publicly he backed Nagy to the hilt on free elections and declared huge enthusiasm for rebuilding a more 'honest' Communist Party that 'was born of the revolution'. He reassured people that from now 'there would be an opposition and no dictatorship ... The new communism will be a Hungarian national communism ... that will have the Hungarian national interest at heart and not those of international communism.' Then he attempted to don the mantle of the revolution. 'Those who prepared this uprising were recruited from our ranks,' he said. 'Communist writers, journalists, university students, the youth of the Petőfi Circle and thousands upon thousands of workers and peasants and veteran fighters who were jailed on false charges, fought in the front line against Rákosi's despotism.'[31]

György Lukács, Minister of Culture in Nagy's government, told Kádár that 'The new Party must not expect rapid success – communism in Hungary has been totally disgraced. In free elections the Communists will receive five per cent of the vote, ten per cent at the most. It is possible that they won't be in the government ... But the Party will continue to exist ... It will be an intellectual centre.'[32] Kádár merely shrugged at the numbers.

TWENTY-SEVEN
Wednesday, 31 October

Nikita Khrushchev stayed up half the night at Stalin's former dacha outside Moscow, Volynoskoye. There was something appropriate about the venue for the discussions being held. They were about whether to slaughter civilians in a European city. The spirit of Stalin 'hovered in the air', according to his successor as Soviet Party leader. For several hours, from about 10.30 the previous night, Khrushchev was in earnest talks with the senior Chinese communist functionary, Liu Shao-chi, and the only item of discussion was Hungary. Khrushchev had a liking and admiration for Liu, a loquacious official who was known to have the ear of Mao Zedong. 'They sat up ... weighing the pros and cons of using force in Hungary. Both sides kept changing their minds. First Liu would suggest waiting to see if the Hungarians could sort the crisis out themselves – then he would suggest taking direct action. Liu phoned Mao regularly – like Stalin, Mao worked at night. They decided not to use force – for the moment.'[1]

Around 3.30 a.m. Khrushchev returned home briefly to his villa in the Lenin Hills. 'I couldn't sleep,' he recalled later. 'Budapest was like a nail in my head.'[2] All the options were fraught with danger for the future of the Soviet bloc and he had to worry about his own position. His enemies in the Kremlin would pounce on any perceived weakness or mistake. He did not want to be the man who 'lost' Hungary. 'All week the pressure had been building,' his son, Sergei, said. He had become withdrawn and irritable.[3] A CIA psychological file records an American psychiatrist describing Khrushchev as 'hypomanic'. There is little in his behaviour to suggest any serious symptoms of manic depression. However, his wife Nina Petrovna Khrushcheva, who kept firmly in the background like most Kremlin wives but was a plain speaker when anybody asked her direct questions, made an interesting revelation about her husband. On a visit to the US in 1961 she told the wife of the then American Ambassador, Llewellyn Thompson: 'He's either all the way up – or all the way down.'

At the start of the crisis, according to Khrushchev's son, the Soviet leader was preoccupied but not grim. Now, 'he would walk around the garden looking silent and he answered questions reluctantly. He said that he was unable to make up his mind. He vacillated throughout the crisis. He agonized not only about Hungary but about what would happen elsewhere in the empire. The Soviet bloc threatened to crumble. Every day the embassy in Budapest sent Moscow an album filled with photographs of people armed with rifles and machine guns running through the streets of Budapest, of broken glass on the pavements and smashed storefronts. Father brought the albums home with him.'[4] He pondered what Soviet history would say about the Communist leader who failed to hold on to the socialist empire but it is unlikely that he considered much Marx's line 'A people that oppresses another people cannot be free'. Nor, probably, did he consult the texts of Lenin: 'We may not use force to compel other nations to ally themselves to Russia. Only a really voluntary, a really free agreement may be used and this is impossible if there is no freedom to repeal the agreement. Only equals may come to an agreement. The parties must have equal rights if the agreement is to be real and not a conquest marked by phrases.'[5]

Restless and agitated, Khrushchev had his chauffeur drive him to his office in the Kremlin at around dawn where he started rereading the latest reports from Budapest. Mikoyan and Suslov still on the spot and for a second time within twelve hours urged the immediate despatch to Hungary of Marshal Konyev. It was the gloomiest message they had sent in a week and they sensed their worst fears were coming true: Hungary could break from the socialist camp. They reported in chilling terms on the bloody attack in Republic Square.

Khrushchev's friend and ally Ivan Serov, head of the KGB, had made his preference known from the start. He had wanted a full-scale invasion of Hungary when the uprising began, using whatever measures were needed to crush the rebels. He thought the problem the Soviets had faced over the past week was that they had used kid gloves. He sent back to Moscow a series of lurid, highly skewed and exaggerated reports which Khrushchev was reviewing again. 'The population is stimulated against Communists. In several cases the armed people search the apartments of Communists and shoot them down,' he wrote in one.[6] 'On buses ... the bandits do checks and prominent

Communists are taken out and shot.'[7] 'In Miskolc the Workers' Council suggested that the employees of the security organs lay down their weapons and go away. Three employees, including the deputy director of the Department, Major [János] Gati, would not comply with the demands. They . . . were all hanged as a group.'[8]

Khrushchev summoned the Kremlin magnates for a crucial session which he said would decide matters on Hungary once and for all. The atmosphere of crisis and tension was sharpened when they met at about 10 a.m. In the room, newsreels were screening scenes from Budapest, including the battle at Republic Square and the lynching of AVO officers.[9]

Khrushchev began by saying he had realised the previous day's decision had been a mistake almost as soon as it had been made. Now he said, decisively: 'We must re-examine our assessment. Our troops must not be taken out of Hungary or Budapest. We must take the initiative in restoring order in Hungary. If we withdraw from Hungary, this will encourage the American, English and French imperialists. They will see this as a weakness on our part and go onto the offensive. In this event our party would not understand us . . . We would give them Hungary, as well as Egypt. We have no other choice . . . We could say we tried to meet them [the Hungarians] halfway, but there is not now any government there.'[10] He had talked with the other most influential Kremlin bosses earlier and they had all approved. Only the dry fifty-six-year-old economic planning official, Maxim Saburov, a nonentity hardly ever known to have uttered an independent view, disagreed. An invasion of Hungary now 'would vindicate NATO', he said.[11]

One thing still had to be decided. The Kremlin potentates were not yet sure whom to install as Hungary's puppet leader. The choices were the faithful old lapdog Ferenc Münnich, well known by the Russians as a Hungarian 'Muscovite', a long-standing KGB agent and a man who could be relied upon to do Moscow's bidding absolutely. The alternative was the younger, more energetic János Kádár, something of an unknown quantity among the Soviet leaders, but a figure whom they had spotted as unsympathetic to the way the revolution in Budapest was going. They decided to take a look at each before making up their minds, but set the wheels in motion to make overtures to them both.

Khrushchev simply ignored his single critic. His arguments were about Soviet prestige, the unity of the socialist camp, and domestic considerations. He said that Party apparatchiks, the army, the 'organs' of the security state would not understand if the challenge posed by Hungary went unanswered. Suez was not the reason for the crackdown in Hungary. The Anglo-French adventure in the Middle East gave Khrushchev added political cover for sending new tanks into Budapest, it made the intervention far easier. But Suez prompted nothing. The Budapest tragedy was inevitable. Moscow was determined to bring the satellites into line.[12]

A series of KGB reports were presented to the magnates that disturbed them deeply. Fear that the Hungarian unrest would spill over elsewhere in the bloc was clearly amongst the principal reasons for the decision. The previous day there had been huge demonstrations throughout Poland in support of the Hungarians – about 300,000 people had taken part in a rally in Warsaw. In Romania, students in Bucharest and in many towns in Transylvania (Cluj, Timisoara and Tirgu Mures) had held big protest marches. As early as 24 October the Romanian leaders had decided to impose strict security measures and visa regulations in an attempt to seal the border with Hungary. The Romanian authorities established extra security to reinforce their defences around key buildings – train stations, airports, broadcasting stations, university campuses, Party and government offices. All leave for soldiers and security services – the Securitate – was cancelled.[13]

Unrest continued, though, and the top Communists were becoming scared. An unofficial student movement formed at Bolyai University in Cluj attracted hundreds of members, including many faculty staff who belonged to the Romanian Communist Party. This had echoes of the beginning of the events in Budapest. They were worried that Party members of Transylvanian Hungarian origin 'were especially likely to succumb to hostile elements'. Some students from Transylvania were intent on joining the Hungarian army. The previous day, the Romanian leaders set up an emergency general command staff headed by the rising Communist star Nicolae Ceausescu, who were given extraordinary powers, including the right to issue shoot-to-kill orders to the police and declare a state of emergency. They contained the troubles in Romania – but the fact that measures like this were needed told Russians leaders loud and clear that revolution in Hungary, if unchecked, could be contagious.[14]

A KGB report from Czechoslovakia described student demonstrations in Bratislava and other provincial cities, and 'a growing

hostility and mistrust of the Soviet Union'. The Czech government
in a top-secret telegram to the Kremlin admitted that events in
Hungary were having a 'deleterious psychological effect' and creating
a 'hostile anti-socialist mood' among some of the Czech troops who had
been sent to reinforce security along the 560-kilometre border with
Hungary.[15] 'If we don't embark on a decisive move, things in Czechoslovakia will collapse,' said the final resolution authorising the invasion
of Hungary. The Russians were entirely realistic. The reports from
their intelligence services, their diplomats, the governments of other
Warsaw Pact states, all seemed to suggest that the Soviet position was
precarious.[16]

They were told also about problems in the USSR itself. De-
Stalinisation had spawned many examples of public disorder that had
been hushed up. In the spring of 1956 there had been disturbances in
Georgia, with riots in Tbilisi and other cities. The Kremlin had declared
martial law throughout Georgia and sent in tanks to quell the trouble.
New riots were being threatened in Georgia and Soviet military forces
had been placed on higher alert when the Hungarian Revolution broke
out.[17]

In Russia, the KGB was concerned about a loosely formed intellectual
dissident movement that had so far been kept in check, but Khrushchev
was worried that, spurred on by the Hungarians, Soviet writers might
try to establish an equivalent of the Petőfi Circle. The Soviet leaders
were not panicking. But even though Khrushchev had begun the
process of reform, and had tried to blur the edges of Stalinism, he
feared the winds of change that were blowing from Budapest. These
fears were reinforced when student protests erupted at colleges, including at the prestigious Moscow State University. KGB troops were
despatched to arrest students and faculty staff who had denounced the
first military intervention in Hungary a week earlier. At Yaroslavl, the
KGB cracked down harshly on demonstrations in which hundreds of
people carried banners throughout the city demanding the withdrawal
of troops from Hungary.[18]

These were among the reasons the Soviets launched their second
invasion. Once decided, the Soviet leaders were determined it would be
done ruthlessly, efficiently and without mercy. Mid-morning Moscow
time, after the meeting was over, Khrushchev requested Marshal
Konyev to see him. He asked the experienced soldier how long it would
take to crush resistance in Budapest if all the necessary reinforcements

were sent. 'Three days, no more,' the Marshal replied. 'We'll do it then,' Khrushchev is reported to have said. The date was fixed to leave enough time to finish the job before Moscow celebrated the 39th Anniversary of the Russian Revolution on 7 November.[19]

Khrushchev had to square his Communist allies outside the USSR, whom he regarded as inferior but whom he needed on his side at such a tricky time. First he talked to the Chinese. When he had last seen Liu Shao-chi, in the middle of the night at Volynoskoye, the decision on Hungary had been to 'wait and see'. Now the Chinese delegation was about to return to Beijing. Unusually, all the top Russian officials were driven in a procession in their Zil 110 limousines to Vnukovo airport. Khrushchev wanted to tell Liu of the volte-face promptly rather than have him and Chairman Mao find out about it much later when the delegation landed in China. He was concerned Liu would be upset about the change of policy. But overnight Mao, too, had come round to the idea of a swift and strong response by the Soviets.[20] Khrushchev then went on a highly secret whistle-stop tour of East European capitals to inform the other socialist leaders of the Kremlin's decision.

The crucial thing, for Khrushchev, was that the Hungarians should be kept in the dark for as long as possible. Nagy must remain in doubt about Russia's intentions, so that the Hungarians would have no time to mobilise their defences. The Soviet troop movements were deliberately confusing. All the Russian soldiers, tanks and armour that had entered Budapest on 24 October had left the city by the middle of Wednesday morning, though it seemed strange to some freedom fighter groups that many Soviet units were heading west and continued towards the Austrian border, when the agreement was that they were preparing to leave the country and return to the Soviet Union.[21] Still, many of the rebels believed in the victory they had declared. Some Americans were convinced, too. The US Legation had doubted the sincerity of Moscow's 'declaration', yet it reported to Washington that there was barely any Soviet military presence left in the city. 'In a dramatic overnight change, it became virtually certain in Budapest this morning that this Hungarian Revolution is a fact of history,' the Legation reported to Washington.[22]

Hungarian leaders, early in the morning, seemed to believe it too. Zoltán Tildy said that Mikoyan had looked him in the eye and assured him that Russian troops would leave Hungary altogether – 'and I believed in his sincerity'. There were doubters, though. János Kádár was less convinced. The previous evening he had attended the same meeting Tildy had with the Armenian and Suslov. Kádár murmured afterwards that it was not them he distrusted but their assurances.

At 10 a.m. the new Hungarian Cabinet met for the first time. The mood was not celebratory. Rumours had been circulating from the early hours that while the Russians soldiers were leaving Budapest, as everyone in the city could see, fresh Soviet troops were crossing back into the country elsewhere. Train signal operators from Záhony, on the border with Soviet Ukraine, reported from early in the morning that they could see soldiers, tanks and armoured vehicles which had returned to the USSR, going back to Hungary. A more precise report said that units from the 114th Parachute Regiment of the 13th airmobile Guards Division had arrived from Lvov at Veszprém airport, eighty kilometres west of Budapest, with 1,120 troops, a dozen 82mm trench mortars and eighteen large cannon.[23] Pál Maléter, promoted to General, who would shortly be appointed Defence Minister in a meteoric career which in a few days seemed to encapsulate the intensity of the revolution, reported the facts to Nagy but said he was not entirely sure if the troop movements meant Hungary was being invaded or not. Béla Király had been placed in charge of Budapest's defences, as well as heading the National Guard. He too was unsure. But he said that even if the numbers of new troops crossing into Hungary were not significant yet, any arrivals broke the terms of the famous Soviet 'declaration' which had been published that day, with much fanfare, in *Pravda*.

If the Russian tactics were to confuse Nagy and his Ministers, they were working. The session rambled on but only one thing became clear: Nagy wanted a news blackout on any information about Soviet troop movements. First, the government did not know exactly what was happening. Second, Nagy did not want the public to be alarmed.[24]

Halfway through the meeting a messenger arrived and handed the exhausted-looking Prime Minister a note. According to deputy Foreign Minister György Heltai, a thirty-five-year-old protégé of Nagy, 'The Premier read it aloud: "British and French forces are bombing Egypt."'

The silence was deafening. 'God damn them,' Losonczy exploded.

Nagy looked at his watch and said, 'Mikoyan expects us, let's go.'

'Aren't we going to put feelers out to the West even now?' someone asked.

'Certainly not now,' Nagy replied.

There is little evidence that Nagy saw the news as much of a blow. He neither wanted nor expected any real help from the West. But he realised that the world would care less about Hungary's struggle now. He thought that if Hungary was ignored, that would make his job a little harder.[25]

Mikoyan and Suslov were waiting for Nagy and his Ministers at Communist Party headquarters to say goodbye. They were about to fly back to Moscow, their job in Budapest, as they explained, nearly done. Though they knew, by now, of the decisions taken earlier in Moscow, they gave nothing away. Both looked cheerful and relaxed, according to Heltai. Nagy asked directly why Russian troops had re-entered Hungary from Ukraine. Nagy told his aides later that the Soviet emissaries had said they meant nothing and were altogether routine. They reaffirmed Moscow's willingness to talk about Soviet troops withdrawing from Hungary and changing the terms of the Warsaw Pact. Then Mikoyan and Suslov left, as they had arrived – dressed in elegant blue wool overcoats, and in two Soviet armoured cars. Nagy had believed them. When they were gone Nagy beamed. 'I think we've done it,' he said to János Kádár.[26]

Imre Nagy, an honourable and decent man, still had a major credibility problem with his own people, however. He was not yet the hero he wanted to be, or would become. He needed to show Hungarians that the patriot in him had taken over from the 'socialist internationalist'. It would not be easy. Many of the revolutionary groups still did not trust him. To them, he was following the revolution, not leading it. Nagy was a Communist, when the great movement on the streets was increasingly anti-Communist. Socialist intellectuals and writers may have started the revolution but they were no longer in the vanguard.

Much of the propaganda beamed into Hungary from the West was deeply hostile to Nagy on the basis, as many Radio Free Europe reports said over the last few days, that 'No Communist is a good Communist'. But RFE continued to go much further, encouraging the insurgents to keep fighting and to increase their demands. 'The Ministries of Defence and the Interior are still in Communist hands,' the station declared that afternoon. 'Do not let this continue, freedom fighters, do

not hang your weapons on the wall ... This little government offers
no guarantee ... it must not be accepted even on a provisional basis. It
is urgent that a new government capable of facing the situation be
formed immediately.'[27]

Nagy realised there was one propaganda claim against him that
was seriously damaging. RFE and many of the local Hungarian radio
stations were continuing to report as fact that it had been Nagy who
had called in the Soviet troops when he became Prime Minister on 24
October. He thought 'nailing this malicious lie' was so important that
he now went on a massive spin offensive to deny it personally and to
persuade other members of the government to help him. At 2.30 p.m.
he spoke in Parliament Square and his words were carried live on Radio
Free Kossuth:

> I address you again, Hungarian brethren, with warm and affectionate
> feelings ... We are living in the first days of our sovereignty and
> independence ... We have expelled from our country the Rákosi and
> Gerő gang. They will answer for their crimes. They tried to besmirch
> me by spreading the lie that I called in the Soviet troops. This lie is
> infamous. Imre Nagy, the champion of Hungarian sovereignty, Hun-
> garian freedom and Hungarian independence, did not call in these
> troops. On the contrary, it was he who fought for their withdrawal. My
> dear friends, today we have started negotiations for the withdrawal of
> the Soviet troops from our country and the abrogation of the obligations
> imposed on us by the Warsaw Treaty. I only ask you to be a little bit
> patient ... you can place that much confidence in me ... Stand by us,
> support us in our patriotic efforts.[28]

An hour later he gave an interview to Radio Vienna when he became
decidedly tetchy:

> Q: 'What about the Warsaw Pact now? Are you in it or not?'
> Nagy: 'At present we are in it.'
> Q: 'Do you wish to leave the Warsaw Pact if the Hungarian people
> desire this?'
> N: 'Today we have begun negotiations on this matter.'
> Q: 'It will now be necessary to reconstruct Hungary economically.
> Will you apply to the Western Powers for aid ...?'
> N: 'It seems to me that we will have to count on all economic
> forces to help us emerge from this situation ...'

Q: 'You said . . . that you were put under pressure to bring in the
Soviet troops, that it was not you who invited the Soviet troops to
move into Budapest. Who invited them?'

N: 'It was not I – that I can say. At that time I was not Prime
Minister. I was not a member of the Central Committee of the Party.'

Q: 'How then did the impression grow that you invited the
troops?'

N: 'I do not know. At that time I was not a member of the
leadership. It may have been this way: at first it was said that it
was the government and then later on, after two or three days, I was
made Premier, and the masses are unable to differentiate. Two days
ago or now – it is all the same to them.'

Q: 'Did you not approve of the invitation to the Soviet troops
afterwards?'

N: 'No.'

Q: 'Did you say it was necessary for the establishment of peace
and order, or did you not?'

N: 'No, no, no. I did not say such a thing, and I must add that this
allegation has caused much damage.'[29]

He spent hours talking to various interviewers during the afternoon.
In a roundabout way that Nagy never made entirely clear he promised
justice against the torturers and murderers in the AVO: 'The guilt of
the AVO is a collective guilt,' he mused. 'We have no intention of not
punishing the criminals. All ranks who belonged to the AVO are
criminals just by virtue of having belonged to it.' Again he was
pressed on who had called in Soviet troops on the first day of the
revolution. 'The Hungarian people did not know so they tried to place
the suspicion on me. But it was not me.' 'Was it Gerő?' he was asked.
'I don't know.'[30]

Just after 8.30 a.m. in Washington DC, Allen Dulles, the bustling head
of the CIA, gave his daily morning intelligence briefing to President
Eisenhower. Almost the whole of their conversation was about Suez
and how the US could best limit the scope and damage of a 'hare-
brained' war in the Middle East. Eisenhower had already decided he
would use all his influence and diplomatic muscle in the UN to put a
stop to the conflict as soon as possible.

Dulles, ever the gentleman spy, had a far more cheerful disposition than his brother, the killjoy Secretary of State. Allen Dulles had been struggling to make sense of the confusing news from Budapest for the last week. An ardent Cold Warrior, he had no illusions about the Soviets and distrusted them on principle. Yet he and his best intelligence analysts seemed now to be convinced that the Russians meant what they said and the crisis in Hungary could be resolved. Everything they were hearing from the Middle East was 'very bad', he admitted. Then he added: 'But there's some good news.' He told the President about the Russians' 'Declaration', and that the Soviets seemed to be fulfilling their pledge to pull forces out of Budapest. 'This utterance is one of the most significant to come out of the Soviet Union since the end of World War Two,' the CIA director said.[31]

Eisenhower was more sceptical. He simply replied: 'Yes, if it's honest.' For the rest of the day he concentrated on Suez. Hungary was barely mentioned except for a brief exchange between Ike and the State Department's Dulles at about 4 p.m. The President was reminded that Hungary was due to be discussed at the next day's National Security Council. Eisenhower told Dulles he thought Suez was the higher priority.[32]

Negotiating with some of the rebel groups was proving an enormous challenge. For Király, now appointed Major-General, it seemed reasonable that the freedom fighters should not trust the Russians, but 'deeply disturbing' that they did not trust him or his deputy, Sándor Kopácsi.[33] It had been the committed revolutionary Kopácsi who on the first day of the uprising opened up the police arsenals and weapons stores so that the insurgents could get hold of arms. Yet now both of them were being grilled by the rebels about their past. Király had been a Communist and some of the rebels distrusted him, despite his long and painful years in Communist jails. Kopácsi still was a loyal Communist, of the Nagy variety. The National Guard was formally established during the afternoon, with headquarters at the Kilián Barracks, spiritual home of the revolution. There were heated exchanges at the launch that revealed major splits among the revolutionaries.[34]

Even the public's hero, Pál Maléter, was loathed by some of the insurgents. At a dramatic point in the meeting, one of the rebel commanders, Gergely Pongrácz, who had now taken over as sole head of the Corvin Passage group, rose to accuse Maléter of being a murderer. 'That is what he was and I told him so,' Pongrácz said. 'For the first day or two of the revolution, his idea of maintaining order in Budapest was to shoot at the Corvin brigade. He won't easily be forgiven by us. Many of our young kids were killed in that fighting.'[35]

Uneasily, amid acrimony and bitter scores that were never settled, the security force was finally formed, with the relieved Király elected as its head. At last, he thought, the revolutionaries had been given a stake in the new dispensation. An agreement had been needed for simple practical reasons – a start could now be made on clearing up some of the wreckage on Budapest's streets. 'It was vital not just to maintain order in the city and the country,' he explained. 'If, as some people were beginning to believe, the Russians were coming back, the National Guard could have been the basis for some sort of defence.'[36]

Nagy, against his better judgment, was persuaded to meet some of the armed freedom fighter leaders. His encounter, the previous afternoon, with 'Uncle' Szabó was almost silent as the former soldier and chauffeur, a legend on the Budapest barricades, was practically tongue-tied in Nagy's presence. According to Jenő Széll, who worked in the Prime Minister's office, Szabó was elaborately polite, 'clicked his heels and said I respectfully report for duty'. That was about all.[37]

His meeting with the tough-skinned Dudás at 6 p.m. on 30 October was bruising. Dudás had been receiving a lot of publicity from Western journalists, some of whom had billed him as the revolutionary alternative to the government. A group of Nagy's supporters convinced the 'old man' to grant Dudás an audience. All he wanted, one of them told the Prime Minister, was to be seen to be important and treated seriously, after which the noisy rebel would cease his stinging attacks on the Prime Minister.[38] Nagy went along with the idea but it was not a success. Dudás and his entourage of tough-looking street fighters walked in brandishing guns. The meeting was brief and evidently distasteful to Nagy, according to one of the participants.[39]

Dudás demanded that the government recognise him as the sole legal representative of the armed rebel groups. He claimed that the government should hand over the task of maintaining order, in collaboration with the police and the army, to the rebels under his orders, i.e. to Dudás himself. Nagy simply refused and said the responsibility of maintaining order was the business of the government 'not the likes of you'. Then Nagy ended the talks but agreed to the publication of a

statement saying the two of them had met. That was all. Then Nagy left
the room before the final draft of the statement had been approved for
he obviously accorded little importance to the whole affair.[40]

Dudás went back to his base at the *Free People* building and in his
newspaper, *Hungarian Independence*, wrote an angry article denouncing
the government as untrustworthy. Dudás halted his personal criticisms
against Nagy, but that was of scant comfort. Nagy felt that dealing with
men like Dudás was beneath him.

Anastas Mikoyan arrived back in Moscow at about 8 p.m. As soon as
his plane landed at Vnukovo airport he tried to reverse the decision
made earlier in the day. Although he knew the invasion of Budapest
was imminent, he did not know exactly when it would start until
Khrushchev told him later that evening. He was bitterly disappointed
and thought the whole venture was wrong. A proud man, he was also
angry that he had not been at the Kremlin when a decision so momentous for the Soviet bloc was made. He wondered what was the point
of despatching him to Budapest for a week if all his advice, as the
acknowledged expert on Hungary, was going to be ignored. In a series
of calls and meetings he argued with Khrushchev and the other senior
Communists in the Kremlin. He said they had misinterpreted the reports
he was sending back from Hungary. The Soviet Union was about to
make a terrible mistake, he told Khrushchev. An invasion of Hungary
would put a new freeze into the Cold War. The damage to the USSR's
prestige would undermine the reputation of the Soviets for years to
come. There were other ways of 'saving face' and ensuring that the
Soviet bloc did not fall apart, the nimble-footed Armenian said.

The hardliners were delighted at the discomfort of Mikoyan, an
incorrigibly soft liberal in their eyes. To the likes of Molotov and
Kaganovich, a defeat for Mikoyan was, by extension, a defeat for
Khrushchev too and would weaken them both. Mikoyan did not give
up, however. Normally he was a calm and cool character who could
gauge accurately when he was beaten and could trim accordingly. But
Hungary was an issue of unusual importance for him. He continued
pleading for a change of mind.

Khrushchev had not slept the night before. He was due to fly early
the next morning, with Molotov and Malenkov, on his goodwill
journey of Eastern bloc capitals. Not long before midnight he returned

to his Moscow apartment, exhausted, and tried to catch some rest. Shortly after he got to sleep the telephone rang by his bedside. It was an agitated Anastas Mikoyan, who began arguing against sending tanks back into Budapest.

'We should not use force and I'm dead set against the whole thing,' said Mikoyan.

Khrushchev, irritated that he had been woken, replied: 'What can I tell you? The decision has been taken and I agree with it.'

Mikoyan desperately said: 'Then I demand another meeting.'

Khrushchev became angrier. 'But the decision has been taken and the timetable has been established. That would have to be changed in order for us to meet again. Our whole plan would be ruined. I can't do it. I personally think we made the right decision and you are wrong,' he said and ended the conversation. He could not get back to sleep.[41]

In Budapest, the celebration parties continued all night. Budapest's squares and streets had been graveyards thirty-six hours ago, scenes of carnage. Now people were dancing, convinced they had won a victory, that their long days as an oppressed colony were over. Joyful music could be heard throughout the city, instead of the insistent cackle of rifle fire heard over the last few days. It was announced late at night that Colonel-General Gyurkó, the soldier who had twice ordered fighter planes to strafe unarmed Hungarian civilians, had deserted and placed himself under the protection of the Russians. The news seemed to symbolise how Hungarian hopes and dreams would be realised. In Parliament Square an impromptu 'cygany' (gypsy) band began playing favourite national melodies. Thousands of people wrapped themselves up to listen, sing, tell stories of the stirring deeds performed over the past days, and to toast victory.

Reports came flooding in throughout the night: Hungary had nothing to celebrate. Shortly after dawn Imre Nagy was woken by a gloom-laden Béla Király with proof that the Russians were returning to Hungary in such massive force that it could mean only one thing: an overwhelming invasion. Troops were sweeping across the Soviet border from Ukraine. A column of 850 tanks had been seen early in the morning outside Miskolc, near the Czech border. They were moving south, had crossed Hungary's second major river, the Tisza, and reached towns controlling the railway lines into the capital. They were beginning a 'slow squeeze' of Budapest, Király said. The Russians had surrounded Ferihegy airport, and only one other in the country, the military strip at Budaörs just outside the city, was left under Hungarian control. Király told Nagy that two planes were at his disposal if need be. Nagy dismissed the idea of fleeing. 'Where would I go?' he asked. Király said that he would order his deputy commander of Budapest's forces, Colonel János Mecséri, to organise an outer defensive ring of the city, but he admitted that it would not be much more than a token force.[1]

The Hungarian air force had about 100 MiG fighter jets, which could have inflicted some damage on the Russians if they had been used at this point – before the Soviets had total control of the country. Király reported that he had flatly refused to let his commanders order them into the sky, as he knew Nagy would disapprove and he thought they could still negotiate a way to prevent turning Budapest into a slaughterhouse. Nagy thought he was right.[2]

Maléter confirmed the same news about troop movements a few minutes later. He told Nagy: 'The tanks are the Soviets' muscle to exact retaliation for their setback. Their hardliners do not care about public opinion in the rest of the world; they intend to use Hungary as a lesson for the other [satellite] states. I assure you the danger has not diminished; quite to the contrary, it is getting worse.' Nagy, despite

After a day of protests, Soviet tanks began rolling into Budapest in the early hours of 24 October. The Russians imagined they were mounting a police operation against a few thousand demonstrators to 'restore order'. Instead, they quickly found themselves in a guerrilla battle against highly motivated bands of freedom fighters. Rebels took up arms under a makeshift new flag – the Hungarian red, white and green tricolour with the circular Communist emblem at is centre removed.

The principal cause Hungarians were fighting for was straightforward. Hundreds of shop fronts in Budapest were daubed with the slogan Russkik Haza (Russians Go Home). The biggest centre of armed resistance to the Soviets was in the warren of alleyways and underground passages around the Corvin, Budapest's biggest cinema, which was screening *Wings*, a romance set on a collective farm, in the week before the Revolution.

The Soviets despatched to
Budapest two of their most
senior Kremlin magnates to
handle the crisis in Hungary.
The shrewd, genial and
Machievellian Armenian,
Anastas Mikoyan (below), who
had been in leadership
positions in the Soviet Union
since the time of Lenin, argued
strongly for a peaceful and
political outcome in Budapest
in 1956. His rival, the dour
Mikhail Suslov (right), had
always forseen that military
action would be needed for
Russia to hang on to its
Hungarian satellite. The pair
stayed in Budapest for nearly a
week, sending back to
Moscow vivid first hand
accounts of the Revolution.

Two days after a ceasefire was agreed between the freedom fighters and the Soviets on 28 October, Russian tanks began to pull out of Budapest. It seemed as though the Hungarians had won an unlikely victory. For three days there were scenes of euphoria in many parts of Budapest, such as these outside the Hungarian Parliament building on the banks of the Danube. But celebrations were short-lived.

Pál Maléter (above), the inspirational military leader of the Revolution, was a much-admired tank corps commander who joined the rebels on the first day of the Revolution, taking most of his officers and men with him. He was in command at the Kilián Barracks before joining Imre Nagy's government as Defence Minister.

One of the best-known leaders of the civilian freedom fighters on the streets was János 'Uncle' Szabó (right) – a chauffeur with a gift for leadership who devised unorthodox, but highly effective, guerrilla tactics against the vastly superior might of Soviet tanks and armour.

Some gory cases of mob violence (left and below), as most of the rebel leaders acknowledged, disfigured the Revolution. The loathed secret police were the targets of vicious revenge attacks. Scores of AVO officers were lynched in the streets of the city and left hanging for days from trees and lamp posts.

János Kádár (left) joined Imre Nagy as one of the political leaders of the Uprising. He was Communist Party boss, but turned coat, went over to the Soviet side, was secretly flown to Moscow and was installed as head of a Soviet puppet regime after the Russian invasion. For years afterwards he was known as 'Judas' Kádár, but over time he gained a measure of independence from the Kremlin and won grudging admiration from Hungarians.

The defendants in the Imre Nagy trial when sentence was passed in June 1958. In civilian clothes, Imre Nagy (left), Zoltán Tildy (front centre) and Miklós Gimes (front right). Head and shoulders above the rest (rear centre) is Pál Maléter and (rear right) Sándor Kopácsi.

After Operation Whirlwind on 4 November, when the Soviet army returned in overwhelming force to crush the Revolution, the Hungarians began counting the cost of their brave but doomed rebellion. It was an heroic failure. More than 2,500 people were killed. Budapest was devastated. Ugly, brutal reprisals continued for years, in which thousands of people suspected of opposition to the regime were jailed. The scars were visible in Hungary for decades afterwards.

the evidence he was hearing, still did not believe it. He kept telling his aides that he was sure he had a deal with the Soviets. He knew the Russians, he had been a Soviet citizen. He was sure they could not be so 'treacherous'.[3]

He tried calling Moscow on the 'K' line. There was no answer and, extraordinarily, nobody would even acknowledge a message from the Hungarian Prime Minister. He tried Mikoyan, who did not call back either. Nagy sensed that his worst fears were proving true.[4]

In Moscow, Khrushchev was preparing, with Molotov, to leave for Brest, near Poland's borders with Russia. He wanted to tell satellite leaders personally of the decision to invade Hungary, partly out of courtesy, but partly, thought some of his advisers, as a way of showing who was boss. Khrushchev's Kremlin apartment was in the same block as Anastas Mikoyan's. At around 7 a.m., almost as Khrushchev was leaving for the airport, the Armenian waylaid him and tackled him once again about Hungary. He repeated all the anguished arguments of the night before and Khrushchev admitted that, much as he respected Mikoyan, he was growing weary of these encounters. They walked along a gravel path in the chilly air while Khrushchev's limousine rolled up the driveway behind them. 'Do you think it's any easier for me?' Khrushchev asked. 'We have to act. We have no other choice.'[5]

Mikoyan kept saying the Hungarian invasion was a foolish decision and eventually, just as Khrushchev made ready to depart, almost shouted, 'If blood is shed, I don't know what I'll do with myself.' The two men misunderstood each other. Khrushchev thought his closest colleague was hinting at suicide and replied, 'That would be the height of stupidity, Anastas. I believe you are a rational man. Think it over, take all the factors into account and you'll see we made the right decision. Even if there's bloodshed now, it will spare us bloodshed later. Think again and you will see the necessity of our decision.' Later, Mikoyan said that his comment meant that, fleetingly, he had considered resigning over Hungary. But he thought better of it.[6]

Finally Nagy managed to find a senior Russian who would talk to him. He telephoned the Soviet Embassy and demanded to see Yuri Andropov urgently. At 9 a.m. the Ambassador arrived at Nagy's wood-panelled office in the Parliament building, where a camp bed had been installed for the last few nights, but had hardly been used. Nagy insisted on being told what was the meaning of the Soviet troop reinforcements.[7] Andropov replied calmly that he did not know what the Red Army's movements were in Hungary, he had no accurate information, but would immediately ask his government for an explanation. After about five minutes he was escorted out and Nagy was left with his chief aides and closest friends, his secretary József Szilágyi, Géza Losonczy and his son-in-law Ferenc Jánosi. Shortly later, Tildy arrived. These were the principal advisers who with Nagy calculated the tactics the government would employ if all the reports about a new Russian invasion were true. Hungary would leave the Warsaw Pact and declare itself neutral. It was a desperate measure and, at this point in the morning, Nagy was unsure that he wanted to increase the stakes by making the threat. He still hoped the Russians would back off if he could establish that Budapest was peaceful, if the strikes were called off, and if Hungary would guarantee to remain a friendly socialist neighbour.[8]

He repeated his instructions on an information blackout about Russian troop movements. He did not want 'the public to be agitated'. Nor did he want any of the armed insurgents to do anything that might provoke the Russians or give them an excuse to return. He also asked Maléter, now deputy Defence Minister, to make a direct appeal for calm and to use his reputation to bolster the government. While Maléter knew the truth – that fresh Russian forces were massing inside the country – he swallowed his pride and did his duty: 'The people of Hungary are mature enough not immediately to regard as a provocation any tardiness in connection with promises made by foreign leaders,' he said.[9] He also agreed to call for an end to the strikes in a plea aimed as directly to the Kremlin as it was to the workers of 'Red' Csepel or other industrial districts of Hungary: 'In the course of the revolutionary fighting every combatant heard with pride that they were supported by the workers' strike,' he said. 'However, as after every battle, the era of peaceful construction must now begin in order to consolidate the achievements of the revolution. The aim of the strike was to weaken the opponent. The present strike weakens not our opponent but ourselves. We must ensure milk for our children, coal for our factories ... Otherwise we shall lose what our revolutionary fighters have won at the cost of so great a sacrifice in blood.'[10]

Nagy waited for good news, unaware that the Russians were now merely stringing him along and had left him no avenue for negotiations.

There was an exodus from Hungary. Western journalists were

leaving as fast as they could, unaware of the tragedy to come. Suez, a war in the Middle East, was filling the front pages and reporters were despatched elsewhere by their news desks. The American reporters began drifting away the previous day. Suez, they thought, was the better story. One of the best-known bylines in British journalism, Sefton Delmer of the (then) best-selling *Daily Express*, declared: 'This is not news any more.'[11] As they drifted from the city – on another clear autumn day, slightly warmer than the last few – they could see life returning to a kind of normality. Some children were still walking around carrying guns, but the process of clearing up the rubble had begun – a task performed by smiling faces and people who looked happier than they had for years.

The first stop on Khrushchev's tour of his satellite states was potentially the most tricky. He was to meet the Polish Communist leader, Gomulka, who had come to power less than a fortnight earlier in a rebellion in Warsaw that in some ways mirrored the uprising in Budapest. The Polish crisis had been settled peacefully. But from Khrushchev's point of view, Poland was still considered turbulent and potentially dangerous. He knew that Gomulka had sympathised with the Hungarians and the Polish people supported the revolution wholeheartedly. He wanted to square Gomulka with the invasion because he did not wish any trouble to come from another flank of the Soviet empire, in Warsaw. Gomulka had encouraged Nagy to seek more independence from Russia, but had privately sent him repeated warnings not to go 'too far' and bring the Soviet axe down on his head.[12] He thought Nagy had ignored all the warnings and reckoned him a poor politician, lacking in judgment.

Yet Gomulka still 'objected strongly' when Khrushchev told him the Russians would settle Hungary with force. Khrushchev thought Gomulka was being 'deliberately difficult' and was not sure that he would refrain from criticising Moscow directly and publicly. The Pole said the Hungarian crisis should be 'resolved by the Hungarian people alone and not by foreign intervention', but went no further than that. He offered Warsaw as a venue for direct Hungarian-Russian talks. But the offer came to nothing. The Russians refused. The time for talking was over. However, Gomulka was shrewd and finally agreed to maintain a discreet silence in public on Hungary to avoid antagonising the Kremlin.[13] It was the best Khrushchev could hope for in Poland and he was content. His other meetings with more servile communist leaders went smoothly. The Czech and Romanian leaders were frightened men desperately worried about Hungary. Antonin Novotny in Prague and Gheorghe Gheorghiu-Dej, the Romanian Communist boss, were so keen on a crackdown against Budapest that they asked if their troops could take part too. Khrushchev refused.[14]

At 11 a.m. Andropov met Imre Nagy again, now at the Communist Party headquarters. Nagy demanded a reply to his question: why are new Russian forces crossing the border? 'What does Moscow say?' he asked.[15] 'The troop movements are routine and not to the prejudice of Hungary,' the Ambassador replied. 'To the contrary, we are doing it to avoid incidents in the pullout of our military units. That is our obligation: to ensure the orderly withdrawal of the forces.' Nagy asked: 'But why have tanks and armoured cars encircled our airports?' Andropov had no ready answer but, under strict orders to play for time, he said 'to ensure the safe evacuation by air of the sick and wounded. You will surely agree, Mr Prime Minister, that things are not very peaceful in your country right now.' This set alarm bells ringing in Nagy's mind. 'For him to be addressed as Mr (Gospodin) was a stab. Andropov and other Russian officials had always called him Comrade until now,' one of Nagy's aides recalled.[16]

Still, he preferred to believe Andropov. There was probably not much else he could do at that stage. He protested formally about Soviet troops crossing the frontier and insisted that Andropov provide him with more accurate and up-to-date information, or Hungary would be left with no alternative but to leave the Warsaw Pact and declare itself neutral.

Nagy had appointed himself Foreign Minister earlier in the day, combining the post with the Premiership. He explained that he was the most experienced man for the job, but he told his keen young deputy, György Heltai, to prepare two documents that he would send the Soviets if necessary.[17] A moment of high farce followed, Heltai recalled. 'When the decision to leave the Warsaw Pact was taken Hungarian officials could not find a single copy of the document,' he recalled. 'Of course we suspected that there might be a clause which makes the entry of foreign troops into the country conditional on a request by the Hungarian government. None of us, including Imre Nagy, had ever seen the Warsaw Pact. We had searched through the

Foreign Ministry registry. No Warsaw Pact. Someone then called the headquarters of the secret police. And there it was, the single copy of the agreement. A messenger brought it over.'[18]

Mikoyan was a realist. Yet despite his dawn assignation with Khrushchev, he still believed he could halt the invasion. Mid-morning in Moscow, he collected all the important magnates remaining in the Kremlin and made a last desperate plea to avoid what he predicted would be a disaster in Budapest. 'In Hungary, the use of force now will not help in anything,' he said. 'We should enter into negotiations instead, wait and see what happens. If the [Nagy] government weakens, then let's decide what to do . . . about taking the troops out or not. Let's wait 10 to 15 days, support the government there and see what happens. If the situation stabilises then everything will be for the better.'[19]

Suslov, when in Budapest, had been indecisive. Now he was absolutely certain of the right response: an invasion in force to show who had the power in Eastern Europe. He disliked Nagy intensely for his weakness. 'Imre Nagy did not organise the uprising, but he has been used by people who did,' Suslov declared. The soldiers were the most forceful in favour of teaching the Hungarians a lesson – and issuing a warning to the other colonies in the empire. A couple of days previously, Minister of Defence Zhukov had been in favour of a diplomatic solution. No longer. 'This is the time for decisive action to catch all the scoundrels. To disarm them,' he told Mikoyan. Marshal Konyev always talked in short breathless sentences, as though issuing orders, even when he was in conference inside the Kremlin. He said simply: 'Budapest is in the hands of the rebels. Anarchy rules. Reaction has the upper hand. The solution: invasion.'

Shortly afterwards, the bull-necked Konyev and his top aides flew to Szolnok, in central Hungary, where he took personal command of the operation to destroy the resistance in Budapest. It was given the codename Operation Whirlwind. By the time the Marshal arrived in Hungary, all the airports had been surrounded by Soviet troops, including the most westerly strip at Veszprém. The families of Soviet officers based in Hungary with the Special Corps had been evacuated.[20]

By 2 p.m. Nagy had heard nothing from the Soviet Embassy. With mounting indignation and frustration, and while the rest of his Cabinet

was in the room, he rang Andropov. He said he now possessed
documentary proof about the movement of Russian troops. 'My military experts have determined as a fact that within the last three hours
even more Soviet troops have crossed the frontier,' he said. 'Your
government is trying to reoccupy Hungary, despite your own Declaration.'[21] Andropov again attempted to say that the new Russian
forces were simply ensuring the safety of the troops which were withdrawing. But now Nagy did not believe him. He announced formally
that Hungary would quit the Warsaw Pact and would ask the four Great
Powers to guarantee Hungary's neutrality 'with immediate effect'.

Hungary's neutrality declaration continues to puzzle historians.
There are some in Russia – no apologists for the Communist era – who
argue that it was the last straw for the Kremlin, the move that convinced
the Soviets to send the tanks rolling back into Budapest.[22] Leaving the
Warsaw Pact was a desperate gamble but the logic was simple. It would
remove the Soviets' treaty rights to intervene in Hungary. Legally,
instead of offering assistance to an ally, they would be attacking an
independent, sovereign state. Some of the freedom fighters' groups
in Budapest, and the revolutionary leaders in the provinces such as
Szigetthy in Győr and Rudolf Földvári in Miskolc, wanted Hungary to
declare neutrality soon after the uprising began.[23] If they had done so,
the argument ran, they would have been in a better position to seek
help from the West. Two days earlier, when he became a Minister and
a member of Nagy's inner Cabinet, the thoughtful Béla Kovács called
for an end to Hungary's 'ties with military blocs'. Nagy was lukewarm.
But his role was to follow the revolution, which he had been doing all
week.

Nagy had hinted to Mikoyan and Suslov two days earlier, when the
Soviet emissaries were still in Budapest, that neutrality was a long-term
goal of the revolution and he hoped to talk about it with the leaders in
Moscow. They reported the comment straight to their colleagues in the
Kremlin – at the time Khrushchev was at Stalin's dacha, turning over
in his mind what to do about Hungary. The neutrality declaration was
an important factor, one of Khrushchev's speech-writers suggested.
'The Soviets knew the momentum in Hungary was building to leave
the Pact. They knew it was likely to happen. They could not permit it.
They had to stop it. Once the Soviet leaders were confronted by the
prospect of Hungarian neutrality they realised how much influence
they had lost.'[24]

The participants on the Hungarian side say that the declaration was a reaction to the Soviets' decision to invade, not the other way round. 'Just look at the dates,' said Béla Király:

The second wave of Soviet aggression started on 31 October. We could see the troop movements . . . We were getting information from various sources, the railway workers for example, who kept us very well informed about the Russian movements. We told Imre Nagy. He began to protest. We were supposed to have a ceasefire agreement with the Soviet Union and they were placing new troops in Hungary, in violation of their agreements. We did protest. On that Thursday, 1 November, Budapest was already surrounded. That is when Hungary declared its neutrality. It was like a drowning man who reaches for a tiny branch of driftwood. That was the spirit in which Hungary made the declaration.

Yes it was desperate. We thought that as a Warsaw Pact member there was nothing any other country could do if we were invaded. The world would regard it as a family quarrel – they won't interfere in . . . internal affairs. But if Hungary was neutral and independent, there was a slim chance that others might just do something, diplomatically anyway. The declaration of neutrality was not the cause of the invasion, but the effect of it. The invasion had already begun by then.

The reason Nagy appealed to the UN to recognise Hungary's neutrality and the Great Powers to protect that status was not because he imagined the Americans would help militarily – Nagy did not ask. The Hungarians, though, did expect the US to employ energetic and peaceful means to defend Hungary's neutrality. In fact they did nothing. Nor did the UN.[25]

In the White House at 9 a.m. President Eisenhower was chairing a meeting of the National Security Council with his foreign policy advisers and intelligence experts. As he entered the room, before sitting down, he announced 'I do not want you to take up the situation in the Soviet satellites today. I want to concentrate on the Middle East.'

The CIA director Allen Dulles was insistent on saying something about Hungary, though, and Ike let him. Dulles said: 'A miracle has occurred in Budapest that has belied our past views that a popular revolt in the face of modern weapons is an utter impossibility. The impossible has happened . . . because of the power of public opinion, armed force could not effectively be used.' Though the President had said the news sounded 'too good to be true', Dulles continued in optimistic vein that he believed in the Soviets' 'declaration'. 'The main problem in Hungary today is the lack of a strong guiding authority to bring the rebels together,' Dulles said. 'Nagy is failing to unite the rebels. Somehow a rallying point must be found to prevent chaos inside Hungary if the Soviets take their leave. In a heavily Catholic nation such as Hungary, Cardinal Mindszenty might prove to be such a leader and unifying force.'[26]

The Primate had been officially rehabilitated by Nagy in a decree signed around the time Mindszenty arrived in Budapest the previous morning. Exuberant crowds had grown, since, outside his palace, but they were smaller than Nagy had predicted. The Cardinal had said very little in public over the last day and a half. He told an Italian journalist that he would use the next couple of days 'to find out what the world has been doing while I have been away' and he gave audiences to Zoltán Tildy and Pál Maléter amongst others. Both urged him to back Imre Nagy and the government but the Cardinal said he would wait and see and make a broadcast in two days. He did not know that the director of the Central Intelligence Agency was putting forward his name to the US President as a potential leader of Hungary, but all Hungary was aware the Primate had backing from America. When he was released, Radio Free Europe 'encouraged Hungarian youth to accept Mindszenty as the leader of the rebellion' and called on them 'to fight with all their strength on the streets to defend the church'.[27]

At 5 p.m. Andropov joined a Cabinet meeting called by Nagy. A few minutes earlier, the decision about neutrality had been unanimously reaffirmed, but not made public. Nagy thought the decision was so momentous he kept putting off announcing it just in case it could be avoided. He realised now it could not wait much longer. Andropov said that he had at last received an official response from Moscow. Nagy himself translated it into Hungarian, for the benefit of his Ministers who knew no Russian, and he dictated it to an aide. The USSR, it said, stood firmly by the declaration of 30 October and wanted to negotiate a full settlement with Hungary. The Soviets proposed establishing two joint commissions, one to deal with the political consequences of Hungary's neutrality, the other to handle the withdrawal of Russian soldiers.

Nagy knew that Andropov was deceiving him and stringing him along, according to aides. He now realised, with a weary fatalism, that there was almost certainly nothing he could do to avoid the catastrophe to come. The Ambassador was acting under instructions from Moscow to gain time – for two reasons. The first was to minimise potential military resistance by the Hungarians and reduce Russian casualties when they invaded. The second was to find Hungarian quislings prepared to set up an alternative government. Lying was the most harmless of the means he could have used.

Nagy and the Cabinet listened to the answer. Nobody looked very convinced. Andropov was again asked, simply, if he could give a guarantee that no fresh troops would cross the border into Hungary. He had lied all day with aplomb, but now remained silent. Then Nagy did a strange thing. He went round the Cabinet table and asked every member individually to state whether they agreed with the decision to quit the Warsaw Pact. They all did.*[28] Andropov reported back to the Kremlin with satisfaction and noted who was enthusiastic about the decision and who was not. He noted that János Kádár 'was reluctant'.

The United Nations deeply disappointed the Hungarians – partly by accident, partly by blunder and partly through wilfulness. When Hungary was resisting the Russians, the free world was stunned and stood in admiration. Now, it was about to stand in idleness. The UN could not, or preferred not to, think seriously about two crises at a time – and it decided that Suez was the more important. Through a series of muddles and misunderstandings, the anguished pleas of Hungary were barely heard in New York.

Imre Nagy had made no contact with the UN until this point, when he appealed for international help. He said later that it had not occurred to him to do so, because he had faith in the Russians. It was too late, of course. He wanted the UN General Assembly to debate Hungary that afternoon, when it was due to hold a session on the Middle East. The Americans, the Soviets and the UN's vastly respected Secretary General, the fifty-one-year-old Swedish moral philosopher and diplomat Dag Hammarskjöld, all colluded to ensure it stuck to one subject, Suez.[29]

---

* According to many reports, at this meeting the most passionate opponent of a second intervention by the Russians was János Kádár. It has been claimed, though never verified, that Kádár looked directly at Andropov and declared that if Soviet troops entered Budapest, 'I don't care about myself. I would fight them with my bare hands.'

Shortly before 4.30 p.m. in Budapest (10.30 a.m. in Manhattan) the teleprinter on the twenty-second floor of UN building received a telex from an operator identified as DIPLOMAG BUDAPEST. 'TO UNITED NATIONS, NEW YORK . . . ARE YOU THERE?' Usually these messages were delivered to a country's UN delegate. But there was a continuing problem with Hungary's representative, Péter Kós, who had been fired but had not vacated his office.* So the message went to the main communications centre. At 10.42, another telex from the Budapest foreign ministry arrived: 'FOR SECRETARIAT UN: IF YOU ARE BUSY I CAN CALL A FEW MINUTES LATER, OUR MESSAGE WILL BE READY OK? PLEASE ANSWER.' The reply came back almost instantly: 'WE ARE NOT BUSY, CAN WAIT IF YOU WANT.' This was after Nagy's Cabinet had approved the neutrality declaration but before the meeting Andropov had attended. Nagy decided to wait and after forty-eight minutes without transmitting, Budapest broke the connection at 11.14.

From New York's end this must have seemed mysterious. Hungary may not have been the number one subject of the day, but it was still a crisis. Nobody warned Hammarskjöld's office that something unusual was happening in Hungary and that a message might arrive at any moment from Imre Nagy.

At 12.21 the UN teleprinter began again. 'BUDAPEST CALLING. ARE YOU READY PLEASE?' The UN replied Yes and Nagy began his plea:

Reliable reports have reached the government of the Hungarian People's Republic that further Soviet units are entering into Hungary. [The Prime Minister] summoned Mr Andropov, the Soviet Ambassador, and expressed his strongest protest against the entry of further Soviet troops into Hungary. He demanded the instant and immediate withdrawal of these Soviet forces.

He informed the Soviet Ambassador that the Hungarian government immediately repudiates the Warsaw Treaty, and, at the same time, declares Hungary's neutrality, turns to the United Nations, and requests the help of the Great Powers in defending the country's neutrality.

Therefore I request Your Excellency promptly to put on the

---

* Hungarians were infuriated when they discovered, on the third day of the revolution, that Péter Kós was in fact a Soviet citizen, Leo Konduktorov. But this was not unusual among the Soviet satellites at the time. Kós was fired by Imre Nagy, but his replacement took some days to arrive and was himself sacked when Kádár took over.

agenda of the forthcoming General Assembly of the United Nations the question of Hungary's neutrality and the defence of this neutrality by the four Great Powers . . .

Signed. Imre Nagy.

The drama and importance of the news was realised by everyone in the teleprinter room and the message arrived in the Secretary General's office eight minutes later. But it was lunchtime at Hammarskjöld's secretariat. It was not until 2 p.m. that the text of Nagy's statement was circulated to delegates. At first Hammarskjöld's aides tried to deny they had ever received the message, although later they had to explain further. It had not been noticed 'through confusion or oversight', they said. The message was not flagged to delegates as urgent. It was placed in their pigeonholes and most of them ignored it. Hammarskjöld's advisers then debated what Nagy meant by 'the forthcoming General Assembly'. That day's session was due to begin in less than three hours. They decided he could not be referring to today; he must have meant the meeting on 12 November.

Amidst so many missed opportunities, misunderstandings and confusions in the Hungarian Revolution, here, now, was another. It should have been clear to which General Assembly meeting Nagy was addressing his desperate plea. Just eighteen minutes after sending his neutrality statement another telex arrived at 42nd Street. I HAVE THE HONOUR TO INFORM YOU THAT MR JÁNOS SZABÓ FIRST SECRETARY OF THE PERMANENT MISSION WILL REPRESENT THE HUNGARIAN PEOPLE'S REPUBLIC AT THE SPECIAL SESSION OF THE GENERAL ASSEMBLY OF THE UNITED NATIONS TO BE CONVENED NOVEMBER IST 1956 AT NEW YORK.[30] The date could not have been clearer, but the UN secretariat overlooked it. More than twenty-four hours later Hammarskjöld did not even know about that telex. Later, during the debate itself, Hungary was barely mentioned in a meeting that dragged on for several hours and ended in a condemnation of the Anglo-British invasion of Egypt. György Heltai said Nagy made a bad mistake by not appealing to the UN earlier. He might have gained some time to raise international support. Ultimately, it probably made little difference, though. 'By now the West was occupied with the Suez crisis and we got no real answer from the UN,' he said. Hammarskjöld did not go to Budapest or Moscow in an attempt to settle a crisis. He went to Cairo.[31]

*

Just before 8 p.m., in the radio studio one floor beneath his office at
the Parliament building, Imre Nagy took a mouthful of honey a radio
technician offered him to sweeten his mouth. Even so, he had a gulp in
his throat when he announced that Hungary was leaving the Warsaw
Pact. He spoke much more emotionally and grandiloquently than was
usual for him:[32]

> People of Hungary! The ... government, imbued with profound
> responsibility towards the Hungarian people and its history, and giving
> expression to the undivided will of the Hungarian millions, declares
> the neutrality of the Hungarian People's Republic. The Hungarian
> people, on the basis of independence and equality and in accordance
> with the spirit of the United Nations Charter, wish to live in true
> friendship with her neighbours, the Soviet Union, and all the peoples
> of the world. The Hungarian people desire the consolidation and further
> development of the achievements of their national revolution, without
> joining any power blocs. The century-old dream of the Hungarian
> people is thus fulfilled. The revolutionary struggle fought by the
> Hungarian heroes of the past and present has at last carried the cause
> of freedom and independence to victory. The heroic struggle has made
> it possible to implement, in our people's international relations, its
> fundamental national interest: neutrality. We appeal to our neighbours,
> countries near and far, to respect the unalterable decision of our people.
> Today our people are as united in this decision as perhaps never before
> in their history.[33]

Then he went home. He told aides he was pessimistic but not without
hope, that the Soviets could be persuaded to change their minds again.
But there was nothing he could do that night. Now he wanted some sleep.
Nagy had barely seen his wife Maria for a week and had caught snatches
of rest in his office. He wanted a decent night in his own bed at his villa
in Buda, a shower, a good meal – and to think of 'normal life for a while'.
He would return to Parliament early the next morning, he said.[34]

Around the time Nagy arrived home, the Party boss, János Kádár, had
just finished a broadcast on the radio. It was rousing stuff: 'In their
glorious uprising, our people have shaken off the Rákosi regime. They
have achieved freedom for the people, and independence for the country,' he declared. The new Hungarian Socialist Workers Party that he
was proud to lead as part of the Nagy coalition 'would take part in

elections and would break away from the crimes of the past once and for all. It will defend the honour and independence of our country against anyone.'[35] The speech had been pre-recorded that morning. By the time listeners heard it, Kádár had betrayed the revolution and defected to the Russians. Between 8 and 9 p.m. he left the Parliament building, telling fellow Ministers and aides that he was going out to dinner. Then he vanished from sight, along with Ferenc Münnich.

Despite his age, Münnich was still an ambitious man. He had lived for years in Russia. He was convinced the Soviets would stamp on the revolution, sooner rather than later, and he wanted to be on the winning side. Though not an old-fashioned Stalinist, he was pro-Russian through and through. Sir William Hayter, who knew him well on the Moscow diplomatic circuit, described him as 'good-tempered and friendly. He seemed to have a cynical sense of humour and was . . . a bon viveur. But I never heard him express an independent opinion about anything.'[36] He had been in close contact throughout the revolution with Andropov and kept his friends in the Kremlin and the Lubyanka well informed about Budapest. Earlier in the day he had said with much authority to a reporter that 'the Russians will not dare to attack Hungary because it could lose them world prestige', but he did not mean it. Münnich had been trying to convince Kádár for a day and a half that they should turn coat together and go over to the Russians. One of his most persuasive arguments was the horrifying slaughter of Kádár's great friend and Münnich's fellow Spanish Civil War veteran, Imre Mező. The other was a passionate conviction they both sharedthat they did not wish to be martyrs, but, rather, should be power-brokers.[37]

Kádár shared his real thoughts with nobody. After the Cabinet meeting attended by Andropov that evening Münnich persuaded Kádár to see the Ambassador privately. Kádár at first was reluctant but finally agreed. The two men tried to be discreet about their intentions. From Parliament, Münnich called for a car and a driver at round 8.30 p.m. He and Kádár stepped into a Mercedes with curtains in the back, and Münnich ordered the chauffeur to take them to a secluded wooded park close to the Kerepesi cemetery, famous in the summer as a rendezvous spot for lovers. When the car drew to a halt, they were met by a black Soviet Zis limousine. The two Hungarians stepped out and walked towards the Russian car, but Kádár seemed to hesitate as if unsure whether to go through with the assignation. They argued in the darkness for a few minutes until finally Kádár was almost pushed by Münnich into the waiting Russian limousine. Neither man ever disclosed exactly what was said between them.

They were driven directly to the Soviet Embassy, where Andropov charmed and threatened Kádár by turns. He was the only Hungarian to whom Andropov told the whole story. He said that the Soviets had decided to invade Hungary with overwhelming force imminently and nothing would stop them, that 'Nagy's game is up and he's done for'. Kádár had little choice, the Ambassador said. If he refused to co-operate with the Russians, he would suffer the same fate as Nagy. Kádár agreed to go to Moscow and talk to the potentates in the Kremlin.[38]

Towards midnight Kádár, Münnich and another defector, the former Hungarian Defence Minister István Báta, were driven to the Soviet military air base at Tököl just outside Budapest, along with a Soviet Embassy official. They were seen by Malaschenko, second in command of Russian troops based in Hungary. The Hungarians, he recalled, 'seemed exhausted. Kádár's shoes had soaked through. We put them up in our air force's only, and none too big, guest house. We gave Kádár a pair of socks and officers' shoes from the supplies department. When we asked what the situation was in Budapest he said he had left Imre Nagy's government and was now wondering what he should do. When he saw a nice-looking chess set on the table he became more animated.'

About two hours later the head of the KGB, the short-fused Ivan Serov, who had been in Budapest throughout the week, arrived. He joined the Hungarians on a flight to Moscow at dawn the next morning on a Russian transport plane.

TWENTY-NINE

Friday, 2 November

The rain poured down from daybreak and a bone-numbing wind swirled across the Danube. It was the first day of winter. There had been no official news from the government about Soviet troops returning to Hungary. Surprisingly, the dozen or so independent newspapers that had sprung up over the last couple of days reported nothing about Russian troops on the move. But word of mouth had travelled and people knew the city was being surrounded by a mass of Soviet troops and armour.

In Budapest, many people fooled themselves into believing that the revolution had been triumphant. Soviet troops had been forced to leave the capital, humbled by ill-organised, poorly equipped but passionate groups of young freedom fighters. The Communists were no longer the only real power in the land. In the reopened cafés, politics was discussed with the kind of openness and intensity few people could remember. New political parties were being formed every few hours. There was a free press, of sorts. Transport was running amongst the debris of shattered glass and masonry of the city centre streets.

Almost all workers had voted to end the strikes. Many had already returned to their factories and offices and schools. More would go back today and the rest promised to return on Monday. The Workers' Councils, which had so quickly taken power as extraordinary examples of direct democracy, assured the government and people that 'On Monday things would get back to normal'.[1]

Yet people did not feel normal. 'Mainly, at that time, we felt a weary sense of helplessness,' said one of the student activists. 'We realised, of course, what seemed sure to happen. But we hoped, while we were apprehensive. Could we believe that the victory we thought we had won would be seized from our grasp? We didn't want to believe it. And of course we were scared.'[2] Many thought of heading to the West, though it would have been difficult now. From the previous day the

Austrians had closed the border, when they saw the size of the Russian military build-up. The Mayor of Budapest, József Kővágó, considered escape carefully. To the disappointment of his wife, Lonci, he decided to stay at his post.³ György Heltai was pondering escape, he said later, even while he was drafting the declaration of Hungary's neutrality.⁴

The rebel fighters, who in their own eyes had beaten off the Russians, were split. Some agreed to join Béla Király's National Guard and support the Nagy government. Maléter, symbolically, had moved his office from the Kilián Barracks, where his own tank still stood outside the main gate, to the Parliament building. Officially his line was that 'neither the government nor I have any reason to doubt the word' of the Russians.⁵ But very few freedom fighters handed over any weapons. Gergely Pongrácz, the leader of the Corvin Passage group, did not. Many of the original fighters who had joined him had drifted away since the Soviet troops left Budapest, 'but they vowed to return if the Russians came back. This period, when we were waiting and seeing, was the worst part of the revolution.'⁶

Through the wet streets Imre Nagy was driven from his home back to his office in the Parliament building at around 7.30 a.m. Immediately he sat at his desk he asked to see the Soviet Ambassador. He had been informed that yet more Soviet troops were crossing the frontier.⁷ Southeast of the capital a giant crescent formation of tanks had formed, presently around 100 kilometres from the city but moving ever closer. Andropov, unusually, looked untidy; he was normally very careful about his appearance. He now looked as though he had been dragged out of bed. He had not shaved, his necktie was skewed, and he seemed exhausted. Nagy read an official diplomatic *note verbale* complaining about the Soviet troop reinforcements and hurled charge after charge at Andropov about the Kremlin's duplicity. The Ambassador shrugged, continued his barefaced lies and played down the military threat. He said: 'When you talk about a massive invasion you are obviously exaggerating. It is just that some units are being replaced by others. But they too will be pulled out. The whole question is not worth a wooden kopeck.'⁸

Andropov, playing for time, insisted that Moscow was serious about negotiations and together he and Nagy worked out the details. The Hungarian and Soviet armies would begin talks about the withdrawal of troops the next day at the Hungarian Parliament. The two sides would soon name their representatives. Diplomatic and political talks about Hungary's neutrality and departure from the Warsaw Pact would follow soon. Nagy nominated Géza Losonczy as the Minister responsible for dealing with those. Nagy decided to act as though Moscow was being genuine about these negotiations. What, he asked, did he have to lose?

At around 10 a.m. the Budapest police chief Sándor Kopácsi entered Imre Nagy's office. Despite Nagy's good night's sleep in his own bed, Kopácsi still thought the Prime Minister's eyes looked withered and strained. He took off his pince-nez and said: 'Comrade Kopácsi, I have to talk to you. My question is simple. Do you have any idea where the Minister of the Interior is?'[9] He replied that he had none. From the previous day, Kopácsi had been unable to reach his immediate boss, Ferenc Münnich. Nagy continued: 'You should know János Kádár also cannot be found. Nothing must disturb the atmosphere of the country at this crucial moment. Can you and Király guarantee nothing will happen that could be labelled an anti-Soviet provocation and used as a pretext for breaking off negotiations?' Kopácsi said he would do his best.

Kopácsi, Losonczy and Szilágyi launched an urgent hunt for the missing Ministers. According to Jenő Széll, who was now placed in charge of Radio Kossuth, even Kádár's forty-two-year-old wife, Maria, who worked as a personnel manager at the Hungarian telegraph agency, MTI, had no idea where he was. 'I had been on pretty good terms with Maria Kádár for a while. She had been there in the Parliament building since the second night of the revolution. She told me she was being treated more or less as a hostage. She said, "My husband's vanished and they won't let me out of here." She thought it was the government who were treating her like that. But they didn't know where he had gone either.'[10] Münnich, who had been a rampant womaniser in his youth and middle age, now had just one mistress, his former secretary. He had spoken to her on the phone shortly before he disappeared, but he gave no hint about where he was going. All morning speculation had grown about their whereabouts. 'The rumours swung between extremes,' said Széll. 'It was said that Kádár had been lured into a trap and was captured, or that he had deserted and gone over to the Russians. The latter gained ground as the day wore on.'[11]

The story about the Hungarian chauffeur taking them to an assignation where they were met by the Russians was still a rumour, unconfirmed until much later, after the revolution was crushed. Nevertheless

Losonczy believed it and tried to persuade Nagy to publicise news about Kádár's disappearance. Nagy was told: 'If Soviet troops attack Budapest, Kádár would be an ideal man to make any new government seem legal. You must broadcast the news . . . immediately.' If they did, it would be harder for the Russians to use Kádár later. Nagy, far too honourable for his own good on some occasions, refused point-blank. 'We can't. We don't really know what happened. We can't publish news based on a driver's unconfirmed story.'[12]

Kádár was in Moscow. He and Münnich were driven from Vnukovo airport straight to a round of meetings at the Kremlin. Khrushchev was not there. He had been joined by Malenkov on the last leg of his whistle-stop tour around Eastern Europe.

The Russians had still not decided whom to set up as the leader of the new Hungarian government after the revolution was crushed. They were careful to make it clear that they might opt for neither of the two Hungarians who had flown to Moscow from Budapest that morning. Kádár did not know the role the Kremlin had cast for him in the future. At this point, as he said later, he believed the Russians could just as easily have decided to bring Rákosi back, which Kádár thought would be a personal disaster for him and a national tragedy for Hungary. He said some odd things for a man in his position, who was in effect being interviewed for a job as a potential dictator. He told old Stalinists like Molotov, Voroshilov and Suslov that he had gone along with the revolution while he thought it was a national independence struggle. He told them 'that everyone in the country demanded the withdrawal of Soviet troops'. That included him, a brave thing to say under the circumstances.[13] Of course he knew the Russians would not now change their minds and the invasion was imminent, but nervously he warned against it. He still thought there was a chance, though a very slim one, for a peaceful settlement 'even though the country is drifting rightwards and heading towards counter-revolution'. He asked what would happen after the destruction and the bloodshed? 'The morale of the Communists will be reduced to zero. The socialist countries will suffer losses. Is there a guarantee that such circumstances will not arise in other countries? If order in Hungary is restored by force, the authority of the socialist countries will be eroded.'

Münnich did not bother with tendentious arguments such as that, which would not appeal to the Communist bosses around the table. Unlike Kádár he knew all the personalities in the Kremlin well and urged them on. 'Anti-Soviet sentiments are being spread. Hungary is in total chaos,' he said.[14]

Around lunchtime at Szolnok, about 100 kilometres from Budapest, Marshal Ivan Konyev, chief of all the Warsaw Pact forces, summoned a war council of his senior officers. He was about to issue the command orders for Operation Whirlwind, which would finally crush the Hungarian rebellion. He also wanted an honest account of what had gone wrong earlier, in the first Budapest intervention, and why the Russians had been forced to leave with their tails between their legs. Konyev was known as an irritable man, if a reliable general, and the exchanges might well have been acrimonious.

The Red Army had not performed with conspicuous glory over the last ten days in Budapest. However, Konyev was an old comrade-in-arms of the commander of the Special Corps stationed in Hungary, Lieutenant-General Piotr Laschenko. They had served together during the Second World War and for the first fifteen minutes or so of their meeting they reminisced of their days together on the First Ukrainian Front in July 1944. When they reached more pressing business, Laschenko explained that the main reason the Russians had failed earlier in the week was that they did not have sufficient forces. The tanks and armoured carriers were incapable of street fighting, he said. 'Why didn't you bring in the air force at all?' asked Konyev. Laschenko replied that air strikes were useless against scattered guerrilla groups and, besides, they would have provoked even further outrage from the civilian population in Budapest. Konyev thought that for the operation to come, that would not matter. The Kremlin had decided this time to act without mercy. Laschenko did admit, though, that 'our officers and soldiers proceeded with uncertainty and lack of skill'. He was told that Operation Whirlwind would proceed more effectively.[15] 'There will be massive reinforcements,' said Konyev. 'Just don't make the same mistakes as before.'

The commander then told his officers of the overwhelming force that had already entered Hungary or would arrive over the next few hours. Two field armies from the Carpathian Military District – the 38th Army and the 8th Mechanised Army – had been sent to Hungary to join the Special Corps, with more than sufficient armour, artillery and air power 'to restore order in Budapest within three to four days'. Konyev issued the operation's codeword: Thunder. Then he reminded his officers that the Hungarians had defences. They had placed, under Király's orders, 50 anti-aircraft guns, and 400 cannon. They had 50,000 soldiers in and around Budapest, as well as National Guard troops and armed rebel groups numbering up to 10,000. The big question was whether they would fight.[16]

We now know that, as far as the Hungarian army went, Imre Nagy had no intention of fighting. He had made the decision two days earlier – though he had not issued the orders. He knew resistance was futile and he wanted to avoid a bloodbath.[17] He believed that even now if he could show the Soviet Union that Budapest was peaceful and calm, the Soviets might yet turn back. There was something noble, if eerily unreal, about the way he carried on at his post, methodically tweaking Cabinet positions, issuing decrees that would never be implemented. He was always an avuncular presence and aides who worked for him were amazed that now, amidst the excruciating tension of those few days, he tried to reassure those around him that all would be well. Some others were allowing themselves to be convinced, too.[18] In the afternoon, Maléter was told to head the talks with the Russian military the next day about the practical details of the promised Soviet troop withdrawals. He said he was optimistic the talks would succeed. Privately, he told his own officers that he thought the Soviet divisions were 'sabre-rattling' over Suez. 'They are concentrating against the West. What matters now is that we must not violate the ceasefire. Not one shot. It could have incalculable consequences.'[19]

Nagy took careful steps to ensure the Soviets were appeased as far as could be. Early in the afternoon, he received an urgent message from Yuri Andropov who said that the Soviet Embassy was besieged by rioters. Nagy phoned Király. 'If anyone ever had an important job you have one now,' he said. 'The Russian Ambassador says Hungarians are raging round his Embassy. If we can't maintain order we will offer an opportunity for a second Russian aggression. Drop whatever you are doing and go there yourself.'[20]

Király ordered a company of men and tanks to proceed to Heroes' Square, near the Embassy. But when Király arrived, within a few minutes of Nagy's call, the streets around the Embassy were deserted. He asked to see Andropov. Once inside, the Major-General told him:

'I have a command from my Premier to check the rioting here but I can see no rioting.'

Andropov replied: 'The Prime Minister, it seems, misunderstood me. Two old women came here to the Embassy. They complained that their flats had burned down during the fighting and they sought a place to stay ... They looked around here but said the rooms were too high and it would be hard to heat them, so the building did not suit them. Then they went away. Before they left we gave them tea ...'[21]

Király was amused by Andropov's continued ability to lie – and by the Ambassador's sense of humour. He said: 'Mr Ambassador, even old women will not step over this threshold without your permission ... I have set up a guard in front of the Embassy and we will guard the building carefully.'

Király went up to Andropov's office to report the incident to Nagy. Andropov pointed to one of the telephones on his desk.

'If you dial 1 Imre Nagy will answer,' said Andropov.

Király dialled 1, spoke to Nagy straight away and said that all was well, there had been no riot.

Andropov rose from his desk, walked over to Király, and made a curious remark as he was showing him out of his office. Ignoring the question of the bogus riots, he simply said, 'We Russians don't want to mix in your business. We understand your troubles and we are on your side.' The whole purpose of the strange performance, 'that wild-goose chase', said Király, was to persuade him that the Russians' wish to negotiate was genuine. He left the Embassy thinking that Andropov was on the side of the revolution. 'He was masterly in conveying the impression that he was sincere and natural,' said Király. 'I'll always remember Andropov's false smiles and grey-blue eyes. Here was this man who clearly knew what was going on. Yet he pretended until the last moment to me and to the Prime Minister and to others that everything was business as usual. Even pirates, before they attack another ship, hoist a black flag. He was absolutely calculating.'[22]

Shortly later, at around six, Király was involved in another tragi-comedy. The top priority for Nagy and his military team was to keep the streets quiet and the Russians thinking that the government could, after all, 'restore order'. The hot-headed Dudás endangered those hopes. Dudás imagined himself the alternative revolutionary leader, who deserved a share of power and was the man to negotiate inter-nationally on behalf of Hungary. He sent an armed detachment from his 'National Revolutionary Committee' to take over the Hungarian

Foreign Ministry, on the Danube riverside near the Parliament building. To the Russians, of course, Dudás was not a mere adventurer, but
one of the chief leaders who had started the 'counter-revolution'. Any
hint that he was near the levers of power in Budapest, let alone in
control of the foreign affairs department, could be used as a pretext by
the Russians to step in. To Nagy it was imperative that Dudás was
ousted. Király ordered a commando team of his National Guard soldiers
to arrest him.[23] When he was under lock and key Dudás's men left the
Ministry. The buccaneering revolutionary was then released. Dudás
was no real threat, but his pathetic attempt at a coup worried Nagy
and infuriated Király. Hungarians 'were being incited towards further
revolt and strikes', he said. He blamed extremists and, specifically,
'the interference of Radio Free Europe' for endangering the gains the
rebellion had made. 'What we really need now is for the workers to
return to work.'[24]

That evening, while Hungary was awaiting its fate, Nikita Khrushchev
feared he would die in a plane crash. The Soviet leader was on the last
leg of his goodwill mission around communist Europe to explain why
it was necessary to invade Budapest. At six, now travelling with
Malenkov, he left Sofia after talks with the Bulgarians. His next stop
was to see Tito. This meeting was potentially problematic. The Marshal
had been Stalin's enemy. Though relations with Yugoslavia had
improved over the last couple of years, they were still tricky, however.
Yugoslavia remained part of the 'socialist camp', even if not a satellite
of Russia, and Khrushchev hoped to persuade Tito to help him stamp
on the rebellion in Hungary. In particular he wanted the Yugoslav
tyrant to ensure that Nagy was out of the way when the Russians
marched back into Budapest.

   The two Soviets were due to meet Tito at the Yugoslav's luxurious
holiday villa on the island of Brioni, off the Adriatic coast. They flew
in a small, twin-engined Ilyushin 14 propeller plane in ghastly weather,
through mountains, at night in a fierce thunderstorm. Lightning flashed
all around them, and Khrushchev admitted to being scared. 'I had
flown a great deal, especially during the war, but I had never flown in
conditions this bad,' he said. When they landed at the small airport at
Pula they had to take a boat to Tito's residence. There was a howling
gale and the conditions on the sea were as bad as in the air. Nobody
was supposed to know about this trip. If it leaked out, the purpose

would certainly have been immediately clear. For the sake of 'secrecy' the officers from the security service and Tito's guard took them on the small motor launch by a longer route than normal through rough seas, a strong wind and pitch darkness. 'Malenkov was as pale as a corpse,' Khrushchev said later. 'He got carsick on a good road. He lay down in the boat and shut his eyes.'[26]

After they arrived, when their stomachs settled, they embarked on eight hours of talks until five the next morning. They were extremely careful about security and secrecy and we still do not know exactly what was agreed at Brioni. But Khrushchev was pleasantly surprised that Tito readily accepted that the Hungarian invasion was inevitable and 'reasonable'. The Soviets did not say exactly when the operation would take place, only that it was imminent. 'What is there left for us to do?' Khrushchev said. 'If we let things take their course, the West would say we were either stupid or weak, and that's one and the same thing. We cannot possibly permit it. We would have capitalists on the frontiers of the Soviet Union.' Tito agreed. He had warned Nagy that Hungary was going 'too far' but he had not listened. Khrushchev said he might not be able to survive against his own hardliners if the Soviets 'lost' Hungary. 'There are people in the Soviet Union who would say that as long as Stalin was in command everybody obeyed and there were no big shocks, but that now, ever since *these* bastards had come to power, Russia had suffered a defeat. And this is happening at a time when we condemn Stalin.'[27]

Suez provided a 'favourable moment' for the operation, Khrushchev said, but it would have happened anyway. 'This will help us. There will be confusion and uproar in the West and in the United Nations, but much less than there would have been because Britain, France and Israel are waging a war against Egypt. They are bogged down there and we are stuck in Hungary.' He said the army were as keen as the politicians were to smash the revolution. 'Twice already the Hungarians have fought alongside the West against us and now they want to join forces with the West against the Russians again.'

Tito and Khrushchev then decided between them who would lead Hungary after the invasion. The Russians wanted Münnich, but were willing to be dissuaded. Kádár was not Khrushchev's first choice. He praised Münnich, who had always been against Rákosi and whom Khrushchev knew in the 1930s when they were 'officers together and on manoeuvres would sometimes share a tent'. The Yugoslavs said

Kádár would be a far better choice. In Rákosi's time Münnich had lived in comfort and style as Ambassador to Moscow, whereas Kádár had been tortured and spent years in jail. For every Hungarian this would be decisively in Kádár's favour and Khrushchev saw the argument. It would be Kádár then.[28]

Many Hungarians were pinning their hopes on the West – or the UN. They knew that if the Russians came back they could not resist for long. 'We believed help was on the way. Of course we wanted to believe it – but everything we were told seemed to confirm it,' said the guerrilla commander at the Corvin Passage group, Gergely Pongrácz.[29] Late in the evening, Budapest time, Ejaz Hussein, the reporter for Pakistan's Karachi *Dawn* newspaper, was walking around Parliament Square, where the revolution had started, with some friends. 'We saw two tanks on guard. As we parked our car, a Hungarian soldier jumped down from the tank, rushed to us and eagerly asked, looking at the UN press sticker on our windshield: "Is the United Nations already there?" We were very sorry to tell him that we did not represent the UN, but were only members of the press corps. "Not enough," said the soldier and went away with marked disappointment all over his face.'[30]

The UN that day did nothing to press the urgency of the crisis in Budapest. Suez was the priority, as it was in Washington where President Eisenhower had just announced a $20 million package of food and medical aid, but limited diplomatic help. The American government did not recognise Hungary's neutrality – a step that would at least have given the Hungarians some support. But Eisenhower thought that was too risky. He believed his consistent line, that America did 'not see the satellite states as potential military allies', precluded going so far diplomatically. The French and the British insisted on raising Hungary at that afternoon's Security Council, but the President and his Secretary of State were unimpressed. Just after 4 p.m. Dulles told Henry Cabot Lodge, his UN Ambassador: 'They want the limelight off them. I think it's a mockery for them to come in, with bombs falling over Egypt, and denounce the Soviet Union for perhaps doing something not quite so bad ... I want no part of it ... We don't have any hard information about what's going on in Hungary.'[31] The orders from Dulles and Ike were that America should try to stop the French tabling any resolution on Hungary at the Security Council, and to delay. The big players were caught up in Suez and nobody agitated for urgent action on Hungary. After more than three hours of mainly procedural wrangling they adjourned and shelved the issue of Hungary for another day.

THIRTY

Saturday, 3 November

The first dusting of snow fell overnight, though it did not settle for long. It was still bitterly cold. The Russians were tightening their noose around Budapest and had begun to move on other towns, including the second main centre of the revolution, Győr. Most people in the capital knew, but still there was no official information. There was no hysteria. Buses began operating, along with more trams. Damaged lines had quickly been mended. Hopes and fears fluctuated wildly, but people 'have decided to behave as though it was a typical Budapest Saturday'.[1] The coffee houses were open, even for pastries, and the warm-chestnut sellers were doing a brisk trade.

Imre Nagy, too, carried on as normal. He was working on forming his new Cabinet. It may have seemed like fiddling while Budapest was about to burn; but now he said he had the balanced government of various parties he wanted and perhaps should have had when the revolution began.[2] Kádár was named on the list of Ministers. Despite all the growing evidence, Nagy did not believe Kádár had betrayed him. Maléter was Defence Minister, a startling rise. When he was officially nominated, he made his politics clear. At a time when all his officers and men had torn off their Soviet-style red stars and epaulettes, 'he still wore the little partisan star of 1944 and another Red Star awarded for successful coal digging. He said "if we get rid of the Russians, don't think we're going back to the bad old days. And if there are people who do want to go back, well we shall see" – and he touched his revolver holster.'[3]

Some of Maléter's colleagues were genuinely optimistic and wanted to lift public spirits, to provide hope. The sophisticated Zoltán Tildy was widely held as a shrewd political judge. He said he was sure the Russians would not invade, but were making threats to exert pressure. 'A tragic clash will not take place,' he said. The talks that were about to be held about Soviet troop withdrawals were genuine and not window-dressing, he insisted. 'I think that if people are willing to talk about their problems, they are willing to settle them.'[4]

Another friend of Imre Nagy was a better judge. 'It is said that when a man is fatally sick, he frequently experiences a day of euphoria a little before his death, when the functioning of his organs seems almost normal, giving him the illusion that recovery is possible. That day was November 3rd.'[5]

In Moscow, Kádár had his second interview for the post of Hungary's new leader. This time, Khrushchev, safely back from his all-night session with Tito, was in the Kremlin carefully sizing Kádár up. The other Soviet bosses went along with the choice, for now, though some of the hardliners close to Molotov considered bringing back Rákosi. Khrushchev said that if Rákosi appeared back in Budapest, 'people would hang him on the spot'.[6]

Towards midday Kádár was told officially that he would be the man to return to Budapest and head a new government. He had not been certain until then. Ferenc Münnich would be number two. Kádár was given the details about when the invasion would be launched and instructions about his role. For the first days, the Russians said, he would not even be in Budapest; the city would be run directly by the Red Army. Kádár said that 'surrendering a socialist country to counter-revolution is impossible. I agree with you.' But he warned that putting down the revolution would not be as easy as the Soviets thought. He wondered what would happen afterwards. 'The whole nation is taking part in the movement. There must be a base for the new government. There must be an answer to the question of what sort of relationship we must have with the USSR,' he told Khrushchev.[7]

They could talk about all of that later, he was told, when the troubles were over. Kádár made one demand, which was instantly granted: that Rákosi and Gerő would not be allowed to return to Hungary. This was very important to Kádár, first because he loathed Rákosi, and second because both the former leader and Gerő would be certain to start plotting against Kádár the moment they landed in Budapest. Then Kádár made a faint gesture of independence. He told Khrushchev that 'this should not be a puppet government'. Khrushchev agreed, but then instantly put Kádár in his place. The Russians decided who all the Ministers would be. Gerő's most ole-aginous toady, the overweight and murderous Moscow-trained István

Báta, who was Defence Minister when the revolution broke out and was in charge while most of the army mutinied, would return, against Kádár's wishes. The declaration setting up the government, its first address to the Hungarian people, and its central programme were all written by the Soviets and composed in Russian. Kádár had no hand in translating it into Hungarian. He would be sent back home accompanied by three high-ranking Soviet plenipotentiaries to keep an eye on him: Malenkov, the up-and-coming Leonid Brezhnev, and, perhaps inevitably, Anastas Mikoyan.[8]

Kádár almost never talked about those two days in the Kremlin. He said later he had little choice but to go along with the Soviets. So fear played a part in his treachery. It was not true, as some of his apologists said, that he was told directly by Khrushchev, that he must take the leadership or go to jail and maybe even the scaffold. But Kádár knew what prison and torture were like and he had a strong survival instinct.[9] Above all he was a realist, as everyone who knew or worked for him said. He knew the Russians would invade. He knew they would win. The only question was on whose head the crown would come to rest. One of the few times he volunteered an opinion on the subject he said, 'if it had not been me it would have been someone else.' He thought he could do Moscow's dirty work with the minimum of brutality.[10]

Shortly after 10 a.m. the much heralded joint Russian-Hungarian talks about Soviet troop withdrawals began. The Soviet delegation, bemedalled and braided, was given full military honours when it arrived at the Parliament building. It was led by the jowly, balding, overweight General Malinin, who knew Hungary well. He was accompanied by Lieutenant-General Fyodor Stepchenko and Major-General Schelbanyin. Maléter headed the Hungarian delegation, which comprised army Chief of Staff General István Kovács, his ambitious young adjutant Colonel Miklós Szűcs, and a political representative, the Minister from the Petőfi Party, Ferenc Erdei. The atmosphere was genial and light. The Russians presented details of their promised withdrawal, down to plans for a full-scale military parade as they left. The Hungarians, for their part, showed goodwill by passing on the decision just made by the National Guard commander Béla Király to order all Hungarian tanks back to barracks. He also called on all 'civilians' with arms and ammunition to hand them in immediately.[11] Nagy and the government were determined to take the talks at face value and they seemed to be going well. At one point Maléter left the room for a few moments with a broad smile over his face.[12]

The first round of the negotiations finished at about 2 p.m. The Soviets asked the Hungarians to be their guests to complete the talks at 10 p.m. at the Russian military base of Tököl, on Csepel Island, twenty kilometres south of Budapest. Maléter agreed to go. Afterwards, Király asked how they were going. 'In fine order,' Maléter replied, but added no details.[13]

During the afternoon Imre Nagy reckoned the day was going well and his spirits rose. An optimistic government statement was broadcast, saying the Soviets had again pledged not to send any troop trains across the Hungarian border. From the countryside it did not look as though the Russians were sticking to the bargain – reports came in from near the Austrian border that Russian troops had now massed in western Hungary, forming a pincer movement against the capital. But Nagy was still hopeful. He could not work out why the Soviets were going through this elaborate display about friendly talks unless they were in earnest. At about four in the afternoon hopes were lifted further. Zoltán Tildy and Nagy's long-term supporter and confidant Géza Losonczy announced the talks were going well and they both tried hard to be accommodating to the Russians. 'In spite of everything that has happened we are striving to achieve true friendship with the Soviet Union,' Tildy said.[14]

Losonczy had supported the revolution with enthusiasm from the first. But he wanted to explain what that meant: 'We shall not give up one single achievement of the last dozen years, such as land reform, the nationalisation of the factories . . . Under no circumstances whatever will [we] tolerate the restoration of capitalism in Hungary.' This was all too late. The Russians were not listening.[15]

At about 6 p.m. Király heard the most positive report so far about the morning's talks, from General Kovács, a Russian-trained officer, who had been a loyal Stalinist. He went over to the revolution at an early stage, but later, like a military Vicar of Bray, began to waver, watching who would come out on top. Király cornered him and asked him what had happened in the first session. It was practically agreed, Kovács said:

First, Russia will evacuate all her armed forces from Hungary. Second, to avoid disrupting transportation, the Russians want to leave by degrees. A committee of experts will be set up to arrange a timetable. Third, the Hungarian garrisons must cease denying the Russians food and fuel. Fourth, the Russians are not prepared for a winter movement and the Hungarians must be patient; the troops will not be able to move until January 15th. Lastly, they say the Russian army did not want to attack the Hungarians but only did what the Hungarian government asked. Therefore, the evacuation must be not only peaceful but friendly. The troops must leave in a festive air and the Hungarians must cheer them as they leave.

In effect, said General Kovács, they had agreed to all the Russian demands, even the friendly farewell, but insisted that departure must be stepped up by a month.[16]

It all sounded, to Király, too good to be true. He warned Nagy that he felt bad omens. The Major-General had assessed the position again and thought that now an attack might come very soon. Nagy doubted it, while the talks were going on. Király went to see his old friend Sándor Kopácsi at the police headquarters a few hundred metres from the Parliament building. 'Everything just seemed ominously quiet that evening for a Saturday night, especially for a Saturday night in the middle of a revolution.' He was depressed and Kopácsi felt the same foreboding. Király said:

'Sándor, there are troop movements everywhere.' He spread a large map of the Budapest area on the table. He said ten divisions were on the move and five heavy-armoured columns were converging on Budapest.

'Has the old man seen it?' Kopácsi asked.

'Yes, he has it.'

'What does he say?'

'He believes in miracles,' said Király.[17]

Millions of Hungarians tuned their radio sets at 8 p.m. to listen to a broadcast by Cardinal Mindszenty. It was a voice most thought they would never hear again. To them he was a hero, a martyr for his faith and his country, and his release seemed the most powerful symbol of the victory of their revolution. His speech had been recorded earlier, in the morning, and half the government – though not Imre Nagy – were watching while he spoke in the Parliament building. A free man for just four days, he was, observed one of the onlookers, 'a fantastic sight; the diehard Primate arriving with an armed guard of honour amongst Communist revolutionaries ... The Cardinal walked in with swaying steps and glaring eyes ... The strange expression may or may not have been the result of his ordeal in AVO imprisonment.'[18]

Mindszenty's broadcast was blamed by the Russians and the Hungarian government later for 'inciting counter-revolutionaries'. He spoke with familiar scorn about the Communists, talked about the Nagy government as 'heirs of the fallen regime' and wondered 'Do not the leaders of the Russians realise that we will respect the Russian people even more if they stop oppressing us?' But nothing he said could have made any difference. By the time he spoke, all the Russian battle plans had already been laid.

Maléter had been warned three times at least to be careful about going to the second round of the talks with his Soviet counterparts. They were scheduled to begin at 10 p.m. at Tököl. Géza Losonczy, highly strung, a nervous figure generally but a good judge of character, was the first to voice misgivings, soon after the morning session of negotiations had ended. Losonczy recalled that it was Andropov who suggested that Maléter should be included in the Hungarian delegation team, and Andropov was not trustworthy. At the Hungarian Parliament earlier in the day the Soviets could do nothing. But a Russian military base was different. There they could do anything. What if the Soviets had laid a trap to keep the top Hungarian army command out of the way if an invasion was launched?

'What if they arrest you?' he asked.

'I cannot imagine such a low betrayal on their part,' Maléter replied. 'Unless of course ... who knows?'

Later, he had dinner with officers at the Kilián Barracks, among them his loyal deputy Captain Lajos Csiba, who had stood by him since the first day of the revolution. He reminded Maléter that the Soviets, in their history, had several times arrested and kidnapped visiting delegations.

'Could this not be a trap?' the Captain asked.

Maléter rejected the warning. 'I don't expect this of Soviet officers. They wouldn't do such a thing. So far the Russians have been frank and understanding.'[20]

A few minutes after eight Maléter's wife Judith called. She was still just twenty-four at the time, and idolised her new husband. She was desperately anxious about him.

'I implored him not to go,' she said. 'It was a scary idea to me, to leave Budapest and go to Csepel Island at that time in the evening, to go to a Soviet barracks. I knew that the Soviet troops had ... entrenched themselves around the city. He had told me that himself, so I was scared. He became annoyed and ended up speaking to me in a military kind of way: "You've got to understand that things will go by the diplomatic rules." The last sentence I heard from him as a free man was "You've got to understand that wife and family don't matter here. I have to go there even if it costs me my life, because the country expects my assistance."'[21]

It would take just over an hour to drive from central Budapest to Csepel. Maléter left at about 8.20. Nagy had given him instructions that after he arrived at Tököl he should phone the Prime Minister's office every half an hour to ensure they knew he was all right.

In Washington, John Foster Dulles woke in the early hours and at 7 a.m. was taken to Walter Reed Hospital. He was undergoing emergency surgery for stomach cancer, from which he never recovered. His illness did not change American foreign policy in the short term, but it had a major, immediate impact on the President, three days away from the election, caught in the middle of a war in the Middle East and uncertain about what to do in Hungary. From Budapest, intelligence was confused about about Soviet reinforcements encircling the city, but was unsure whether the Russians would use force. A new head of the US Legation arrived the previous day. He was fifty-three-year-old Tom Wailes, the former Ambassador in South Africa. He was an experienced diplomat, but to take over in a crisis as complex as Hungary's was no easy task. He could add very little insight to news from Budapest.[22]

Late the previous night Ike, Dulles and Lodge in New York had discussed some refinements to their 'active non-involvement' policy in Hungary. But it was of little practical help to Budapest. Imre Nagy had not heard any word directly from the UN – or from the US government – about recognition of Hungary's neutrality. However, Eisenhower decided that at last he would censure the Russians. At 3 p.m. in New York, Lodge introduced a motion at the UN Security Council 'deploring the use of Soviet military force to suppress the efforts of the Hungarian people to reassert their rights'. It was never put to a vote, though. The Americans agreed to an adjournment to see if the talks at

Tököl amounted to anything. The Americans said they would raise the matter again the following week. After ten days of crisis in Hungary the UN had decided – absolutely nothing. The failure would damage the reputation of the organisation and of its Secretary General, Hammarskjöld.[23]

Maléter arrived for the second round of talks with the Soviets at about 9.45 p.m. He had the same team as before – General Kovács, the popular, thirty-six-year-old Colonel Szűcs and an edgy Ferenc Erdei, who was looking very nervous. They, too, were given an honour guard, as the Russians had received in the morning. Maléter reported to Nagy's office twice and he spoke once to Király, at 11 p.m., saying everything seemed to be in order. Király, in charge of Budapest's defences, relaxed and announced he was going to bed.[24] The talks seemed friendly. Sándor Horváth, one of Maléter's bodyguards who was waiting outside, said: 'Everything appeared to go off perfectly in the office where the talks were taking place. At least that was our impression in the ante-chamber, from the noise of the conversation we could hear.'[25]

Then just before midnight a dozen Soviet policemen wearing green caps stormed into the room and trained their guns on the Hungarian delegation. A tall, well-built man in civilian clothes with blond hair and bright blue eyes followed the policemen into the room. It was Ivan Serov, head of the KGB. He said to the Hungarians: 'I am placing all of you under arrest.' Maléter stood up and all he said, calmly, was: 'Oh, that's it, then.' Horváth had been watching through a crack in the door: 'I seized my own gun, thinking I could shoot a few rounds at the men in the green caps, but it was too late. The boss called out "stop. It's useless to resist" and I obeyed orders.'

Malinin was an honourable, decent, professional soldier, who had clearly not been told about this coup. He was indignant and demanded to know what was going on. Serov went close to him and whispered into his ear. Malinin shrugged his shoulders and left the room, ordering his junior officers to follow him. They had all been ruthlessly tricked. The Russians had used Andropov's lies and the so-called military 'negotiations' to give them time to finalise their military plans and to capture Maléter, the soldier who might have organised some effective resistance against them.[26]

They were now at the tender mercies of Serov. The three soldiers and the fifty-one-year-old politician who had managed to survive throughout all the purges of the Rákosi-Gerő era were led to the court-yard of the barracks at Tököl. They were convinced they were all going to be executed straight away. Then they were separated, taken to the prison complex and thrown into individual cells. A short while later the cells were opened one by one. After each door opened they heard a salvo of gunfire. The Russian soldiers were firing into the air to make them believe that their companions were being killed. Each thought he was the sole survivor.[27]

THIRTY-ONE
Sunday, 4 November

Shortly after midnight Major-General Király was woken with reports that Russian troops had penetrated Budapest's outer defence ring. They had fired no shots yet, but Soviet tanks were on the move. Some were less than ten kilometres from the centre of the city. He immediately rang Imre Nagy at his office in the Parliament building for 'the most dramatic conversation of my life'.[1]

He said: 'Prime Minister. It is now certain that the Soviet Union has launched a war against us. The first Soviet waves are already attacking. We do not have reliable contact with every defence position and zone. Until now we have ordered our troops not to shoot, so now many commanders may be very uncertain. It is possible that they will act only when it is too late, that Soviet troops will storm them. We have only one choice: either you, Prime Minister, or I must immediately make a radio broadcast. We must inform our troops that we are at war with the Soviet Union and they must start their defensive struggle.'

Nagy replied: 'This is a political affair. As a General Staff officer, you must know that such a declaration is a thing for the government, not the military. I forbid you to make such a pronouncement.'

'I am completely aware of this. That is why I proposed that you ... make the declaration, or if you prefer I will do it with your consent,' Király declared.

'No,' Nagy insisted. 'We will not issue such a declaration whatever the case. That would mean war and we don't want that. We cannot undertake war against the Soviet Union. Please continue to inform me of events.'

Marshal Konyev had speedily put together a huge force to mount Operation Whirlwind. There were nearly 150,000 troops from ten divisions, 2,500 of Russia's most modern tanks and plenty of air support. He had assured Khrushchev that he could 'restore order' in Budapest in three days and he intended to be as good as his word. He issued the order for his men to advance on Budapest at midnight,[2] from north and south along the Danube, slicing the city in half. By three in the morning a few tanks – a small advanced guard – had begun to rumble into the centre of Pest. Three were spotted by Sándor Kopácsi's office at the city's police headquarters.[3] The officer placed in charge of the attack on Budapest was Major-General Kuzmin Yevdokimlovic Grebenyik, fifty-six, an old-school Stalinist who was a close friend of the KGB's Ivan Serov. But there was another key element of the operation from Moscow's point of view. The Russians deployed more than 20,000 troops along the border with Austria to forestall any possible Western intervention. The Soviets did not imagine they would be needed – Nato headquarters, on the orders of Eisenhower, had been given particular instructions to do nothing that could be interpreted as provocative[4] – but the Russians erred on the side of caution. Major Grigori Dobrynov, a tank regiment commander who was about to enter Budapest, was told his orders: 'We were going in as saviours to protect the people from terrorism,' he recalled. Then he was 'warned that the Americans might also enter the city from the west. We asked our divisional commander, "Could this mean war?" and he said "Yes. This could be the beginning of World War Three."' It was a way of impressing on the Russian troops the importance of their task.[5]

At 4 a.m. Konyev issued the code word Thunder and a few minutes later that was the sound everywhere in Budapest. 'I felt the ground shake, and I saw the horizon light up, and I heard explosion after explosion after explosion,' said Eva Walko of that dawn. 'So much for our victory.'[6]

Five minutes later, when he heard the shelling, Király grabbed his direct phone to Nagy. 'I told him the city was being invaded and begged for the orders to open fire . . . "No, no," Nagy said. "Calm down. The Russian Ambassador is here in my office. He is calling Moscow right now. There is some misunderstanding. You must not open fire." I hung up, bewildered.'[7] He need not have been.

Nagy had no intention of ordering large-scale, bloody armed resistance with no possibility of victory. Most of the government were not there with Nagy. Tildy was an exception and some other Ministers made attempts to reach the building. Among them was the Minister of State, István Bibó, who had been appointed just the previous day. The short, wiry, forty-five-year-old sociologist managed make his way to Parliament through the lines of Russian tanks.

Nagy was calm as his dreams were shattered. He said he had to do something, but what? Every moment the noise of shelling was reaching nearer the heart of Budapest and the hubbub in Parliament was growing more frenetic. Nagy's deputy Tildy, who genuinely did not believe this moment would come, suggested making a broadcast – it might be the last opportunity. Nagy agreed. His long-time friend Ferenc Donáth noted a few words down in pencil on a scrap of paper. Nagy took his jacket, walked down one flight of stairs and entered the makeshift radio studio to make his final broadcast. Nostalgic tunes were being played on Radio Kossuth. At 5.20 a.m. the music was interrupted. 'Attention. Attention. The Prime Minister Imre will address the Hungarian people.' Then he began, in a firm, clear, calm voice: 'This is Imre Nagy speaking. Today at daybreak Soviet troops attacked our capital with the obvious intention of overthrowing the legal Hungarian democratic government. Our troops are in combat. The government is at its post. I notify the people of our country and the entire world of this fact.'

When Nagy returned to his office Király rang again. He said: 'Prime Minister, Soviet troops have broken the defence ring in several places and have penetrated deep into the capital. One tank column is now advancing past our building and heading for Parliament. I will count the tanks . . .'. Nagy paused, sighed deeply and said very decisively, 'I do not wish any more reports.' Király decided to leave central Budapest and head for a National Guard headquarters at Szabadhegy (Freedom Hill), in the wooded suburbs north of the city, 'to see what we could salvage'.[8] Király was baffled that Nagy was specific he did not want to hear from his own military chief more reports about the invasion of the country. What the Major-General did not know was that Nagy, even before his dramatic appeal on the radio, had accepted the offer of sanctuary from the Yugoslav Embassy.

The offer had come at 1 a.m., from the Yugoslav Ambassador, Dalibor Soldatic, through Zoltán Szánto, an old Stalinist turned Communist reformer and a wily, grey-haired figure well known as one of Budapest's great wits and political intriguers. Szánto had at one time been Hungary's Ambassador to Yugoslavia, where he still had good contacts. Tito had agreed with Khrushchev at the Brioni meeting to get Nagy out of the way when the invasion was launched. He delivered on his pledge. It was a lifeline for Nagy and his entourage, which eventually numbered forty-one, and equally convenient, at the time, for Moscow. Szánto met Soldatic in the early hours of the morning and he told Nagy about the agreement when he heard the tanks begin to shell the city.[9]

They were not the only ones to flee from the building. Just before 5.30 a.m. Cardinal Mindszenty was called from Nagy's office and warned that the Primate's life was in serious danger if he stayed at his palace. He should find a way of reaching Parliament. The Cardinal woke his private secretary, the elderly Monsignor Egon Turchányi, and told him to get dressed as quickly as he could. The Monsignor, in his black cassock, drove. Russian tanks were already ringing the square when they arrived, though the Soviets had not yet attacked the building. Mindszenty remained hidden in the car, while Turchányi got out and explained to one of the officers: 'The Hungarian government has asked us to come.' The Russian soldier smiled and replied: 'I am afraid we are in control here, not the Hungarian government.'

They drove to a side door which had been left unguarded and found their way inside, but did not feel much safer there. Tildy told them the government would do all it could for him. But that gave him little confidence. Mindszenty decided to see if he could reach the American Legation. He put on his overcoat and rolled up his cassock above the hem so it could not be seen. Three young Hungarian soldiers led the Cardinal to a side door, shielding him from the sight of the Russians. They got into the car, dodged the tanks by staying on small side roads and reached the sanctuary of the US mission where Mindszenty would stay, a *cause célèbre* for fifteen years.*[10]

Andropov left Parliament a contented man. He had been summoned by Nagy well before dawn when the tanks started firing. The Ambassador had heard a stream of invective from Nagy about Soviet duplicity. Nagy is reported to have told Andropov that 'today it is Hungary and tomorrow or the day after tomorrow it will be the turn of other countries because the imperialism of Moscow knows no borders and is only trying to play for time'.[11] But it washed over the smooth, deceitful diplomat-spy. Andropov could feel well pleased with his performance

* He proved to be major irritant, not just for the Hungarian regime but also for the Vatican, which from the mid 1960s wanted to improve relations with the Hungarian Communists. Mindszenty stayed sequestered at the US Embassy despite Kádár's willingness to let him go. Eventually he was pressurised to leave by the American President, Richard Nixon, and, finally, he was ordered to go by Pope Paul VI in 1971. He lived in Rome briefly and retired to Vienna in 1973. He died in 1975.

during the revolution. He had split the Hungarian leadership. He had dealt brilliantly, from the Soviets' point of view, with Nagy, lulling him into a false sense of security. The Hungarians, partly because of Andropov's bold lies, took no defensive action until it was too late. He had helped to entrap Hungary's military leadership. He had advised the Kremlin on who the Hungarian leader should be – and his advice had been accepted. His own KGB minder in Budapest, Vladimir Kryuchkov, praised him. 'He was so calm – even when bullets were flying and when everyone else at the Embassy felt like we were being besieged in a fortress.'[12]

At 6 a.m., on a Soviet-controlled radio station, Hungarians heard the voice of János Kádár proclaiming the formation of a new Hungarian Revolutionary Worker-Peasant government. He claimed to be speaking from Szolnok. 'Acting in the interests of our people, our working class and our country, we requested the Soviet army command to help the nation in smashing the dark reactionary forces and restoring order and calm in the country,' he declared. Münnich joined him. He said they had broken with Imre Nagy because he had proved 'impotent'. The broadcast had been pre-recorded: neither man was even in Hungary. They were still in Russia, arrived in Hungary only later that evening, and would not reach Budapest for days.[13]

Nagy's simple, brief and emotional final broadcast seemed straight-forward enough. But it contained one minor and one major inaccuracy. The 'legal government', which he said was at its post, was about to decamp to seek refuge at a foreign embassy. More serious, Hungarian troops were not 'in combat'. The arrest of Maléter and his most senior officers a few hours earlier decapitated the army command. It could never recover from the blow. They were soon joined by another well-known Hungarian soldier, Colonel János Mecséri, the thirty-five-year-old deputy commander of Budapest's defences. He, too, had been arrested the night before.[14] The one-time Stalinist Defence Minister Lieutenant-General Károly Janza, who had been sacked two days earlier by Nagy, had that morning moved into the Ministry again, on his own initiative. Most Hungarian soldiers were confined to barracks on 4 November and were systematically disarmed when Soviet forces re-entered Budapest. There was some brief resistance at the Petőfi Barracks and Military Academy, but when the Hungarian troops realised they were hopelessly outnumbered they laid down their arms. Outside

Budapest, the Hungarian army barely put up a struggle – except in one small battle about fifty kilometres north-west of Budapest at Soroksár. Malaschenko, second in command of the Special Corps of Russian troops, said operations against the Hungarian army were over in less than half a morning.[15] Király had been instructed by Nagy not to fight, so the National Guard took no action until it was far too late.

The only real resistance was offered by the rebel bands who had made the revolution twelve days earlier. They fought hard and courageously. But the struggle was completely different now. This time the Russians were not mounting a police operation; they were waging war, with ruthless savagery. They had overwhelming force – three times the number of troops, five times the number of tanks and heavy guns. Molotov cocktails and light weapons were of no use against the T54 tanks the Soviets had sent to Budapest as reinforcements. They were newer, faster, more manoeuvrable and had been built with heavier armour-plating.

This time, as Malaschenko said, the Russians knew what to expect. 'The insurgents no longer had the element of surprise on their side.'[16] The tactics were altogether more brutal. The Russians did not wait to be the targets of guerrilla bands. If they were attacked, they launched devastating bombardments towards the vicinity of the shots being fired against them. They demolished any buildings where they suspected revolutionaries might be hiding. Young people rushed to the barricades, but there were fewer of them. Many of the freedom fighters had drifted away from the main resistance centres after the ceasefire on 28 October and had not returned.

The Russians launched savage assaults on the main battle centres of a week earlier – the Kilián Barracks, the Corvin Cinema and its connecting passageways, the Eastern Railway Station, Üllői Avenue, in central Pest, and in Buda at Széna Square, Zsigmond Móricz Square and Moscow Square. And this time they used jets. From early in the morning, Russian fighter planes were making a deafening noise overhead, strafing rebel strongholds without concern for the 'collateral damage'. By 10 a.m. the Russians had control of all the bridges across the river and two of the better-known resistance centres had fallen: Baross Square and the Eastern Railway Station. But there was no question of the revolutionaries giving up.[17]

'That Sunday was devastation, disaster,' said Gergely Pongrácz. 'Against a few infantry and the old tanks they had, we could survive where we were fortified. But no longer. We fought on, as well as we could, but we knew it was hopeless. We couldn't hope to win against heavy guns hammering us from three kilometres away.'[18] What was the purpose? 'We were not suicides. We never thought we could win a military victory by ourselves. That wasn't the point now. It was an impossibility. We thought that if we could hold out, we could cause international outrage. We really believed we would get help, moral support from the UN and real practical help from the West. So we carried on fighting for as long as we could.'[19]

Most people, terrified, simply hid during the relentless fury of the Russian cannonade – in cellars and basements if they had them. Tamás Foty, a ten-year-old at the time, lived with his family in an apartment block on Rákóczi Avenue, a main road in the heart of Budapest's commercial centre. 'Some revolutionaries thought it would be a good place from which to hit passing Soviet tanks. So down we went, the family, and the pet parakeet,' he said.[20] Soon a tank took aim at the building and the snipers shooting from inside. They levelled the entire block, leaving the former residents huddled in the basement. Rubble was everywhere. The exit was cut off. Hungarians had planned for the attack. Older ones remembered the war and the bloody three-month siege of Budapest. Foty recalled: 'In the candlelight below, someone suggested trying to dig a tunnel underground to an adjoining bomb shelter on the other side of a small side street. Using picks and shovels stocked in the shelter the adults hammered away. Finally they did it. The tunnel was made.'

A joke had travelled fast through the rebel centres, the barracks and the basements of Budapest. 'The Russians say they have come as our friends. Imagine if they had said they were our enemies.'

Radio Free Kossuth, broadcasting from a transmitter at the Parliament building, went dead at 8.07. The last words listeners heard was a message from the elderly playwright Gyula Háy, a friend of Nagy from their years of exile in Moscow, a Communist all his life and one of the intellectual leaders of the short-lived revolution. He spoke to 'all writers, scientists . . . and academics in the world. We appeal for help to all intellectuals in all countries. Our time is limited. You all know the facts. There is no need to review them. Help Hungary. Help!'[21]

Soon afterwards the Russians threatened to demolish the Parliament building. Nagy had fled with his closest advisers, his aides and their families. Some Ministers departed in the direction of the West. Tildy, Nagy's deputy, remained, as did István Bibó. Tildy was determined to save the vast, ornate, neo-gothic building from destruction. He told the Hungarian guards, some of whom were willing to fight: 'I can't give you orders. Only the Defence Minister can do that. But I can give you advice. The best thing to do is send a senior officer with a white flag and a Russian interpreter to the Soviet commanding officer in Parliament Square and tell him they won't be fired at and ask them not to fire on us.'[22]

Soviet officers arrived at Tildy's room around 8.30 a.m. and demanded to see Nagy. Tildy said he had no idea where he was – the truth, as the Prime Minister had not told his deputy about the offer of sanctuary by the Yugoslavs. The Russians demanded an official signature on a document of surrender by the Hungarian armed forces. It had to be signed by István Dobi, the President, a titular office held by a nonentity. The thin, bespectacled Dobi had sworn in governments led by Rákosi, Gerő and Nagy, had few opinions and was known for being fond of the bottle. He muttered 'if the Soviet representatives desire to speak with me I'll be in my office' and then stumbled out.[23] The piece of paper was later duly signed.

Tildy managed to leave the building in safety (though he was arrested later). Only one Hungarian official remained in Parliament at his post, the extraordinarily courageous Bibó. 'If I refuse to yield I shall be demonstrating to the world that the new government was installed in place of Nagy's legal government by force,' he said.[24] He found a typewriter and, with shooting going on all around him in central Budapest, quickly set down one of the most moving and well-argued testimonies against tyranny ever written by a Hungarian, which has stood as a manifesto for social democracy in central Europe since. He wrote also – 'as a legal representative of the Hungarian government' – a passionate plea directly to President Eisenhower for help. 'At this moment, the kind of help most urgently needed is political not military,' he said. Refusing such aid 'would bankrupt the liberation policy which the United States of America has pursued ... with such firmness and wisdom'.[25]

In Moscow, the Soviet leaders might have felt comfortable, easier in their minds, perhaps even pleased with themselves. But they did not. Late in the afternoon, as Marshal Zhukov was reporting to his colleagues that, helped by their elaborate deception, the operation to crush the rebellion in Hungary was progressing well, the Russian leaders continued to fight amongst themselves. There was an extraordinary clash between the titans in the Kremlin. Hours after the Soviets launched their invasion, when Kádár had already declared himself head of Hungary's new government, they fought again over who should be installed as Communist leader in Budapest. Molotov and Kaganovich, the leading hardliners, were wary of Kádár, whom they regarded still as a furtive supporter of Nagy. They fought a rearguard campaign against giving Kádár a top post. Molotov said they should reconsider and restore one of the older, 'reliable' Stalinists to power as Soviet proconsul in Budapest. Khrushchev refused to listen. It was those Stalinists who had caused all the trouble in Hungary, he said. He declared angrily: 'I simply cannot understand Comrade Molotov: he always comes up with the most pernicious ideas.' Molotov flashed back that Khrushchev 'should keep quiet and stop being so overbearing'.[26]

In America nobody in authority was listening to the Minister/ academic Bibó, Major-General Béla Király, nor the freedom fighters waging a hopeless struggle against the overwhelming Russian invasion. President Eisenhower, now without his Secretary of State who was gravely ill, made an immediate decision: to do nothing to risk any confrontation with Russia. When the Russian tanks began the invasion of Budapest, Nikolai Bulganin wrote to the President, warning him about Suez, that 'if this war is not stopped it contains the danger of turning into a Third World War'. Eisenhower wrote of his 'inexpressible shock' when he heard the news from Budapest, but made it clear he would not do anything to intervene.[27] Frank Wisner in the CIA made desperate pleas for the Agency to send covert assistance to the freedom fighters. He was instantly slapped down. There was never a real possibility that anybody in the West would make a move, militarily.

But Ike made sure. The US had heard that General Franco in Spain was intending to offer help to Hungary. The fascist dictator was not allied to America, but Ike went out of his way to ensure nothing came of Franco's idea. Of course, the *caudillo* might have been playing to the gallery and never had any real intention of taking action in Hungary. But for a while the US took the Spanish seriously. According to Robert Murphy, number two at the State Department in the absence of Dulles,

the Spanish Cabinet wanted to send a 'volunteer force' to Budapest on
4 November, led by a former top commando. The Spanish Foreign
Minister Alberto Martin Artajo warned the US and told his good
contact Henry Cabot Lodge that Spain 'stood ready to send an armed
force to Hungary'. Artajo suggested the US might 'send two planes to
Spain to be loaded with arms to be dropped into Hungary'. He said
he was speaking with the full authority of Franco and his Cabinet.
Washington's response was instant and unequivocal: 'The US Government can lend no support, either overt or covert, to any military
intervention in Hungary in the present circumstances. We hope that
Spain will take no precipitate action of its own.'[28]

The American Legation in Budapest and its new Minister, Tom
Wailes, were sending powerful reports about the fighting – 'a good
flight of jets overhead – we plan to send staff to basement,' he telegrammed towards midday to the State Department. But his instructions
were to act cautiously. Mindszenty had been given asylum at about
seven that morning. But Wailes was in a quandary when a government
Minister, Béla Kóvacs, asked for refuge later in the day. He was told he
could give 'shelter tentatively' to Kovács and his lieutenants, but they
would have to leave the Legation the next day.[29]

In New York, the UN Security Council met and at last at 3 a.m.
passed a resolution condemning the Soviet aggression. By that time
Budapest was an occupied capital – and the Secretary General
Hammarskjöld was making preparations for his visit to Egypt.

PART THREE
AFTERMATH

THIRTY-TWO
Friday, 7 November

After two days of ruthless bombardment, people began to emerge from their hiding places. Budapest was a mass of debris. Some commercial districts which had been rebuilt only after the devastation of the war lay in ruins again. József Kővágó ventured out on the Tuesday morning to find his wife, Lonci, who had taken refuge in a hospital when the invasion began: 'I reached the main boulevard which looked like a battlefield. Houses were wrecked, destruction was all around. The only people you could see were in front of stores. Suddenly two Soviet tanks appeared. People tried to hide. I fled into a house. The tanks opened fire on the people standing in the food line.'[1]

One by one the main resistance centres were crushed. Széna Square fell on the 6th. 'Uncle' János Szábo was captured trying to escape to Austria. Dudás's headquarters were overrun on the same day. He had been one of the first casualties of the Soviet blitz on Sunday. Wounded, he was hidden by some of his loyalists in a northern suburb of the city. Zsigmond Móricz Square, where the old-style Soviet T34 tanks had been so vulnerable, was devastated by shellfire and the insurgents gave up on Tuesday. An unusual leader surfaced at the defence of the Castle District. He was Vazúl Végyvári, a twenty-eight-year-old Franciscan monk. Before the uprising he had been working at an orphanage in Esztergom, the cathedral city seventy-five kilometres north of Budapest. Now, when the Russians invaded, he wore a machine-gun round his neck and clutched grenades close to him. 'A monk who stays outside the monastery for twenty-four hours without permission of the Superior will get punished, possibly suspended. But I considered the fight of the people to be a holy war,' he said.

After the revolution broke out Végyvári had gone to the Kilián Barracks and asked Maléter for a job as a chaplain 'but he turned me down'. He went to the Castle District when the Soviets launched their dawn attack and decided to fight:

There were a few dozen of us, no more. Before becoming a priest I had
been a cadet in military school, so I knew something about weapons.
We tried to turn the area into a fortress. We still hoped then that under
UN or Western pressure the Russians might be forced to enter into
negotiations. But it was hopeless. On Tuesday we received an ultimatum: leave. We stayed. Our headquarters were discovered and
shelled heavily – we moved into an eszpresso bar nearby. That was
discovered, too. All resistance seemed useless against this kind of attack.
There were many secret underground passageways under the Castle –
we used those to make an escape.[2]

At the Corvin Cinema, a few fighters were left but they decided to
leave on 6 November to try to make an escape to the West. 'It was
utterly hopeless,' Gergely Pongrácz told his followers. The Kilián Barracks held out for a little longer – there was fighting in the basement
after the building had been all but demolished by the remorseless
shelling from tanks and cannon and fire from MiG jets.

Major-General Király, in command of Hungary's only official fighting
force, the National Guard, tried to resist while he could. During Sunday
morning he moved his headquarters to a small monastery on Freedom
Hill, high above the city, and with his men considered his options.
Should they 'call on the nation to resist the Soviet aggression in a
guerrilla war, or start negotiations or just lay down arms?'[3] One of his
commanders, General Daniel Görgenyi, an old friend of Király, said
they should try to make a truce with the Russians, offer a ceasefire on
the condition that the Russians promised not to initiate any criminal
proceedings against anyone and especially to guarantee the personal
safety of Maléter and Király. Király said he thought the idea naive: 'At
this point everybody must listen to their own conscience. If somebody
tries to save something that is salvageable, that is laudable. If someone
wants to fight, he should. If someone decides to take a road that leads
straight to the West that is also acceptable . . . I now ask all those who
want to join General Görgenyi to leave immediately. Let us not stand
on ceremony or be emotional. Those who want to go should go, but
right away.'

Just under half went. The rest stayed, formed a command unit under
Király and tried to resist for as long as possible. 'They felt, even if
further fighting seemed in the final outcome hopeless, they would not
be willing to place their arms or themselves at the mercy of Soviet

troops.'[4] He explained: 'Even if it does not sound heroic, I have to say that I did not keep the ... command together in order to organise a guerrilla war, or to prolong Hungarian suffering with stubborn warfare. My only aim was that, if Imre Nagy did make an acceptable compromise, there would be some sort of organisation upon which he could rely. That is why I ... was willing to fight on to keep the Supreme Command alive until such a moment arrived.'

But they could not hold out for long. The Russians prepared for an all-out assault on the headquarters so over the next few days Király retreated, moved away from Budapest and headed west. 'We bivouacked on various ridges of the Pilis, Vértes and Bakony mountains while Soviet helicopters hovered overhead, tracking our line of retreat. Anxiously we listened to foreign broadcasts, waiting and hoping for an eventual change, that somehow at some point something would force the Soviet Union to negotiate with Imre Nagy after all.' He left Hungary 'because while the first death sentence passed on me was not carried out, there would be another one, and it would be executed. There are times when a soldier has to sacrifice his life for his duty. On the other hand, if they want to kill you and absolutely no tangible result would come of it, why run the risk?'[5]

János Kádár arrived in Budapest on 7 November when the Soviets were celebrating the biggest day in the Communist calendar – the anniversary of the Russian Revolution. Not long after the traditional parade in Moscow's Red Square had finished, the new Hungarian leader entered his capital. He knew he would not be welcomed back in triumph. He arrived in a Russian armoured car, escorted by two Soviet tanks to the Parliament building. Nobody apart from a few Soviet troops was anywhere near him. Parliament Square had been cleared hours earlier.

Sporadic gunfire was still heard across the city when Kádár took office. But it was not the fighting that most concerned him; he knew that soon armed resistance would be over – and he was right. It continued in isolated places for a few days. The Kilián Barracks held out until 9 November, when the last serious shots were exchanged. At 'Red' Csepel, where 70,000 people had been besieged by the Russian army for five days, determined rebel groups bravely hung on until 11 November.[6] About 2,600 Hungarians had died since the revolution began on 23 October, roughly two-thirds of them since the second invasion on 4

November.[7] Warfare was useless, but the nation found other ways to fight back. A profound, sullen, passive resistance began – along with a general strike that brought the country to a complete halt.

Kádár was loathed as a Judas. He could not leave the Parliament building safely so he would not have seen the myriad placards that went up around the city. 'Lost: the confidence of the people. Honest finder is asked to return it at once to János Kádár, at 10,000 Soviet tanks Street'[8] was a common one. Also, Kádár was still under probation by the Kremlin. Two KGB officers followed his every move, ostensibly for his security, but really to keep an eye on him. Serov and Grebenyik wielded the real authority in Budapest, one as the secret police chief, the other as military commander. Budapest was under martial law.[9]

The Russians gave little more than moral support for their choice as Hungary's leader. Kádár tried, at first, to be conciliatory. On 11 November he said 'as a former Minister in the Nagy government' that he knew Nagy had not 'led a counter-revolution'.[10] He had been under pressure. Kádár repeatedly said that when 'order had been restored' he wanted Soviet forces to leave.[11] On 14 November he promised that nobody would come to harm as a result of 'the great popular movement of the last few weeks'.[12] He repeated that pledge several times during November.

Kádár knew how damaging the strike could be to him. The Soviets had changed their proconsuls in Budapest several times in the last few years. He could easily be removed at the whim of his liege lords in the Kremlin, if he could not get Hungary working again. He tried to negotiate with the strike leaders of the Central Workers' Council of Greater Budapest, based in Csepel. The Soviets did not like the idea of talking to strikers – particularly as their central demand was the withdrawal of Russian troops. However, they were willing to let Kádár try. Serov authorised Kádár to meet the tall, languid, twenty-three-year-old Sándor Rácz, a toolmaker who had emerged from the revolution as the most charismatic workers' leader in Hungary. They met for the first time on 14 November and the encounter went well, up to a point. Rácz agreed to lift the strike so that food could be delivered and heating was supplied. However, they quarrelled.[13] Rácz said his members regarded the CWC as the sole representative of Hungary's working class. Kádár said the Communist Party did that job: 'Workers' power can be killed not only by bullets but by ballots,' he replied, in answer to a call for free elections. Kádár decided that when the time was right he would find a way to deal with the Workers' Councils.

While Kádár was trying to show moderation, the Russians displayed no such restraint. Arrests began. On 8 November Sándor Kopácsi was tricked into handing himself over to the KGB, by an old Russian friend. 'He told me that the Ambassador wanted to meet me, that he was anxious to discuss the possibility of a truce. He said I could be of service to his country and save Hungarian lives.' Naively, Kopácsi agreed to go. The moment he reached the Embassy he was arrested in the garden and thrown into the basement, which was set up as a prison with Soviet guards. Kopácsi said he thought the arrangement was fitting: 'The cellar had no heating and we were shivering with cold. Once a day we were taken to unspeakably filthy toilets. On the main floor was the ballroom; four metres away was the gulag. That was as good an image as any of Soviet sovereignty.' Kopácsi was reunited with Maléter and the other three who had been trapped by the Russians the midnight before the invasion. 'Maléter behaved with dignity. He gave a dressing-down to a KGB guard, in fluent Russian, who was not showing him sufficient respect. "Stand at attention. It's the Minister of Defence of a socialist country that you have the honour to push into this cell."' They were soon transferred to Budapest Central Prison.[14]

Wild rumours circulated the city that the Russians were deporting thousands of people, including many children, to the Soviet Union. In the first few days after the invasion, 846 Hungarians, mostly ordinary civilians who had been found near fighting, were sent to Russia, including sixty-eight young people under eighteen. They had been despatched to Ukraine, but the deportations stopped on 15 November and they were all returned a few days later. The Soviet official in charge said they could just as easily and efficiently be dealt with back in Hungary.[15]

In the early part of November Kádár was telling friends and supporters that he did not like these tough measures. Serov and Grebenyik had the authority, particularly on security, and they sometimes took decisions without informing him. He said later that commitments he made in good faith were frequently countermanded by the Soviets. It was a mask, but at this point he thought it would be an advantage to try to appear a conciliator.[16]

Münnich rarely showed what he thought. But even he tried to distance himself from what the Soviets were doing in his name. According to the journalist István Szábo, who fled to America as a refugee and

had no obvious reason to lie, Münnich 'disliked the cruel manifestations of terror. But instead of standing up against it he preferred
to shut his eyes and not notice. He drank very heavily – and this helped
him to maintain a sort of "couldn't care less" attitude. He did not
enforce his will. I used to share a drink with him on occasions and
found him a jolly fellow. At the height of the "mopping up" operations
after November 4th . . . he sat in his office, not answering the phones.
If a visitor was with him, he would remark simply *"they're* doing it",
meaning the Russians.'[17]

On 4 December a month after the Soviet tanks began to pulverise
Budapest, the anger, bitterness and resentment of the Hungarians
reached what the great philosopher Hannah Arendt described as the
most moving moment of the revolution. All demonstrations had been
banned under Russian martial law controls. Yet 30,000 women, dressed
in black, marched through central Budapest in silent protest against
the invasion and in mourning for the lost revolution.[18]

The reality of defeat, the death and the destruction, were painful
enough for the Hungarians. As serious, was a huge exodus out of the
country. It began with a trickle on the morning that Russian tanks
rolled into Budapest to smash the revolution. Within a few months
180,000 people had gone – often young, energetic, well-educated, ambitious people whose absence created a significant problem for Hungary
later. Throughout most of November and the first week of December,
the Soviets and the Kádár regime were relaxed about the emigration.
Russian troops left large parts of the frontier with Austria unguarded,
almost as though they were willing potential 'troublemakers' to leave.
Scores of thousands simply walked out of the country, or took a train
as near to the border as they could and then trudged through muddy
fields to Austria and freedom. Later, when Kádár tightened his grip,
Hungary turned into a prison again. It became a risky and hazardous
business to escape.

Some prominent revolutionaries were fleeing from death sentences,
Béla Király and Gergely Pongrácz among them. Others would certainly
have been jailed for long terms if they had stayed, for example György
Heltai, the deputy Foreign Minister, and József Kővágó, the Mayor of
Budapest, who had been released from jail just a few days before the
revolution began. Some, like the writer Paul Ignotus, had broken out
of prison during the uprising and would have gone straight back inside.

For a few, it was the second time in their lives that they had been forced to emigrate; the poet György Faludy had fled from the fascists in the 1930s and now faced exile again. People feared another Great Terror as appalling as the Rákosi years; the Russians, they thought, would seek revenge on the Hungarians for daring to rebel. Many families just took the first opportunity to leave that they could. The gifted Faludy, as so often, hit on another fear of living under totalitarian dictatorship: the fear of collaborating. 'I wanted to write in freedom,' he said. 'But I had another reason for leaving. I was scared. I had a wife and young son. I was afraid that if I stayed I would break, join the Communist Party in order to survive and protect my family.'

Western countries were remarkably generous. The refugee camps hastily set up in Austria to deal with the influx of Hungarians were closed by early 1957. Hungarian émigré communities have been a feature of big cities throughout the world, but these new refugees were absorbed with remarkable ease. The US accepted about 150,000, Britain and France each about 30,000.

Soon the façade disappeared and Kádár showed his brutal side. The trap he set Imre Nagy shows a politician with a ruthless ability to deceive.

The Khrushchev-Tito agreement made at Brioni was a partial success. The Yugoslavs managed to 'neutralise' Nagy, and keep him out of the way while the Russians invaded. But they could not persuade him to resign as Prime Minister and offer his support to the Kádár government. Nobody envisaged that the group of forty-two including several Ministers' wives and seventeen children, would stay for nearly three weeks and again sour relations between the Soviets and Yugoslavia.

The Embassy was a white stucco three-storey building standing in its own garden on Stalin Avenue. Two-metre-high iron railings surrounded the compound. Deflated, depressed and deposed, Nagy made it clear from day one that he would not resign 'and make things easy for Kádár'. The Yugoslav Ambassador, the experienced and sophisticated Dalibor Soldatic, acted as a go-between – a job he disliked intensely.[1] His dealings with the Russians were tense almost from the start. On 7 November a Soviet tank fired on the Embassy, killing one of his diplomats. The Soviets apologised, saying the shots were accidental, but Soldatic was not entirely convinced.[2] He thought it might have been done deliberately to put more pressure on him.

Each day the Ambassador would hold separate talks with Nagy and his group and with Kádár. After three days Kádár realised that the stubborn Nagy would not budge. He told Soldatic that he wanted them all to seek refuge in Romania until the situation was back to normal in Hungary. The Yugoslav said he had nothing against that idea, but it would be up to the refugees. Nagy and his entourage wanted to stay in Hungary, if they could obtain written guarantees of their safety. If not, they would prefer to go to Yugoslavia, a socialist country that was not under Russian domination. Tito vetoed asylum in Yugoslavia itself. He was worried about the Soviets' reaction. However, he was prepared to let the refugees stay in the Embassy.[3]

In public Kádár gave repeated guarantees that no harm would come to Nagy. On the morning of 14 November he told Sándor Rácz: 'I would gladly bring him back into the government ... Let Nagy come to this Parliament building, then we can talk to him.' Later the same day he said he wanted to negotiate, but 'how can I talk with Imre Nagy while he is in the embassy of a foreign power?'[4]

Nevertheless, on 16 November Kádár said he would give Nagy the guarantee he wanted. But when Soldatic went to Kádár to discuss the details, Kádár presented a new set of requirements. Nagy and his closest associate, Losonczy, would have to recognise the new government, they would have to give up any claims to ministerial office and they would have to make a public confession of error.[5] Nagy rejected the deal at once. Tito, exasperated and impatient for a solution, sent his deputy foreign minister, Dobrivoje Vidic, to Budapest for talks with Nagy and Kádár. Finally, on 21 November Kádár, in a letter addressed to the Yugoslav government, he confirmed in writing a guarantee that Nagy and his friends could live in Hungary without conditions. Released after Tito's death in the 1980s, it could not be plainer: 'In order to settle this affair the Hungarian government, in conformity to the Yugoslav letter to me ... repeats herewith the assurances already given several times by word of mouth that it has no desire to punish Imre Nagy and the members of his group in any way for their past activities. We therefore expect the asylum granted by the Yugoslav Embassy to be withdrawn and that its members will return to their homes.'[6]

The refugees decided to leave. Three had already gone (the philosopher György Lukács, for example). Some had considered going but rejected the idea. Júlia Rajk, who had taken a limited role in the revolution but was close to Nagy and was far distant from Kádár, was depressed at the Embassy and wondered if she should leave with her seven-year-old son. She sent a letter to her husband's old friend Béla Szász, carried by the diplomat Milan Georgievic, wondering whether she should go home. Szász, who would himself soon leave Hungary for a new life in the West, replied 'Come out. There is no point in staying with the Yugoslavs. Nobody would dare touch you of all people.' She did not take his advice.[7]

What persuaded them now? Nagy obviously did not trust Kádár. But he believed that the man who usurped him was still too weak

politically to take the chance of breaking such a public promise as a
written guarantee. Again, Nagy showed a fatal naivety and mis-
judgment about people. He believed the Russians would not harm him,
even if they had deposed him. There was another factor in his decision.
Nagy did not feel comfortable in the Yugoslav Embassy. A week after
giving them sanctuary Tito made a speech highly critical of Nagy and
his handling of the 'Hungarian crisis'. He said:

> If Imre Nagy's government had been more energetic, if it had not
> always vacillated instead of taking a strong stand against the chaos and
> against the fact that Communists were killed by reactionaries . . . if it
> had energetically opposed reaction, then perhaps things could have
> been straightened out and perhaps the intervention of the Soviet army
> could have been avoided. But what did Imre Nagy do? He asked people
> to take weapons against the Soviet army and he asked the Western
> countries for help. This intervention was exploited enormously by the
> West. We have to protect the Kádár government and give it help . . . I
> can tell you that I know the men who are now the members of the new
> government and, in my opinion, they represent the most honest forces
> of Hungary . . .[8]

This exasperated Nagy. He could not trust Tito either.

At 6.30 p.m. on 22 November, eighteen days after arriving at the
building, Nagy and the thirty-nine refugees remaining with him left
the Embassy. Nagy genuinely believed he would be allowed to return
home. He called friends to tell them the family would be back for
dinner at Orsó Street.

Münnich had said he would send a bus to take them from the
Embassy to their homes. Nagy went for a final walk in the garden to
hand Soldatic a letter of thanks for treating him and his friends so well
over the last days. He walked to the street looking cheerful. Doubts
began to surface only when it became obvious that there were KGB
officers on the bus. As he was climbing aboard, the driver warned him,
'Be careful, Comrade Nagy, you will not be taken to the place they
have promised.' Astonished, Nagy stepped out of the vehicle and went
to the Ambassador, who sent the two Milans, Georgievic, the First
Secretary, and military attaché Drobac, to check what was happening.
The Ambassador himself followed a few moments later. Nagy insisted
he 'would not board the bus while Soviet spies are on it'.[9]

The KGB men said they were there only to ensure the safety of the passengers and climbed off the bus as requested. The women and children boarded, followed by Nagy who, whether he now believed the Russians or not, took a window seat on the right-hand side of the bus. The two Yugoslav diplomats sat near the door. As the driver revved up the engine to drive off, the Soviet police jumped back on board. A Soviet car appeared as if from nowhere, and drove alongside the bus. Another trailed it. The Yugoslav diplomats protested but were forced to leave the bus. As Milan Georgievic told a close friend of Nagy, the writer Miklós Molnár, later that evening over a drink at the Hotel Duna bar: 'We had hardly gone 200 metres when the bus stopped and the Russians physically pulled us from the bus.'[10]

After driving along Gorki Street, the party reached the house of one of the Hungarian refugees. The bus drove straight past the front door. Two armoured vehicles joined the convoy. Eventually the bus drew to a halt at the Rákóczi Military School on the edge of the city. Guards warned that anyone trying to escape would be shot. Nagy at first refused to get out of the bus. Two burly soldiers climbed aboard, pulled him out and hustled him through the front door of the building. The abduction had clearly been planned to the last detail. We now know that the idea of the kidnap was Andropov's, and it was enthusiastically approved by the KGB chief Serov. Three top Kremlin officials were in Budapest overseeing their colonial domains in Hungary: Malenkov, Suslov and a third who had arrived a few days earlier, the little-known 'organisation' man, Averiky Aristov, who stayed in Hungary for less than a week. They were involved in the kidnap plot.

The Yugoslavs knew of the plan, though they firmly denied it. Kádár always claimed that he had a verbal understanding with the Yugoslavs that Nagy would never reach home. The Yugoslavs issued an indignant statement, though, expressing anger at the treatment of their diplomats, which caused renewed tension between Tito and Khrushchev.[11] Kádár's version of events three days later was scarcely credible: 'It was for their own safety that the passengers of the coach in question were not driven back to their homes. The government had good reason to suppose that there were counter-revolutionary elements in hiding in the country who might resort to an act of provocation, murdering Nagy or one of his collaborators and trying to fix the responsibility before the public on the Hungarian government.'[12]

Münnich met the kidnap victims at about 7.30 p.m. The ghastly irony that this act of treachery should be his was not lost on Nagy or his wife. When they had been émigrés in Moscow in the 1930s they had been friends. While Münnich was away fighting in Spain, his wife lived with them for two years. Münnich's purpose now was to see if Nagy had been frightened enough into dropping his obstinacy and would be prepared to support Kádár. He went away dissatisfied. Four days later Nagy and his entourage were flown to Romania. For more than eighteen months ordinary Hungarians had no idea if he was alive or dead.

Next it was the turn of Kádár's less well-known opponents. The AVO did not return in its old form, but its 40,000 members had not simply disappeared over the last fortnight. Many joined the Kádár regime's new security force, the Karhatalom, whose special 'R Section', Riado Csopart (Alarm Groups), had the job of organising massive reprisals against revolutionaries. It was headed by László Mátyas, a dry and dull apparatchik, thin and gaunt, who for a short period shared one of Rákosi's prison cells with Kádár. The 'R' groups' methods were not as brutal; they did not practise torture. They managed to be ruthlessly efficient though. They did not instigate an indiscriminate purge, but from late November they began hunting down anyone who had been directly involved in the uprising.[13]

Kádár himself favoured lies and deceit to entrap victims. On 11 December he invited the Central Workers' Council leader Sándor Rácz and his deputy, the thirty-two-year-old tool-fitter at the Standard Electrical plant Sándor Bali, for another round of talks. Kádár was no longer willing to compromise with the workers' leaders. When he tried to abolish the CWC, they called another strike which again brought the country to a virtual full stop. Every worker downed tools and Kádár said he would negotiate. When Rácz and Bali arrived at Parliament for the meeting, police arrested them. It was a replay of the treatment meted out to Maléter and Kopácsi. Rácz and Bali were in jail for six years. The strike was called off.

Dudás was tricked in a similar way at the end of November. He had managed to stay in hiding, but through an intermediary got word through to Kádár that he would be prepared to talk. Kádár promised him safe conduct. Instead of meeting him, when Dudás turned up at the Parliament building at the appointed time for the talks, he was arrested. He was one of the first to be hanged after the revolution – on 19 January 1957, the same day as 'Uncle' Szabó. Lajos Steiner, twenty-six, a casual labourer, was one of the leaders of the rebel group near the Eastern Railway Station. He had the chance to escape after the Russians invaded, but he returned. From the safety of Austria he was lured back. The Hungarian Embassy in Vienna traced him, gave him assurances that he would be granted an amnesty, and he was persuaded to return. Within days, he was arrested and sent to the scaffold.

Tildy was arrested within a few weeks and was sentenced to six years' imprisonment. After Attila Szigetthy, leader of the revolution in the provinces, was captured in Győr, he killed himself. Then student leaders and the intellectuals who began the revolution were rounded up. Tibor Déry was the first, followed by journalists such as Gyula Obersovsky, editor of *Truth*, the tabloid that lived up to its name for ten days. He was sentenced to death, but after widespread indignation from the West the sentence was commuted to life in jail. An all-out hunt went on for Nagy's friend Miklós Gimes, one of the inspirational voices of the uprising. He started an underground movement, with a newspaper called *October 23rd*, which tried to keep alive the spirit of revolution. He was caught in mid December, was tried with Nagy and executed. Writers went on strike, refusing to bring forth words of any kind for publication. They existed on royalties from old books and stood firm for months.[14]

Kádár set up new 'People's Courts' with extraordinary powers, supervised by carefully screened judges and overseen by Communist Party functionaries, reinforcing the point that the Soviets were back and Hungary was still a Communist colony. Around 22,000 people were jailed after the revolution in a dark era of reprisals that lasted throughout the rest of the 1950s. Death sentences were imposed on 229 people, but more were carried out. In some ghastly cases, victims who were originally sent to jail had their sentences increased on appeal. About 330 were executed.

Settling the score was vicious and cruel. Mária Wittner, a nineteen-year-old factory worker and a single mother, joined the Corvin group of rebels, after the second day of the revolution. She did no fighting to speak of. 'I had just one gun. We learned to shoot on a vacant lot but the recoil hit me on the cheek, so I said I would give it up before it knocked a tooth out.' She gave the weapon away. She was wounded when the Corvin Passage was attacked by mortar shells on 4 November. 'I was hit in three places – on my thigh, on my leg, and on my back, one centimetre away from my spine.' When she got out of hospital on

9 November she returned to the Corvin, but the rebels had been defeated and had all gone. She tried to leave the country but she was captured by the Russians, interrogated and, to her amazement, released.

She managed to reach safety in Austria, but returned after a few weeks. 'The message from the Kádár government at that time was that those who were active in the first part of the revolution – before the second Russian invasion – were safe from retaliation. I believed it. I thought if that was the case I wasn't going to have any problems, otherwise they would have to lock up half of Budapest.' She was arrested again a few weeks later. In jail she met up with a friend from the Corvin group, a petite brunette called Kati Stickler, twenty-six who reached Switzerland after the Russians invaded, but came back: 'Her fiancé had sent her a message saying she wouldn't be harmed in any way, because Kádár had promised everyone immunity. We were stupid to believe them.'

Mária and her friend were held for more than a year without trial but were then prosecuted on the basis of a photograph that had been taken of them on 30 October 1956 carrying weapons, even though there was plenty of evidence that they had fired no shots. Their trial in May 1958 lasted a month, before the well-known People's Court judge Gusztáv Tutsek. They were found guilty. At the appeal the following February in front of Judge János Bórbely the verdict stood. These were well-known judges, famed for their harshness, who sent many victims to their deaths after the revolution. Both young women were sentenced to hang. A few days later Mária and her friend were in their condemned cell: 'The door opened and her name was called. We hugged each other then two guards came in, took hold of her arm and led her out. I just stared after them until the cell door slammed shut. Kati was a tiny little woman. She walked out upright, with her head held high.'

For three months Mária thought every day would be her last. Then she heard that, because she was a mother, they had decided to be 'lenient' and her sentence was reduced to life imprisonment. She remained in jail for thirteen years, almost the last to be released in the reprisals following the revolution.[15]

THIRTY-FOUR

16 June 1958

Betrayed, humiliated and abducted, Imre Nagy and his fellow kidnap victims were held for four days at Russian military headquarters in Budapest. Each day Ferenc Münnich visited and tried to persuade his erstwhile friend to resign, recant and declare his support for the new government. Nagy refused.[1] He was by turns morose and outraged, but according to most witnesses who saw him, he was not frightened. He was convinced that Kádár was in too weak a position to have him killed – and the Russians, despite everything, would back away from the final step of murdering him. When Münnich was finally convinced that his persuasive charms would not work, Nagy, his family and now thirty of his friends were flown out of Hungary and were held in Snagov Castle, on a lake close to Bucharest. It was well appointed, and they were treated decently, but nevertheless they were in prison.

Kádár still seemed to want a compromise and he repeatedly gave assurances of Nagy's safety. On 26 November, in a radio broadcast, Kádár declared: 'We have promised not to institute any court action against Imre Nagy or his friends on account of the crimes they committed ... We shall keep this promise. We do not regard their departure as permanent, but, in the present situation, we think that it is preferable for Nagy and his followers to leave Hungarian territory for a while.'[2]

Then, early in the New Year, the temperature changed. Between 1 January and 4 January 1957 the leaders of the Soviet bloc states met at a summit in Budapest. Two days later, for the first time, they used the word 'treason' to describe how 'Imre Nagy and his government ... opened the way to the fascist counter-revolution'.[3] In mid January, Zhou Enlai, second in command to Mao among China's Communists, on a visit to Hungary, several times referred to Nagy and his companions as 'traitors and renegades'. He would not have done so if it was likely to embarrass his host.[4] Still, Kádár in public issued denial after denial that he would bring Nagy to trial. On 27 February a Foreign Ministry statement declared: 'The Government has no intention of bringing Imre Nagy to trial.'[5] On 4 April Kàdar, speaking to foreign journalists off the record, said that 'in view of the delicacy of the situation there will be no trial'.[6]

For many years it was assumed that the Russians bore most of the responsibility for the murder of Imre Nagy. Khrushchev, the argument went, was determined to make an example of the Hungarian, to show other satellite leaders the line they could not cross if they wanted to survive. There is little proof of that. Speaking to his son Sergei later, Khrushchev defended the arrest of Nagy because he 'presents too great a danger to be left free in Budapest. Disaffected people would gather around him.'[7] But Khrushchev junior said his father was 'disheartened' when Kádár requested that Nagy be handed over to the executioner. Many of Khrushchev's critics doubt that, but documents kept secret until the late 1990s suggest that Kádár was more eager than his masters in Moscow on a hanging. He saw that Nagy alive, even in jail, would always be a rival and he had to eliminate him. In private Kádár was determined on the death of Nagy from an early stage.[8]

Kádár knew that on such a serious issue for the future of the whole Soviet bloc he needed approval from the highest levels of the Kremlin. He received it at a Hungarian-Soviet summit in Moscow between 21 and 27 March. He told aides later that he took full responsibility:

> The question of Imre Nagy and the others ... arose. We raised it. The comrades think it proper that we call him to account with suitable severity ... Whether this happens sooner or later may be debated, but they endorse its execution.
>
> Of course, bearing in mind our past experiences, nothing can be invented – our starting point must be the facts known by hundreds of thousands of people. This matter demands conscientious preparatory work ... I don't mean playing for time, but it is impossible to imagine the whole country's political situation without us establishing suitable order in this matter ... Work should start on this ... within the foreseeable future. We cannot wait 8–10 months, or years, to pull out the bad tooth.[9]

On 14 April 1957 Nagy was arrested by Hungarian police at Snagov. He was returned to Budapest and held at the Central Prison, along with his fellow accused, Pál Maléter, Miklós Gimes, József Szilágyi, Sándor

Kopácsi and Géza Losonczy, who Kádár decided would hang at the same time. But the wheels ground slowly, partly because they all pleaded not guilty. Kádár had declined the use of torture to extract confessions, which ruled out an old-fashioned Communist show trial.[10] They were kept in solitary confinement. Nagy refused to answer a single question put by his interrogators until late May 1957. But that was pointless. He held an ideal about the printed record, and he thought posterity would acquit him, so he decided to answer direct factual questions, but little else. He knew by then almost certainly the fate that awaited him. Szilágyi was tried separately and executed two months earlier than the others. Géza Losonczy collapsed psychologically and physically. He suffered terribly and broke down as he had done in Rákosi's jails. He went on hunger strike and died following forced feeding.

Kádár was deeply frustrated by the slow pace of events, caused mainly by diplomatic concerns in Moscow. On 19 June 1957 he was summoned by Khrushchev for talks in Moscow but they were inconclusive. The Russians wanted to wait, so the murder would take place at the least inconvenient moment for them. But Kádár was eager to press ahead. In early August, the Hungarian Interior Minister Béla Biszku, who was to remain in senior positions in Kádár governments for decades, again went to Moscow to ask for the process to be hastened so the hangings could proceed. Andropov had been promoted. He was now the Kremlin official in charge of ties with the 'fraternal' parties in the Soviet bloc. He agreed with the proposed candidates for the gallows. However, he urged a further delay to the trial. The Hungarians wanted it to proceed in September. The Soviets postponed it until after November 1957, when celebrations were planned in Moscow for the fortieth anniversary of the Bolshevik Revolution.[11]

Kádár's impatience grew but he could do nothing. On 21 December he regretted privately that they had not killed Nagy immediately after the revolution was crushed. 'Retaliation would have been more justifiable between November 4th–5th, but it was then that we were weakest.'[12] The trial was put back until 5 February 1958. The preliminary hearings had already begun when the Russians again asked for a deferral. Soviet diplomats were hoping that there would soon be an East-West summit and a big trial of Nagy would be a public relations disaster. Kádár became increasingly annoyed. He noted on 14 February: 'At the time when we could have settled this case we had not the strength to do so. Now we have the strength but cannot settle the case.'[13]

Khrushchev in December had shown interest in a reprieve for Nagy.[14] Kádár was appalled. He told Moscow's new Ambassador, Yevgeny Gromov: 'Should we grant an amnesty now, it would include the principal criminals which would weaken the people's democratic order.' Kádár was desperate to ensure that Moscow would not insist on a lighter sentence. He was not a bloodthirsty man; but he was convinced that he could never establish himself as a legitimate leader if Nagy was still alive. He thought a dead martyr was better than a living rival. To one doubter in his circle, Márton Valkó, who suggested that after pronouncing the death sentence there should instantly be a pardon with a reduced penalty, Kádár said indignantly: 'No. This is not feasible.'[15]

In late May 1958 Kádár flew to Moscow for a final summit on the Nagy issue when Khrushchev told him the trial could go ahead. It took place between 9 and 15 June. However, the big show trial designed to bring down the curtain on the revolution had to be held in secret. Nagy denied the charges of plotting to overthrow the state, and refused to acknowledge the competence of the court. When he was addressed by the prosecution – and the judge – as the 'former' Prime Minister of Hungary, he insisted that he was 'still' the Premier. Kopácsi was spared hanging at the eleventh hour; Kádár commuted his sentence to life imprisonment. Maléter and Miklós Gimes were hanged with Nagy. Maléter's last recorded words were: 'Long live independent and socialist Hungary.'

After Nagy was sentenced he declined to plead for mercy. During the ordeal of his last eighteen months he had lost a little weight but he still looked a jovial figure as he made a last statement to the court:

> I have twice tried to save the honour and image of communism in the Danubian valley, once in 1953 and again in 1956. Rákosi and the Russians prevented me from doing so. If my life is needed to prove that not all Communists are enemies of the people, I gladly make the sacrifice. I know there will one day be another Nagy trial, which will rehabilitate me. I also know I will have a reburial. I only fear that the funeral oration will be delivered by those who betrayed me.

He was hanged at dawn on 16 June 1958, but the fact was made known to Hungarians in a terse statement on the radio the next day.

Nagy, Maléter and Gimes were buried in the prison courtyard, face-down and wrapped in tar paper. Four years later they were secretly reburied in the Rákoskeresztúr, the cemetery opposite the jail, in unmarked graves on a remote corner of the graveyard reserved for the remains of hardened criminals. Their families were not allowed to tend the graves until the late 1980s. It was difficult to identify their bones when, after the collapse of communism, they were reburied in public as national heroes.

POSTSCRIPT

In Washington, the post-mortems began. Though President Eisenhower exclaimed to one of his speech-writers, Emmet John Hughes, that 'I just don't know what got into these people, it's the damndest business I ever saw',[1] he acknowledged there had to be a further and more detailed explanation of the Hungarian Revolution. He won re-election easily on 6 November. Ike was still hugely popular at home. The sight of Soviet tanks rumbling into the centre of Budapest would not change that. But he knew that the Hungarian Revolution had been a major setback for US credibility as the leader of the free world. The President's image had received a battering, whatever the polls might have said.

Public attention in the West had been diverted to the Middle East, but it was now directed back to central Europe and the Soviet Union. Sympathy for Hungary as a victim nation was overwhelming. Aid flooded in for the refugees. Insistent questions were asked of the US and inside the US. This had been a bitter blow against liberty. The Russians stood condemned as barbaric tyrants; but how had the Soviets got away with it so easily? The Americans had always said they wanted to liberate captive peoples. Now they had been given a chance, and it looked to outsiders as though they had done nothing. The gap between words and deeds seemed immense.*

President Eisenhower was highly sensitive to the criticism. A week after the election, Henry Cabot Lodge was the first to raise the charges directly with Ike. The next day the UN General Assembly was sched-

---

* Some voices in the intelligence establishment were deeply disappointed. Frank Wisner never recovered from the 'loss', as he put it, of Hungary. The 1956 revolution was not the only reason, but he went downhill fast soon afterwards. He resorted increasingly to the bottle, had a psychological breakdown in 1957 and early the next year committed suicide.

uled to consider another resolution condemning the Soviet invasion. Lodge called the President. An old, patrician Republican, Lodge had been an isolationist before the war but had changed his views. He said, nervously, to Eisenhower: 'There is a feeling at the UN that for ten years we have been inciting the Hungarians through our [propaganda] and now that they are in trouble, we turn our backs on them.' Eisenhower protested strongly. 'We have never incited anybody to rebel,' he declared.[2] John Foster Dulles was by then an ill man but, recovering from surgery, was back at his Foggy Bottom desk. After his frosty conversation with Lodge, Ike complained bitterly at the presumed rebuke he had just heard and Dulles assured him 'we always said we are against violent rebellion'. However, it was a charge that never went away.

The next day Eisenhower defended his administration firmly: 'Our hearts have gone out to them [the Hungarians] and we have done everything that is possible in the way of alleviating their suffering, but we must make things clear,' he said. 'The US does not now and never has advocated open rebellion by an undefended populace against force over which it could not possibly prevail. We, on the contrary, have always urged that the spirit of freedom be kept alive; that people do not lose hope. But we have never, in all the years that I think we have been dealing with problems of this sort, urged or argued for any kind of armed revolt which could bring about disaster to our friends.'[3]

The issue of American propaganda lies at the heart of complaints by so many Hungarians that they were let down by the Americans. Some of the despairing denunciations sounded like the bitterness of defeat. Some were more reasoned and worried American policy-makers. Gergely Pongrácz, one of the Budapest rebel leaders who made his home in America for thirty years after the revolution, said just before he died in 2005 that 'the US sold us out. We were promised help. It never arrived.'[*][4] Béla Király, another exile in America, used to say, 'People hear what they want to hear.'[5] Some of the Radio Free Europe broadcasts without a doubt encouraged Hungarians to take up arms against the Soviets. Its so-called 'military expert' said during the revolution: 'Soviet forces deployed against Hungary are not irreversible . . .

---

* Pongrácz returned to Hungary in 1990, after the collapse of communism, and went into politics, launching a curious right-wing party – half Hungarian nationalist, part American neo-con.

their troops available have been used up . . . The Hungarian forces are superior to those.'[6] What else could that mean except – 'fight'?

The CIA countered. Towards the end of 1956 the Agency asked the old Cold Warrior William Griffith, the psychological warfare expert who helped set up the station, to investigate whether any of the charges were valid. In a long report he produced transcripts, including some quoted earlier here, that clearly broke CIA guidelines. But it happened unintentionally, he said, and he cleared the station. 'After the revolution was well under way a few of the scripts do indicate that RFE occasionally went beyond the authorised factual reports . . . to provide tactical advice to the patriots to the course the rebellion should take and the individuals best qualified to lead it . . . As soon as these deviations from policy were noted, steps were taken to impose rigid supervision of broadcasting content . . . Radio Free Europe did not incite the Hungarian people to revolution, which was the result of ten years of Soviet repression.'[7]

A thousand Hungarian refugees were polled by American academics immediately after the revolution. Ninety-six per cent thought the foreign radio broadcasts made them believe help would come from the West.[8] Among them were extremely intelligent writers like Tamás Aczél, who became a literature professor at an American university: 'Our heart was in the right place. The trouble was we imagined the West had similar feelings towards us, would reciprocate our confessions of love. This probably foolish notion was greatly strengthened by the slogans and propaganda of the US. "Liberation" and "rolling back" of Soviet domination. Since then we learned what we didn't know – that the West had written off these countries and only their propaganda machines pretended otherwise.'[9] And the passionate liberal intellectual József Köböl, who argued that the US did not support the revolution until after it failed, said:

When . . . America finally spoke . . . it was a message of condolence. Of course no Hungarians expected a nuclear war on their behalf but probably we believed too deeply political rhetoric in election campaigns that we weren't supposed to take seriously. The wrong was partly our fault for twisting words. It was partly America's fault for thinking that words can be used loosely. Words like 'freedom', 'struggle for national independence', 'rollback', 'liberation' have meanings. If America wants to flood Eastern and Central Europe with these words it must acknowledge a responsibility for them. Otherwise you are inciting nations to commit suicide.[10]

An acute American observer asked a good question. 'For years we have held aloft the torch of liberty. At what point does the torch become an incendiary weapon?'[11]

Eisenhower gave plain reasons for not intervening.

'There was no European country, and I don't believe ours, ready to say that we should have gone into this thing at once and try to liberate Hungary from Communist influence,' he said. 'I don't believe we had the support of the UN to go and make this an all-out war ... We had no government [in Hungary] that was asking us to come in and it wasn't until there was a, sort of, I think, very brief revolutionary government was set up that we had any communication with them. So I don't know. The thing started in such a way that everybody was a little bit fooled, I think, and when suddenly the Soviets came in strength with their tank divisions, and it was a fait accompli, it was a great tragedy and disaster.'[12]

There were critics of the policy as well as the propaganda. Henry Kissinger was an academic at Harvard at the time, before he went into politics. He was a cynical, hard-headed opponent of communism. He blamed Eisenhower for inaction. 'He behaved like a spectator,' said Kissinger, 'without any direct interest in the outcome of the Hungarian Revolution and its abject failure to extort any price from Moscow, diplomatic, economic, military. There were no diplomatic notes, no pressure, no offers to mediate. Nothing.'[13] The judgment of the Republican-controlled Congressional Committee on Foreign Affairs the next year stung. It had an echoing ring of truth: 'The failure of the US to have a plan, or plans, of action concerning the Hungarian events indicates either a serious weakness in our intelligence services or a serious misapplication by the administration of our foreign policy ... There was no evidence that passivity would induce a spirit of compromise in the Soviet leaders.'[14]

In his second term, Eisenhower remained popular, but became more realistic in his rhetoric. He had learned lessons from Hungary. Propaganda to Eastern Europe was toned down. The Cold War went into deep freeze for a while, but the following year the first halting steps towards coexistence and détente were made. He sounded less of a hero, perhaps. But less of a hypocrite, too.

*

The UN, not for the first or last time, looked impotent as a peacekeeping body after the Hungarian crisis. There was probably nothing it could have done, as the world's two superpowers had decided matters between them. Russia had tanks in Budapest, and the power of veto in New York. America had accepted the status quo in central Europe, and President Eisenhower concentrated on the Middle East instead, where he could make a difference. However, the UN managed to look inefficient as well as powerless. The desperate missing messages from Budapest on critical days, the lack of urgency in dealing with Nagy's pleas, all made the UN appear worse than it was.

Dag Hammarskjöld fulfilled the role of scapegoat – unfairly. Asked later why he did not go to Budapest at the beginning of November, when he might have begun negotiations with the Russians, he replied: 'At that time no one on the Security Council knew what the situation was in Budapest. But we did know what the situation was in Suez.' He was telling the truth.[15] Canada's Prime Minister, Lester Pearson, asked the upright Swede on 7 December 1956: 'What can we do?' He replied, very little: 'It would be a cruel deceit to pretend that force could have been used. The people who would suffer first and foremost by that kind of action would be the Hungarians themselves.'[16] Hammarskjöld consistently maintained that there was nothing more he could have done to help Hungary. Eighteen months later he reflected from a distance: 'I did what I could. And it did not yield the results I was hoping for. That can ... happen in public diplomacy. It certainly happens in private diplomacy.'[17]

The Russians had sent a terrible warning to all their vassal states. They were prepared to crush any sign of rebellion with ruthless savagery. The lesson was learned; there was barely a hint of open resistance in the Soviet satellites for more than a decade. But 'victory' in Hungary came at a price.

In the Kremlin, Khrushchev had left himself open to attack for nearly 'losing' Hungary. He admitted he had not handled the crisis decisively enough,[18] by which he meant that he thought the Soviets should have marched into Budapest earlier. Molotov, Kaganovich and other hardliners mounted increasing challenges against him. They failed to depose him. The following June, with the help of his old ally Mikoyan, Marshal Zhukov and the intelligence chief Serov, he turned the tables and mounted a coup against them. Khrushchev survived until 1964, continuing to rule by a mass of contradictory impulses – shrewd, brutal, occasionally decent by turn. He tried to liberalise the Soviet empire, but when he perceived a threat to its existence he returned instinctively to repression. After 1956 he, and many close to him in the Kremlin, had what one of his advisers later called a 'Hungary complex'. He was left acutely aware of the speed with which an apparently all-powerful one-party state could crash.[19] He claimed to have increased Soviet prestige, but that has always been debatable. Prestige can be illusory.

Russia was loathed as much as feared after the Hungarian Revolution. There was outrage in the rest of the world, tinged with remorse that so little had been done by the West to help. All major cities outside the Soviet bloc saw big demonstrations against the invasion. In London thirteen bricks were thrown at the Hungarian Legation in Belgravia on the night of 4 November – the Hungarian-born writer Arthur Koestler claimed credit for the protest. Large demonstrations were held outside the Embassy each day for a week. In Luxembourg, the Soviet Ambassador and his family hid in the basement of the Embassy when protesters stormed inside the building and set it on fire just before a cocktail party was about to begin. In Bonn demonstrators threw bricks at the Russian Legation and flags on official buildings flew at half mast. In The Hague, grocers refused to deliver food to the Soviet Embassy and a hotel declined to let the Russians hold a reception that had been booked weeks previously. In Rotterdam dockworkers would not unload Soviet ships.[20]

None of these protests disturbed the Soviet leadership. The respect they seemed to receive in the rest of the world outweighed the anger of the West. However, one effect that barely entered the calculations of the Kremlin potentates when they sent their tanks into Budapest, had a profound impact on the Cold War. Soviet savagery in Hungary fractured the Left throughout the world, particularly in Europe. The Soviet Union always thought it important to ensure that in the West there remained Communist Parties utterly loyal to Moscow. They were valuable for propaganda purposes, obviously. In Italy and France since the end of World War II the Communists had been almost strong enough to take power in fair elections. Not after Hungary. The Communist Parties split down the middle – a serious blow to the USSR's reputation and influence. The French CP lost around half its members and the schismatic Italian Communists broke with Moscow. In Britain, where the Party was always weak, two-thirds of the members left. The Danish CP ceased to exist altogether.[21]

Fellow travellers broke ranks. The most powerful denunciation written against the Soviet crackdown on Hungary came in a brilliant pamphlet entitled *The Ghost of Stalin* by the Marxist philosopher Jean-Paul Sartre, usually the most reliable apologist for the Soviet Union. He wrote: 'Before Hungary they [the Russians] were winning across the board; they looked like coming out victors in the Cold War. They were reconciling themselves with Tito and restoring unity in the socialist camp. They were extending their influence as far as India and the Middle East. In the bourgeois democracies their cultural offensive was bearing fruit. Now ... the Budapest massacres have destroyed years of efforts for détente, for co-existence, for peace. Never in the West have communists found themselves so isolated. Never has their confusion been greater ... '[22]

Few people would have any illusions left about the imperial pretensions of Moscow. For some optimists in the West, Hungary 1956 was 'the beginning of the end of the Soviet empire'.[23] The hope was premature. But the Hungarians gave the Soviets a jolt from which they never entirely recovered.

János Kádár was the most hated man in Hungary for years. Even Khrushchev, when he visited Budapest in January and April 1957, seemed less unpopular than the Hungarian collaborator, as Kádár was called in private. After the crackdown, a partial thaw began. From the spring after the revolution, Soviet soldiers were confined to barracks near Budapest, or tried to be less noticeable in other towns and cities. Officers wore civilian clothes. Over the next three years the occupation army was halved. With the help of huge Russian loans, wages went up by 15 to 20 per cent by the summer of 1957.[24]

In time, and in stages, Kádár relaxed his iron grip. He tried to show that he was not tied to the Kremlin's puppet strings. In the summer of 1959, while the People's Courts were continuing to hang some revolutionaries, there was an amnesty for some others, though many thousands were still in jail. He released more prisoners the following April. The Communist Party took back its old power and soon its membership was again at about 800,000.[25] However, Kádár discouraged any personality cult around himself and he loathed publicity. It was hard to find a picture of him anywhere in Hungary.

Kádár maintained that if he had not taken power in November 1956 someone worse would have been imposed. Hungarians came, grudgingly, to believe him. He very seldom talked, either in private or public, about the revolution (or the attempted 'counter-revolution', as he always called it). In November 1962 he said 'those who are not against us are with us', and promised a full amnesty to prisoners arrested after the uprising. Everyone knew what he meant. Almost all the prisoners were released. 'We breathed a sigh of relief after that moment,' Ágnes Gergely, a victim of the repression on a limited scale, said. It was not only terror of arrest that made life so ghastly in those post-uprising years, she explained. She was fired from her job as a teacher for saying once in a class that in 1956 there had been a 'revolution' in Hungary – a forbidden word.[26]

After the amnesty the mood eased. But as for revolution, or counter-revolution, neither was talked about. Imre Nagy's name could not be mentioned, except in hushed tones, in privacy amongst families and friends.

The psychologist Ferenc Mérei, who spent four years in jail after 1956 as one of the leaders of the rebel student movement in Budapest, said a 'collective amnesia' took hold of Hungarians from the 1960s onwards. It was a willing conspiracy of silence. There was no democracy, the Communist Party was in power and Soviet troops still occupied Hungary. In return, Kádár abandoned the most creaking parts of the Soviet-style command economy and the police state was relatively unobtrusive. Hungary was 'the merriest barracks in the prison camp',[27] as one who had escaped from the country said. In many ways Hungary was the most relaxed and most prosperous of the Soviet satellites – except that memories of 1956 continued to haunt. With Soviet backing, Kádár instituted a uniquely Hungarian 'gulyas communism' – a peculiar brand that got rid of the worst features of East European socialism but kept the Communist Party in power.

Kádár became a widely respected figure, admired for his political dexterity. He had not been forgiven, but there was some acknowledgement of his achievements. He hung onto office too long. He was beginning to go senile when he was relieved of power by younger Communist claimants in 1988. In his last year he confessed to guilt about the deaths after the revolution was suppressed.[28] He died the following July – a fortnight after Imre Nagy was reburied at a funeral attended by thousands of people in Budapest. Communism did not survive him long. Nor did the presence of Russian troops on Hungarian soil. The new democratic, free-market, multi-party Hungary officially replaced the People's Republic on 23 October 1989, thirty-three years to the day after the first anti-Soviet demonstrations of the revolution.

APPENDIX
The Sixteen Points

1. We demand the immediate evacuation of all Soviet troops, in conformity with the provisions of the Treaty of Peace.
2. We demand the election by secret ballot of all Party members, from top to bottom, and of new officers for the lower, middle and upper echelons of the Hungarian Workers' Party. These officers shall convoke a Party Congress as early as possible in order to elect a Central Committee.
3. A new Government must be constituted under the direction of Comrade Imre Nagy; all the criminal leaders of the Stalin-Rákosi era must be immediately relieved of their duties.
4. We demand a public inquiry into the criminal activities of Mihály Farkas and his accomplices. Mátyás Rákosi, who is the person most responsible for all crimes of the recent past, as well as for the ruin of our country, must be brought back to Hungary for trial before a people's tribunal.
5. We demand that general elections, by universal secret ballot, be held throughout the country to elect a new National Assembly, with all political parties participating. We demand that the right of workers to strike be recognised.
6. We demand revision and readjustment of Hungarian-Soviet and Hungarian-Yugoslav relations in the fields of politics, economics, and cultural affairs on a basis of complete political and economic equality and non-interference in the internal affairs of one by the other.
7. We demand the complete reorganisation of Hungary's economic life under the direction of specialists. The entire economic system, based on a system of planning, must be re-examined in the light of conditions in Hungary and in the vital interests of the Hungarian people.
8. Our foreign trade agreements and the exact total of reparations that can never be paid must be made public. We demand precise and exact information on the uranium deposits in our country, on their exploitation, and on the concessions accorded the Russians in this area. We demand that Hungary has the right to sell her uranium freely at world market prices to obtain hard currency.
9. We demand complete revision of the norms in effect in industry and an immediate and radical adjustment of salaries in accordance with the just requirements of workers and intellectuals. We demand that a minimum living wage be fixed for workers.
10. We demand that the system of distribution be organised on a new basis and that

agricultural products be utilised in a rational manner. We demand equality of treatment for individual farms.

11. We demand reviews by independent tribunals of all political and economic trials as well as the release and rehabilitation of the innocent. We demand the repatriation of prisoners of war and civilian deportees in the Soviet Union, including prisoners sentenced outside Hungary.

12. We demand complete recognition of freedom of opinion and expression, of freedom of the press and radio, as well as the creation of a new daily newspaper for the MEFESZ Organisation (Hungarian Federation of University and College Students organisations).

13. We demand that the statue of Stalin, symbol of Stalinist tyranny and political oppression, be removed as quickly as possible and be replaced by a monument to the martyred fighters for freedom of 1848/49.

14. We demand the replacement of emblems that are foreign to the Hungarian people by the old Hungarian arms of Kossuth. We demand for the Hungarian Army new uniforms conforming to our national traditions. We demand that 15 March be declared a national holiday and that 6 October be a day of national mourning on which schools will be closed.

15. The students of the Technological University of Budapest declare unanimously their solidarity with the workers and students of Warsaw and Poland in their movement towards national independence.

16. The students of the Technological University of Budapest will organise as rapidly as possible local branches of the MEFESZ and they have decided to convoke at Budapest on Saturday 27 October a Youth Parliament at which all the nation's youth will be represented by their delegates.

SOURCES

Chapter One (pp. 7–15)

1. Winston S. Churchill, *The Second World War*, vol. 6, *Triumph and Tragedy* (Houghton Mifflin, Boston, 1953), p. 174.
2. David Dilles (ed.), *The Diaries of Sir Alexander Cadogan, OM, 1938–1945* (Cassell, London, 1971), p. 233.
3. See Admiral Horthy's Papers (Corvina Press, Budapest, 1965).
4. Ibid.
5. Krisztián Ungváry, *The Siege of Budapest* (Yale University Press, New Haven and London, 2005), pp. 30–36.
6. Ibid.
7. Ibid.
8. Ferenc Nagy, *The Struggle Behind the Iron Curtain* (Macmillan, New York, 1948), p. 42.
9. Sándor Márai, *Memoir of Hungary, 1944–1948* (Corvina/Central European University Press, Budapest, 1996), pp. 36–40.
10. Ungváry, *The Siege of Budapest*, p. 45.
11. Christine Arnothy, *J'ai Quinze ans et je ne veux pas mourir* (Fayard, Paris, 1981).
12. Alaine Polcz, *A Woman's War*, Hungarian Quarterly, Budapest, 1991.
13. László Borhi, *Hungary in the Cold War, 1945–1956* (Central European University Press, Budapest, 2004), pp. 37–41.

14. Cited in Eduard Mark, 'Revolution By Degrees: Stalin's National Front Strategy for Europe', Cold War International History Project (Woodrow Wilson Center, Washington, 2001).
15. See Borhi, *Hungary in the Cold War*. Also, Charles Gati, *Hungary and the Soviet Bloc* (Duke University Press, North Carolina, 1986).
16. Bennett Kovrig, *Communism in Hungary from Kun to Kádár* (Hoover Institution Press, Stanford, Calif., 1979), p. 80.
17. Cited in Borhi, *Hungary in the Cold War*, p. 58.
18. László Mravik, *The 'Sacco di Budapest' and the Depredation of Hungary, 1938–1949* (The Hungarian National Gallery, Budapest, 1998).
19. Tamás Aczél and Tibor Meray, *The Revolt of the Mind* (Thames and Hudson, London, 1960), pp. 40–41.

Chapter Two (pp. 16–19)

1. Arpád Pünkösti, *Rakosi a Csúcson* (Europa, Budapest, 1996).
2. Gyula Háy, *Born 1900* (Hutchinson, London , 1974), p. 194.
3. See Pünkösti, *Rákosi a Csúcson*, also Miklós Molnár, *From Béla Kun to János Kádár; Seventy Years of Hungarian Communism* (Berg, Oxford, 1991).

4. György Páloczi-Horváth, *The Undefeated* (Secker and Warburg, London, 1959) p. 122.
5. Ibid, pp. 136–7.
6. Cited in Pünkösti, *Rákosi a Csúcson*.

Chapter Three (pp. 20–26)

1. Paul Lendvai, *The Hungarians*, (Hurst, London, 1999), pp. 481–4.
2. Cited in Peter Unwin, *Voice in the Wilderness* (Macdonald, London, 1991) p. 37.
3. Borhi, *Hungary in the Cold War*, p. 78.
4. Rákosi to Dimitrov, cited in István, Feitl (ed.), *Documents from Rákosi, on Rákosi'*, Múltunk, Budapest, 1991.
5. Borhi, *Hungary and the Cold War*, p. 92.
6. Nagy, *The Struggle Behind the Iron Curtain*, p. 197.
7. Paul Ignotus, *Hungary* (Benn, London, 1972), p. 326.
8. See Oscar Jászi, *Homage to Danubia* (Rowman and Littlefield, Lanham, Md, 1995).
9. Hugh Seton-Watson, *The Times*, 15 June 1946.
10. Quoted in Borhi, *Hungary in the Cold War*, p. 86.
11. Ibid.
12. Paul Zinner, *Revolution in Hungary* (Columbia University Press, New York, 1962), p. 177.
13. Borhi, *Hungary in the Cold War*, pp. 82–90.
14. David Pryce-Jones, *The Hungarian Revolution* (Benn, London, 1969), pp. 33–40.
15. Speech made at the Academy of the Hungarian Workers' Party, 29 February 1952. Quoted in Lendvai, *The Hungarians*.
16. Cited in Miklós Molnár, *From Béla Kun to János Kádár* (Berg, Oxford, 1991).
17. Quoted in Borhi, *Hungary in the Cold War*, p. 109.

Chapter Four (pp. 27–33)

1. People's Republic of Hungary Constitution, *Szabad Nép (A Free People)*, 20 August 1949.
2. Mátyás Rákosi, speech, 29 February 1952.
3. Pünkösti, *Rákosi a Csúcson*.
4. Ibid.
5. Paul Ignotus, *Political Prisoner* (Routledge and Kegan Paul, London, 1959) p. 135.
6. Cited by György Faludy, *My Happy Days in Hell* (André Deutsch, London, 1962), pp. 166–7.
7. Ignotus, *Political Prisoner*, p. 137.
8. Faludy, *My Happy Days in Hell*, p. 173.
9. Páloczi-Horváth, *The Undefeated*, p. 139.
10. Béla Szász, *Volunteer for the Gallows* (Chatto and Windus, London, 1971), p. 144.
11. Faludy, *My Happy Days in Hell*, pp. 180–81.

Chapter Five (pp. 34–7)

1. See Cardinal József Mindszenty, *Memoirs*, translated by Richard and Clara Winston (Macmillan, New York, 1974).
2. Quoted in Ignotus, *Hungary*, p. 204.
3. Ibid, pp. 204–6.
4. Interview Number 227 (Box 12) with János Ödön Péterfalvy, Bakhmeteff Archive, Columbia University Oral History Project (CUOHP), New York.
5. Quoted in Lendvai, *The Hungarians*, pp. 482–4.

Chapter Six (pp. 38–46)

1. Szász, *Volunteer for the Gallows*, p. 167.
2. Borhi, *Hungary in the Cold War*, pp. 208–12.
3. Ibid.
4. Interview with Péter Kende, Oral History Archive, Institute for the Study of the 1956 Hungarian Revolution, Budapest.
5. Miklós Molnár, *Budapest 1956* (Allen and Unwin, London, 1971), pp. 69–73.
6. Szász, *Volunteer for the Gallows*, p. 112.
7. Interview by the author.
8. Lendvai, *The Hungarians*, p. 483.
9. Borhi, *Hungary in the Cold War*, p. 117.
10. Lendvai, *The Hungarians*, pp. 481–2.
11. Ibid.
12. Interview with Péter Kende, Oral History Archive, Institute for the Study of the 1956 Hungarian Revolution, Budapest.
13. Interview with Miklós Vásárhelyi, Oral History Archive, Institute for the Study of the 1956 Hungarian Revolution, Budapest.
14. Pálocz-Horváth, *The Undefeated*, p. 165.
15. Ignotus, *Political Prisoner*, p. 177.
16. Interview with Vladimir Farkas, Oral History Archive, Institute for the Study of the 1956 Hungarian Revolution, Budapest. Also, Vladimir Farkas, *No Excuse: I was a Colonel in the AVO* (Corvina, Budapest, 1991).
17. Klara Skakasits, *Fent es Lent (Up and Down)* (Magveto, Budapest, 1985).
18. Conversation between Kisilev and Zagar, 4 December 1956, cited in Borhi, *Hungary in the Cold War*, pp. 203–4.
19. Pünkösti, *Rákosi a Csúcson*.
20. Veljko Micunovic, *Moscow Diary* (Doubleday, New York, 1980), pp. 86–8.

Chapter Seven (pp. 47–53)

1. George Mikes, *The Hungarian Revolution* (André Deutsch, London, 1957), pp. 62–5.
2. András Klinger, *Társadálomstatisztikal álapismerétek (Social Statistics)* (Budapest KSH, 1998).
3. Ignotus, *Hungary*, p. 238.
4. Miklós Nyarádi, *My Ringside Seat in Moscow* (Crowell, New York, 1952).
5. Ibid.
6. Cited in Borhi, *Hungary in the Cold War*, pp. 175–9.
7. Páloczi-Horváth, *The Undefeated*, p. 181.
8. Péter Kende interview, Oral History Archive, Institute for the Study of the 1956 Hungarian Revolution, Budapest.
9. George Schöpflin essay in György Litván (ed.), *The Hungarian Revolution: Reform, Revolt, Represssion, 1953–1956* (Longman, New York, 1996), pp. 12–19.
10. *Szabad Nép*, 4 July 1950.
11. Ivan Péto and Sándor Szákacs, *A házai gazdasag négy évizédenek törtente (A History of Four Decades of the Hungarian Economy)* (Közgazdasági és Jogi Kiadó, Budapest, 1985).
12. Ferenc Váli, *Rift and Revolt in Hungary* (Oxford University Press, 1961), pp. 70–75.
13. Péto and Szákacs, *A házai gazdasag*.
14. Váli, *Rift and Revolt*, pp. 70–75.
15. Mikes, *The Hungarian Revolution*, pp. 41–4.
16. The Simon Papp Affair is recounted in papers at the Magyar Országos

Levéltár (The Hungarian National Archives), 276. F. 67.

17. Borhi, *Hungary and the Cold War*, pp. 179–82.

18. Radio Free Kossuth, 1 November 1956.

19. Klinger, *Social Statistics*.

20. Péto and Szákacs, *A házai gazdasag*.

21. Litván, *The Hungarian Revolution*, pp. 51–9.

Chapter Eight (pp. 54–60)

1. See Stephen Ambrose, *Eisenhower: Soldier and President* (Simon and Schuster, New York, 1990), pp. 123–7.

2. Stephen Ambrose, *Ike's Spies: Eisenhower and the Espionage Establishment* (Simon and Schuster, New York, 1981), pp. 113–25.

3. Ibid.

4. Richard Immerman, *John Foster Dulles: Piety, Pragmatism and Power in US Foreign Policy* (SR Books, Wilmington, Del., 1998), pp. 90–110.

5. Ambrose, *Eisenhower: Soldier and President*, p. 192.

6. *Full Circle: Memoirs of Sir Anthony Eden* (Cassell, London, 1960), pp. 98–9.

7. National Security Archive, Cold War Interviews, CNN, Episode 7, November 1998.

8. Immerman, *John Foster Dulles*.

9. Sir John Colville, *The Fringes of Power, Downing Street Diaries 1939–1955* (Hodder and Stoughton, London, 1985), p. 662.

10. Lord Moran, *Winston Churchill: the Struggle for Survival 1940–1965* (Houghton Mifflin, New York, 1966), p. 292.

11. *Memoirs of Sir Anthony Eden*, pp. 98–9.

12. For example, speech on 15 May 1952 in Pittsburgh, Pennsylvania.

13. Peer de Silva, *Sub Rosa. The CIA and the Uses of Intelligence* (Times Books, New York, 1980), pp. 121–6.

14. Tamás Pásztor, Interview Number 484, Bakhmeteff Archive, CUOHP.

15. James McCargar (writing as Christopher Felix), *The Spy and His Masters* (Secker and Warburg, London, 1963), p. 137.

16. National Security Council Staff Study, 'United States Policy Toward the Soviet Satellites in Eastern Europe', 11 December 1953 NSC 144. *Foreign Relations of the United States 1955–57* (FRUS), Washington DC.

17. Ibid.

18. Walter Hixson, *Parting the Curtain: Propaganda, Culture and the Cold War 1945–1961* (Macmillan, London, 1997), pp. 63–4.

19. Hungarian Refugee Opinion, Radio Free Europe, Munich, Audience Analysis. National Security Archive, Washington.

20. Hixson, *Parting the Curtain*, pp. 63–70.

21. George Urban, *Radio Free Europe and the Pursuit of Democracy* (Yale University Press, London and New Haven, 1998).

22. Hixson, *Parting the Curtain*, pp. 90–98.

23. Frances Stonor Saunders, *Who Paid the Piper? The CIA and the Cultural Cold War* (Granta, London, 1999), pp. 140–52.

Chapter Nine (pp. 61–2)

1. Farkas, *No Excuses*, pp. 82–90.

2. Paul Ignotus, Interview Number 503, CUOHP, and also in *Political Prisoner*.

3. Sándor Kopácsi, *In the Name of the Working Class* (Grove Press, New York, 1986), p. 129.

4. Vladimir Farkas interview, Oral History Archive, Institute for the Study of the 1956 Hungarian Revolution, Budapest.

Chapter Ten (pp. 63–6)

1. Váli, *Rift and Revolt in Hungary*, pp. 126–30.
2. Tibor Meray, *Thirteen Days that Shook the Kremlin* (Thames and Hudson, London, 1959), pp. 3–7.
3. Notes of a meeting between the Communist Party of the Soviet Union Presidium and the Hungarian Workers' Party Political Committee delegation in Moscow, 13–16 June 1953. Hungarian National Archives, Budapest. First published *Múltunk* No. 37, 1992. Translated by Monika Berbely and Csaba Békés.
4. Meray, *Thirteen Days*, pp. 3–7.

Chapter Eleven (pp. 67–76)

1. *Szabad Nép*, 5 July 1956.
2. Páloczi-Horváth, *The Undefeated*, p. 178.
3. William Shawcross, *Crime and Compromise: János Kádár and the Politics of Hungary since Revolution* (Weidenfeld and Nicolson, London, 1974).
4. See János Rainer, *Imre Nagy Politikai, életrajz* (1956-os Intézet, Budapest, 1996–9) and Peter Unwin, *Voice in the Wilderness: Imre Nagy and the Hungarian Revolution* (Macdonald, London, 1991).
5. Unwin, pp. 41–50.
6. *Népszabadság*, Budapest, 9 May 1957.
7. Johanna Granville, *Agent Volodya: The Halo Slips*, Cold War International History Project. East Europe, Autumn 1995.
8. Ibid.

9. György Lukács, *Record of a Life* (Verso, London, 1983), p. 278.
10. Quoted by Rainer, *Imre Nagy*.
11. *Szabad Nép*, 9 March 1953.
12. Bennett Kovrig, *Communism in Hungary from Kun to Kádár* (Hoover Institution Press, Stanford, Calif., 1979), p. 92.
13. Mátyás Rákosi, *Visszaémlékezések* (Napvilag Kiadó, Budapest, 1997).
14. Zinner, *Revolution in Hungary*, p. 137.
15. Meray, *Thirteen Days*, pp. 30–36.

Chapter Twelve (pp. 77–8)

1. Pünkösti, *Rákosi a Csúcson*.
2. Vladimir Solovyov and Elena Klepikova, *Yuri Andropov: A Secret Passage into the Kremlin* (Robert Hale, London, 1984), pp. 12–13.
3. Notes of discussion between the CPSU Presidium and a Hungarian Workers' Party delegation in Moscow on 8 January 1955. Hungarian National Archives. Published *Múltunk*, 37, 1992. Translated by Csaba Farkas.

Chapter Thirteen (pp. 79–83)

1. Aczél and Meray, *The Revolt of the Mind*, p. 162.
2. Eva Walko in conversation with the author.
3. Jenő Széll interview, Oral History Archive, Institute for the study of the 1956 Hungarian Revolution, Budapest.
4. Háy, *Born 1900*, p. 197.
5. Tamás Aczél, Interview Number 500, CUOHP.
6. Dmitri Volkogonov, *The Rise and Fall of the Russian Empire – Political Leaders from Lenin to Gorbachev* (HarperCollins, London, 1998), pp. 228–49.

7. Imre Nagy, *On Communism* (Praeger, New York, 1957).
8. Eva Walko in conversation with the author.
9. Volkogonov, *The Rise and Fall of the Russian Empire*, pp. 228–49.
10. Paul Kecskeméti, *The Unexpected Revolution: Social Forces in the Hungarian Uprising* (Stanford University Press, 1961), pp. 57–8.
11. From *The Plough and the Pen: Writings from Hungary 1930–1956*, ed. Elena Duczynska and Karl Polany (Peter Owen, London, 1963).
12. Miklós Molnár, *Budapest 1956*, pp. 61–4.
13. Eva Walko in conversation with the author.
14. István Vizinczey in conversation with the author.

Chapter Fourteen (pp. 84–5)

1. William Taubman, *Khrushchev: The Man and his Era* (The Free Press, London, 2003), pp. 294–9.
2. Litván, *The Hungarian Revolution*, pp. 78–86.
3. Pünkösti, *Rákosi a Csúcson*.
4. In conversation with the author.
5. Molnár, *Budapest 1956*, pp. 68–72.

Chapter Fifteen (pp. 86–7)

1. Simon Bourgin, 'The Well of Discontent,' *Hungarian Quarterly*, Numbers 142 and 143, Spring and Autumn 1996.

Chapter Sixteen (pp. 88–91)

1. NSC 174. FRUS, 1953.
2. NSC 5608. Dwight D. Eisenhower Library, Abilene, Kansas.
3. Minutes of the National Security Council, 12 July 1956, National Security Council, Washington.

4. Ibid.
5. US Army Military History Institute, Carlisle Barracks, Pennsylvania. Also National Security Archive, Washington.
6. Bourgin, 'The Well of Discontent'.
7. Leslie Fry to Foreign Secretary Selwyn Lloyd, 2 January 1956, Public Record Office, London. Foreign Office. 371.122372.NH.1013/1. Published in Eva Haraszti-Taylor, *The Hungarian Revolution: A Collection of Documents from the British Foreign Office* (Astra Press, Nottingham, 1995).
8. Fry to Foreign Office, 9 April 1956. PRO.FO.371.122373.NH.10110/6.
9. Fry to Foreign Office, 15 June 1956. PRO.FO.371.122373.10110/31/28.

Chapter Seventeen (pp. 93–5)

1. Fedor Burlatsky, *Khrushchev and the First Russian Spring* (Weidenfeld and Nicolson, London, 1991), pp. 88–94.
2. Cold War History, CNN, Episode 7, interview with András Hegedüs, 8 November 1998.
3. Report from Anastas Mikoyan to the CPSU Presidium, 14 July 1956. Archive of the President of the Russian Federation, Moscow. Also published in *Sovietskii Soyuz i vengerskii krizis, 1956*, (ROSSPEN, Moscow, 1998). Translated by Svetlana Savranskaya.
4. Ibid.
5. Ibid.
6. Mikes, *The Hungarian Revolution*, pp. 85–93.
7. Ibid.
8. Introduction, Jenő Györkei and Miklós Horváth (eds), *Soviet Military Intervention in Hungary*

1956 (Central European University Press, Budapest, 1999).

9. Lieutenant-General Yevgeny Malaschenko, 'Memoirs of an Eyewitness', in Györkei and Horváth, *Soviet Military Intervention*, pp. 210–42.

Chapter Eighteen (pp. 96–103)

1. Mikes, *The Hungarian Revolution*, p. 72.
2. Váli, *Rift and Revolt in Hungary*.
3. Jenő Széll interview, Oral History Archive, Institute for the Study of the 1956 Hungarian Revolution, Budapest.
4. Ibid.
5. Ibid.
6. Quoted in Burlatsky, *Khrushchev and the First Russian Spring*, p. 90.
7. Report by Yuri Andropov on conditions in Hungary to the CPSU Presidium, 29 August 1956. Foreign Policy Archive of the President of the Russian Federation, Moscow. Published in *Sovietskii Soyuz i vengerskii krizis, 1956* (ROSSPEN, Moscow, 1998).
8. Mark Kramer, *The Soviet Union and the 1956 Crises in Poland and Hungary: New Evidence on Soviet Decision Making*, Journal of Contemporary History, Vol. 33, 1998, p. 14.
9. Top Secret Urgent Telegram from Andropov to CPSU Presidium, 27 September 1956. Centre for the Storage of Contemporary Documents, Moscow.
10. Ibid.
11. Strictly Secret Urgent Telegram from Andropov to CPSU Presidium, 12 October 1956. Archive of the President of the Russian Federation, Moscow.
12. Kramer, 'The Soviet Union and the

1956 Crises in Poland and Hungary', p. 17.
13. Ibid.
14. Nagy, *On Communism*.
15. Ibid.
16. Quoted by Tibor Meray, Interview Number 567, CUOHP.
17. Malaschenko, 'Memoirs of an Eyewitnes', pp. 232–5.
18. Ibid.
19. Ibid.
20. Csaba Békés, Malcolm Byrne and János Rainer (eds), *The 1956 Hungarian Revolution: A History in Documents* (Central European University Press, Budapest, 2002).
21. Imre Mécs, interviewed in *The Revolution Goes Home*, 30th anniversary of the Hungarian Revolution, BBC Television, London, 1986.
22. Ibid.

Chapter Nineteen (pp. 107–25)

1. Kecskeméti, *The Unexpected Revolution*, p. 97.
2. Aczél, Interview Number 500, Bakhmeteff Archive, CUOHP.
3. Meray, *Thirteen Days*, pp. 78–82.
4. Ibid.
5. Ibid.
6. Tibor Meray, Interview Number 567, CUOHP.
7. Ibid.
8. Ibid.
9. Kopácsi, *In the Name of the Working Class*, pp. 73–7.
10. Ibid.
11. Sándor Petőfi, *60 Poems*, translated by Eugenie Bayard Pierce (Petőfi Society, Budapest, 1948).
12. Interview with the author.
13. Lenin, *Collected Works*, Vol. 10 (Foreign Language Publishing House, Moscow 1960–80).
14. Györkei and Horváth, *Soviet*

Military Intervention,
pp. 22–5.
15. Malaschenko, *Memoirs of an Eyewitness,* p. 251.
16. Working Notes of the CPSU Presidium, 23 October 1956, 11 p.m. Centre for the Storage of Contemporary Documents, Moscow.
17. Malaschenko, 'Memoirs of an Eyewitness', pp. 242–7.
18. George Gábori, *When Evils Were Most Free* (Deneau and Company, Ottawa, 1981), pp. 280–84.
19. Ibid.
20. Meray, *Thirteen Days.*
21. See Tamás Aczél (ed.), *Ten Years After* (MacGibbon and Kee, London, 1966), pp. 13–19.
22. Ibid.
23. See four articles under the title 'A Radio Ostrama', in *Népszabadság,* 22–6 January 1957. Also John MacCormac, *New York Times,* 25 October 1956.
24. Ibid.
25. Noel Barber, *Seven Days of Freedom* (Macmillan, London, 1973), pp. 13–21.
26. *Népszabadság,* 23 January 1957.
27. Mátyás Sarközi in conversation with the author.
28. Kopácsi, *In the Name of the Working Class,* pp. 121–37.
29. Interview with István Vizinczey, BBC documentary, 'The Hungarian Revolution: 30 Years After', 1986.
30. Gábori, *When Evils Were Most Free.*
31. *Thirteen Days,* pp. 149–55.
32. Aczél, Interview Number 500, CUOHP.
33. Péter Kende interview, Oral History Archive, Institute for the Study of the 1956 Hungarian Revolution, Budapest.
34. Working notes of the CPSU Presidium, 23 October 1956.

35. Györkei and Horváth, *Soviet Military Intervention,* pp. 15–20.
36. Király, *Life* magazine, February 1957.
37. Kopácsi, *In the Name of the Working Class,* p. 135.
38. Tibor Meray, Interview Number 567, CUOHP.
39. András Hegedüs interview, National Security Archive, CNN, Episode 7, November 1998.
40. Kopácsi, *In the Name of the Working Class,* pp. 131–42.
41. Various accounts: Meray, as above; Molnár, *Budapest 1956;* Mikes, *The Hungarian Revolution.*
42. Meray, *Thirteen Days,* pp. 86–90.
43. András Hegedüs interview, National Security Archive, CNN, Episode 7, November 1998.

Chapter Twenty (pp. 126–37)

1. Malaschenko, *Memoirs of an Eyewitness,* pp. 230–42.
2. Ibid.
3. In conversation with the author.
4. Radio Kossuth, 24 October 1956.
5. Ibid.
6. Sergei Khrushchev, *Nikita Khrushchev and the Creation of a Superpower* (Penn State University Press, 2000), pp. 192–4.
7. Notes by Jan Svoboda of meeting of the CPSU Presidium with leaders of the Satellite States, 24 October 1956. Originally published in *Ekonvy 1992* (ed. János Rainer), and in the Cold War International History Project Bulletin 5, Spring 1995.
8. Maléter material from Péter Gosztonyi, *The General of the Revolution, The Review,* Brussels, Vol. 5, 1963 and *Föltámadott a tenger . . . 1956* (*Népszava,* Budapest, 1986).
9. Ibid.
10. Ibid.
11. Ibid.

12. Barber, *Seven Days of Freedom*, pp. 26–31.
13. Gasztonyi, *Föltámadott a tenger*, pp. 70–90.
14. Ibid.
15. Radio Kossuth, 24 October 1956.
16. Meray, *Thirteen Days*, p. 86.
17. Péter Kende interview, Oral History Archive, Institute for the Study of the 1956 Hungarian Revolution, Budapest.
18. Miklós Vásárhelyi, interview, ibid.
19. Report from Anastas Mikoyan and Mikhail Suslov to the CPSU Presidium, Top Secret, 24 October 1956. Foreign Policy Archive of the Russian Federation. F. 059a Op.4, Pap. 6 D. 5. Published in Cold War International History Project Bulletin 5, Spring 1995. Translated by Johanna Granville.
20. Ibid.
21. Ibid.
22. Malaschenko, *Memoirs of an Eyewitness*, pp. 245–52.
23. Ibid.
24. FRUS 1955–57, Vol. 25.
25. Malaschenko, *Memoirs of an Eyewitness*, pp. 245–52.
26. Béla Király, in conversation with the author, April 2004.
27. Veljko Micunovic, *Moscow Diary*, pp. 126–9.

Chapter Twenty-one (pp. 138–48)

1. Radio Kossuth, 25 October, 1956.
2. Gergely Pongrácz, National Security Archive, Cold War Interview, CNN, 1998.
3. Ibid.
4. Ambrose, *Eisenhower the President*, pp. 348–9.
5. Dwight Eisenhower, speech, 25 October 1956, Madison Square Garden, New York.
6. Ibid.
7. Telephone notes to Dulles, Eisenhower Diaries, Eisenhower Library, Abilene, Kansas.
8. Ibid.
9. Reported by Nagy to Meray, *Thirteen Days*, p. 89.
10. Tibor Huszár, *János Kádár: Politikai életrajza 1912–1956* (Szabad Ter Kiadó, Budapest, 2001); Shawcross, *Crime and Compromise*.
11. Ibid.
12. Mikes, *The Hungarian Revolution*, pp. 131–8.
13. See Lendvai, *The Hungarians*, p. 391.
14. György Páloczi-Horváth, Interview Number 578, CUOHP.
15. Ibid.
16. Mikes, *The Hungarian Revolution*, p. 136.
17. Lendvai, *The Hungarians*, pp. 490–91.
18. József Kővágó, *You Are All Alone* (Praeger, New York, 1959).
19. UN Special Report on the Events in Hungary (New York, 1957), pp. 30–35.
20. Ibid.
21. Alexander Kirov, essay in Györkei and Horváth, *Soviet Military Intervention*, pp. 143–52.
22. Ibid.
23. Ibid.
24. Ágnes Gergely, in conversation with the author.
25. Barnes to State, FRUS 1955–57.
26. Ibid.
27. As quoted in Barber, *Seven Days of Freedom*, p. 51.
28. Lodge, telegram, FRUS, 1955–57.
29. Gergely Pongrácz, National Security Archive, Cold War Interview, CNN, 1998.

Chapter Twenty-two (pp. 149–60)

1. CUOHP Interview Number 243 with István Kovács.

2. Ibid.

3. Ibid.

4. As quoted by Barber, *Seven Days of Freedom*, p. 76.

5. CUOHP Interview Number 242 with István Kovács.

6. Author in conversation with László Eörsi.

7. CUOHP Interview Number 243 with István Kovács.

8. Ibid.

9. Gergely Pongrácz, National Security Archive, Cold War Interviews, CNN, November 1996, and in conversation with the author.

10. Interview with Anikó Vajda, National Security Archive, Cold War Interviews, CNN, 1998.

11. CUOHP Interview Number 467 with György Szabó.

12. In conversation with László Eörsi. See also Eörsi, *A Széna tériek 1956* (1956-os Intézet, Budapest, 2004).

13. Molnár, *Budapest 1956*, pp. 163–73.

14. Report by Mikoyan to CPSU Presidium, Moscow, 26 October 1956. Archive of the President of the Russian Federation. F.3. Op.64. D. 484. And published in *Sovietskii Soyuz i vengerskii krizis, 1956 goda*, ed. E.D. Orekhova, T. Sereda et al. (ROSSPEN, Moscow, 1998).

15. Ibid.

16. Author, in conversation with Mária Vásárhelyi.

17. Molnár, *Budapest 1956*, pp. 166–73.

18. László Eörsi, in conversation with the author.

19. Radio Kossuth, 26 October 1956.

20. Radio Free Győr, 27 October 1956.

21. Radio Free Miskolc, 27 October 1956.

22. Kecskeméti, *The Unexpected Revolution*, pp. 78–82.

23. Radio Free Miskolc, 26 October 1956.

24. Accounts of Mosonmagyaróvár massacre from Bruno Tedeschi, *Il Giornale d'Italia*; Peter Fryer, *Hungarian Tragedy* (Dobson Books, London, 1957); CUOHP Interview Number 515 with Ernő Garnadi, and Erik Durschmied, *Unsung Heroes* (Hodder and Stoughton, London, 2003).

25. Fryer, *Hungarian Tragedy*, pp. 74–82.

26. Memorandum of discussion at National Security Council, 9–10.42 a.m., Washington DC. FRUS 1955–57, Vol. 25.

27. Ibid.

28. Stassen to Eisenhower, Eisenhower Library, Abilene, Kansas.

29. William Colby, *Honorable Men: My Life in the CIA* (Simon and Schuster, New York, 1978), pp. 134–5.

30. Archive of the Russian President. F.3. Op.64. D. 484. Published in the Cold War International History Project Bulletin 5, Spring 1995. Translated by Johanna Granville.

31. FRUS 1955–57, Vol. 25.

Chapter Twenty-three (pp. 161–72)

1. Radio Kossuth, 27 October 1956.

2. In conversation with the author.

3. Ágnes Gergely in conversation with the author.

4. Dora Scarlett, *Window onto Hungary* (Broadacre, Bradford, 1959), p. 224.

5. Ibid.

6. Fryer, *Hungarian Tragedy*, p 96.

7. Author's conversation with Csaba Békés, April 2004.

8. Ibid.

9. For a life of Tildy see Károly Vigh, *Zoltán Tildy életútja* (Tevan Kiadó, Békéscsaba, 1991). Also Kővágó, *You Are All Alone*.

10. For biographical material on Béla Kovács see Mária Palasik, *Béla*

Kovács 1908–1959 (Occidental Press, Budapest, 2002).

11. Lendvai, *The Hungarians*, pp. 489–92.
12. Meray, CUOHP Interview Number 567.
13. Radio Free Miskolc, 27 October 1956.
14. Gosztonyi, *Föltámadott a tenger*.
15. Ibid.
16. Malaschenko, *Memoirs of an Eyewitness*, pp. 241–8.
17. Quoted by Ilaria Fiore, journalist in Italian Legation.
18. CUOHP Interview Number 227 with János Péterfalvy.
19. Alexander Kirov, in Györkei and Horváth, *Soviet Military Intervention*, pp. 140–45.
20. Ibid.
21. Ibid.
22. Peer de Silva, *Sub Rosa*.
23. Kecskeméti, *The Unexpected Revolution*, pp. 80–84.
24. See Mikoyan and Suslov telegrams to Kremlin, Archive of the President of the Russian Federation.
25. Béla Király, National Security Archive, Cold War Interviews, CNN, 1998 and in conversation with the author in Budapest, April 2004.
26. Litván, *The Hungarian Revolution*, pp. 92–8.
27. Spencer Barnes to State Department, Telegram Number 168, FRUS 1955–57, Vol. 20.
28. Ambrose, *Ike's Spies*, pp. 128–34.
29. Speech made by John Foster Dulles, 27 October 1956.
30. Radio Kossuth, 27 October, 9 p.m.
31. Molnár, *Budapest 1956*, pp. 135–9.
32. Radio Free Győr, 27 October 1956.
33. György Kövér, *Géza Losonczy 1917–1957* (1956-os, Budapest, 1998) and Meray, *Thirteen Days*, pp. 107–10.
34. Heard and reported by Péter Kende, Aczél, Meray, Losonczy.

Chapter Twenty-four (pp. 173–83)

1. See Tibor Meray, CUOHP Interview Number 567, and author's conversation with Béla Király, April 2004, in Budapest.
2. Malaschenko, *Memoirs of an Eyewitness*, pp. 241–8.
3. Ibid.
4. Barber, *Seven Days of Freedom*, pp. 88–91.
5. Györkei and Horváth, *Soviet Military Intervention*, pp. 63–72.
6. Ibid.
7. See various telegrams from Mikoyan and Suslov, Archive of the President of the Russian Federation.
8. Ibid.
9. Ibid.
10. Ibid.
11. Alexander Kirov, in Györkei and Horváth, *Soviet Military Intervention*, pp. 130–34.
12. Malaschenko, *Memoirs of an Eyewitness*, pp. 240–48.
13. Györkei and Horváth, pp. 41–6.
14. Working notes of the CPSU Presidium, 28 October 1956. Centre for the Storage of Contemporary Documents, Moscow. 'The Malin Notes' F.3. Op.12. D.1005. Published in Cold War International History Project Bulletin 8/9, Winter 1996–7.
15. Ibid.
16. Hegedüs interview in National Security Archive, Cold War Interviews, CNN November 1998.
17. Békés, Byrne and Rainer, *The 1956 Hungarian Revolution*, pp. 203–7.
18. Solovyov and Klepikova, *Yuri Andropov*, pp. 16–18.
19. Kopácsi, *In the Name of the Working Class*, pp. 159–68.
20. *Solovyov and Klepikova, Yuri Andropov*, pp. 18–19.
21. Author in conversation with Béla Király.

22. Kopácsi, *In the Name of the Working Class*, pp. 159–68.
23. Taubman, *Khrushchev*, pp. 294–9.
24. Békés, Byrne and Rainer, *The 1956 Hungarian Revolution*, pp. 203–7.
25. Ambrose, *Eisenhower*, pp. 351–60.
26. Békés, Byrne and Rainer, *The 1956 Hungarian Revolution*, RFE transcripts, pp. 286–90.
27. Ibid.
28. Ibid.
29. RFE, 28 October 1956.
30. Ibid.
31. Records of telephone conversations, Eisenhower Library, Abilene, Kansas.

Chapter Twenty-five (pp. 184–98)

1. Litván, *The Hungarian Revolution*, pp. 91–7.
2. Hungarian refugee opinion poll carried out by RFE, November 1957. National Security Archive, Washington.
3. In conversation with the author.
4. Meray, *Thirteen Days*, pp. 111–15.
5. Author's interview with Béla Király, April 2005.
6. *Life* magazine, February 1957 and Király article in *East Europe* No. 7, 1958.
7. Ibid.
8. Ibid.
9. Ibid.
10. Kopácsi, *In the Name of the Working Class*, pp. 177–85.
11. For Maléter's politics, see Péter Gosztonyi, *General Maléter, a Memoir*, in Problems of Communism, March/April 1966 and Péter Gosztonyi, 'The General of the Revolution'.
12. George Gábori, *When Evils Were Most Free*, pp. 270–76.
13. See telegrams of Mikoyan and Suslov.

14. Gábori, *When Evils Were Most Free*, pp. 270–76.
15. Eörsi, *A Széna tériek*.
16. Gábori, *When Evils Were Most Free*, pp. 270–76.
17. Ibid.
18. Ibid.
19. *Magyar Függetlenség* (*Hungarian Independence*), 3 October 1956.
20. Jenő Széll interview, Oral History Archive, Institute for the Study of the 1956 Hungarian Revolution, Budapest.
21. György Szabó Interview Number 470, CUOHP.
22. Ambrose, *Eisenhower*, p. 359.
23. Charles Bohlen to State Department, Moscow, Telegram 992, FRUS 1955–57.
24. Ibid.
25. Barnes to State Department, Telegram 180, FRUS 1955–57.
26. Ambrose, *Eisenhower*, pp. 355–7.
27. Tibor Meray Interview Number 567, CUOHP.
28. In conversation with the author, April 2004.
29. Meray, *Thirteen Days*, pp. 142–9.
30. Kopácsi, *In the Name of the Working Class*, pp. 177–85.
31. See Gosztonyi, *The General of the Revolution*.
32. Kopácsi, *In the Name of the Working Class*, pp. 177–85.
33. Leslie Bain, *The Reluctant Satellites: An eyewitness report from Eastern Europe and the Hungarian Revolution* (Macmillan, New York, 1960), pp. 92–8.
34. Ibid.
35. Litván, *The Hungarian Revolution*, pp. 86–9.
36. Ágnes Gergely in conversation with the author.
37. *Népszava*, 1 November 1956.

Chapter Twenty-six (pp. 199–213)

1. A.J. Cavendish, United Press, 30 October 1956.
2. Ibid.
3. First published *Pravda*, 31 October 1956.
4. Nikita Khrushchev, ed. Strobe Talbott, *Khrushchev Remembers: The Glasnost Tapes* (Little, Brown, New York, 1990), pp. 180–96.
5. Ibid.
6. Working Notes from the CPSU Presidium, 30 October 1956. Centre for the Storage of Contemporary Documents, Moscow. 'The Malin Notes', F.3. Op. 12.D. 1006. Published in the Cold War International History Project Bulletin 9, Winter, 1996–7.
7. Kopácsi, *In the Name of the Working Class*, pp. 190–98.
8. Ibid.
9. Ibid.
10. John Sadovy, *Life* magazine, December 1956.
11. Ibid.
12. *New York Herald Tribune*, Paris, 16 December 1956; also Cardinal Mindszenty, *Memoirs*.
13. Ibid.
14. Monsignor Egon Turchányi's testimony, *New York Herald Tribune*, 15 June 1958.
15. Mindszenty, *Memoirs*.
16. Radio Kossuth, 30 October 1956.
17. Paul Zinner, *National Communism and Popular Revolt in Eastern Europe* (Columbia University Press, New York, 1956), pp. 126–34.
18. Radio Free Győr, 30 October 1956.
19. Tibor Meray Interview Number 567, CUOHP.
20. Free Radio Kossuth, 30 October 1956.
21. Ambrose, *Eisenhower*, pp. 356–60.
22. Eisenhower Diaries, Eisenhower Library, Abilene, Kansas.
23. Telegrams in Archive of the Russian President, Moscow.
24. Ibid.
25. Békés, Byrne and Rainer, *The 1956 Hungarian Revolution*, pp. 203–7.
26. Bohlen to State Department, Telegrams 1040 and 1044, FRUS 1955–57, Vol. 20.
27. Hungarian News Agency, 31 December.
28. Rainer, *Imre Nagy*.
29. Quoted in Pryce-Jones, *The Hungarian Revolution*, pp. 92–3.
30. Ibid.
31. Free Radio Kossuth, 30 October.
32. Huszár, *János Kádár*.

Chapter Twenty-seven (pp. 214–27)

1. Sergei Khrushchev, *Nikita Khrushchev: An Inside Account of the Man and his Era* (Little, Brown, New York, 1990), pp. 196–9.
2. Ibid.
3. Ibid.
4. Ibid.
5. Ibid.
6. Ivan Serov, Top Secret Telegram to CPSU Presidium, 28 October 1956. Centre for the Storage of Contemporary Documents, Moscow. F.89. Per.45. Dok 10. Translated by Johanna Granville.
7. Ibid.
8. Ivan Serov, Top Secret Telegram to CPSU Presidium, 29 October 1956. Centre for the Storage of Contemporary Documents, Moscow. F.89. Per.45. Dok 11. Translated by Johanna Granville.
9. Taubman, *Khrushchev*, p. 297.
10. Working notes of the CPSU Presidium, 31 October. Centre for the Storage of Contemporary

Documents, 'The Malin Notes'. F.3.
Op. 12.D. Ll 1006. Published in Cold
War International History Project
Bulletin 8/9, Winter 1996–7.

11. Ibid.

12. Ibid.

13. Protocol Number 54. Archive of the
Central Committee of the Romanian
Communist Party, Bucharest. F.
Biroul Politic. Doc 355/56.

14. Corneliu Mihai Lungu, *1956
Explozia Bucharest* (Editura Univers
Enciclopedic, Bucharest,
1956).

15. Report from Colonel-General Vaclav
Kratochivil, chief of the
Czechoslovak General Staff, 29
October 1956 Top Secret. Archive of
the Czech Defence Ministry, Prague.
GS/OS 2/8–39 b.

16. Kramer, *The Soviet Union and the
1956 Crises in Poland and Hungary*,
pp. 39–42.

17. Ibid.

18. Ibid.

19. Taubman, *Khrushchev*, p. 297.

20. Ibid.

21. Malaschenko, *Memoirs of an
Eyewitness*, pp. 248–53.

22. Barnes to State Department
Telegram 200, 31 October 1956,
FRUS 1955–57.

23. Király, *Life* magazine, February
1957.

24. Király, National Security Archive,
Cold War Interviews, CNN,
1998.

25. George Heltai, *The End in Hungary*,
East Europe No. 6, 1958.

26. Tibor Meray, Interview Number
567, CUOHP.

27. Radio Free Europe, 31 October
1956.

28. Radio Free Kossuth, 31 October
1956.

29. Radio Vienna and Rias (Berlin), 31
October 1956.

30. Radio Free Kossuth, 31 October.

31. Eisenhower Diary, Eisenhower
Library, Abilene, Kansas.

32. Ibid.

33. Kopácsi, *In the Name of the Working
Class*, pp. 203–9.

34. Király in conversation with the
author.

35. Gergely Pongrácz, National Security
Archive, Cold War Interviews,
CNN, November 1998.

36. Király in conversation with the
author, April 2004.

37. Jenő Széll interview with Oral
History Archive, Institute for the
Study of the 1956 Hungarian
Revolution, Budapest.

38. Tibor Meray, Interview Number
567, CUOHP.

39. Jenő Széll interview, as above.

40. Ibid.

41. Nikita Khrushchev, *Khrushchev
Remembers*, pp. 180–84.

Chapter Twenty-eight (pp. 228–42)

1. Király in *Life* magazine, February
1957.

2. Ibid.

3. Tibor Meray, *Thirteen Days*, pp.
203–15.

4. Rainer, *Imre Nagy*.

5. Nikita Khrushchev, *Khrushchev
Remembers*, pp. 421–5.

6. Ibid.

7. Report by Yuri Andropov to CPSU
Presidium in Moscow. Top Secret.
Archive of the President of the
Russian Federation, Moscow, RF.
059a. Op.4, p.6. D. 5. Published by
János Rainer, 'The Other Side of the
Story', *Hungarian Quarterly* No. 129,
Spring 1993.

8. Heltai, *The End in Hungary*.

9. Maléter speech, Radio Free Kossuth,
1 November 1956.

10. Ibid.

11. Barber, *Seven Days of Freedom*, pp. 145–51.
12. Kramer, *The Soviet Union and the 1956 Crises in Poland and Hungary*, pp. 38–43.
13. Ibid.
14. Ibid.
15. Report by Andropov to the Kremlin, as above.
16. Tibor Meray, Interview Number 567, CUOHP.
17. Heltai, *The End in Hungary*.
18. Ibid.
19. Györkei and Horváth, *Soviet Military Intervention*, pp. 55–61.
20. Ibid.
21. Report by Andropov to the Kremlin, as above.
22. Borhi, *Hungary in the Cold War*, pp. 243–9.
23. Ibid.
24. Burlatsky, *Khrushchev and the first Russian Spring*, pp. 88–94.
25. Király in National Security Archive, Cold War Interviews, CNN, November 1998.
26. Memo of the 302nd National Security Council meeting, Washington. FRUS 1955–57, Vol. 25.
27. Radio Free Europe, 31 October 1956.
28. Report by Andropov to the Kremlin, as above.
29. Brian Urquhart, *Hammarskjöld* (Bodley Head, London, 1973), pp. 241–4.
30. United Nations Special Committee Report on the Problems in Hungary, New York, General Assembly Official Records, 1957.
31. Heltai, *The End in Hungary*.
32. Ibid.
33. Radio Free Kossuth, 1 November 1956.
34. Meray, *Thirteen Days*, pp. 213–19.
35. Radio Free Kossuth, 1 November 1956.
36. Quoted in Haraszti-Taylor, *The Hungarian Revolution*, p. 210.
37. Huszár, *János Kádár*.
38. Malaschenko, 'Memoirs of an Eyewitness', pp. 243–51.

Chapter Twenty-nine (pp. 243–53)

1. Litván, *The Hungarian Revolution*, pp. 119–24.
2. Mátyás Sárközi in conversation with the author.
3. Kővágó, *You are All Alone*, pp. 160–72.
4. Heltai, 'The End in Hungary'.
5. Radio Free Kossuth, 2 November 1956.
6. Gergely Pongrácz in conversation with the author.
7. Béla Király in *Life* magazine, February 1957.
8. György Heltai, interview in Westdeutsche Rundfunk TV programme, 'Die Toten kehren wieder', June 1968.
9. Kopácsi, *In the Name of the Working Class*, pp. 192–8.
10. Jenő Széll interview, Oral History Archive, Institute for the Study of the 1956 Hungarian Revolution, Budapest.
11. Ibid.
12. Tibor Meray, Interview Number 567, CUOHP.
13. Notes from meeting of the CPSU Presidium, with János Kádár and Ferenc Münnich, 2 November 1956. Centre for the Storage of Contemporary Documents, Moscow. 'The Malin Notes'. F.3. Op. 12. D. 1006. Ll 23–30. Published in the Cold War International History Project Bulletin 8/9, Winter 1996/7. Translated by Mark Kramer.
14. Ibid.
15. Alexander Kirov in Györkei and

Horváth, *Soviet Military Intervention*, pp. 152–7.

16. Malaschenko, *Memoirs of an Eyewitness*, pp. 246–53.
17. Király, *Life* magazine, February 1957.
18. Colonel Lajos Csiba, interview in Westdeutsche Rundfunk TV programme, 'Die Toten kehren wieder', June 1968.
19. Ibid.
20. Király, *Life* magazine, February 1957.
21. Ibid.
22. Ibid.
23. Király in conversation with the author, April 2004.
24. Ibid.
25. Nikita Khrushchev, *Khrushchev Remembers*, pp. 180–84.
26. Ibid.
27. Micunovic, *Moscow Diary*, pp. 138–42.
28. Ibid.
29. Gergely Pongrácz, National Security Archive, Cold War Interviews, CNN, November 1998.
30. Ejaz Hussein, *Dawn* (Karachi), 15 November 1956.
31. Dulles Papers, Eisenhower Library, Abilene, Kansas, box 18.

Chapter Thirty (pp. 254–62)

1. Meray, *Thirteen Days*, pp. 232–5.
2. Ibid.
3. Maléter interview with Noel Barber, London, *Daily Mail*, 4 November.
4. Press conference with Zoltán Tildy, also on Radio Free Kossuth, 3 November 1956.
5. Meray, *Thirteen Days*, pp. 240–45.
6. Notes of CPSU Presidium meeting, 3 November 1956. Centre for the Storage of Contemporary Documents, Moscow. 'The Malin Notes'. F. 3. Op. 12. D. 1006. L. 31-

330b. Published in Cold War International History Project Bulletin 8/9, Winter 1996–7.
7. Ibid.
8. Ibid.
9. György Páloczi-Horváth, 'János Kádár and Schizophrenia', *Der Monat*, Berlin, March 1957.
10. Huszár, *János Kádár*.
11. Király, *Life* magazine, February 1957.
12. Ibid.
13. Ibid.
14. Tildy and Losonczy press conference and on Radio Free Kossuth, 3 November 1956.
15. Ibid.
16. Király *Life* magazine, February 1957.
17. Kopácsi, *In the Name of the Working Class*, pp. 210–18.
18. Ignotus, *Hungary*, pp. 250–51.
19. Péter Gosztonyi, *The General of the Revolution*.
20. Lajos Csiba interview in Westdeutsche Rundfunk TV programme, 'Die Toten kehren wieder', June 1968.
21. Judith Gyenes interview in Oral History Archive, Institute for the Study of the 1956 Hungarian Revolution, Budapest.
22. Dwight Eisenhower Diaries, Eisenhower Library, Abilene, Kansas.
23. Urquhart, *Hammarskjöld*, pp. 242–3.
24. Király, *Life* magazine, February 1957.
25. In Gosztonyi, *The General of the Revolution*. Kopácsi article, 'Maléter's Last Days', in *Irodalmi Ujsag*, Paris, May 1978. In the United Nations Special Committee Report on the Problems in Hungary, New York, General Assembly Official Records, 1957.

26. Kopácsi, *In the Name of the Working Class*, pp. 210–18.
27. Ibid.

Chapter Thirty-one (pp. 263–72)

1. Király, *Life* magazine, February 1957 and in conversation with the author, May 2004.
2. Malaschenko, *Memoirs of an Eyewitness*, pp. 258–63.
3. Kopácsi, *In the Name of the Working Class*, pp. 210–18.
4. Borhi, *Hungary in the Cold War*, pp. 243–51.
5. Malaschenko, *Memoirs of an Eyewitness*, pp. 258–63.
6. Eva Walko in conversation with the author.
7. Király, *Life* magazine, February 1957.
8. Király, in conversation with the author.
9. See Békés, Byrne and Rainer, *The 1956 Hungarian Revolution*, pp. 214–16.
10. Barber, *Seven Days of Freedom*, pp. 190–98.
11. Written by Nagy, but never published or broadcast, according to CNN, Cold War History, June 1998.
12. See Solovyov and Klepikova, *Yuri Andropov*, pp. 22–4.
13. Kádár, Government Radio, Szombathely, 4 November 1956.
14. Litván, *The Hungarian Revolution*, pp. 121–4.
15. Malaschenko, *Memoirs of an Eyewitness*, pp. 258–63.
16. Ibid.
17. Alexander Kirov in Györkei and Horváth, *Soviet Military Intervention*, pp. 164–8.
18. Gergely Pongrácz, National Security Archive, Cold War Interviews,

CNN, 1998 and in conversation with the author.
19. Ibid.
20. Interview with Radio Free Europe, 18 October 1996.
21. Radio Free Kossuth, 4 November 1956.
22. See Vigh, *Zoltán Tildy*.
23. Kopácsi, *In the Name of the Working Class*, pp. 219–25.
24. István Bibó, *Összegyujtott munkai (Collected Works)* (Európai Protestáns Magyar Szabadegyetem, Bern, 1993).
25. Ibid.
26. Notes of CPSU Presidium meeting, 4 November 1956. Centre for the Storage of Contemporary Documents, Moscow. 'The Malin Notes'. F. 3. Op. 12. D. 1006. Published in the Cold War International History Project Bulletin 10, March 1998.
27. Eisenhower letter to Mikhail Bulganin, FRUS 1955–57.
28. Robert Murphy, *Diplomat among Warriors* (Collins, London, 1964), p. 380.
29. Wailes to State, FRUS 1955–57.

Chapter Thirty-two (pp. 275–81)

1. Kővágó, *You Are All Alone*, p. 245.
2. Interview Number 478 with Vazúl Végyvári, CUOHP.
3. Király, *Life* magazine, February 1957. Also in conversation with the author, April 2004.
4. Ibid.
5. Király in conversation with the author.
6. Litván, *The Hungarian Revolution*, pp. 120–24.
7. Ibid.
8. Mikes, *The Hungarian Revolution*, pp. 146–52.
9. Györkei and Horváth, *Soviet*

Military Intervention, pp. 98–104.

10. *Népszabadság*, 12 November 1956.
11. Huszár, *János Kádár*.
12. *Népszabadság*, 15 November 1956.
13. See Békés, Byrne and Rainer, *The 1956 Hungarian Revolution*, pp. 213–15.
14. Kopácsi, 'Maléter's Last Days'.
15. Report by Soviet Deputy Interior Minister M.N. Holodkov to Interior Minister Duddorov, 15 November 1956. Archive of the President of the Russian Federation. F. 3. Op.4. D. 486. Published in *Sovietskii Soyuz i vengerskii krizis 1956* (ROSSPEN, Moscow, 1998).
16. Huszár, *János Kádár*.
17. István Szabó, Interview Number 249, CUOHP.
18. See Hannah Arendt, *The Origins of Totalitarianism* (Meridian, New York, 1958), pp. 12–17.

Chapter Thirty-three (pp. 282–8)

1. See Békés, Byrne and Rainer, *The 1956 Hungarian Revolution*, pp. 366–72.
2. Ibid.
3. Micunovic, *Moscow Diary*, pp. 132–41.
4. *Népszabadság*, 15 November 1956.
5. See Békés, Byrne and Rainer, *The 1956 Hungarian Revolution*, pp. 366–72.
6. Ibid.
7. Szász, *Volunteer for the Gallows*, p. 198.
8. Tito's speech at Pula, 11 November 1956. Published in *Borba* (Belgrade), 16 November 1956.
9. Accounts taken from UN Special Report on Hungary. Dalibor Soldatic interview with *Vjesnik* (Zagreb), 28 November 1977. Accounts of Júlia Rajk to Béla Szász and Miklós Molnár, *Budapest 1956*.

10. Ibid.
11. See Békés, Byrne and Rainer, *The Hungarian Revolution*, pp. 366–72.
12. *Népszabadság*, 26 November 1956.
13. Litván, *The Hungarian Revolution*, pp. 131–6.
14. Molnár, *Budapest 1956*, pp. 219–26.
15. Mária Wittner interview, Oral History Archive, Institute for the Study of the 1956 Hungarian Revolution, Budapest.

Chapter Thirty-four (pp. 289–93)

1. Meray, *Thirteen Days*, pp. 252–6.
2. *Népszabadság*, 27 November 1956.
3. See Békés, Byrne and Rainer, *The 1956 Hungarian Revolution*, pp. 366–72.
4. Ibid.
5. *Népszabadság*, 27 February 1957.
6. See Békés, Byrne and Rainer, *The 1956 Hungarian Revolution*, pp. 366–72.
7. Sergei Khrushchev, *Nikita Khrushchev*, pp. 201–5.
8. See Békés, Byrne and Rainer, *The 1956 Hungarian Revolution*, pp. 366–72.
9. János Kádár, Report to the Hungarian Socialist Workers Party Executive Committee, 2 April 1957. Hungarian National Archives, 288. f. 5/20.
10. See Békés, Byrne and Rainer, *The 1956 Hungarian Revolution*, pp. 366–72.
11. Ibid.
12. Minutes of the Hungarian Communist Party Central Committee, 21 December 1957. Hungarian National Archives, 288. f. 4/14/1. Published Károla Nemthne Vagyi et al., *Á Maghar Szócialista Munkáspárt Központi Bizottságnak 1957–58* (Magyar Országos Levéltár, Budapest).

13. Huszár, *János Kádár*.
14. Sergei Khrushchev, *Nikita Khrushchev*.
15. Minutes of the HSWP Central Committee, 21 December 1957, as above.

Postscript (pp. 294–302)

1. See Ambrose, *Eisenhower*, pp. 358–61.
2. Records of phone conversations, in Eisenhower Library, Abilene, Kansas.
3. *New York Times*, 14 November 1956.
4. Gergely Pongrácz, National Security Archive, Cold War Interviews, CNN, 1998.
5. In conversation with the author.
6. William Griffith report, Policy Review of Voice for a Free Hungary, National Security Archive, Washington. 'Flashpoints' series.
7. Ibid.
8. Radio Free Europe Monitoring Study, cited in Békés, Byrne and Rainer, *The 1956 Hungarian Revolution*, pp. 464–72.
9. Aczél, *Ten Years After* and in Interview Number 500, CUOHP.
10. In Archive of the Institute for the Study of the 1956 Hungarian Revolution, Budapest.
11. *The New Republic*, New York, 7 January 1957.

12. Interviewed by Walter Cronkite, CBS, 23 November 1961.
13. Henry Kissinger, *Diplomacy* (Simon and Schuster, New York, 1994), p. 566.
14. Findings of the US Congressional Committee on Foreign Affairs into Hungary. Library of Congress, Washington, 1957.
15. Quoted in Urquhart, *Hammarskjöld*, p. 246.
16. Ibid.
17. Ibid.
18. Nikita Khrushchev, *Khrushchev Remembers*, pp. 180–84.
19. Burlatsky, *Khrushchev and the First Russian Spring*, pp. 92–3.
20. Barber, *Seven Days of Freedom*, pp. 226–9.
21. Jean-Paul Sartre, *The Spectre of Stalin* (Hamish Hamilton, London, 1969), pp. 23–4.
22. Ibid.
23. Richard Milhous Nixon, 20 November 1956, in Austria.
24. Litván, *The Hungarian Revolution*, pp. 156–60.
25. Ibid.
26. In conversation with the author, April 2004.
27. George Mikes, in Reg Gadney, *Cry Hungary* (Weidenfeld and Nicolson, London, 1986), p. 13.
28. Lendvai, *The Hungarians*, pp. 498–503.

BIBLIOGRAPHY

Aczél, Tamás, (ed.), *Ten Years After* (MacGibbon and Kee, London, 1966)

Aczél, Tamás, and Meray, Tibor, *The Revolt of the Mind: A Case Study of Intellectual Resistance Behind the Iron Curtain* (Thames and Hudson, London, 1960)

Aldrich, Richard, *The Hidden Hand, Britain, America and Cold War Secret Intelligence* (John Murray, London, 2001)

Ambrose, Stephen, *Eisenhower: Soldier and President* (Simon and Schuster, New York, 1990)

Ambrose, Stephen, *Ike's Spies: Eisenhower and the Espionage Establishment* (Simon and Schuster, New York, 1981)

Arendt, Hannah, *The Origins of Totalitarianism* (Meridian, New York, 1958)

Bain, Leslie, *The Reluctant Satellites: An eyewitness report from Eastern Europe and the Hungarian Revolution* (Macmillan, New York, 1960)

Barber, Noel, *Seven Days of Freedom* (Macmillan, London, 1973)

Békés, Csaba, Malcolm Byrne and János Rainer (eds), *The 1956 Hungarian Revolution: A History in Documents* (Central European University Press, Budapest, 2002)

Békés, Csaba, *Cold War, Detente and the 1956 Hungarian Revolution* (Ekonvy III, Budapest, 1996–7)

Békés, Csaba, *The 1956 Hungarian Revolution in World Politics* (1956-os lntézet, Budapest, 1996)

Borhi, László, *Hungary in the Cold War, 1945–56. Between the United States and the Soviet Union* (Central University Press, Budapest, 2004)

Bourgin, Simon, 'The Well of Discontent', *Hungarian Quarterly*, Numbers 142 and 143, Spring/Summer 1996

Burlatsky, Fedor, *Khrushchev and the First Russian Spring*, translated by Daphne Skillen (Weidenfeld and Nicolson, London, 1991)

Coutts, Charles, 'Eyewitness in Hungary', *Daily Worker*, 1957

Cox, Terry (ed.), *Hungary 1956 – Forty Years On* (Frank Cass, London, 1997)

Eörsi, László, *Corvinsatak, 1956 A VIII kerulet fegyveres csoportjai (Corvinists 1956: Three armed groups of the Viiith District* (1956-os Intézet, Budapest, 2001)

Eörsi, László, *Ferencvaros 1956: The armed groups of the district* (1956-os Intézet, Budapest, 1997)

Eörsi, László, *A Széna tériek 1956 (The Szena Ter People)* (1956-os Intézet, Budapest, 2004)

Faludy, György, *My Happy Days in Hell* (André Deutsch, London, 1962)

Ferrell, Robert, *The Eisenhower Diaries* (Norton, New York, 1981)

Fontaine, André, *La Guerre Froide* (Fayard, Paris, 1970)

Fryer, Peter, *Hungarian Tragedy* (Dobson Books, London, 1957)

Gábori, George, *When Evils Were Most Free* (Deneau and Co., Ottawa, 1981)

Gadney, Reg, *Cry Hungary* (Weidenfeld and Nicolson, London, 1986)

Gati, Charles, *The Bloc that Failed. Soviet-East European Relations in Transition* (Indiana University Press, 1990)

Gosztonyi, Péter, *Föltámadott a tenger . . . 1956: A Magyar Október története (The Sea Rose . . . 1956: A History of the Hungarian Revolution*, 3rd edn (Népszava, Budapest, 1986)

Gosztonyi, Péter, 'The General of the Revolution', *The Review*, Brussels, Vol. 5, 1963

Grose, Peter, *Gentleman Spy, The Life of Allen Dulles* (André Deutsch, London, 1995)

Györkei, Jenő and Miklós Horváth (eds), *Soviet Military Intervention in Hungary 1956* (Central European University Press, Budapest, 1999)

Hajdu, Tibor, 'Soviet Foreign Policy towards Hungary 1953 1956', in *20th Century Hungary and the Great Powers*, ed. I. Romsics (Highland Lakes, New Jersey, 1995)

Háy, Gyula, *Born 1900* (translated by J.A. Underwood) (Hutchinson, London, 1974)

Hixson, William, *Parting the Curtain: Propaganda, Culture and the Cold War 1945–1961* (Macmillan, London, 1997)

Hodos, George, *Show Trials: Stalinist Purges in Eastern Europe 1949–56* (Praeger, New York, 1987)

Huszár, Tibor, *János Kádár: Politikai életrajza [Political Biography] 1912–1956* (Szabad Ter Kiadó, Budapest, 2001)

Ignotus, Paul, *Hungary* (Benn, London, 1972)

Ignotus, Paul, *Political Prisoner* (Routledge and Kegan Paul, London, 1959)

Kecskeméti, Paul, *The Unexpected Revolution: Social Forces in the Hungarian Uprising* (Stanford University Press, 1961)

Khrushchev, Sergei, *Nikita Khrushchev and the Creation of a Superpower* (Penn State University Press, 2000)

Kissinger, Henry, *Diplomacy* (Simon and Schuster, New York, 1994)

Konrád, György, *Loser* (Harcourt Brace International, New York, 1984)

Kopácsi, Sándor, *In the Name of the Working Class* (Grove Press, New York 1986)

Lasky, Melvyn (ed.), *The Hungarian Revolution, A White Book* (Secker and Warburg, London, 1957)

Lendvai, Paul, *The Hungarians* (Hurst, London, 2003)

Litván, György (ed.), *The Hungarian Revolution: Reform, Revolt, Repression 1953–56* (Longman, New York, 1996)

Lomax, Bill, *Hungary, 1956* (Allison and Busby, London, 1976)

Lukács, György, *Record of a Life* (Verso, London, 1983)

Marchio, James, Resistance Potential and Rollback, US Intelligence and the Eisenhower Administration's Policies on Eastern Europe 1953–56, *Intelligence and National Security*, 10, Vol. 2, April 1995

Márton, Endre, *The Forbidden Sky* (Little, Brown, Boston, 1971)

Medvedev, Roy, *Khrushchev* (Blackwell, Oxford, 1982)

Medvedev, Roy, Zhores Medvedev, *Khrushchev, the Years in Power* (Oxford University Press, 1977)

Meray, Tibor, *Thirteen Days that Shook the Kremlin* (Thames and Hudson, London, 1959)

Micunovic, Veljko, *Moscow Diary* (Doubleday, New York, 1980)

Mikes, George, *The Hungarian Revolution* (André Deutsch, London, 1957)

Molnár, Miklós, *Budapest 1956* (Allen and Unwin, London, 1971)

Molnár, Miklós, *From Béla Kun to János Kádár; Seventy Years of Hungarian Communism* (Berg, Oxford, 1991)

Nagy, Imre, *On Communism, In Defence of the New Course* (Praeger, New York, 1957)

Nyarádi, Miklós, *My Ringside Seat in Moscow* (Crowell, New York, 1952)

Palasik, Mária, *Béla Kovács 1908–59* (Occidental Press, Budapest, 2002)

Páloczi-Horváth, György, *The Undefeated* (Secker and Warburg, London, 1959)

Páloczi-Horváth, György, *Khrushchev, the Road to Power* (Secker and Warburg, London, 1960)

Polcz, Alaine, *One Woman in the War* (Central European University Press, Budapest, 2002)

Pongrácz, Gergely, *Corvin Koz 1956* (*Corvin Passage 1956*) (Magyar Szinkor Kisszovetkezet, Budapest, 1989)

Prados, John, *Lost Crusader, The Secret Wars of CIA Director William Colby* (Oxford University Press, 2003, 1989)

Pryce-Jones, David, *The Hungarian Revolution* (Benn, London, 1969)

Pünkösti, Árpád, *Rákosi a Csúcson* (*Rákosi in Power*) (Europa, Budapest, 1996)

Rainer, János, *Nagy Imre, Politikai életrajz* (*Imre Nagy, A Political Biography*), 2 vols (Intézet, Budapest, 1996 and 1999)

Rákosi, Mátyás, *Visszaémlékezések 1944–56* (*Memoirs 1944–56*) (Napvilag Kiadó, Budapest, 1997)

Ripp, Zoltán, *Otvenhat Oktobere es a hatalam* (*Fifty-six and Power*) (Napvilag Kiadó, Budapest, 1991)

Sartre, Jean-Paul, *The Spectre of Stalin* (Hamish Hamilton, London, 1969)

Saunders, Frances Stonor, *Who Paid the Piper? The CIA and the Cultural Cold War* (Granta, London, 1999)

Scarlett, Dora, *Window onto Hungary* (Broadacre, Bradford, 1959)

Shawcross, William, *Crime and Compromise: Janos Kadar and the Politics of Hungary since Revolution* (Weidenfeld and Nicolson, London, 1974)

Solovyov, Vladimir and Klepikova, Elena, *Yuri Andropov: A Secret Passage into the Kremlin* (Robert Hale, London, 1984)

Strodes, James, *Allen Dulles, Master of Spies* (Regency Publishing, New York, 1999)

Szász, Béla, *Volunteer for the Gallows* (Chatto and Windus, London, 1971)

Taubman, William, *Khrushchev: The Man and His Era* (The Free Press, London, 2003)

Téglás, Csaba, *Budapest Exit* (Medianix Kiadó, Budapest, 1998)

Unwin, Peter, *Voice in the Wilderness: The Life of Imre Nagy* (Macdonald, London, 1991)

Ungváry, Krisztián, *The Siege of Budapest* (Yale University Press, New Haven and London, 2005)

Urban, George, *The Nineteen Days, A Broadcaster's Account of the Hungarian Revolution* (Heinemann, London, 1957)
Urban, George, *Radio Free Europe and the Pursuit of Democracy* (Yale University Press, New Haven and London, 1997)
Urquhart, Brian, *Hammarskjöld* (Bodley Head, London, 1973)
Váli, Ferenc, *Rift and Revolt in Hungary* (Oxford University Press, 1961)
Vigh, Károly, *Zoltán Tildy életútja* (biography) (Tevan Kiadó, Békéscsaba, 1991)
Walker, Martin, *The Cold War* (4th Estate, London, 1993)
Zinner, Paul, *Revolution in Hungary* (Columbia University Press, New York, 1962)

INDEX

Ács, Lajos, 107

Aczél, Tamás, 83, 114, 120, 124, 189, 296

Ada Szadabka, 16

air force, Hungarian, 197, 228

airports, 220, 228, 232–3

American War of Independence, 59

Andropov, Yuri: reports back to Moscow, 77, 92, 98; appearance, 77, 178–9, 244; ambition, 98, 179; Gerõ confides in, 99; and 23 October demonstrations, 112–13; war service, 113; and Nagy, 174, 179; deals with missing letter, 178, 180; political career, 179; family, 179; character, 179–80, 249, 266–7; backs Rákosi, 179; discussions with Nagy, 229–30, 232, 234, 236–7, 241, 244, 266–7; and Kádár's defection, 241–2; plays for time, 248–9, 261; and withdrawal talks, 259, 261; content with role in invasion, 266–7; and kidnapping of Nagy, 285; promoted, 291

Angyal, István, 196

Angyalföld, 143

Apor, Bishop Vilmos, 12

Arendt, Hannah, 280

Aristov, Averiky, 285

army, Hungarian: Sovietisation, 28; reorganised, 28; ability to contain uprising, 95, 113, 115, 120, 134; granted unlimited powers, 125; divided loyalties, 122–3, 128–30, 168, 210; and Great Terror, 131–2; units join rebels, 111, 124, 145, 155, 168; newspaper, 162; and Soviet offensive, 173–5; numbers, 182, 248; and National Guard, 186, 194; uniform, 197; and attack on Communist Party headquarters, 202, 210; Transylvanians seek to join, 217; and

Soviet invasion, 248, 267–8; surrenders, 270

Army Academy, 186

Arnothy, Christine, 11

Àrpád, 9

Arrow Cross, 9, 24, 29, 31; government, 34, 39

Artajo, Alberto Martin, 272

Austria, 16–17, 25, 275, 287–8; Hungarian refugees in, 58n, 281; border with Hungary, 59, 126, 154, 156, 219, 244, 257, 264, 280; and 1848 revolution, 82, 96, 103, 139; peace treaty with Soviet Union, 94; basis of neutrality, 158–9

AVO, 28–33; name, 28n; tortures, 32; salaries, 32; informers, 32–3; targets, 38, 47, 81, 83; arrests Rajk, 40; and Great Terror, 41, 43–4, 132, 143; increasing autonomy, 43, 64; Gerõ on, 49; in rural Hungary, 53; counter-espionage successes, 56–7; identities revealed, 59; and Péter's arrest, 61; and Jewish doctors, 62; power reduced, 73, 85; Losonczy and, 87; and 23 October demonstrations, 115–17, 121–4; fighting in Budapest and Parliament square massacre, 133, 144–6, 148; outside Budapest, 154–7, 162–3; Kovács and, 165; disbanding of, 172, 194, 201; officers allegedly tortured, 189; documents, 190–1; lynchings and executions of, 196–7, 203–4, 216; in Communist Party headquarters, 201–4; Mindszenty and, 205, 259; justice against, 223; reorganised into Karhatalom, 286

Baczi, Pista, 151